DEBUSSY: HIS LIFE AND MIND
VOLUME II: 1902–1918

Méthode, Méthode, que me veux-tu?
Tu sais bien que j'ai mangé du fruit
de l'inconscient.

Jules Laforgue

Debussy, by Nadar, 1909

DEBUSSY: HIS LIFE AND MIND

VOLUME II

1902–1918

EDWARD LOCKSPEISER

THE MACMILLAN COMPANY

NEW YORK

1965

Published in the United States by The Macmillan Company, 1965
Library of Congress Catalog Card Number: 62-52835

Printed in Great Britain

Contents

Illustrations

Acknowledgements

In the planning of a work of this kind the greater part of the source material has obviously to be collected at the outset. Accordingly, I was happy to acknowledge in Volume I the help generously given to me by friends, colleagues, libraries, and other institutions. The material thus made available has been used throughout the work, and it remains for me to renew my thanks to all those who, having made it possible for me to embark on this work in the first place, have also contributed to its completion.

Several new fields of investigation were of course indicated as the work developed. I have had much valuable advice from Miss Mary Chamot and Mr. Ronald Alley of the Tate Gallery on matters relating to Debussy and Turner. Mr. Ceri Richards, many of whose paintings have been inspired by Debussy, has helped me to a keener understanding of parallel lines of thought in the works of painters and musicians. Monsieur Léon Guichard, whose works on Wagner and Proust are well-known, has helped me to interpret many obscure references and has generously allowed me to publish, in Appendix E, his study on Debussy and the Occultists. Debussy's friend Dr. Pasteur Vallery-Radot, who possesses the largest single collection of unpublished letters of Debussy, kindly placed this collection at my disposal, thus providing me with many new and invaluable sources of biographical and critical material. Other fields of investigation were suggested by several publications issued on the occasion of the Debussy centenary in 1962. These are listed in the Bibliography on page 301. The lively discussions that took place with colleagues from many countries at the international conference, *Debussy et l'Evolution de la Musique au 20ᵉ Siècle*, held at the University of Paris in 1962, encouraged me to interpret aspects of Debussy's character in a new light or develop lines of thought that might otherwise have seemed irrelevant. Dorothy Partington gave me valuable information on Shakespeare editions, and Dr. Gerald Abraham kindly lent me the papers of M. D. Calvocoressi.

I offer my thanks to Maria Isabel de Falla for permission to publish a translation of the article by Manuel de Falla on Debussy and

Spain; to Madame Marie Romain Rolland and the Editions Albin Michel for a letter from Richard Strauss to Sofia Gonzaga; William Heinemann Ltd. and Holt, Rinehart & Winston, Inc. for a passage from Romain Rolland's *Jean-Christophe* translated by Gilbert Cannan; John Calder Ltd. for permission to make translations of extracts from the correspondence between Romain Rolland and Richard Strauss; Longmans, Green & Co. Ltd. and A. L. Rye for permission to quote a passage from *Farewell, my youth* by Sir Arnold Bax; Madame Aglaé de la Blanchetai for a letter from Paul-Jean Toulet to Debussy; Monsieur Jean de Buzelet for unpublished letters from Paul-Jean Toulet to Debussy; Madame Cahen Martineau for information on the libretto by Toulet based on *As You Like It*; to Kenneth Cavander for his translation of lines from Euripides; to Messrs. Durand & Cie. for permission to quote from the following works of Debussy: *La Cathédrale engloutie; Et la lune descend sur le temple qui fut; Feuilles mortes; Voiles; Des Pas sur la neige; Boîte à joujoux; Pour les sonorités opposées; Le Faune; Je tremble en voyant ton visage; Colloque sentimental; Jeux; Gigues; Khamma; Epigraphes antiques, II; Pour les Notes répétées; La Damoiselle élue; Le Jet d'eau; Ce qu'a vu le Vent d'Ouest; La Puerta del Vino;* and to the Editions Jean Jobert to quote from *En Sourdine* and *Syrinx.*

The completion of this work has naturally demanded the sacrifice of time from other professional activities and I record with gratitude the award kindly made to me of the Leverhulme Research Fellowship.

Introduction

In the feverish musical world of the beginning of the century the production of *Pelléas et Mélisande* had the effect of wholly transforming Debussy's status. A shadowy, obscure figure until then, hardly known outside certain exclusive Paris circles, Debussy was now proclaimed the most progressive force in contemporary music. The greater part of his work belongs to this second part of his life. It was a short period, a mere sixteen years, much of it devoured by illness.

Any view of Debussy's evolution during this period must take into account the historical fact that these years preceding the first World War were among the most decisive in the history of western music. Our long musical civilization reached its height during these years. In this first decade of the twentieth century—in a sense it was an additional, exquisite decade of the previous century—it was possible to believe that composers were writing music that was more imaginative, more immediately satisfying than any music of an earlier period. Even today no one will question that Debussy and his contemporaries, Strauss and Stravinsky, disclosed realms of musical expression that had never before been glimpsed. Like explorers in other fields, musicians at that time still passionately believed in progress, and they also believed that contemporary music represented, if not the whole of music, at any rate its most vital manifestation. Later generations were unable to maintain this faith. A disillusionment set in and the very works of Debussy and his contemporaries which had been held to crown the long development of European music were now also seen to contain the seeds of its decline. Later musical developments, deriving from these final explorations and conquests of Debussy, leave no doubt about the magnitude of the crisis into which composers, performers, and critics alike were swept; it is a crisis which has no parallel in western music.

The first task of the biographer, as of the historian, is to reconstruct contemporary ideas. The history of the career of Debussy after *Pelléas* is the history of the many conflicting ideas developed in Paris at that time not only in the world of music and the arts, but in spheres of social and political thought. I am not suggesting that Debussy was essentially a product of these external influences. Like

Marcel Proust's Jean Santeuil and Romain Rolland's John-Christopher, he was inclined to shun the harsh realities of the outer world and, like these idealists too, he himself helped to create our image of the period. All the same he was profoundly affected by certain deepseated movements. Religious values in those last turbulent years of peace tended to be replaced by searching enquiries into the workings of the unconscious mind; and at the same time, though there was apparently no direct connexion between these manifestations, an unnatural emphasis, as it seems to us now, was placed on the virtues of nationalism. I have considered it essential to reconstruct the main features of these social and political movements and to show their impact on Debussy's thought.

Shortly before the first World War Debussy became intimately associated with Stravinsky. As we saw in Volume I, Debussy in his earlier years had plunged into the heart of the main artistic movements of his time; and he remained until the end of his life identified with exploratory, forward-looking ideas. With Stravinsky, however, there was a parting of the ways. Perhaps Debussy felt that Stravinsky's works of genius contained also the seeds of a decline. Perhaps he was aware that future generations would sense this same element of decline in his own still unfinished work. One is, of course, unable clearly to mark the point at which a musical civilization falls away from the highest point of its development. Over a whole area of time the zenith and the golden decline of our western musical civilization did indeed appear to be indistinguishable; and they appear so still. If this study of the mind of one of the last great musicians of the era before the first World War helps us to see more clearly this dual nature of a problem that is with us still it will have achieved its purpose.

E. L.

PRELUDE

Preliminary Survey

PRELUDE
Preliminary Survey

Je me persuade, de plus en plus, que la musique n'est pas, par
son essence, une chose qui puisse se couler dans une forme
rigoureuse et traditionelle. Elle est de couleurs et de temps
rythmés.

Letter to Jacques Durand

The production in 1902 of *Pelléas et Mélisande* radically altered the
whole of Debussy's subsequent career. Until then, despite the success
of his earlier works, he had remained relatively unknown to the
larger musical world. Works were written only when the mood
compelled him to write; he made the minimum effort to present his
achievements to the public and he was content to become merged
with the main stream of the artistic movements of his time, a self-
exiled, almost an anonymous figure disdainful of the concrete,
exterior world. By a curious piece of irony the success at the
Opéra-Comique of *Pelléas*, the most tenuous and introspective of
all Debussy's works, drove him out of the secluded backwaters
of the world of art and letters. Innocuous as *Pelléas* may seem to us
today, something in this all too simple work had struck deep into
the minds of the public of that time, and as a result of fierce controversies Debussy was now mercilessly held in the limelight, the
unwilling leader of a school, the creator of a 'system', the musician
of the present and the future. The remaining sixteen years of his life
were spent battling with this public image. He was seldom able to
accept it; more often this preconceived notion of his role merely
drove him to retire into further depths of his inner being. The
development of his career was also determined by material factors.

In 1907 Emma Bardac, whom he was to marry the following year, was disinherited by her wealthy uncle, the financier Osiris. Heavy financial commitments had now to be met and though by the beginning of 1909 Debussy was already a sick man he was obliged, during the five years preceding the first World War, to undertake lengthy and fatiguing concert tours.

We may thus divide this second part of Debussy's life into two sections. The first, from 1902 to about 1907, is the period of 'Debussyism'; the second, from 1908 until his death ten years later, is the period of his travels abroad and of his principal commissioned works. These two sections overlap, of course, and in regard to certain of his activities there is no question of this division at all. Partly to meet his obligations to his publisher Durand, Debussy produced a vast number of works, written over the whole of this second period of his life, and indeed the bulk of his finest works, including the three orchestral works, *La Mer*, the *Images*, and *Jeux*, the late chamber works and the main piano works, belongs to this period as a whole. This survey, in the form of an amplification of the chronology at the end of the volume, is therefore conceived as a guide to Debussy's activities from the latter part of 1902 onwards, and it is also designed as a framework for the many interlocking æsthetic problems raised by Debussy's work which will be dealt with in the chapters that follow.

Stage works on *The Devil in the Belfry* and *As You Like It* occupied Debussy during the latter part of 1902. For the former he wrote a detailed scenario; a version of *As You Like It* was devised for him by Paul-Jean Toulet but delays and doubts prevented their further collaboration. His main concern after *Pelléas* was to branch out in a new direction and his correspondence regarding both these projects shows how anxious he now was to write music that should be vivacious and sharply exteriorized. In July 1902 he paid his first visit to London, and later in the year went to Bichain in Burgundy to spend the remainder of the summer at the modest country home of his parents-in-law.

The first completed work after *Pelléas* is the *Danses* (*Danse sacrée* and *Danse profane*) for chromatic harp and string orchestra, commissioned early in 1903 by the firm of Pleyel as a test piece for the Brussels Conservatoire. The cross-strung chromatic harp, as opposed to the pedal harp, enjoyed a short vogue at this period and Debussy's

two pieces with their curious Spanish and Portuguese associations
are one of the few works written for this form of the instrument
(see Appendix B). The first series of *Images* for piano was begun at
Bichain during the summer and so were *La Mer* and the *Rapsodie*
for saxophone. In the meantime, in May and June 1903, Debussy
had again been in London where at Covent Garden he heard for
the first time a complete performance of Wagner's *Ring*. The
overwhelming impression it created on him is evident from his
articles in *Gil Blas*. This was also the year he met the cultivated
amateur singer Emma Bardac, who became his second wife.[1]
Though determined to progress beyond the style he had established
in *Pelléas* he glanced backwards, at any rate momentarily, at this
period, contemplating a setting of another play of Maeterlinck,
Joyselle. The three *Estampes* for piano were published towards the
end of the year and, characteristically, Debussy's correspondence
with his publisher on this work deals exclusively with the design,
the choice of type for the title page, and the colouring of the letter-
press. He insisted on particular shades of blue and gold. For the
admirer of Hokusai and Hiroshige the publication of these Japanese
prints in music was required to be as pleasing to the eye as to the ear.

Darkened by the emotional crisis in Debussy's personal life,
leading to the attempt at suicide of Lilly Debussy, the years 1904
and 1905 saw the production of some of Debussy's most powerful
works. *La Mer* was written at this time and the first series of piano
Images was completed. The year 1904 opened with the first performance in January of the *Estampes*. Two short song-cycles, the
second set of *Fêtes galantes* and the *Trois Chansons de France*, both
dedicated to Madame Bardac, were completed before the summer.
In June Debussy abandoned his wife Lilly Debussy, whom he had
married five years earlier, and the summer months were spent with
Madame Bardac, first in Jersey and later at Dieppe. The piano works
Masques and *L'Isle joyeuse* were written during this idyllic escapade.

---

[1] Beyond a few biographical details little is known of the character or personality
of this dominating figure in Debussy's life. A Jewess, she was born at Bordeaux in
1862, her maiden name being Emma Moyse. In 1881 she married a banker, Sigismond
Bardac, by whom she had two children, Raoul who became a pupil of Debussy, and
Dolly who inspired the piano suite of this name by Fauré. Chouchou, her second
daughter, by Debussy, inspired *Children's Corner*. Besides Fauré, who dedicated to
Emma Bardac his song-cycle *La Bonne chanson*, her friends among musicians and
writers included Charles Koechlin and Albert Samain. The portrait of her by Léon
Bonnat shows her as a woman of commanding presence.

In October, shortly after Debussy's return to Paris, Lilly's histrionic attempt at suicide created a mountainous scandal in the artistic world of which there are echoes in Henry Bataille's play *La Femme nue*, known to have been based on this episode in Debussy's private life. Fauré's bitter criticism of the harp *Danses* ('the same profusion of harmonic singularities . . . sometimes frankly disagreeable') also reflects the anger provoked by this incident in Debussy's personal life. Several of Debussy's friends accused him of seeking material advantages in his association with Madame Bardac and it was under a considerable moral strain that the piano score of *La Mer* was completed by March 1905. Orchestrated later in the year, it was first performed at the Concerts Lamoureux in October. The scandals of the preceding year were by no means forgotten and it was clear to Debussy that the hostile reception of *La Mer*, particularly by critics who had proclaimed the qualities of *Pelléas*, was motivated by personal rather than musical reasons. One critic, he tells Louis Laloy, accuses him of having become an Americanized Debussy, another of being the Impalpable Musician.[1] Madame Bardac was divorced in May, Debussy the following August. Judgement went against him with the result that he was harassed by law-suits in connexion with Lilly Debussy until the end of his life.

In October, two weeks after the first performance of *La Mer*, the daughter of Madame Bardac and Debussy was born and named Claude-Emma ('Chouchou'). During the next two years (1906–7) Debussy was principally dependent on the financial resources of Emma Bardac. These were, in fact, the only years throughout the whole of his life when he was able to claim some freedom from material anxiety.[2] And they were the last years in which he enjoyed good health. According to Monsieur Dietschy's admirable analysis of his state of mind during the first six months

[1] To Pierre Lalo, critic of *Le Temps*, Debussy wrote with much dignity: 'I have no objection to your not liking *La Mer*, nor have I any complaint to make on this matter. I may perhaps be sorry that you have not understood me and astonished to find you, for once, sharing the opinion of your critical colleagues. . . . You say "that you neither see nor feel the sea in these three sketches". This is saying rather a lot. I love the sea and I have listened to it passionately. . . . You will concede that not all ears are capable of perceiving in the same way. In short, you uphold traditions which for me no longer exist, or at any rate they seem to me to belong to a period when they were not as fine and as true as one supposes. If in future we continue to disagree I shall not forget your warm defence of *Pelléas* which is indeed my main reason for writing to you.'

[2] In conversation with me in 1935 Louis Laloy revealed the extent to which Debussy was humiliated by the dependent position in which he found himself. Debussy's words were: 'Vous savez de quoi ça me donne l'air.'

of 1906 'he sunk into a great lassitude, into a feeling of well-being too, to the extent that all idea of work was abandoned'. In fact he published only one small piece in 1906, the *Sérénade à la poupée* from *Children's Corner*, and in 1907 wrote only the three pieces forming the second set of the *Images* for piano. He hardly seems to have looked upon the house belonging to Madame Bardac in the Avenue du Bois de Boulogne as a home of his own; his many journeys to the Normandy coast and to England indicate a growing restlessness. 'You are living in an old house which has been a friend to you from childhood', he writes somewhat enviously to Laloy in 1906. Nor was he greatly entranced with the personality of Richard Strauss who at a luncheon party earlier in the year had spoken incessantly to the impecunious composer about money matters. The following year Debussy gives a picture of mingled restlessness and dejection, almost an evocation of one of the greyer moods of Verlaine: 'Rain, destined for us all, though what its purpose is one does not quite see, falls on Paris. There is no quiet in my soul. Is it the character of this quarter of Paris? Am I just not made for a domestic life? These are questions to which I have not even the strength to reply.'[1] Long conversations are indulged in with Paul-Jean Toulet; bridge parties are continuously being arranged with Louis Laloy. With Gabriel Mourey, Debussy proposes to write a stage work on the subject of Tristan; with Victor Segalen he plans a Buddhist drama, *Siddharta*. But these are among the many plans or projects of Debussy destined to come to nothing.[2] He tells his friends

[1] Henri Büsser notes in his diary, under the date 5 July 1909: 'Long visit paid to Debussy in his private house in the Avenue du Bois de Boulogne. He seems to be bored there! He must often think of his little apartment in the Rue Cardinet where he wrote *Pelléas*.'

[2] The plan for the libretto of Debussy's *Tristan*, of which some details are given in Vol. I, p. 108 and which Mourey adapted from *Le Roman de Tristan* by the remarkable medievalist Joseph Bédier, is published in the conversations between Debussy and Victor Segalen (*Segalen et Debussy*, 1961, p. 74). The first act consists of three tableaux. The dwarf Froncin reveals to King Mark that Tristan has become the lover of the Queen. Isolda is thereupon handed to the lepers from whom she is eventually delivered by Tristan. The second act, a forest, presents the misfortunes of the lovers. The scene of the third act is a desolate heath. The final act presents Tristan in a state of madness followed by the betrayal of Isolda of the White Hands and the death of Tristan. Debussy was greatly moved by the line of Tristan in the last act: 'Je ne puis plus tenir ma vie.' Unfortunately, although Mourey had adapted the work of Bédier the theatrical rights of this play had earlier been assigned to a minor writer, Louis Artus, whom Debussy found wholly unacceptable. The *Tristan et Iseut* of Bédier and Artus was eventually performed in 1929 with music by Paul Ladmirault.

The publication *Segalen et Debussy* also contains an account of the project for *Siddharta*. Debussy describes it as a 'wonderful dream', but poet and musician were

that he now has 'a stony mind', a 'blind mind'. Yet in the meantime
the relatively few works he had produced had made a wholly
revolutionary impression. The age of 'Debussyism' had arrived and
in 1906, before the appearance of the piano Preludes or any of the
later works, Pierre Lalo could write: 'At the time of the first
performance of *Pelléas et Mélisande* a small public greeted the art of
Debussy with indifference, hostility, even contempt. Who would
have thought that in no more than two or three years this hostility
would be replaced by an ardent fervour and that the mere name of
Monsieur Debussy would be enough to draw enthusiastic, almost
fanatical crowds. This is in fact what has now happened. The
Debussyist religion has replaced the Wagnerian religion. . . . The
sight of the faithful leaves no doubt that Debussy has bewitched
them and that by his magic he reigns over them.'

Eventually, in January 1908, two years after their respective
divorces, Debussy and Madame Bardac were married. The
numerous concert tours now begin, and in February in London
Debussy conducted his first concerts abroad. *Pelléas* was given in
New York in February and in Milan in April. In June he returned
to his old project of a dramatization of Poe's *Fall of the House of
Usher*, later signing a contract for its production, together with the
Le Diable dans le beffroi and *Tristan*, at the Metropolitan Opera,
New York. He had cherished the project of *Usher* throughout his
life, and it was to remain with him as a dream-vision determining
the nature of several of his other works.

As we have seen, an opera on the subject of Orpheus, was
concurrently outlined in collaboration with Victor Segalen. The
major part of the libretto was submitted by Segalen during the
summer but no music was composed for it. By the end of 1908
Ibéria, the central panel of the orchestral *Images*, had been completed
and also the piano suite *Children's Corner*. It had been on the whole

---

unable to agree on the form the drama should take. 'Je ne connais pas de musique
capable de pénétrer cet abîme', Debussy comments. Victor Segalen was strongly
drawn to exotic civilizations and at Debussy's suggestion his study of Maori music,
'Voix mortes: musiques maori', a piece of imaginative literature rather than a musico-
logical document, was published in the *Mercure Musical* of 1907. In its original form
this study included a project for a play, *Le Maître du jouir*, in which the principal
character is Gauguin, who had come to New Zealand to revive the ancient Maori
traditions. Finally, Segalen proposed to Debussy a work inspired by Greek mythology.
His charming story, 'Dans un monde sonore', based on a modern version of the legend
of Orpheus, led to the operatic project with Debussy mentioned in Vol. I, p. 111.

a confident and a productive year. After so many disappointments something of the sweetness of success did seem within sight. 'Do not believe that I have become a pessimist; I have a horror of this outlook', one reads with pleasing astonishment in one of Debussy's letters to Durand of this period.

The optimism engendered by these successes was short-lived. The piano duet version of *Gigues* was completed at the beginning of January 1909, but before going to England the following month the first signs of cancer were declared. They took the form of haemorrhages, not producing excessive concern, and were only later diagnosed as rectal cancer. Nevertheless the doses of cocaine and morphine which Debussy was obliged to take made it difficult for him to fulfil his conducting engagements in London and he was obliged to cancel later engagements on this tour at Manchester and Edinburgh. Despite this alarming experience he steeled himself to conduct in Paris in March and April. The final section of the orchestral *Images* was completed in May and in the summer he returned to London to supervise the rehearsals of *Pelléas* at Covent Garden. Diaghilev had now appeared in Paris and Debussy wrote for him the scenario of *Masques et Bergamasques*, planned as the first of Diaghilev's French ballets. By December five Preludes from the first book were written and the publication of the controversial *Le Cas Debussy*, containing replies from leading musicians and other artists who had been questioned on Debussy's significance, lifted the æsthetic problems associated with his work from the national to the wider European scene.

In 1910 Debussy met both Mahler and Stravinsky. In April he dined with Mahler at a soirée organized for him by the Comtesse de Greffühle before the performance at the Trocadéro of Mahler's Second Symphony, which Debussy also attended, at any rate in part, for, with Paul Dukas, he was seen to walk out of the concert-hall after the first movement. Two months later the young Stravinsky was introduced to Debussy by Diaghilev after the performance of his first ballet for Diaghilev, *L'Oiseau de Feu*. In the same year the Société Musicale Indépendante was founded as a progressive offshoot of the Société Nationale and at its first concert, in April, Ravel introduced Debussy's *D'un Cahier d'esquisses*. Journeys abroad were planned during the year. In Vienna, where Debussy conducted the Konzertverein Orchestra, the Austrian musicians, who were associated with Mahler, Bruckner, and Schoenberg and who had expected the representative of the new French music to be a tall, aristocratic figure of commanding presence, were amazed at his informal and somewhat gnomish appearance. Two of Debussy's finest song-cycles were written in this crowded year, *Le Promenoir des deux amants* and the *Trois Ballades de François Villon*.

Despite a widening reputation in many countries royalties accruing from performances were limited. Anxieties were not relieved by mounting debts and ill-health was beginning to make serious inroads. At this stage a flamboyant figure, the poet, playwright, and soldier, Gabriele d'Annunzio, fleeing from his creditors in Italy, settled in Paris, where he planned an ambitious production of a mystery play, *Le Martyre de Saint-Sébastien*, with elaborate scenery, mime, and music. Debussy, together with Léon Bakst and Ida Rubinstein, was associated with d'Annunzio in this farrago which, as a theatrical enterprise, was doomed to failure. During the early part of 1911 the sick and impecunious composer slaved at the substantial score of *Saint-Sébastien*, the orchestration of which was undertaken at Debussy's dictation by André Caplet. Produced in May, this huge venture left him exhausted, with the result that a concert he conducted at Turin later in the year was a fiasco. He was now walking with difficulty and at the rehearsals was manifestly unable to control the hostile Italian orchestra. He hurried back to Paris and was soon caught up in the intrigues of the Diaghilev Ballet.

At the end of 1912, at the age of fifty, Debussy was able to join in the celebrations held in Paris at the Café Riche for the hundredth performance of *Pelléas*. But his state of health was making it impossible for him to meet his commitments unaided. In addition to his friend André Caplet, who served as amanuensis in *Saint-Sébastien* and *Gigues*, Henri Büsser and Charles Koechlin lent their support in the completion of orchestral scores. The former orchestrated the early *Printemps*, the latter the ballet commissioned by Maud Allan, *Khamma*. In the meantime Debussy had reluctantly given his consent for Diaghilev's controversial production in May 1912 of *L'Après-midi d'un faune* with choreography by Nijinsky. Financial reasons also caused him to accept Diaghilev's commission for the ballet *Jeux*, his final and one of his greatest works for orchestra, completed in September. It was produced in May of the following year, 1913, during the same season as Stravinsky's *Le Sacre du Printemps*, which Debussy and Stravinsky had earlier played together in a piano duet version. Towards the end of 1913 Debussy's resources were drained to the extent that he was obliged to pledge future royalties with a mutual insurance company. In December he managed to drag himself for the third time to Russia where, at the invitation of Koussevitzky, he conducted concerts in Moscow and St. Petersburg.

In the seven months before the outbreak of war in 1914, repeated journeys were made to Italy, Holland, Belgium, and England. Fighting valiantly against adversity, Debussy nevertheless complained that he was fast becoming 'a travelling salesman'. He threw himself into the preparatory work required for these tours, but he was becoming increasingly aware that his many concert tours were devouring the energies of his last few years. Resolved since his youth to retire from the outer world, he now found himself inextricably caught up in the machinery of the concert world.

The *Trois Poèmes de Mallarmé* was his last new work to be given before the war. He was deeply affected by the cataclysm of the first World War and for some months became almost incapacitated. Apart from an arrangement of a score of incidental music dating from 1901 and a short war piece which he supplied for a London publication, he wrote nothing until the summer of 1915. Determined then that he should not himself become a war casualty, he wrote in rapid succession the twelve Studies, *En blanc et noir*, and the first two of a series of sonatas. His style changed; the harmonic ambiguities of the earlier works were replaced by an harmonic sense which, if not more strictly tonal, showed a keener affinity with eighteenth-century harmony. The period of neo-classicism was in sight and Debussy was himself beginning to contribute to what was soon to be described as an anti-Debussyan style.[1] But this last intense period of activity was to be cut short. At the end of the year he underwent an operation from which a complete

[1] Pierre Boulez presumably had this period of Debussy's works in mind, and also the early neo-classical period of the 1920s, when he wrote: 'The shade of Debussy must have drunk a bitter poison in witnessing the debauchery of "classicism" which raged after his death. All those badly-tempered harpsichords on which were let loose an orgy of fugues, variations, and sonatas. . . . In this great *retraite aux flambeaux* of history did not Debussy himself momentarily carry a dubious torch. . . ?'

recovery could no longer be expected. Nevertheless by the middle of the following year, 1916, he was slowly able to resume some musical activities, chiefly concert-giving. In the last two years of his life Debussy frequently appeared as pianist and conductor at charity concerts and other activities connected with the war. But it was clear to all who saw him that he was now gravely ill. During this period he was able to write only the Violin and Piano Sonata and to complete the libretto of *La Chute de la Maison Usher*. When he died, in March 1918, during the most critical week of the war, many works were left either unfinished or abandoned.

The corpus of Debussy's later piano, vocal, chamber, and orchestral works, that is to say those written after *Pelléas*, is not only large; it is extremely varied. Adversity produced in the seemingly indolent composer a stoic determination to overcome his growing material and physical handicaps with the result that in this short period of sixteen years he produced most of his finest works. He lived with intensity throughout this short period and the evolution of his style was rapid. It is imperative, therefore, to investigate his ideas and his achievement on several different levels. Debussy's evolution was not all of a piece nor did it proceed unswervingly to its goal. His musical nature was complex, and one has often to go far afield to see how it was affected by external factors. The internal factors present other problems; they must be judged with great caution. In the pages that follow we must attempt to bring into focus the merging background and foreground of Debussy's world and to judge the interplay of the many different æsthetic and social influences that determine his often bewildering evolution.

PART I

The Years of Debussyism
1902–1914

I

Turner, Monet, and Hokusai

La musique souvent me prend comme une mer.

Baudelaire

The origins of Debussy's principal orchestral works after *Pelléas*, namely *La Mer* and the *Images*, have so many visual associations that it will be convenient to consider them together in this chapter under the heading of the three painters whom Debussy particularly admired. It is true, as we shall see, that the *Images* were also inspired by specific literary subjects. Nevertheless the manner, in *La Mer*, in which Debussy's musical and pictorial ideas become merged persists in the five movements of the *Images* which thus form a pendant to his great musical seascape.

The first performance of *La Mer*, on 15 October 1905 at the Concerts Lamoureux, took place at the time of the Paris Autumn Salon of that year at which were exhibited the startling pictures by Matisse, Derain, Van Dongen, Rouault, and Friesz. This was the first exhibition of the Fauves, so called by the art critics of the period since these painters had created something of a scandal by their spontaneous, almost wild use of colour. Derain was told that he had dipped his brush in dynamite and the fresh singing colours of Matisse, notably in his three female figures entitled, after Baudelaire, *Luxe, calme, et volupté*, caused Picasso to exclaim, 'He has a sun in his belly.' Beyond the fact that they were inspired by the intensity and brilliance of colour the Fauves had no common æsthetic nor were they painters to whom Debussy was especially attracted.[1]

[1] It was Othon Friesz, one of the original Fauves, however, who did the two pen-and-ink drawings of Debussy on his death-bed. One is in the collection of André Meyer, the other at the Musée de l'Opéra, Paris.

[15]

Yet it was possibly because of the powerful impact made by this exhibition that the anonymous writer of the programme note introducing *La Mer* at the Concerts Lamoureux drew a parallel between Debussy's technique of orchestration and the approach to primary colours of the Fauves, more vital and arresting than that of the Impressionists. The orchestral effects of *La Mer*, he stated, were procured by means of a 'palette of sounds and by skilful brush-strokes designed to convey in gradations of rare and brilliant colours the play of light and shade and the *chiaroscuro* of the ever-changing seascape'. Earlier Debussy had himself compared his manner of working to that of certain painters. Informing André Messager on 12 September 1903 that he had begun work on *La Mer* at Bichain in Burgundy, he states: 'You will say that the Ocean doesn't exactly wash the hills of Burgundy and that what I am doing might be like painting a landscape in a studio.'[1] Shortly after the first performance of *La Mer* he seems to have maintained that music was able to express the Impressionist theories more completely than painting. 'Music has this over painting', he wrote to his stepson Raoul Bardac[2] on 25 February 1906, 'it can bring together all manner of variations of colour and light—a point not often observed though it is quite obvious.' Probably Debussy was thinking of the experiments made by Monet in the latter part of his career in which series of pictures of ponds, cathedrals, and haystacks, painted at different times of the day, were designed to illustrate the changing play of light on form. But between the art of the painter and that of the composer there was an essential difference, Debussy pointed out. Whereas the play of light, in a painting, can only be rendered in a static manner—hence the series of pictures, painted by Monet, showing different intensities of light—in music, a continuous, fluid art, all these effects of light can be combined. Though light and

[1] Debussy was referring to an opinion commonly held at this time that the Impressionist paintings of Monet and Pissarro, unlike the earlier Romantic paintings, those of Delacroix, for instance, owed their appeal to the fact that the Impressionist painters worked in the open air. In fact, pictures had been painted direct from nature long before the Impressionists, notably by Corot and Constable, and later critics showed that the Impressionist technique derived not from the fact that they painted out-of-doors but from a new theory of light.

[2] The son of Madame Bardac by her first marriage, Raoul Bardac (1881–1950) was a composer who had studied at the Paris Conservatoire and who later took lessons from Debussy. Two letters written to him by Debussy in 1901 and 1906, the second giving advice on æsthetic matters ('From time to time forget music altogether. "Practice makes perfect" is a schoolmaster's notion.') appear in my *Debussy* in the 'Master Musicians' Series (4th ed., London, 1963).

colour are normally metaphysical terms in music, *La Mer* clearly presents the equivalent in sound of pictorial symbols, and Debussy implies that such a work was able to convey the fleeting nature of these symbols more adequately than painting, since music exists not in space but in time.

This view of *La Mer*, in terms associated with contemporary painting, is suggested by a new departure in art criticism. 'The art of the colorist is evidently in some respects related to mathematics and music', Baudelaire had tentatively declared in his essay on Delacroix. We see now that this judgement was more precisely applicable to the use of colour by the later Impressionist painters. *La Mer* is certainly the first great Impressionist work in music though, as we shall presently see, its underlying ideas and range of expression are more closely associated with Turner, the forerunner of Impressionism, than with the Impressionist painters themselves. However this may be, it is desirable at this point to investigate the nature of musical impressionism, its relation to Impressionism in painting and also to assess the many changing ideas that were beginning to draw painting and music closer together.

Between 1895 and 1902 several studies appeared proclaiming parallels between colour and sound. Some of the theories put forward were sterile and merely resulted in the short-lived colour-organ, used by Scriabin, and the cultivation of a vocabulary in music criticism that was merely misleading. But it is certain that a new province of the imagination was being explored. 'In describing a picture', observed Paul Souriau, 'art critics speak of roaring reds, shrill greens, singing blues, a noisy note of yellow and of chromatic harmonies and dissonances. A symphony, on the other hand, is described in terms belonging to painting: the melodic line is coloured with different hues ... the three colours of the wind instruments in the upper register are harmoniously combined. Above is the luminous blue of the flutes, the bright red of the oboes is in the centre and the warm, brownish tints of the clarinet are in the bass.' Far from indicating 'a morbid experience of coloured hearing', these metaphors, Souriau states, 'are based on a true relationship of sensations'.[1] Another critic pursuing this line of thought, Lucien Favre, sees painting as a kind of static music: 'La peinture est, si l'on veut, une musique des couleurs sans mouvement,

[1] 'Le Symbolisme des couleurs' in *La Revue de Paris*, 15 April 1895.

[17]

une musique morte mais c'est déjà une sorte de musique.'¹ Analysing the uses of colours in shadows, Camille Mauclair suggested that light is used in Impressionist painting in the manner that a theme in music is symphonically developed. 'The landscapes of Claude Monet are in fact symphonies of luminous waves', he writes, 'and the music of Monsieur Debussy, based not on a succession of themes but on the relative values of sounds in themselves [*la puissance comparée des sons en eux-mêmes*], bears a remarkable resemblance to these pictures. It is Impressionism consisting of sonorous patches [*taches sonores*]'.²

It is well known that the term Impressionism derives from the picture of Monet, *Impression: lever du soleil*, painted at Le Havre in 1872, in which water and sky merge imperceptibly into each other, creating a formless 'impression' of these elements shrouding the rising sun.³ The main period of the Impressionist movement in painting dates from 1870 to 1880, that is to say, long before a comparable movement had arisen in music. The last exhibition of the Impressionist group took place in 1886, in the very year when Debussy made his desperate but unsuccessful attempt to return from Rome to Paris in order to see the pictures of Manet.⁴ Though there were important differences in outlook the Impressionists were

¹ *La Musique des couleurs*, 1900.
² 'La Peinture musicienne et la fusion des arts' in *La Revue bleue*, 6 September 1902.
³ Commenting on the origin of the term in his *Claude Monet*, translated by J. Lewis May (London, 1935), Camille Mauclair says: 'It was but a word and nothing more, devoid of any significance although the attempt has since been made to assign it one. . . . Had it not been for the title which Monet, by the merest chance, happened to bestow on his picture, some totally different term might have been employed to describe the general tendency of artists whose efforts, while originating in realism, were directed towards presenting scenes of modern everyday life in the light of atmospheric colour effects . . .' The principal representatives of the æsthetic movements of the period were often bitterly critical of the terms by which these movements were described. Writing to Jacques Durand in March 1908 of the orchestral *Images*, Debussy says: 'J'essaie de faire autre chose, en quelque sorte des *réalités*—ce que les imbéciles appellent "impressionisme".' Verlaine was similarly suspicious of the use of the term Symbolism: 'Les symbolistes? Ça doit être un mot allemand!' A more appropriate term, he suggested, would be 'Les cymbalistes.' Nor did Picasso support the arbitrary labelling of the periods in his development. Questioned on the African influence in his work he almost incredibly replied, 'L'Art nègre? Connais pas . . .'
⁴ The production of *La Mer* in 1905 occurred in a decade in which the Impressionists, though no longer a unified group, still exhibited remarkable works. The main exhibitions in Paris were: 1903, Founding of the Autumn Salon; 1904, Renoir and Cézanne rooms at the Autumn Salon; Monet exhibits a set of views of London; 1905, The Fauves at the Autumn Salon; 1909, Monet exhibits a series of 'Water-lilies' at Durand-Ruel; 1912, Monet exhibition at Bernheim Jeune (Venice pictures); 1913, Renoir exhibition at Bernheim Jeune.

principally concerned to convey the sensations of light, and they believed, according to contemporary theorists, that the realistic rendering of an object mattered less than the opportunity provided by sun on water or sun on snow, to juxtapose the seven colours of the solar spectrum. Their preoccupation with the sensuousness of texture caused them to seek colour in shadows and it also caused them to see a picture not primarily as an image but as a composition of volumes and surfaces. While there could be no conscious imitation of the technique of the Impressionist painters by composers, new conceptions became common to the two arts. When in 1882 Renoir spoke to Wagner 'of the Impressionists in music', probably the first time the term was applied to music, he may have alluded not only to the works of French composers[1] but to Wagner's own *Forest Murmurs*, a true Impressionist evocation of nature in music by which, around 1893, Debussy was surely influenced in the central section of *L'Après-midi d'un faune*. In 1887 the *Journal Officiel* had criticized the 'vague Impressionism' of Debussy's *Printemps* and the term was again associated with his music on the occasion of the concert of his works in 1894 at the gallery of the Libre Esthétique in Brussels, which was hung with pictures by Renoir, Pissarro, Sisley, Gauguin, and others.

The Impressionists of painting and music also resemble each other in their choice of subjects. Both Renoir and Monet were most moving when painting a dreaming young woman gazing at reflections in water or into the water's depths. The reflections are of course of images reversed, reaching depths that are unfathomable. Hence the sense of mystery and the fragmentation of colour.[2] Renoir's *The Boat* (1867) and Monet's *Argenteuil-sur-Seine* (1868) are pictures of this kind and so are their two pictures painted in

---

[1] See Vol. I, p. 92n. Renoir was himself one of the early visitors to Bayreuth.

[2] In his book on Monet Camille Mauclair writes of the theory of Impressionism: 'All things that exist are enveloped and coloured by the solar atmosphere. It follows that a picture is not the representation of a set of objects, but rather of the atmosphere in which these objects are immersed, as in a living fluid. Our eyes receive the impression of various colours. . . . What we call coloration is due to the juxtaposition of the luminous waves. Disintegrated by spectral analysis, the coloration reveals variable combinations of the seven primary colours, or at least as many of them as our retina is capable of perceiving. . . . Nothing has a fixed colour. There is no such thing as "local tone", that is to say a particular and stable colour proper to, and inherent in, a given object, independent of the enveloping atmosphere.' The corresponding theory in music challenged the fixed tonality. Debussy's frequent use of the word *couleur* in music ('la musique est de couleurs', 'une fois la couleur admise') refers, however, not to tonality but to the mood of the work.

1869 of the riverside café *La Grenouillère*. In each of these pictures the Impressionist technique allowed the state of reverie to be boldly explored. Renoir's *The Seine at Argenteuil* and Monet's *Sail-boats at Argenteuil*, both of 1873–4, are other water-pieces which are brighter in tone and more extrovert. The water-pieces of Debussy which convey the spirit of these Impressionist pictures are specifically *En bateau* (1889), *Sirènes* (1899), *Reflets dans l'eau* (1905), *Voiles* (1910), and *La Cathédrale engloutie* (1910).[1]

La Mer is a work on a completely different scale. Not for nothing did Debussy proclaim Turner, the artist who first painted the sea in an Impressionist manner, 'the finest creator of mystery in art'. We cannot say with certainty which of Turner's pictures Debussy saw nor have we his first-hand impression of any of them. But the fact that Turner is twice mentioned in Debussy's correspondence, first in 1891 when he was hardly known in France, and again, in superlative terms, in 1908[2] clearly indicates the extent to which his work had aroused Debussy's imagination. As a background to the history of *La Mer*, therefore, Turner's reputation in France during Debussy's lifetime must at any rate be outlined.

In 1871 Monet and Pissarro made a memorable journey to London where they saw the Turners at the National Gallery. By no means all the Turners now to be seen at the National Gallery and the Tate Gallery were then on view though the exhibits included the famous *Snowstorm* of his later period. The extent to which these painters were influenced by Turner has frequently been discussed

---

[1] About twenty pictures by Monet of the west front of the cathedral at Rouen created a great stir when they were exhibited in Paris in 1895. The blurred outlines of many of them, particularly the one entitled *Symphonie en gris*, convey both a watery and a musical effect strikingly evocative of *La Cathédrale engloutie*. Many other works of Debussy, including *Pelléas*, were inspired by images associated with the impenetrable depths of water or reflections in water. The symbolical associations of water in dreams, illustrated in literature and painting, are discussed in Gaston Bachelard's *L'Eau et les rêves*. The application of Bachelard's theories to music is dealt with in Appendix F. By contrast with Debussy, Ravel contributed only three water-pieces to this particular style, *Jeux d'eau* (1900), *Une Barque sur l'océan* (1905), and *Ondine* (1908), owing more to the style of Liszt than to the spirit of Impressionism.

[2] Writing to Robert Godet in London on 13 February 1891, Debussy says: 'Et vous, cher, que devenez-vous dans cette ville si peu faite pour vous? (Quel stupéfiant hasard qui vous fait tomber de Java dans Londres!) Brayer m'a raconté une lettre de vous où vous disiez une belle admiration pour Turner et Rossetti: j'en ai été très heureux, à juste titre, comptant sur ceux-là pour vous masquer les autres!' We have seen that in a letter of March 1908 on the subject of the orchestral *Images*, Debussy strongly criticized the use of the word 'Impressionism'. (See page 18, note 3.) This is a term, he says, 'aussi mal employé que possible, surtout par les critiques d'art qui n'hésitent pas à en affubler Turner, le plus beau créateur de mystère qui soit en art!'

but it remains a matter of conjecture. Debussy may have seen the exhibition of some twelve pictures of Turner at the art-dealer's Sedelmeyer in Paris in 1894, and it is extremely likely that he saw the Turners on his visits to London in 1902 and 1903, that is to say at about the time when he began to work on *La Mer*. We may imagine their significance for him from the fact that many passages in early French and English criticisms of Turner might be applied to aspects of the work of Debussy. Gustave Geffroy speaks of the effects of 'iridescence' in Turner's misty pictures of the Thames and of the sudden blazing flashes of sunlight. *Brouillards* comes to mind in this description, and also the end of the first movement and the opening of *Jeux de vagues* in *La Mer*. 'Precious stones stud the atmosphere', says this critic, 'and Turner succeeds in giving the impression of a fairy-play enacted in the air.'[1] A much earlier critic, Hazlitt, in 1816 recorded impressions of Turner's works in terms which, a hundred years later, were applied to Monet and Debussy: 'His pictures are too much abstraction of aerial perspective.... They are pictures of the elements of air, earth, and water.... All is without form and void.' And Hazlitt quotes a paradox of which we may today see the full significance: Turner's works were said to be 'pictures of nothing, and very like'.

Even more than to Turner's expressions of fantasy, Debussy was apparently drawn to the dream aspects of his work. In an early appreciation of Turner by Philip Gilbert Hamerton,[2] which appeared in a French translation in Paris in 1889, these dream qualities, particularly of his later works, were strongly emphasized: 'After *The Golden Bough* of 1834 he was more and more inclined to be inspired by dreams rather than by reality. His dream

---

[1] A similar comparison with the colours of precious stones is made by Edmond and Jules de Goncourt. On 12 August 1891 they describe one of the first pictures of Turner seen in Paris, an imaginary view of ancient Rome: 'Ah . . . cette mer, ce ciel aux transparences roses . . . tout celà vu comme dans une apothéose, couleur de pierres précieuses! Et de la couleur par coulées, par larmes, par congélations telles qu'on en voit sur les flancs de poteries de l'Extrême-Orient. Pour moi c'est un tableau qui a l'air fait d'un Rembrandt né dans l'Inde.' The attraction to precious stones is a curious feature of the æsthetic of the period. 'What a marvellous subject for pictorial music is the cascade of scattered jewellery', wrote Gabriel Fauré on Dukas' *Ariane et Barbebleue* in *Le Figaro*, 11 May 1907. 'What invention in this phantasmagoria of rich stones falling in a cataract: emeralds, sapphires, pearls, rubies.'

[2] Hamerton was editor of *The Portfolio* and had published the English edition of his book in 1879. Debussy may have read Hamerton's comments on Turner's publication, *The Rivers of France*, including those on Turner's manner of painting the sky and clouds.

conception was that of a painter-poet dazzled by light, drunk with colour and who seems no longer to be in contact with the material world.'

More recently, in his study of Turner's *The Snowstorm*, Sir Kenneth Clark similarly draws attention to this painter's pre-occupation with 'visions' and 'dreams'. These words, he says, 'were commonly applied to Turner's pictures in his own day, and in the vague, metaphorical sense of the nineteenth century they have lost their value for us. But with our new knowledge of dreams as the expression of deep intuitions and buried memories, we can look at Turner's work again and recognize that to an extent unique in art his pictures have the quality of a dream. The crazy perspectives, the double focuses, the melting of one form into another and the general feeling of instability: all these forms of perception which most of us know only when we are asleep, Turner experienced them when he was awake.'

Allied to this idea of the dream was the current idea of mystery. In his description of Turner as 'the finest creator of mystery in art' Debussy was echoing the well-known opinion of Ruskin, who is also mentioned in Debussy's writings.[1] Mystery, in the sense in which the word is used by Ruskin and Debussy, has nothing of a sentimental meaning. It denotes that which, for æsthetic reasons, must deliberately remain unsaid or unseen. 'Of all modern artists', Ruskin writes in *Modern Painters*, 'Turner is the one to whom most people would first look as the great representative of nineteenth century cloudiness . . . every one of his compositions being evidently dictated by a delight in seeing only part of things rather than the whole, and in casting clouds and mist around them rather than unveiling them.' And he goes on: 'Not only is there a partial and variable mystery thus caused by clouds and vapours throughout great spaces of landscape; there is a constant mystery caused throughout all spaces, caused by the absolute infinity of things. We never

[1] In the first scene of Debussy's unpublished play *F.E.A.* (*Frères en Art*) Redburne, the English art critic, greets the painter Hildebrand with the words: 'Oh Monsieur! les librairies de Londres m'ont déja appris votre physionomie; vraiment votre portrait se vend chez nous aussi fort que ceux de Ruskin ou. . . . Miss Langtry!' Ruskin is mentioned in connexion with the pre-Raphaelite movement in Louis Laloy's *Claude Debussy*, published in 1909 with Debussy's approval, and is discussed at length in Robert de la Sizeranne's *Ruskin et la religion de la beauté* (1897), known to Marcel Proust, where he is said to have anticipated the later techniques of Impressionism and Pointillism.

see anything clearly.' Ruskin was here almost using the language of Mallarmé. The tonal ambiguities in the music of Debussy similarly create the impression that we 'never see anything clearly'. By its nature the dream, as both Turner and Debussy were aware, was essentially vague.[1]

Another pictorial influence has to be assessed before dealing with the circumstances which led to the composition of *La Mer*, that of the nineteenth-century Japanese artists, Katsushika Hokusai and Ando Hiroshige. All students of Impressionist and Post-Impressionist painting agree on the important impact made by the prints and drawings of these artists on the painters of the time, particularly on Degas and later on Gauguin and Van Gogh. Though he used rather crude colours, Hokusai had himself experimented in his prints of Japanese landscapes and seascapes with effects of light, and what appealed to the later French painters in his work was—apart from the exotic character of his subjects—the strong element of patterning, the flattened shapes and silhouetted forms. Curiously there were no shadows in his work. Nor were there shadows in the work of Hiroshige, remarkable for his impressionistic landscapes. Here an unsuspected link was established with contemporary European painters. 'The pioneering work done some years earlier by Turner', writes J. A. Michener on this subject, 'prepared the way for Hiroshige. The similarities between Turner and Hiroshige were remarked by most writers of the day.'[2] Hiroshige also introduced an original method of depicting rain, by means of bold, parallel lines. In one of his pictures, Mr. Michener observes, 'the rain comes down in lonely and unrelieved power'. In another 'it slants down in heavy gusts not parallel to one another'. In a third it 'drifts down in silvery mist'. Elsewhere 'it comes as white rain, disappearing before it strikes earth'.

Such fantasies were undoubtedly appreciated by Debussy. So much we gather from the fact that the cover of the full score of

[1] In his study *Les Grands Imprécistes du 19e Siècle: Turner, Wagner, Corot* (1930) Léon Arnoult attempts to define an æsthetic principle, common to these artists, based on ambiguity: 'L'Imprécisme en art réside donc dans la tendance à voiler l'expression afin d'obtenir un effet sensoriel ou émotionnel allant du désir réalisé jusqu'au monde du rêve.' Imprecision or vagueness in this sense does not imply inaccuracy; on the contrary, the ability to bring into relief the precise note or chord in harmony of an ambiguous tonality was Debussy's supreme quality. To Milhand, analysing his harmonies, André Gédalge emphatically declared, 'Debussy ne pouvait pas se tromper!'
[2] *The Floating World* (London, 1954).

La Mer consisted, at the composer's request, of a reproduction of Hokusai's print, *The Hollow of the Wave off Kanagawa*, or rather of part of it. This is the best-known and the most admired of all Hokusai's designs. The picture as it is reproduced on the cover, however, shows only the curve of the huge wave breaking into stylized designs of spray and foam. It is important to stress, moreover, that this is a copy made by an unknown contemporary artist which in no way does justice either to the form or the detail of Hokusai's print. In its original form, seen in the background of a contemporary photograph of Debussy and Stravinsky, the subject is much more dramatic. Three boats, manned by desperate crews, are almost submerged in what appears to be a terrifying storm. The construction of the picture is also arresting. In his manner of contrasting the different planes of the picture Hokusai was apparently experimenting with novel effects of perspective.

In any view of the development of Debussy's ideas at this period it is essential to reconstruct the impression made by Hokusai on the artists of his generation. Hokusai's reputation in France was largely established by Edmond de Goncourt. His study of the painter's work, which appeared in 1896, has a description of the print entitled *L'Intérieur du flot en face de Kanagawa* which is entirely appropriate to the spirit of Debussy's work: 'The design for *The Wave* is a sort of deified version of the sea', Goncourt writes, 'made by a painter who lived in a religious terror of the overwhelming sea surrounding his country on all sides: it is a design which is impressive by the sudden anger of its leap into the sky, by the deep blue of the transparent inner side of its curve, by the splitting of its crest which is thus scattered into a shower of tiny drops having the shape of animals' claws.' Goncourt also gives a description of the erotic works of Hokusai and elsewhere, in regard to a gentler aspect of Hokusai's work, conveys the pale but sensuous impression of an album of his prints: 'I allowed my eyes to be seduced by its blues which are really greys made slightly blue by a soapy azure, by its pinks which again are only hardly pink, by its colorations which seem to have been absorbed by the paper, by its faded harmony, its discreet polychromy.' Colorations 'absorbed by the paper' are indeed suggestive of some of the water-colour effects in Debussy's piano works.

Debussy knew the albums of Hokusai through his association

with the sculptress Camille Claudel.[1] They were to inspire him over many years. Returning to Paris after hearing *The Ring* in London in 1903 he published in *Gil Blas*, at the end of his article on Wagner, a description of the apple trees in blossom in Normandy: 'En ce moment la Normandie, toute revêtue de la délicate floraison blanche des pommiers, ressemble à une estampe japonaise . . . si l'on veut bien cette constatation sera tout à l'honneur de la France.'[2] The colours of Japanese prints inspired the precision of his directions for the publication in the same year of the *Estampes* in lettering of pale gold and blue: 'Isn't the colour originally chosen for the lettering a little hard? . . . The blue should be of the address printed above and the gold pale yellow.' The decorative, pictorial aspects of Debussy's published works were frequently the main subject of his correspondence with Durand. All these influences were not allowed to act independently of each other; they often merge, and in an unpredictable manner. One expects the poetic representation of nature—trees, wind, and the sea—to change from one period to another. Frequently it does; but there are sometimes hidden connexions which compel us to see works of an older period in a new light.[3]

There remains the appeal, which Debussy shared with the painters of his time, of Hiroshige. In 1888 Gauguin wrote to Emile Bernard: 'Look at the Japanese who draw so admirably and you will see there life in the open air and in the sun, without shadows.' At about the same time Van Gogh, who had himself organized an exhibition of Japanese prints and who became intimately acquainted with the

[1] Writing of the artistic relationship between Debussy and Camille Claudel, Robert Godet refers to 'une attention constante aux exemplaires de la virtuosité japonaise qui passaient par leurs mains et où ils admiraient, en l'absence fréquente de valeurs humaines intelligibles sans traduction, les miracles des mises en places ou les paradoxes des perspectives'. Linking the work of Hokusai with that of Ruskin he adds, 'La *Mangwa* de Hokusai leur fut une petite *Bible d'Amiens* exotique.' The *Mangwa* of Hokusai, literally, thousands of sketches, appeared in fifteen volumes (1812–75). Ruskin's *The Bible of Amiens* was translated in 1904 by Marcel Proust.

[2] Writing to his sister from Arles, Van Gogh similarly speaks of Wagner and Japanese art in the same letter and was apparently inspired by the same associations as Debussy: 'By strengthening all colours one obtains . . . something similar to Wagner's music. . . . As for me here, I have no need for Japanese art, for I always tell myself that here I am *in Japan* and that consequently I have only to open my eyes and take in what I have before me.' The Japanese influence is noticeable in Van Gogh's pictures of fruit trees in blossom, painted in 1888.

[3] There is a curious resemblance, for instance, between a passage in the article entitled *Notes sur l'art japonais* by the Japanese critic Tei San, which appeared in the *Mercure de France*, 15 October 1905, and a letter of Debussy to Durand of 12 September

work of both Hokusai and Hiroshige at Samuel Bing's gallery of oriental art in the Rue de Provence, made a copy of Hiroshige's woodcut *The Ohashi Bridge in Rain*. It is clear from this copy how the curious effects of geometrical design and perspective in Hiroshige's woodcut prompted similar ideas in the work of Van Gogh. Eight years later, in 1896, Debussy presented his friend René Peter with a print of Hiroshige, one of the *Stages on the Road to Tokaido*, consisting of small groups of people playing games, and remarkable also for its strange effects of perspective and geometrical design.[1] If, by comparison with *Pelléas et Mélisande* and *L'Après-midi d'un faune*, *La Mer* has a firmer strength of design, a brittleness even, a contributing factor may well have been the assimilation within the Impressionist vision of the æsthetic of Hokusai and Hiroshige.

La Mer is first mentioned in Debussy's letter, referred to earlier, of 12 September 1903 to André Messager. Here he denies the rumour that he was working at a quintet and states: 'I am working on three symphonic sketches under the title *La Mer: Mer belle aux Iles Sanguinaires; Jeux de vagues;* and *Le Vent fait danser la mer.*' Recalling experiences from his childhood years, before his talents had been discovered by Madame Mauté, he goes on: 'You perhaps do not know that I was destined for the fine life of a sailor and that it was only by chance that I was led away from it. But I still have a great passion for the sea.' He was deeply moved by the project for he speaks of the 'endless memories' which it aroused. These he maintains 'are worth more than reality which generally weighs down one's thoughts too heavily'.[2]

1903. Writing of *La Mer* from Bichain Debussy gives the title of the third movement as *Le Vent fait danser la mer* and comments: 'Le vent qui fait danser la mer n'a-t-il pas abimé les arbres de Bel-Ebat [the country home of Durand]?' Tei San writes on *The Wave*: 'Hokusai montre comment le vent fait jaillir l'eau en écume et courbe les arbres.' Elsewhere we discover that the trees in Burgundy happened to have been an object of particular admiration to both Debussy and Ruskin. In the same letter Debussy tells Durand that he is able 'to do nothing but admire the different kinds of trees around Bichain'. From Burgundy, too, Ruskin had written to his father more than fifty years earlier, in 1845: 'Ran out and made a sketch in the market place, and then down to the river side (Yonne) to see the sun set. Such an avenue! Every tree a perfection! Turners, and better than Turner, at every step. . . .'

[1] It bears the dedication: 'Pour la fête de mon petit René et en témoignage de ma sûre amitié. Claude Debussy, le 11 Novembre 1896.'

[2] A letter of the same date to Jacques Durand announces the work in identical terms and also, in the manner of Marcel Proust, draws attention to the many memories aroused: 'C'est à quoi je travaille d'après d'innombrables souvenirs.' It is possible that Debussy was influenced in his choice of the title by earlier works bearing this title:

Though this major work was the main product of the years 1903 to 1905, that is to say of the period immediately following the production of *Pelléas et Mélisande*, we now have evidence that if the work was not actually begun at an earlier date, ideas associated with it had long been in the composer's mind. In the first place the curious title *Mer belle aux Iles Sanguinaires*, later changed to *De l'Aube à midi sur la mer*, is also the title of a short story by Camille Mauclair which, according to Monsieur Henri Borgeaud, appeared in the *Echo de Paris Illustré* of 27 February 1893. The calm seas of the Iles Sanguinaires, the French name for Corsica and Sardinia, appear to offer a haven in this story from the mists and tempests of the north to which the voyager remains nostalgically drawn.[1] This association indicates that the work had perhaps taken shape in Debussy's mind at the time of the beginning of *Pelléas*, or even before, and while we possess no sketches of it from this period it is reasonable to assume that there may have been earlier attempts to give expression to his 'endless memories' of the sea.

Debussy certainly had reason to remember the Mediterranean, both from his childhood visits to Cannes and from his stay at Fiumicino at the time of his residence at the Villa Medici in Rome. He knew the Atlantic from his visit to Arcachon with Madame von Meck. In his memoirs on Debussy René Peter has a chapter entitled *La Mer* in which he describes a visit undertaken with Debussy and his brother Michel Peter to Saint-Lunaire on the north coast of

the symphonic ode *La Mer* for mezzo-soprano, chorus, and orchestra written about 1890 by Victorin de Joncières, and *La Mer, esquisses symphoniques*, by the Belgian composer Paul Gilson, first performed in Brussels in 1892 and subsequently in Paris, Germany (where it was conducted by Richard Strauss), and London.

[1] Unfortunately, the file of the *Echo de Paris Illustré* containing the story is missing from the Bibliothèque Nationale and other French libraries and efforts to trace this story have been unsuccessful. Monsieur Borgeaud has, however, kindly allowed me to consult the extracts which he made from a copy of it which he had seen. The Mediterranean journey described in it appears to have been a disillusionment: 'N'allons-nous plus revoir la tempête assourdissante . . . la hurlante omnipotence de l'Océan? Ah! demeurerons-nous, Seigneur, dans l'écœurement de ce pays rouge, ainsi pour jamais renonçant le quai brumeux de la crique natale, la douceur des brumes du Nord et le cher frisson de la vaste mer, soyeuse d'algues et de chevelures?' There can be no doubt that Debussy knew this story of Camille Mauclair and that he took its title for the first of the three 'sketches' forming *La Mer*. An unpublished letter from Mauclair to Pierre Louÿs in the possession of Monsieur Borgeaud and written about 1893, that is at the time of the publication of the story, proves, moreover, that Debussy and Mauclair were known to each other at this time. Mauclair regrets in this letter that he was unable to be present at one of the evenings devoted to Debussy's music at the home of Louÿs: 'Dire que voilà un temps immémorial que je voudrais entendre la musique de Debussy, que j'en demande à tous les échos. . . .'

Brittany. From the collation of Debussy's correspondence we may presume that the date of this visit was April–June 1889. During their stay a dramatic voyage was made by Debussy and his friends in a fishing-boat from Saint-Lunaire to Cancale, a distance of some twenty miles, in a terrifying storm. The skipper had advised against putting out to sea and consented only on Debussy's insistence. 'As a result of a cloudburst', Peter writes, 'we were flooded. The boat jumped about like a porpoise.' Before long the lives of the party were in danger and a critical situation had developed which Debussy appeared to relish. He is said by René Peter to have philosophically mused on the storm, declaring, 'Now here's a type of passionate feeling that I have not before experienced—Danger! It is not un-pleasant. One is alive!' About fifty years earlier, in 1842, Turner had similarly put out to sea in a storm, off the east coast of England. 'I got the sailors to lash me to the mast to observe it', Turner recorded. 'I was lashed for four hours and I did not expect to escape but I felt bound to record it if I did.' The result of this experience was the greatest of his seascapes, *The Snowstorm*, which, said Turner, 'no one had any business to like.' 'I did not paint it to be under-stood,' he explained. 'I wished to show what such a scene was like.'[1]

Such is the network of associations, pictorial, literary, and psycho-logical, as well as musical, which prompted the composition of *La Mer*. It would be foolish to attempt to define any one of these associations more closely or even to suggest, in one passage or another of the music, a reflection of one of the many sources of Debussy's inspiration. *La Mer*, laconically described by the com-poser as a set of 'Three Symphonic Sketches', is in reality a three-movement symphony inspired by the interplay of these visual and aural associations. Memories and associations merge in the artist's

[1] Other sources affirm that part of *La Mer* was composed during an early stay that Debussy is said to have made at the Pré des Oiseaux, Judith Gautier's country home at Saint-Enogat, also on the Brittany coast, not far from Saint-Lunaire, a trustworthy authority here being Suzanne Meyer-Zundel, the intimate friend of Judith Gautier, quoted by André Billy in *Le Figaro Littéraire*, 5e année, No. 234. No early sketches of *La Mer* have come to light and this testimony cannot therefore be substantiated. On the other hand, it is tempting to think that Debussy was inspired to write *La Mer* in this retreat of a writer who divided her interests between Wagner, Poe, and the Orient, whose home, the very name of which, Le Pré des Oiseaux, was conceived in homage to Wagner—in *Meistersinger* Walter, in love with Eva, evokes the work of Walther von der Vogelweide—and who had visited Wagner in the company of two writers, Catulle Mendès and Villiers de l'Isle Adam, with whom Debussy was closely asso-ciated.

mind, and out of their marriage an artistic experience is born, bringing with it a technique of expression. It may at first sight seem desirable to follow through the underlying ideas of *La Mer* on the purely musical level, to attempt to see their illustration in the form of melodic designs, in the evocative use of instruments, in the use also of the ambiguous chords of the seventh and the ninth, and of principles of the cyclic form. But I do not think much would be gained by an investigation of this kind. We know as yet too little about the psychology of musical expression to attempt a definition of the symbols of music. We may sense them—and therein lies the poetry of music—but we must remain chary of too literal a definition of them.[1]

La Mer is the greatest example of an orchestral Impressionist work. As we shall see, later examples of musical Impressionism were primarily conceived by Debussy for the piano which, on account of the illusory nature of its tone duration, became the Impressionist instrument par excellence. It is significant, therefore, that Debussy's principal orchestral works written after *La Mer*, namely the three *Images* (*Gigues*, *Ibéria*, and *Rondes de Printemps*), were originally conceived not for orchestra but for two pianos or piano duet.[2] Though the orchestral *Images* are not strictly Impressionist works in the sense of *La Mer* or even in the sense of the two sets of *Images* for piano, they retain much of the Impressionist character, the visual imagination is kept constantly alive by their kaleidoscopic succession of images and, as we have seen in the extracts quoted from Debussy's letter to Durand of March 1908, when the work was beginning to take shape, the spirit of Turner was still prominently in his mind.

The order of the pieces set out in the published edition of the orchestral *Images* (*Gigues*, *Ibéria*, *Rondes de Printemps*) is purely arbitrary. Their order of composition and also the order in which

---

[1] See 'Debussy's Musical Language', p. 244 for the opinion of Ernest Ansermet on Debussy's ideas of form.

[2] The following extracts from the correspondence with Durand show that the orchestral *Images* were conceived as a two-piano or a piano–duet pendant to the *Images* for piano solo. 29 September 1905: 'I am now going to complete as quickly as possible the *Images* for two pianos.' 9 July 1906: 'I hope to have finished *Ibéria* next week and the two other pieces in the course of the month.' This can only mean the piano version of *Ibéria*, the orchestral score of which was not completed until two years later. 11 October 1911: 'I can send you the arrangement for piano duet of *Gigues*, but the orchestral version is not yet completed.'

they were first performed have no relation to this sequence. The following table sets out the main facts:

	COMPOSED	FIRST PERFORMED
Ibéria	1906–8	20 February 1910
Rondes de Printemps	1908–9	2 March 1910
Gigues	1909–12	26 January 1913

Each of these three works uses or recalls folk tunes. *Ibéria*, divided into three sections, *Par les Rues et par les chemins*, *Les Parfums de la nuit*, and *Le Matin d'un jour de fête*, does not make use of specific folk tunes, but the folk-music character is clear enough. *Rondes de Printemps* uses the French folk tunes *Nous n'irons plus au bois* and *Do, do l'enfant do*, and *Gigues* a curious version, sometimes in augmentation, sometimes in diminution, of *The Keel Row*. The character of *Ibéria*, perhaps the greatest of the numerous Spanish works written by French composers, is discussed by Manuel de Falla (see Appendix B).

We have finally to investigate the literary ideas which underline the *Images*. *Rondes de Printemps*, which, Debussy insisted, 'is different from other music in that it is immaterial', bears a quotation which he had come across in the book on Dante published in 1908 by Pierre Gauthiez:

> Vive le mai, bienvenu soit le mai
> Avec son gonfalon sauvage!

This is a French translation of one of the *Canzoni a ballo* of Politian, the Italian fifteenth-century humanist, beginning 'Ben venga maggio/E'l gonfalon selvaggio' ('Welcome May and the woodland banner'). It is quoted by Gauthiez in a description of a medieval May-day scene in Tuscany, the joyousness of which Debussy apparently wished to convey in *Rondes de Printemps*: 'On the first day of May the whole country scene awakens and rejoices. Women and girls form processions and pair off with joyous dancers or musicians, their heads encircled with garlands of flowers. Games and contests take place and lovers carrying the May banners, branches brought from the woodlands, leave them at their sweethearts' doors and proceed to sing the May-song, *La Maggiolata*.'[1]

[1] The Andrieux catalogue (1933) of the sale of Debussy's manuscripts and possessions refers to a manuscript note of Debussy in his copy of Pierre Gauthiez' *Dante*: 'Petite Ballade, page 172' (followed by the lines of Politian). The 'Petite Ballade'—

The orchestration of *Gigues*, originally entitled *Gigues tristes*, the first in the set in the published form but the last in order of composition, was completed by André Caplet, who also made the transcription for piano duet. Léon Vallas quotes an article by Caplet, published in 1923, in which he writes:

Gigues . . . sad *Gigues* . . . tragic *Gigues*. . . . The portrait of a soul in pain, uttering its slow, lingering lamentation on the reed of an oboe d'amore. A wounded soul, so reticent that it dreads and shuns all lyrical effusions, and quickly hides its sobs behind the mask and the angular gesture of a grotesque marionette. Again, it suddenly wraps itself in a mantle of the most phlegmatic indifference. The ever-changing moods, the rapidity with which they merge, clash and separate to unite once more, make the interpretation of this work very difficult. . . . Underneath the convulsive shudderings, the sudden efforts at restraint, the pitiful grimaces, which serve as a kind of disguise, we recognize . . . the spirit of sadness, infinite sadness. . . .'[1]

In fact the 'spirit of sadness' which runs through this work derives from the affecting poem of Verlaine entitled *Streets* (from the *Aquarelles*), written in Soho, and which had been set to the tune of *The Keel Row*, under the title *Dansons la Gigue*, by Charles Bordes in 1890. Director of the Chanteurs de Saint-Gervais, Bordes was well known to Debussy and it was only natural that in planning an English counterpart to the Spanish and Franco-Italian *Images* he should have remembered this early example of an English folk-song set by a French composer. The spirit of *Gigues*, one of the most

---

on page 178, not page 172—of Gauthiez' *Dante* is the tragic *Ballata*, written in exile by Guido Cavalcanti on his approaching death, of which the opening lines, in the translation of E. H. Wilkins, are:

Because I think not ever to return
Ballad, to Tuscany,—
Go therefore thou for me
Straight to my lady's face,
Who, of her noble grace,
Shall show thee courtesy . . .

These are lines which form a gruesome contrast to the May Song of Politian, a contrast which may conceivably have been in Debussy's mind at the time of the composition of *Rondes de Printemps*.

[1] Translation by M. and G. O'Brien.

moving and subtly ironic of Debussy's larger works, is, however, determined by Verlaine's poem, catching, as in a vignette, the *douceur de vivre* of the period with its indulgent and sometimes alarming nostalgia:

Dansons la gigue!

J'aimais surtout ses jolis yeux,
Plus clairs que l'étoile des cieux,
J'aimais ses yeux malicieux.

Dansons la gigue!

Elle avait des façons vraiment
De désoler un pauvre amant,
Que c'en était vraiment charmant!

Dansons la gigue!

Mais je trouve encore meilleur
Le baiser de sa bouche en fleur,
Depuis qu'elle est morte à mon cœur.

Dansons la gigue!

Je me souviens, je me souviens
Des heures et des entretiens,
Et c'est le meilleur de mes biens.

Dansons la gigue!

2

The Technique of Illusion

L'impression est la source de l'art: la réflexion l'aide mais la
suppose.

Eugène Lefébure, letter to Mallarmé

It has not perhaps been sufficiently noticed that the latter part of
Debussy's life coincided with a golden age of piano music in which
he played the most important part. This age, in which a new conception of the piano was triumphantly established, was short: it
consisted of barely more than a decade and came to an end with the
first World War. Yet not since the era of the great works of Chopin
had there been a period in which the piano was transformed into
what amounted to another instrument. Many of the piano works of
Fauré belong to this period, but it cannot be claimed that they
seized upon the newly discovered expressive resources of the
instrument in the manner of the piano works of Debussy. Only
Ravel was able to vie with Debussy in this sphere. As we see now,
the emergence of this new piano style, in many ways the joint
achievement of Ravel and Debussy, was one of the most important
events in early twentieth-century music. We must try to discover
its origin and its significance.

The personal and artistic relationship between Debussy and
Ravel was complex, but there is one aspect of this relationship
which is immediately striking: it was largely centred on their
common friend, the Spanish pianist Ricardo Viñes. No pianist of
the twentieth century, nor indeed of the nineteenth, enjoyed the
privileges of Viñes. Chopin and Liszt and the other great nineteenth-
century pianists were themselves composers for the piano who
interpreted their own and other composers' works. Apart from his

Hommages to Satie and Séverac, Viñes was nothing of a composer and he did not claim to be a pianist of this towering order. Yet within the short period of twelve years, from his first performance in 1901 of Ravel's *Menuet antique*, to his first performance of three Preludes of Debussy in 1913, he had introduced almost the entire piano repertory of Debussy and Ravel. This itself was a phenomenal achievement, and though it is difficult to discover the extent to which the novel conceptions of keyboard-writing of both Debussy and Ravel were inspired by the style of piano playing of Viñes, his association with the two composers was so close that we must at least endeavour to reconstruct his artistic character and principles.

Born at Lerida, Catalonia, in 1875, he came to Paris as a youth and in 1891 played with Ravel the *Valses romantiques* for two pianos by Chabrier to the composer.[1] Ravel and Viñes were both at this time pupils at the Paris Conservatoire of the pianist Charles de Bériot, son of the Belgian violinist of the same name. They were no doubt drawn to each other by their common attraction to the music of Spain, and somewhere near the heart of the music not only of Ravel but also of Debussy there remained a nostalgia for the Spanish scene which the very presence of Viñes must have encouraged.[2] The life and soul of the 'Club des Apaches', the gatherings of artists at which Ravel and M. D. Calvocoressi were prominent figures, Viñes, with his long oval head and penetrating look, was said by the poet Léon-Paul Fargue to have created the impression of an 'El Greco who might have been gay'.[3] He was drawn to literature and painting as much as to music; and it was he who introduced Ravel to the lugubrious prose poems of Aloysius Bertrand, *Gaspard de la Nuit*, which inspired his amazing virtuoso piano suite. Viñes's manner of playing was based on a subtle and complex use of the two pedals. The Spanish pianist Gonzalo Soriano claimed that he was double-jointed, and this, it was said, enabled

[1] At Rome about four years earlier, this fresh, exuberant work, with its novel rhythmic and melodic ideas, was played by Debussy and Paul Vidal to Liszt. (See Vol. I, p. 82.)

[2] It was clearly in Paris that the school of twentieth-century Spanish music arose. The Franco-Spanish musical connexions of this period are discussed in Appendix B.

[3] The arresting thumb-nail sketch of Viñes by Fargue from which this description is taken is worth reproducing: 'Je le vois monter d'un bond du fond du souvenir, attachant comme personne, drôle et fin, vif et noir, un Greco qui eût été gai ... volubile, emballé, sautant littéralement sur ses amis, les empoignant avec force par un bouton de leur veston, par un bout de leur sensibilité dans sa hâte à leur faire partager son amour des êtres et des choses.'

The Deep-Sea Wave off Kanagawa, by Hokusai

Ravel and Stravinsky

Ricardo Viñes and Ravel

him to stroke the keys in a way that produced an unusually evoca-tive tone. The last work of Ravel which Viñes introduced was *Gaspard de la Nuit*, in 1909. After the death of Debussy he continued to bring forward new French piano works, and at a series of concerts appropriately called *Lyre et Palette* he was the first to play the *Mouvements perpétuels* by Francis Poulenc, whose piano teacher he was. 'He was some kind of a strange hidalgo with an enormous moustache, a brown sombrero in true Barcelona style and button boots with which he used to kick me on the shins whenever I was clumsy at the pedals', Poulenc affectionately recalled. 'No one could teach the art of using the pedals, an essential feature of modern piano music, better than Viñes', this composer, who was also a remarkable pianist, went on to explain; and he emphasized the fact that Viñes 'somehow managed to extract clarity from the very ambiguities created by the pedals'.

On a score of Ravel's *Jeux d'eau* Viñes is admiringly described by the composer as 'the guardian of the key of the waters'. The special delight of these two sophisticated musicians, drawn to each other by their common love of Baudelaire, was to discover an old out-of-tune piano hidden away in some ancient provincial mansion. Chopin played on such a piano was felt by these seekers of strange sensations to reach the heights of poetic nostalgia.[1] Ravel, who deliberately put forward a most deceptive image of himself—one thought of him as a *gaillard* (a lad), said Colette; a jockey, said Viñes—responded to certain works in a hypersensitive manner. At a performance of the Prelude to *Tristan* this remote detached figure melted into tears, as he did again on hearing *Le Sacre du Printemps*. Two works of Debussy and Ravel are dedicated to Viñes, *Oiseaux tristes* from Ravel's *Miroirs* and *Poissons d'or* from the second set of Debussy's *Images*.

Though, as we shall presently see, the piano styles of Debussy and Ravel are radically different they have nevertheless points of re-semblance, some of which have been exaggerated in the past in order to ascribe to the one composer or the other the priority of a technical discovery. In 1898 a work for two pianos entitled *Sites auriculaires* by the twenty-three-year-old Ravel was performed, consisting of two pieces, *Entre cloches* and *Habanera*. The former is

---

[1] There is perhaps an anticipation here of the out-of-tune cottage piano used by another admirer of Baudelaire, Alban Berg, in *Wozzeck*.

lost but an orchestral form of the latter appeared as the third movement of Ravel's *Rapsodie espagnole* of 1907, where a note on the score states that it had been composed twelve years earlier. The reason for this note, Léon Vallas states, was that Ravel wished to establish the authenticity of a particular harmonic device, a persistent pedal figure, which he had originated. In the meantime, according to Vallas, Debussy's curiosity had been aroused by Ravel's *Habanera* to the extent of his asking the younger composer to lend him the score.[1] *Lindaraja*, a piece for two pianos which Debussy wrote in 1901, and the *Soirée dans Grenade* both bear a resemblance to Ravel's *Habanera*, the first of the many Spanish pieces by both Ravel and Debussy, though there had been many opportunities for Debussy to become acquainted with the harmonic and melodic peculiarities of Spanish music other than through this early piece of Ravel.[2]

If in fact Debussy's imagination was kindled by this early *Habanera* it is equally true that Ravel was stimulated by certain of Debussy's later piano works. Echoes of *D'un cahier d'esquisses*, of which Ravel himself gave the first performance, are to be found in Ravel's *Oiseaux tristes*, and something of Debussy's *Hommage à Rameau*, of 1905, is reflected in the opening of *Le Gibet* (from *Gaspard de la Nuit*) composed three years later. We should not, however, attach too much importance to these points of resemblance. The detection of melodic or harmonic similarities of this kind is easy enough. Indeed, such resemblances between the works of two composers exploring the same territory are inevitable. Ultimately they do not really detract from the originality of the one or the other.

We have also to take into account an important personal aspect of their relationship. It was long held that though Debussy and Ravel greatly esteemed each other an estrangement had developed

---

[1] There is no known correspondence between Debussy and Ravel, nor have we any precise knowledge of a meeting or meetings between them. In his *Ravel* (1938) Roland Manuel says that in about 1902 the two composers enjoyed 'un commerce amical et spirituel'. About 1912 Ravel said of his relationship with Debussy: 'Il vaut peut-être mieux, après tout, que nous soyons en froid pour des motifs inconsistents.' Debussy's alleged entreaty to Ravel on his String Quartet, 'In my name and in the name of the gods of music do not alter a single note of your Quartet', is supported by no known document. Debussy's stepson, Raoul Bardac, informed me that it was he who introduced Ravel to Debussy around 1901. This seems to be confirmed by Ravel's letter to Florent Schmitt of 8 April 1901 (*Ravel au miroir de ses lettres*, p. 21).

[2] Notably through his knowledge of the Spanish folk-songs collected by Pedrell. See Appendix B.

between them as a result of certain journalistic battles of which both composers had become victims. There was perhaps an element of truth in this, but what is striking to us today is the emptiness and futility of this critics' war, vainly waged on the matter of the respective merits of Debussy and Ravel; it could hardly have inflamed feelings that had not previously existed. There was of course rivalry between Debussy and Ravel. It turned sometimes to jealousy and even envy. The adjacent or overlapping fields explored by the two composers were rich and it would be foolish not to expect severe and often persistent clashes between them. Recently published material, particularly the correspondence between Debussy and the critic Louis Laloy, allows us to see their relationship more closely and to assess those altogether natural elements of rivalry which, far from being concealed, were openly admitted in the form of a challenge.

In the opening years of the twentieth century Debussy and Ravel had presented some of their greatest works. By the end of 1905 *Pelléas* and *La Mer* had been heard and also Ravel's piano works, *Jeux d'eau* and *Miroirs*. Ravel, however, was still relatively unknown. In January 1907 Jane Bathori, accompanied by the composer, gave the first performance of Ravel's *Histoires naturelles*, a song-cycle on the miniature portraits by Jules Renard of birds and animals. The work achieved a *succès de scandale* and represented a turning-point in Ravel's career. Praising this amazing little song-cycle in *La Revue S.I.M.* of 15 February 1907, Laloy drew a comparison between the character of Ravel's music and that of Japanese landscapes, and he also claimed that the *Histoires naturelles* owed something to the spirit of Moussorgsky: 'I freely admit', he wrote, 'that the whole spirit of Moussorgsky's *Nursery* is in this work, but combined with an infallible sense of taste and with wonderful skill. . . . Moussorgsky showed the way, but he had neither the courage to follow it to its logical end nor the talent to endow such a natural, freely conceived text with real, pure music.' Provoked by this comparison of Ravel with Moussorgsky, Debussy's letter to Laloy of 22 February contains a caustic reproach: 'I have received the second number of the *S.I.M.* and am amazed to see that a man of your taste deliberately sacrifices such a pure instinctive master-piece as *The Nursery* to the artificial Americanism [*l'américanisme voulu*] of the *Histoires naturelles* of Monsieur Ravel. Despite Ravel's unquestionable skill, these songs only consist of music that we must call unwarranted.' And in a rage he adds, 'Leave such things to the lackey Calvocoressi. . . .'[1]

Publishing this correspondence in *La Revue de Musicologie*, François Lesure reasonably wonders whether Debussy had been animated not by Laloy's opinion in itself but by the fact of his having published it, since three days later, on 25 February, Debussy offers a rather different assessment of this work of Ravel to Durand: 'Thank you for the *Histoires naturelles*. It's extremely interesting [*excessivement curieux*]! It's artificial and imaginative, rather like the house of a magician. *Le Cygne* [the third of the *Histoires*] is all the same very lovely music.' On 2 March, having received no reply from Laloy, Debussy angrily writes: 'Forgive me for breaking a silence which you seem to value, and also for telling you that I am nonplussed by your attitude. You don't even take the trouble to reply. . . . I confess that my affectionate feelings for you are some-what hurt and I have been fruitlessly seeking the reasons which allow you to act in this way.' In his memoirs Laloy, naturally concerned about the rivalry between his two friends, states: 'I did everything possible to avert a misunderstanding between them, but too many silly meddlers seemed to delight in making such a misunderstanding inevitable, sacrificing, for instance, the Quartet of Debussy to that of Ravel, or by bringing up absurd questions of priority between the *Habanera* and the second of the *Estampes*. The two musicians thus stopped seeing each other. Since each esteemed the other I was aware of the fact that they both regretted this rupture.' Some kind of courteous or perhaps an embarrassed apology must have been sent by Laloy to Debussy, as we gather from Debussy's anxious letter to him of 8 March:

Nervous people are unbearable and you must therefore forgive me [. . .]. Concerning Ravel, I am aware of your usual cleverness. If, as it seems to me, he hasn't finally found the direction he should pursue, he may be grateful to you for having shown it to him. . . . But between ourselves do you sincerely believe in 'humorous' music? There is no such thing as humorous music in

[1] M. D. Calvocoressi was one of Ravel's earliest admirers. His article 'Maurice Ravel et l'imitation debussyste' was to appear in the *Grande Revue of* 10 May 1907. Despite its title, chosen to lure Ravel's opponents, it emphasized the radical differences in style and technique of the two composers.

itself; it may become so as a result of being associated with certain words or a certain situation. Two chords stuck in the air, or in any other absurd position, are not necessarily humorous. Only by association can they become so. I agree with you in recognizing that Ravel could not be more gifted, but what annoys me is his attitude of a mountebank [*faiseur de tours*] or rather of an oriental magician who is able to make flowers grow out of a chair. Unfortunately a trick of this kind is always well prepared and can only astonish once![1] However, I want nothing more than that people should be amused—an art calculated to restore the smiling face of music would be a rather polite gesture since there have been such efforts to torment music and weigh it down.[2]

Ravel's appreciation of Debussy was hardly ever curdled by irony of this kind. Nearly all the references to Debussy in his correspondence and writings show not only respect and admiration for the older composer but a frank recognition of his stature. The Preludes are 'wonderful masterpieces'. Despite 'the croakings of his perfidious admirers, Debussy is still very much alive'. In 1903 Ravel's orchestration of Debussy's *Sarabande* (from *Pour le Piano*) was given at the Concerts Lamoureux. Romain Rolland, who met Ravel in 1904, found him 'plus Debussyste que Debussy', and when, together with Richard Strauss, they heard *Pelléas et Mélisande* at the Opéra-Comique, Ravel was said to be noticeably unaffected by his quarrel with Debussy. In 1909 and 1910 Ravel transcribed for two pianos Debussy's *Nocturnes* and *L'Après-midi d'un faune* and in 1923 his orchestration of Debussy's early piano piece, *Tarantelle styrienne*,

[1] It is significant that in an unpublished letter of 1909 to Calvocoressi Debussy uses the same expressions of Rimsky-Korsakov, whose sense of the orchestra manifestly influenced Ravel in *Daphnis et Chloé*. Calvocoressi had sent Debussy his translation of *Coq d'or*: 'Très sincerement merci pour l'envoi du *Coq d'or*', Debussy writes. 'C'est la musique d'un vieux faiseur de tours qui fut très fort et qui s'en souvient.' If there was rivalry between Debussy and Ravel in regard to their piano works they were apparently unable to see eye to eye on the matter of their orchestral works. One would dearly love to know in regard to which work Ravel declared to Emile Vuillermoz: 'Debussy est un musicien admirable mais comme il est fâcheux qu'il orchestre si mal!'

[2] In the 15 March issue of *La Revue S. I. M.* Laloy wrote again about the *Histoires naturelles*, standing firmly by his original judgement: 'His light ironic touch, far from diminishing the emotional value of his music, enlivens and sharpens its appeal. Nothing could be nearer tears than the smiles which he provokes, smiles which belonged to Cervantes and Dickens before they were appropriated by Jules Renard.... Monsieur Ravel is a humorist among composers, a born humorist.'

appeared under the title *Danse*. In all this there is ample proof of Ravel's sincere devotion to Debussy. On the other hand, the name of Ravel is not once mentioned by Debussy without a note of sarcasm, irony, or concern, certainly never with any sort of unreserved admiration.[1] Yet of the French piano music written in the decade before the first World War Debussy was easily able to claim the lion's share. The following table shows the rapid succession of works by the two composers, most of them introduced during this short golden age of French piano music—a mere seventeen years extends from Debussy's *Pour le Piano* to Ravel's *Le Tombeau de Couperin*—by the alluring 'hidalgo' Ricardo Viñes.

DATE OF FIRST PERFORMANCE	WORK	COM-POSER	PERFORMER
11 Jan. 1902	*Pour le Piano*	Debussy	Viñes
5 Apr. 1902	*Pavane pour une infante défunte*	Ravel	Viñes
	Jeux d'eau	Ravel	Viñes
9 Jan. 1904	*Estampes*	Debussy	Viñes
18 Feb. 1905	*Masques*	Debussy	Viñes
	L'Isle joyeuse	Debussy	Viñes
6 Jan. 1906	*Miroirs*	Ravel	Viñes
3 Mar. 1906	*Images* (First Series)	Debussy	Viñes
10 Mar. 1906	*Sonatine*	Ravel	Paule de Lestang
21 Feb. 1908	*Images* (Second Series)	Debussy	Viñes
18 Dec. 1908	*Children's Corner*	Debussy	Harold Bauer
9 Jan. 1909	*Gaspard de la Nuit*	Ravel	Viñes

[1] Asked by Laloy in 1906 to write for *Le Mercure Musical*, he refused, expressing a note of disillusionment: 'Il y a certainement des choses à dire, mais à qui? Pour qui? Pour des gens qui oscillent de Beethoven à Maurice Ravel!' Calling on his publisher in 1908, he finds Ravel seated in his armchair: 'Votre fauteuil occupé par Monsieur Ravel ne devait certes pas trouver cela plus drôle que moi.' In 1913 the two composers, both published by Durand, happened each to write the songs *Soupir* and *Placet futile* on the same two poems of Mallarmé. 'The story of this Mallarmé-Ravel connexion is not amusing', Debussy wrote to Durand in an annoyed mood. 'Is it not strange that Ravel happens to have chosen the same poems as myself?' Finally, we have evidence of Debussy's feelings from the letters of Robert Godet, which must be read with the knowledge of this persistent feud in mind. To encourage Debussy at the most acute period of his illness—in 1917 during the last months of his life—Godet assures him how easily he can surpass Ravel. Debussy was staying at Saint-Jean-de-Luz in the Basque country, near Ravel's birth-place. 'Laissez venir à vous l'inspiration des petits enfants, si c'en est l'heure', Godet writes, 'bien assuré—quoi que vous fassiez—de ravir d'un seul geste à Ravel le mérite qu'il ambitionnait, d'immortaliser sa patrie.' And he adds à propos of Ravel's gift for musical caricature: 'Son Pickwick articulé ne sera jamais mû que par des ficelles.'

DATE OF FIRST PERFORMANCE	WORK	COM- POSER	PERFORMER
20 Apr. 1910	*D'un Cahier d'esquisses*	Debussy	Ravel
	Ma Mère l'Oie (piano duet)	Ravel	J. Leleu and G. Durony
25 May 1910	Four Preludes (*Danseuses de Delphes, Voiles, La Cathédrale engloutie, La Danse de Puck*)	Debussy	Debussy
14 Jan. 1911	Three Preludes (*Les Collines d'Anacapri, La Fille aux cheveux de lin, La Sérénade interrompue*)	Debussy	Viñes
11 Mar. 1911	*Hommage à Haydn*	Debussy	—
	Menuet sur le nom d'Haydn	Ravel	—
29 Mar. 1911	Four Preludes (*Les Sons et les Parfums, Le Vent dans la plaine, Des Pas sur la neige, Minstrels*)	Debussy	Debussy
9 May 1911	*Valses nobles et sentimentales*	Ravel	Louis Aubert
12 Mar. 1912	Preludes (not specified)	Debussy	Debussy
– Mar. 1913	Three Preludes (*Bruyères, Feuilles mortes, La Puerta del Vino*)	Debussy	Debussy
5 Apr. 1913	Three Preludes (*Les Fées sont d'exquises danseuses, La Terrasse des audiences, Feux d'artifice*)[1]	Debussy	Viñes
10 Dec. 1913	*A la Manière de . . .*	Ravel	Casella
15 Oct. 1915	*Berceuse héroïque*	Debussy	—
14 Dec. 1916	Twelve Studies	Debussy	Walter Rummel
21 Dec. 1916	*En blanc et noir* (for two pianos)	Debussy	Debussy and Roger-Ducasse
17 Mar. 1917	*Six Epigraphes antiques*	Debussy	—
11 Apr. 1919	*Le Tombeau de Couperin*	Ravel	Marguerite Long

It would be wrong to deduce from this account of the Debussy-Ravel relationship that it was only Debussy who was envious or jealous. A close artistic relationship of this kind is largely motivated by rivalry—the healthy, productive force at the root of whole areas

---

[1] Debussy gave the first performance of eleven of his Preludes; Viñes of six. The first performances of the remaining seven have not been traced.

of human behaviour—and where there are no overt manifestations of rivalry it is likely, according to psychological theory, that this is because jealousy or envy has become so intense, indeed so threatening and dangerous, that by a trick of nature it is suppressed and relegated to the unconscious. The tremendous forces of rivalry are then obscured and appear to be replaced by the gentler (and safer) manifestations of love and admiration. Yet the situation created for Ravel, great artist as he was, was to some extent false since the underlying element of rivalry was neither met nor resolved.[1] In a sense it was also a paralysing situation for perhaps we may see here how it was that the exquisite art of Ravel did not evolve, unlike the more probing art of Debussy who was bold enough frankly to admit the gifts of his rival, his attraction and his stature.[2] However this may be, after writing Le Tombeau de Couperin, the prelude of which recalls the first of Debussy's Studies, Ravel produced no further works for piano solo. Ravel's piano works of genius, which had amazingly opened with Jeux d'eau in 1902, were equally amazingly concluded only seventeen years later with Le Tombeau de Couperin. It was only towards the end of his life, in 1931, after having heard the piano concertos of Stravinsky and Prokofiev, that Ravel wrote his two piano concertos, glancing back to those brief magical years before the first World War which in spirit still belonged to the preceding century.[3]

This preoccupation of Debussy and Ravel with the piano is an

[1] The suppression of rivalry is a well-known device of the unconscious mind, and recognition of this device frequently illuminates aspects of an artist's work and his behaviour. Without looking too far, I am sure that Francis Poulenc, known to be rightly jealous of a leading position, was, like Ravel, unconsciously concealing the truth from himself in the letter which, some months before his death, he spontaneously wrote to Benjamin Britten on the occasion of his fiftieth birthday: 'Cher Ben, A 50 ans vous voici glorieux comme un jeune Verdi. Nul ne s'en réjouit plus que moi car, en plus de la réelle affection que j'ai pour vous, j'ai toujours été émerveillé par la multiplicité de vos dons. Si j'étais de nature jaloux, ce que, Dieu merci, je ne suis pas, je crois bien que je serais déjà mort!'
[2] Debussy's self-knowledge must certainly have served him in Pelléas et Mélisande. The scene in which Golaud seizes Mélisande by her long fair hair and drags her to her knees (Act IV, Scene i) is one of the great explosions of jealousy in music.
[3] At the end of his life Ravel's work, so frequently stylized, forked out in two directions: to the emptiness of Boléro and to the powerful inspiration of the piano concerto for the left hand in which Ravel came nearest to bursting the vein of his genius. The contrast between these two works is alarming, and indeed they were shortly to be followed by the mental collapse from which Ravel never recovered. Tension had been brought to breaking-point, and beyond. We may form some idea, however, of Ravel's potential range from the fact that during these final, sterile years, he continued to be convinced that his finest music was still to be written.

interesting development in itself and is worth investigating. Not for nothing did the piano, at once the most mechanical of instruments, the most illusory and the most evocative, become the cherished instrument of both Debussy and Ravel during these years. Broadly speaking, the style of the piano works of Ravel derives from Liszt while Debussy's piano music is closer to the spirit of Chopin. Ravel's *Jeux d'eau* is no doubt the most original work in this renaissance of the piano, and its particular value at the time was that it explored realms of expression entirely different from those associated with the more austere piano styles of both César Franck and Brahms. These styles were largely based on the capacity of the ten fingers to sound heavy chords. In recent years the piano works of Brahms have regained favour, but at the beginning of the century his manner of writing for the piano was regarded as a model of how not to write for this instrument, at any rate outside Germany.[1] Nor was the genius of the piano understood by Franck, who regarded the resonant grand piano as a substitute for the organ. On the other hand Liszt, in his transcriptions, showed his perception of the illusory character of the piano when he declared that at least ten fingers were required to do justice to the deceptively simple accompaniment to the opening theme of Mozart's G Minor Symphony. The fact that the piano could sound ten notes simultaneously was not always an advantage.

Jeux d'eau is the first of Ravel's Lisztian works and it marks a distinct advance on Liszt's *Jeux d'eau à la Villa d'Este*. The elaborate arpeggios of Liszt's water-piece are the musical counterpart of a display of hydraulic fireworks. Ravel adopted the Lisztian technique but his aim, says Roland Manuel, 'was to extend Liszt's experiments in the high register of the piano and also to introduce the vivacity of the sonatas of Scarlatti'. Clarity in this Lisztian work of Ravel was of course essential, but there was another aspect of piano sonority with which Ravel was concerned. If sustained notes on the piano are an illusion, piano tone has, by its nature, a quality of indefiniteness. According to Ricardo Viñes Ravel recommended the use of the pedal in the higher register of the piano in *Jeux d'eau* in order to bring out 'not the clarity of the notes, but the hazy impression [*l'impression floue*] of vibrations in the air'. As we have seen,

---

[1] In 1916 Edward Dent could declare that 'Brahms's piano writing is in many ways nothing short of barbarous'.

Jeux d'eau appeared between the works of Debussy, *Pour le Piano* of 1902 and *Estampes* of 1904.[1] It was this haziness, this *impression floue*, remarkable in other aspects of Debussy's work, which Debussy must have found attractive, together with a development of the Lisztian manner, in *Jeux d'eau*.[2]

In her memoirs Marguerite Long repeatedly asserts that Debussy claimed Chopin as his principal model: 'He was impregnated with the spirit of Chopin, inhabited by it.' His knowledge of Chopin's manner of playing, which he derived from his first piano teacher, Madame Mauté, could not, however, have been extensive; it was principally concerned, as we saw earlier (Vol. I, Ch. 2, on Debussy's childhood) with Chopin's advice on the use of the sustaining pedal.[3] We shall presently return to Debussy's use of the two pedals in his piano music. For the moment we may note that his life-long attraction to Chopin resulted in his editing a collection of Chopin's works and the dedication of his last piano works, the twelve Studies, to Chopin's memory.[4]

In his study, published in 1916, on the influence of the piano in modern music, Edward Dent presents a strong case for considering the piano as the typical instrument of the romantic movement.

[1] A frequently quoted letter of 5 February 1906 from Ravel to the critic Pierre Lalo shows Ravel's awareness of the novelty of his work: 'You propound at length on a rather special kind of piano writing, the invention of which you ascribe to Debussy. But *Jeux d'eau* appeared at the beginning of 1902, when the only known works of Debussy were the three pieces forming the suite *Pour le Piano* which, I need hardly say, I deeply admire, but which from a purely pianistic viewpoint conveyed nothing really new.'

[2] Louis Laloy reproduces an illuminating conversation between Debussy and the conductor Camille Chevillard at the final rehearsal of the *Nocturnes* in 1901. Dissatisfied with the tonal balance and the character of one of the movements, no doubt *Nuages*, Debussy from the back of the hall shouted out: 'Je voudrais ça plus flou.' 'Plus vite?' Chevillard enquired. 'Non, plus flou.' 'Plus lent?' 'Plus flou.' The uncomprehending conductor was nonplussed. 'Je ne sais pas ce que vous voulez dire', he declared to the composer in a huff. 'Reprenons, Messieurs!'

[3] 'I have heard only two fine pianists,' Debussy told Victor Segalen in 1908, 'my old piano mistress, who plunged me straight away into Bach and who played Bach as he is never played now, and Liszt whom I heard in Rome.'

[4] In his last letter to Debussy, of January 1918, Robert Godet asks Debussy for his approval of a series of lecture-recitals on Chopin and Debussy. This series was planned by Marie Panthès with Godet's co-operation. Marie Panthès 'intends playing some of the Preludes and, I believe, the whole set of Studies to show resemblances and differences in style in both inspiration and technique (you and Chopin, in my opinion, mark the two main stages in the evolution of piano technique)'. Godet's lecture, *Chopin, Debussy*, published in Geneva, was conceived as a guide to the many affinities in the Preludes and Studies of the two composers. Antecedents are suggested among Chopin's Studies, for Debussy's five-finger Study, for his Studies in thirds, sixths, and octaves, in arpeggios, chords, and chromatic harmony.

This came about, Dent suggests, since the romantic movement, devoted to the poetry of associations, found that the piano was unique among musical instruments in being able to provide these associations. The piano alone could convey military effects, ecclesiastical effects, chromatic winds, waves in arpeggios, and many other realistic effects. Dent also stressed the fact that Beethoven in his writing for the piano assumed that his interpreters would realize that he was imitating the orchestra or even a singer.[1]

No one will question the validity of these conceptions of the piano in the early part of the nineteenth century. But together with realistic associations of this kind the piano was required to produce a type of tone for which, as Dent convincingly argues, it was utterly unsuited. He provides an amusing description of the school of late nineteenth-century pianists who constantly endeavoured to produce a 'singing tone' although this, at the piano, is a physical impossibility. These pianists 'systematically accepted the doctrine that the sounds of the piano were equivalent in value to the sounds of sustaining instruments'. Realizing that notes on the piano cannot be real sounds but only indications of them, Chopin and Liszt had established a different tradition. These were the true pianist-composers. Their styles were based on a realization of the fact that as the hammer strikes the strings notes are created percussively and their duration can therefore only be maintained artificially. Debussy boldly developed this illusory quality of the piano. To both Marguerite Long and Louise Liebich he insisted that the piano was to sound as if it were 'an instrument without hammers' and he wanted the fingers on the keyboard to appear to 'penetrate into the notes'.[2] The illusion was to be complete. Nothing was to be allowed to destroy the impression that the mechanical piano, a

---

[1] Though Debussy played Beethoven in his youth, in his later years, when he had evolved his original conception of the piano, he found himself wholly out of sympathy with Beethoven's piano works. After listening to students of the Paris Conservatoire playing Beethoven in 1909 he wrote to André Caplet, 'I became finally and completely convinced that Beethoven definitely wrote badly for the piano.' With the exception of Chopin, earlier composers for the piano left him unmoved. To Marguerite Long he confessed, 'Je déteste bien les concertos de Mozart, mais moins que ceux de Beethoven.'

[2] Marguerite Long writes of her study of *L'Isle Joyeuse* with the composer: 'L'illusion persiste toujours en moi de sentir, pressant mon épaule, les doigts du Maître commandant aux miens d'être *de plus près* encore *dans le clavier*.' If the fingers were to appear to enter into the very mechanism of the piano, the instrument itself was to become ethereal, 'ce piano surnaturel', as Laloy describes it, 'où les sons naissant sans choc des marteaux, sans frôlements, s'élèvent dans un air transparent'.

mere 'box of hammers and strings', was not a piano. It was sometimes to be an instrument that drew music from the circumambient air, or that could project patterns made up of myriads of little sounds. It was never admitted to be an instrument inferior, in the range or shadings of its dynamics, to wind or string instruments. Its defects were its virtues.[1]

At this point we may try to reconstruct the function which Debussy ascribed to the two piano pedals. In his letter to Durand of 1 September 1915, in which he recalls that his piano teacher, Madame Mauté, had told him that Chopin, like Liszt, used the sustaining pedal 'as a kind of breathing', he goes on to suggest a notation for the use of the pedals: 'The simple truth is, perhaps, that the abuse of the pedal is only a means of covering up a lack of technique, and it is also useful in making a great deal of noise, thus preventing people from realizing how music is massacred. In theory we should be able to find a graphic means of representing this "breathing" pedal—it should not be impossible. Moreover, I think there is a work by Marie Jaëll who was meticulous in her approach to the piano on this matter.' I think that the work Debussy had in mind was not one of the theoretical works of Marie Jaëll but Les Pédales du piano published in 1892 by a pupil of Massenet, Georges Falkenberg. Brought out in several later editions, this interesting treatise indicates methods of detailed notation for the use of the two pedals, in Chabrier's Sous Bois among other works, both separately and together.[2] Debussy's ideas on pedalling were

---

[1] The few orchestral arrangements that have been made of Debussy's piano works have been no more successful than the orchestral arrangements of works of Chopin—and for the same reason: they lose their evocative appeal. Several of Ravel's piano works, on the other hand, were orchestrated by the composer (though curiously not Scarbo from Gaspard de la Nuit, the most orchestrally conceived of them all). Several skilful piano versions, by Ravel himself among others, were made of Debussy's orchestral works, some of them extremely elaborate, such as André Caplet's arrangement of La Mer for three pianos.

[2] The Alsatian pianist Marie Jaëll (1846–1925) was a renowned teacher and a typical figure of her period in that she sought to establish in her teaching a relationship between tactile and visual sensations. Liszt, to whom Marie Jaëll acted as secretary, said that she possessed 'the brain of a philosopher and the fingers of an artist'. Most of her work consists of investigation into the nature of touch. Debussy's interest in her theoretical works, of which the principal one is Le Mécanisme du toucher (1897), indicates, if not one of the origins of his conception of the keyboard, at least a parallel line of thought. Her teaching was remarkable for her searching analyses of tone-colours depending, as she believed, on the degree of sensitiveness in the finger-tips. She described and analysed 'the unconscious reasoning at the root of instinctive works of art' and co-operated with the psychologist Charles Féré in La Musique et la psycho-physiologie and in other works not primarily concerned with music, among them

passed on by the pianists, Viñes, Marguerite Long, and Cortot, who played his work during his lifetime, but strangely enough we do not find a theoretical treatise on the use of the pedal in his work until *Pedalling the Modern Pianoforte* in 1936 by the English pianist York Bowen. Though Bowen was not known as an interpreter of Debussy he certainly came near to the heart of the problems of pedalling in his work. He first of all points out that the sustaining pedal is the only means of obtaining a legato in a sequence of chords; that a half-pedal which reduces vibrations but does not obliterate them is useful in achieving a diminuendo; and that a 'vibrato' pedal, produced by a rapid but limited movement of the foot (for which he indicates a special notation), provides for a more gradual diminuendo than a series of half-pedals which, by comparison, 'may seem to take chunks out of the sound'. He also describes a 'swirl' pedal, used in quick running passages and which consists of 'short patches of pedal calculated to help in the form of a swirl towards certain spots', and finally the 'hazy pedal', on which Bowen writes with great insight. There are occasions, he says, when 'we have deliberately to use a truly unclean form of pedalling. There are numerous examples in modern French music where it is essential to hold the pedal through passages of mixed harmonies. . . . The strangest of them is Debussy's *Cathédrale engloutie* where all kinds of diatonic combinations of notes are intended to be merged together. Indeed, in order that the last page should create the illusion of something seen hazily through a depth of water, the pedal is hardly changed at all—at any rate not fully—and an occasional "flick" pedal is all that is necessary.'

The well-known passage to which York Bowen refers consists of a series of chords of the seventh overlaid, as it were, with a chord of the ninth at the second bar, the merging of these harmonies creating the illusion, as Bowen rightly says, 'of something seen hazily through a depth of water'. (See example on p. 48.)

During Debussy's lifetime Dent was the first to perceive that the peculiar properties of the piano helped to establish twentieth-

---

L'Intelligence et le rythme dans les mouvements artistiques. In 1909 the names of Falkenberg and Debussy appear together as composers of simple pieces for children commissioned for publication by the piano teacher Théodore Lack in his *Méthode de piano*. Debussy's contribution was a Cake-Walk, *The Little Nigar*, in the style of the *Golliwog* from *Children's Corner*.

century harmony. Although Dent was writing at a time when it was still too early to realize the full significance of Debussy's innovations—he associates Debussy not only with Satie but with the forgotten Leo Ornstein—he was able to discover one of the underlying reasons for the new harmony and the manner in which it functioned.

Discords of modern harmony [he maintained] arise out of . . . the acceptance of chords, dissonant and consonant alike, as effects of timbre. . . . We know that any single note may be split up into its component harmonics, and that timbre depends on the relative intensities of these; then why should we not construct new timbres synthetically by sounding several notes together? If the organist may harmonize a melody in consecutive major thirds, fifths and octaves [which he does by using a mixture or a mutation stop] why should not the pianist, or anyone else, harmonize it in consecutive seconds, fourths or sevenths? It amounts to no more than pulling out a different stop. The pianoforte is obviously the most practical instrument on which to try experiments of this kind, and so about 1887 there rises in the world of music that delightfully quaint and entertaining composer Erik Satie, followed by Debussy, Ravel, Leo Ornstein, and others.

In an earlier chapter (Vol. I, Ch. 6) we saw how Debussy's early improvisations so impressed the organist at the Madeleine that he determined to reproduce them at this famous church, precisely in the manner that Dent half-humorously suggests, namely by using mutation stops to convey the impression of parallel successions of chords. Passages frequently met with in Debussy's music, such as this from *Et la Lune descend sur le temple qui fut*, use chords, as Dent states, principally for an effect of timbre.

The use of dissonance has no place in this seemingly more uniform music. Hitherto certain intervals were regarded, more or less arbitrarily, as consonant or dissonant. A dissonance was prepared or anticipated in a consonant chord, brought into relief by means of an ordered clash, and finally resolved into another consonance. This method of preparing and controlling tension was foreign to Debussy. In its place he provided degrees of dissonance or consonance, decided upon in advance—Debussy called this process *arrêter la couleur*—and calculated to attract a range of decorative or harmonic refinements.

This leads us to the technical question of form in Debussy's music, in the sense of the sequence and organization of musical ideas. In principle these ideas are (1) based on accepted theories of musical construction, or (2) follow an instinct for construction based on the interplay of contrast and association. The various forms of absolute music, the chief of which is the sonata form, derived their logic from the principles of diatonic harmony. It followed, therefore, that towards the end of the nineteenth century when these principles were challenged the forms which depended on their validity were likewise challenged.[1] In his youth Debussy wrote a String Quartet the form of which, as we saw, was based on the cyclic principles of César Franck. But this was an exceptional work in his evolution. In his later years he wrote a series of Sonatas 'for various instruments', the forms of which in no sense adhere to conventional principles. The very titles of their movements, *Prologue et Sérénade* (from the Cello Sonata) and *Pastorale et Interlude* (from the Piano and Violin Sonata), indicate their rhapsodic nature. There are, however, samples in Debussy's work of the classical type of thematic development, notably in *Jeux de vagues* from *La Mer* and in the scene of Golaud and Yniold in *Pelléas et Mélisande* (Act III Scene iv). In both cases these prolonged development passages are used to heighten dramatic effects. But in general, in view of the greater subtleties of harmony, 'development' for Debussy had come to be regarded as a mechanical procedure or a form of padding.[2] The piano with its essentially evocative qualities offered experiment with new principles of form based on contrasts of register, sonority, and figurations, and also on associations of aural imagery. Monsieur Jankélévitch draws attention to the several piano works of Debussy such as *Mouvement, Les Fées sont d'exquises danseuses,* and *Le Vent dans la plaine,* in which some kind of circular, whirlwind rhythm does not progress towards a goal but, on the contrary, remains static, emphasizing, by means of its spiral figurations, a preoccupation with the present moment (*le perpétuum mobile de l'immobile*). Rhetoric or even eloquence is not part of the technique of Debussy's musical language ('Take hold of Eloquence and wring her neck' proclaimed Verlaine in his search for the deeper instinctive

---

[1] Understandably, Debussy in his conversations with Guiraud on his return from Bayreuth failed to see why Wagner should retain methods of symphonic development. In his view the chromatic nature of Wagner's harmony had rendered symphonic development incongruous.

[2] In his *Debussy et le mystère* Vladimir Jankélévitch goes so far as to suggest that the logic of classical form is itself an illusion. Recalling the challenging eighteenth-century dictum of Fontenelle, 'Sonate que me veux-tu?', he writes: 'Une sonate n'a pas de "sens". Une fugue n'est pas un raisonnement. Un thème n'est pas la majeure d'une déduction; et l'on ne parle ici de syllogisme que par manière de dire. Une "pensée" musicale (si pensée il y a) ne "progresse" pas, c'est-à-dire: n'est pas plus avancée au milieu qu'au début. Plutôt que les moments successifs d'un plaidoyer ou d'une démonstration, nous vivons avec Debussy les épisodes et les événements décousus d'une histoire qui est rhapsodie de fait divers . . . , qui n'est pas "symphonie-Jupiter", mais plutôt "symphonie-Dionysos"!'

German and
Austrian
caricatures:

Richard Strauss
    by J. J. Vrieslander
Claude Debussy
    by Rudolf Herrmann

Turner, self-portrait

Edgar Allan Poe, by Thomas C. Corner

truth) but reticence is, and together with reticence a ruthless paring away of superfluous trappings.[1]

The elements of Debussy's musical language, to be dealt with in a later chapter, derive from many different sources: medieval sources (Gregorian chant and plainsong), the ecclesiastical modes, pentatonic scales in their different modes, folk songs of several countries, European and Oriental, unresolved discords of nineteenth-century harmony. But all these elements are merged together and moulded into an unmistakably personal language. Ultimately, since the great bulk of Debussy's music is associated with literary or pictorial ideas, his technique of composition, consisting in the first place of the discovery of thematic symbols or aural images, must be classed with that of the composers of programme music. Thematic symbols have, however, by their nature, a variety of meanings. A horn solo in the music of Weber signifies a romantic forest, in Berlioz a hunt, in Wagner heroism. Debussy invented many new symbols, but he gave us no clue to their meaning apart from some vague observations: 'The sight of a sunrise is a more valuable experience than listening to the Pastoral Symphony' or 'Listen to no one unless to the passing wind which tells us the history of the world.'[2] Debussy sometimes uses imitation—in *La Cathédrale engloutie*, *Feux d'artifice*, and even the opening of *L'Après-midi d'un faune*—but nearly always it is evocation with which he is principally concerned and which, as Brailoiu observes, he achieves by means of thematic symbolism. More than any other single instrument it was the romantic, evocative piano, the instrument with sonorities of ill-defined duration and lingering vibrations,[3] that provided Debussy with those 'mysterious concordances' in sound and sight and that most convincingly enabled him to define his musical language.

[1] Jankélévitch suggests that Debussy took this admonition of Verlaine literally: 'Tantôt par la poignante monotonie, tantôt par la discontinuité, Debussy coupe court à l'inclination rhétorique. A la brusque suspension du discours un motif spécial d'étranglement est souvent préposé.' Examples of this 'strangulation' of development are to be found in *La Sérénade interrompue*, *La Danse de Puck*, *Minstrels*, and *Général Lavine*.

[2] 'This is all very well', observes the ethnologist Constantin Brailoiu in one of the most penetrating analyses of Debussy's musical language, 'but the wind is able to teach us neither harmony nor counterpoint.' Brailoiu was a pupil of André Gédalge who, though one of the earliest of Debussy's admirers, insisted to his pupils that music should be 'ni littérature ni peinture'.

[3] 'Laissez vibrer' is a frequent direction given by Debussy.

3

Monsieur Croche and Monsieur Teste

A quoi bon votre art presque incompréhensible?

M. Croche

Debussy's activities as a critic began before Pelléas, in 1901, when he wrote regular articles for *La Revue Blanche*, and they continued almost until the beginning of the first World War. During this period he was also critic of *Gil Blas* and *La Revue S.I.M.* and wrote occasional articles for other journals. The scope of these articles, covering many æsthetic and technical aspects of the music heard in Paris at that time, is wide but Debussy's writings on music have not so far been brought out in a collected edition. The well-known collection entitled *M. Croche antidilettante* consists of twenty-five more or less arbitrarily selected articles, many of them abridged, and drawn entirely from the earlier series written between 1901 and 1906. The more controversial articles on the crisis of French music, art, and nationalism, and on musical taste, published in the later series in *La Revue S.I.M.* do not appear in *M. Croche*. Moreover, though the proofs of this collection of early articles were seen by Debussy and corrected by him, his corrections were not taken into account by the publisher, who was unable to bring the book out until after Debussy's death, in 1921. It cannot therefore be said that *M. Croche* is representative of Debussy's work as a critic. Though it contains the valuable articles on Rameau and Gluck, on Moussorgsky, and on Wagner and Strauss, it is desirable, in assessing Debussy's critical work, to refer to their original form and also to collate them with other often contradictory opinions expressed in Debussy's letters and conversations.[1]

Apparently Debussy had intended publishing a book containing his critical ideas shortly after *Pelléas*. Infuriated by Jean Lorrain's malicious article *Les Pelléastres*, Pierre Louÿs wrote to Debussy in 1904: 'Your best reply will be your book. It will enable your ideas to become known among people who need to know them.' Probably Debussy wished at this time to re-edit his early articles together with his theories on criticism and music set out in his *Entretien avec M. Croche*.[2] This particular article, the key to Debussy's manner of thinking on music, may in fact have been written earlier, for we have evidence not only that the creation of the searching philosophical character of Monsieur Croche was based on a similar figure, Monsieur Teste, created by Paul Valéry, but that Debussy was associated with Valéry at the very time when Valéry's *Soirée avec M. Teste* was first published.

In 1896 there appeared a new literary review, *Le Centaure*. The signature of Debussy appears on a copy of this first number together with the signatures of Valéry, Léon-Paul Fargue, Pierre Louÿs, and Lord Alfred Douglas,[3] who, on 18 May of that year, had dined together to celebrate its publication. The first number of *Le Centaure* contained two poems by Valéry, *Vue* and *Eté*. The second number contained *La Soirée avec M. Teste*, originally entitled

---

[1] In 1927 Léon Vallas listed all the articles and essays of Debussy which had been discovered up to that time under the title *Les Idées de Claude Debussy* (translated by Marie O'Brien as *The Theories of Claude Debussy*, London, 1929). Corrections and additions to Vallas's compilation appear in Appendix G. Lengthy extracts from Debussy's critical writings together with commentaries are ingeniously grouped together in this publication, though Vallas's selection tended to over-emphasize Debussy's nationalist ideas.

[2] This was first published in *La Revue Blanche*, 1 July 1901. Writing to Louis Laloy five years later regarding contributions to the *Mercure Musical*, Debussy says: 'For the future I am thinking of a series of notes and opinions left by our poor Monsieur Croche who has finally decided to die. This most sensitive gentleman came to the conclusion that I really could not go on producing dialogues between Nothingness and some vague kind of Emptiness. He left me the option therefore either of publishing his papers or of burning them. We must consider the best thing to do together.' Laloy was unable to persuade Debussy to write for the *Mercure Musical*. Nor was André Gide any more successful in his approach to Debussy as a contributor to *La Nouvelle Revue Française*. Gide, after hearing *Pelléas* ('Quel bien vous nous faites de nous prouver que l'art n'est pas mort') writes to Debussy on the matter of the *N.R.F.*: 'Doit-elle vraiment perdre tout espoir de voir jamais votre nom à son sommaire?'

[3] It was no doubt only a coincidence that Debussy, who had met Louÿs in 1893, was to meet Lord Alfred Douglas ('Bosie') with Louÿs three years later. Douglas was in Paris at this time for the publication of his poems by the *Mercure de France*.

Mémoires du Chevalier Dupin, a title chosen as a homage to Poe and
to his celebrated hero who became the prototype of the scientific
detective. In *The Art of Paul Valéry* Francis Scarfe makes it clear
that Poe's analytical characters were a powerful inspiration to
Valéry in his creation of Monsieur Teste. 'The *Soirée*', he writes,
'is written in the form of a monologue, in the first person, with
occasional reported speech. . . . Poe in *The Murders in the Rue
Morgue* and *The Mystery of Marie Roget* . . . had already presented
the formula of the strong silent man, the unusual analytical mind
presented through a first-person narrator; but the *Soirée* differs
from these in the sense that the narrator has substantially the same
thoughts, the same type of mind as the one he is describing.'[1]

The similarities between Monsieur Croche and Monsieur Teste,[2]
both wizened, cigar-smoking observers, are striking not only in
their philosophical approach to criticism but even in their physical
appearance. Monsieur Teste 'was perhaps forty years old. His
speech was extraordinarily rapid, and his voice quiet. Everything
about him was fading, his eyes, his hands. . . . When he spoke he
never raised an arm or a finger; he had *killed his puppet*. He did not
smile, and said neither hello nor good-bye.'[3] And here is Debussy's
Monsieur Croche. He 'was a spare, wizened man whose gestures
were apparently calculated to make some point in a metaphysical
discussion. His appearance is best suggested by recalling those of
Tom Lane, the jockey, and of M. Thiers.[4] He spoke very softly
and never laughed, occasionally emphasizing his remarks with a
quiet smile which, beginning at the nose, proceeded to wrinkle the
whole face, the effect being of a still pond disturbed by a pebble.
These smiles of his were interminable and also unbearable.'

They were both aware of the evils of vanity, and they were also
aware of the narrow borderland between vanity and rivalry. 'If I
had gone on as most men do', says Monsieur Teste, 'not only
would I have believed myself their superior, but would have seemed

[1] Five years before the publication of *M. Teste* Valéry had written to Gide: 'Pour
lectures surtout et toujours sans pouvoir m'arracher à cet opium vertigineux et comme
mathématique: Poe, Poe!'
[2] 'Teste' has the allied meanings of 'head' (old French) and 'witness' or 'spectator'
(from the Latin *testis*). 'Croche' has also a double meaning. It is the musical term for a
quaver, while the expression 'les mains croches' means 'to be close-fisted'.
[3] The translations of these extracts from *M. Teste* are by Jackson Mathews.
[4] Resolute and grim in appearance, Louis Thiers, President of the Republic, was the
most gifted of the French literary statesmen of the nineteenth century. The well-
known English jockey at this time was not Tom but Frederick Lane.

so. I have preferred myself. What they call a superior being is one who has deceived himself. To wonder at him, we have to see him—and to be seen he has to show himself. And he shows me that he has a silly obsession with his own name. Every great man is thus flawed with an error.' In his first conversation with Monsieur Croche Debussy is similarly aware of this element of play-acting in an artist's career.

What is the point of defining one's aims, even of finishing a work in hand? [he asks]. These are questions prompted by childish vanity or by a craving to be rid of too powerful an obsession [besoin de se débarrasser à tout prix d'une idée avec laquelle on a trop vécu]. All this is a thin disguise for the foolish yearning to be superior to others. No great effort is required to surpass others if one is not at the same time absorbed in surpassing oneself. Here one must be prepared to sacrifice one's whole nature and to submit to a transformation. Moreover, superiority over others is an illusion and leads nowhere. As for public success this can only be procured at the expense of a great waste of time and by sedulous self-advertisement. In the end one merely belongs to a collection of great men whose names are bandied about to revive dreary conversations on art. But I don't want to labour the point. Some people are inclined that way.

Elsewhere these analytical, Poe-like characters discourse on the nature of discipline, divinity, and genius. 'Discipline is not bad', Monsieur Teste concedes. 'It is at least a beginning.' The values of inspiration are unreliable. 'Will you deny', he is asked, 'that there are trees that intoxicate us, men that give us strength, girls that paralyse us, skies that stop our speech?' To which Monsieur Teste replies: 'But, sir, what is the "talent" of your trees—or of anyone to me! I am at home in MYSELF. I speak my language, I hate extraordinary things. Only weak minds need them. Believe me literally: genius is easy, divinity is easy. . . . I mean simply—that I know how it is conceived. It is easy.' The same search for a novel, instinctive art drives on Monsieur Croche.

Music is a gathering together of impulsive expressions [La musique est un total de forces éparses]. And these impulsive expressions are turned into a formal song! I prefer a few notes on the flute of an Egyptian shepherd; he at any rate belongs to his native scene and has a knowledge of harmony not to be found in theoretical treatises. Musicians listen only to sophisticated music, never to the music of nature. The sight of a sunrise is a more valuable experience than listening to the Pastoral Symphony. What is the use of your almost incomprehensible art? Is it not time to abolish those parasitical complexities which have turned music into an instrument as ingenious as the lock of a safe? The reason you are merely marking time is that you have no knowledge of anything beyond music and because you are willing to submit to barbarous laws the origin of which no one knows. You are acclaimed in terms of high praise but in fact you are rather crafty: something between a monkey and a lackey.

These heights are not of course maintained indefinitely. Once the character of Monsieur Croche is established Debussy often jots down any idea or association that happens to cross his mind, sometimes writing in the precious and even the verbose style cultivated by some of the lesser writers of the period, sometimes maliciously annihilating a discussion with a waspish sting, or plunging headlong into some matter that has aroused his anger with bitter and vociferous sarcasm. Willy, who was Debussy's contemporary, was a master of the type of penetrating criticism written in a light style, in short, sharp sentences. Debussy had not the literary gifts of Willy though he favourably compares with Colette, who under the name of Claudine happened to write a musical column in *Gil Blas* in the same year, 1903, as Debussy.[1] Colette, in her best tomboyish manner, was nothing if not outspoken.[2] She was aware that though Debussy was in two minds about Strauss he recognized the abundant qualities of the German composer. All the same Colette could not abide the love-scene in *Feuersnot*: 'Even if Debussy were to stone me to death I will persist in saying that I don't like

[1] Editors of French journals sometimes employed two music critics not of complementary but of contrasting views. In the *Revue S.I.M.* a double column was shared by Debussy, who wrote on the Concerts Colonne, and Vincent d'Indy, who wrote on the Concerts Lamoureux. It thus came about that these two composers wrote in a single issue (February 1914) of the first performances in France of *Parsifal* and Mahler's Fourth Symphony.

[2] Of a performance of Beethoven's *Missa Solemnis* she wrote: 'Croire en Dieu, comme ça pendant trente-cinq minutes sans ronfler, c'est trop pour la mediocrité de ma foi.' And of Tchaikovsky's Pathetic Symphony: 'Me réfugier dans le sommeil? J'ai bien essayé, mais zut! je ne peux pas dormir sur des rhythmes à cinq-quatre.'

this kind of music. My ears go *bzi, bzi*, and if I allowed myself to become so ecstatic I wonder what my neighbours downstairs would say!' The soft, faint smile is evident enough on her knowing face.

Among foreign conductors visiting France at the beginning of the century, Weingartner, who in later years was noted for the sobriety of his gestures, was one of the first figures to use the extravagant physical gestures associated with the conductor who had become a king of musical supermen. Nikisch, belonging to the older school, believed that for orchestral musicians to give of their best the arm of the conductor should not be raised above the level of the shoulders. The new conducting technique, encouraging wild, fantastic gestures, seemed to the French to be play-acting in rather doubtful taste. Colette and Debussy accordingly vied with each other in describing Weingartner's spectacular manner. 'Tall, clean-shaven and with that colourless complexion, suddenly turning crimson, of an enlightened Jesuit', Colette amusingly observes, 'Weingartner conducts with gestures that are magnificent or ridiculous. His short coat jumps up with the ataxic jerks of his arms or flies around to the rhythm of his hammering fists. In opening the flood-gates of music this German works himself up to a state of epilepsy.' Weingartner's tall, lean figure seemed to Debussy to be as sharp as a knife. 'He has an almost rectilinear elegance; and then, all of a sudden, unrelenting gestures draw moans from the trombones or drive the cymbals crazy. It is most impressive and belongs to the art of the miracle-worker.' Seen for the first time, the spectacular gestures of the modern conductor must indeed have been alarming.[1]

One of the most arresting chapters in *M. Croche* is the extremely concise description, a mere five hundred words, of Moussorgsky's *The Nursery*, originally part of an article written for *La Revue Blanche* in 1901. Debussy was exaggerating when he baldly stated

[1] One of Debussy's celebrated tirades was directed against Cortot who, before the first World War, had established a reputation as a Wagnerian conductor. 'Cortot is the French conductor who has most successfully appropriated the usual pantomime technique of the German conductors', Debussy caustically remarks. 'He advances on the orchestra, directing at them a threatening baton like a banderillero at a bull-fight determined to undermine the confidence of the bull. (The members of the orchestra remain as cool as Icelanders; they have seen displays of this sort before.) Like Weingartner, Cortot leans affectionately over the first violins, murmuring intimate secrets, then swoops round to the trombones whom he exhorts with a gesture which apparently means, "Courage! Put some go into it! Try to be supertrombones!" Whereupon the obedient trombones conscientiously swallow their brass tubes.'

at this time that 'Moussorgsky is not well known in France'.[1] How far *The Nursery* may have prompted *Children's Corner* may be judged from Debussy's immediate response to the purely intuitive aspects of Moussorgsky's art: 'It is like the art of an enquiring savage discovering music step by step, dictated only by his feelings. There is never question of a particular form, or at any rate the form is so varied that it is impossible to relate it to the established or, as one might say, the official forms. It is music which is built up by means of a succession of little touches mysteriously linked together, the sense of unity being achieved with remarkable shrewdness.'[2]

The two chapters in *M. Croche* on Rameau and Gluck, originally criticisms, both written in 1903, of *Castor et Pollux* at the Schola Cantorum and *Iphigénie en Aulide* at the Opéra, should be read in conjunction with a later article by Debussy on Rameau. This remained unpublished in Debussy's lifetime and appears in the *Lettres inédites à André Caplet*. Debussy, as opposed to Berlioz and other early nineteenth-century French musicians, believed that Gluck had on the whole a stifling influence on French music. Gluck's ideas on French prosody, he declared, were clumsy and primitive, his classical ideals were pompous, and his inspiration, deriving from Greek mythology, suspect. Rameau, whose operas were only beginning to be revived in France at this time, appeared to Debussy to be 'infinitely more Greek' in spirit and certainly more lyrical. It may seem strange to us that a musician of that time was able to admire both the spontaneity of Moussorgsky and the theoretical mind of Rameau, but the breadth of Debussy's sympathies allowed him to embrace them both.

Debussy's revolutionary ideas on the merits of Rameau and Gluck shocked the contemporary musical world, but in recent times they have been endorsed. To present-day ears the subtleties of Rameau have become more apparent while the so-called classical style of

---

[1] Moussorgsky may not have been widely known in France at this time, but as early as 1896 he was certainly well known to both French musicians and writers (see Vol. I, pp. 48–9). Debussy himself knew Moussorgsky's works well at this period. 'Il en parlait à tout le monde', writes René Peter, 'à tout instant, comme de l'un des plus grands musiciens contemporains, peut-être le plus grand; il le répandait autour de lui de cent façons, le donnant à chanter à ses élèves.'

[2] Though the child-like qualities of *The Nursery* and *Children's Corner* illustrate deep-seated differences between the Russian and the French musical characters, there is an obvious similarity in the tenderness and naïvety of their approach. 'Vous y êtes, Debussy?' enquired Jules de Brayer, Debussy's Moussorgskian friend on hearing *Children's Corner*. 'Oui', conceded Debussy. 'J'y suis et j'y reste.'

Gluck strikes us as increasingly severe and remote. Debussy's article on Rameau, sent to André Caplet in Boston in 1912, possibly for publication in an American magazine, has not hitherto appeared in English and even in its original form has remained almost unknown. Since it sets out Debussy's main ideas, inspired by the Rameau revival in the first decade of the twentieth century, largely the work of his friend Louis Laloy, it is worth reproducing in full:[1]

Rameau was fifty when he began to write for the theatre yet almost nothing at that time was known about his life. Thanks to French scholarship we know much more about him today than his contemporaries did, at any rate from the biographical view-point. Musically he is still for many people nothing more than the composer of the *Rigaudon* from *Dardanus*. In appearance he was tall and thin. He had a difficult character but he was quickly fired by enthusiasm. He disliked social life at a time when fine manners happened to be cultivated and when not to be obsequious or flattering in manner was a peculiarity not greatly appreciated.

At the Opera musicians and singers both feared and loathed him. He never forgave them for the passages in his works which they compelled him to suppress for the reason that they were unable or unwilling to perform them adequately. His devotion to music allowed him to overcome all the vexations with which, when the fashion was for sublime indifference, he was inflicted.

He was a born philosopher, yet he was not indifferent to fame. He valued even more, however, the beauty of his works. Towards the end of his life he was asked 'if the sound of applause did not please his ears more than the music of his operas'. He reflected a few moments and then said, 'I like my music even better.'

A compelling curiosity—rare among artists—was part of Rameau's nature. In response to this curiosity he wrote his Treatise on harmony where he attempted to restore the 'rights of reason' and also to bring into music the order and clarity of

---

[1] Debussy's earlier articles on Rameau were '*Castor et Pollux* at the Schola Cantorum' (*Gil Blas*, 2 February 1903) and 'A propos d'*Hyppolyte et Aricie* (*Figaro*, 8 May 1908). He was aware of carrying on a campaign in favour of Rameau. 'This article is written in a style favoured by the prophets', he tells André Caplet in 1912, 'or nearer our time Louise Michel [the political revolutionary deported for her anarchistic activities].'

geometry. In the preface to this Treatise we read that 'music is a science which must have established rules'. These rules must be based on an obvious principle and this principle can hardly be known without the help of mathematics.[1]

In a word he does not for a moment doubt the truth of the old dogma of Pythagoras. The whole of music must be reduced to a combination of numbers. This combination forms the arithmetic of sound as optics form the geometry of light. It is clear that Rameau uses the terms, and also outlines the development, of modern harmony—and of his own art. He was perhaps wrong to set down his theories before composing his operas for it allowed his contemporaries to conclude that his operas were devoid of feeling. He had hardly reached the end of his career before other fashions invaded the musical world. They were at first triumphant, in the works of Lully, but later, under the influence of the considerable figure of Gluck, they became stifling. It thus came about that French music was long dominated by Gluck and that even today it has hardly emerged from his influence.

Over an inexplicably long period nothing was heard of Rameau. His charm and his subtle formalities were to be replaced by a musical style in which all that mattered was dramatic effect. Harmonic novelties, appealing to the ear, were replaced by massive conventional harmony easy to listen to and easily grasped. Music thus strangely branched off in the direction that led to Richard Wagner, another tyrannical genius.

The great contribution of Rameau is that he discovered an harmonic sensibility and that he was able to give expression to certain moods and certain shades of feeling of which earlier musicians had only a vague idea.

Like Nature, Art becomes transformed and branches out into bold developments, but eventually there is a return to the starting-point. Rameau's work forms one of the great foundations of music and one can fearlessly pursue the road he opened up

---

[1] 'La musique est une mathématique mystérieuse dont les éléments participent de l'infini', says Monsieur Croche, though this does not imply the desirability of a rigid system. Elsewhere Debussy remarks, 'There is nothing more mysterious than the perfect chord. Despite both old and recent theories one is not at all sure that it is perfect nor why some other chord has the misfortune to be called imperfect or dissonant.'

despite hesitations and errors likely to distract us. This is reason enough to love him with that tender respect due to our ancestors, sometimes a little forbidding, but who knew how tellingly and beautifully to give expression to that which was true.

The value for us today of Debussy's critical articles, apart from their amusing conversational style and the shrewdness or provocative nature of their judgements, is that they show us the composers or the works which nourished his musical mind. Instinctively, he was drawn to the original spirits of the great artistic movements of his own and earlier times: to Turner and Poe as the godfathers of the Impressionist and Symbolist movements; to Rameau as one of the principal figures of the classical movement; and, in a reassessment of the Romantic movement, to Weber. The distinction drawn by Debussy between Gluck and Rameau was prompted by the same motives as the distinction which he drew between Berlioz and Weber. Which of these composers, he appears to ask, makes the bolder, more immediate appeal—and which is the truer artist?

In recent years less enthusiasm for Berlioz has been shown in France than in England and America, but at the beginning of the century the main works of Berlioz were frequently given in Paris, and Debussy often had occasion to write of the *Symphonie Fantastique*, the *Damnation of Faust*, *Roméo et Juliette*, and *L'Enfance du Christ*. There were many aspects of the art of Berlioz which Debussy profoundly admired, notably the lyrical manner of *L'Enfance du Christ*. But there were also many that were inimical to him, particularly his brazen, rhetorical manner. Berlioz is then 'a tremendous humbug who managed to believe in his own hoaxes'.[1] Elsewhere he is described as 'an exception, a monster; he is not a musician at all'.

Berlioz had always been recognized as one of the great orchestrators of the nineteenth century. But Debussy provided reasons for considering Weber's conception of the Romantic orchestra to be even more evocative and imaginative. However this may be, of the Romantic composers before Wagner, Weber, together with

[1] See the letter to Prince Poniatowski (Vol. I, p. 171). Possibly Debussy was thinking of the extravagant *Lélio*, or of the *Symphonie funèbre et triomphale* performed in the streets of Paris by Berlioz himself, dressed in his uniform of the National Guard and conducting with his sword.

Chopin, was certainly the figure to whom he was most strongly drawn. In a review of the opera *Titania* by Georges Hüe, Debussy evokes several other characters from *A Midsummer Night's Dream*, among them Puck and Oberon, and eventually presents a portrait of Weber which is half-truth, half-fantasy:

I am particularly reminded of a man now nearly forgotten, at least in the theatre. I saw him trudging along the London streets, his body consumed by some kind of vivid light [*un corps usé par la lumière aiguë*], while his radiant brow proclaimed that he belonged to those who have known beauty. On he went, sustained by a feverish desire to delay death until he had heard his final work born in the fiery pangs of his ebbing life. By what miracle was he able to revive that wild passion, those galloping, romantic rhythms which marked his youthful genius? No one will ever know. His work had a sort of dreamy melancholy, characteristic of his time, though never marred by the crude German sentimentality in which nearly all his contemporaries indulged.

He was perhaps the first to face the problem of establishing a relationship between the infinite spirit of nature and the finite spirit of the individual. The legend, he felt, would allow music to find its natural course. For music alone has the power of evoking imaginary scenes [*les sites invraisemblables*] and of revealing that real yet elusive world, the home of fantasy and nocturnal poetry, where a thousand nameless sounds are produced by leaves in the moonlight.

Weber was master of every known means of conveying the fantastic in music. Even in our time, rich as it is in orchestral chemistry [*en chimie orchestrale*] he has hardly been surpassed. If he attached too much importance to flourishes and vocalizations we must not forget that he married a singer. Probably he adored her. This is a sentimental matter but not to be despised. Though he was able to tie a lovers' knot with ribbons made of semi-quavers, his musical language was simple and beautiful. This man, as you must now know, was Karl Maria von Weber. The opera, the final product of his genius, was *Oberon*, first performed in London—there were thus many good reasons for thinking of that city.

This romantic vision of Weber must be assessed in conjunction with a record of an illuminating conversation on the subject of Weber's orchestration between Debussy and Robert Godet. It took place at the conclusion of the dress rehearsal of *Pelléas et Mélisande* in April 1902. A new vista was opened up and Debussy seems suddenly to have glimpsed the magic of Weber's orchestration. 'Night was falling when the composer of *Pelléas* was accompanied to his door', Godet recalled in an article written on the occasion of the centenary of Weber's death in 1926.[1] 'He insisted that I should go up for a cup of tea. . . . It was then, in a quiet tête-à-tête in which he did not make the slightest allusion to his work or the tumultuous reception it had received, that he began to praise with all his heart and all his soul the "horn" of *Oberon*.'

Debussy was particularly fascinated by the three distant notes forming the melancholy horn call at the opening of *Oberon*. 'What a refuge for an artist of this world', he told Godet. 'Only in *Parsifal* is there anything comparable to the eternal youthfulness of *Oberon* and *Freischütz*.' And Debussy proceeded to supply Godet with a catalogue of Weber's orchestral effects, his manner of writing for each of the woodwinds, the brass instruments, and the strings. In this monologue, delivered to Godet on Weber, the illustrations were calculated to appeal to an imaginary visitor wholly ignorant of music.

Now supposing a visitor from Mars were to come this evening to pay us a musical call [Debussy began], all the stars having fallen, as you are aware. . . .[2] Apart from one or two supplementary notes, Weber's work presents us with the best treatise on instrumentation. What is a clarinet? I would refer the Martian to the aria of Agatha where he would hear the instrument in its virgin state, and also to the *Konzertstück* where he would learn the secrets of its lower register. The flute? Here I should be embarrassed in my choice but the flutes in thirds in the scene of the 'Casting of the Bullets' are remarkable, and so are those in Agatha's aria in the second act of *Freischütz*. In the same act,

[1] The extracts from Robert Godet's article in *The Chesterian*, presumably translated from the French by himself, are abridged.
[2] The reference is to the line of *Pelléas* 'Oh, oh! Toutes les étoiles tombent', at the end of Act IV, Scene iii, where Pelléas and Mélisande, having been discovered together by Golaud, throw themselves into each other's arms for the last time.

in the 'Hunting Scene', he would hear the fierce, brilliant piccolos and a wild horn quartet, whilst the horn quartet of the overture is a model of sylvan charm and bird-like sweetness. Anticipating the modern style of writing for brass instruments, there is a trumpet solo symbolizing the sunrise in *Oberon* and a breathless passage for trombones in the overture of *Freischütz*. . . . Who has used the strings more effectively than Weber, who has more vividly brought into relief their tone colours, particularly the colour of the E string? He is aware of different kinds of bowing, of different methods of attack, and of the dramatic value of the tremolo. His string writing is sometimes brilliant, it is sometimes delicate and his use of the mutes is remarkable. Look at the muted violins in the Overture to *Oberon* contrasted with the answer from violas and cellos; or the ethereal violins in the aria of Agatha or the octet of *Euryanthe*, so mysteriously sombre, at the appearance of the ghost. . . . Only one example more—a minute but a delectable example, and then good-night (already the Martian has vanished). Look again at the four or five introductory bars to Max's air in G, after the Waltz in *Freischütz*, and listen to the introduction of the clarinets between the flutes and oboes. And then let me know—but not on the evening of a dress rehearsal.[1]

Godet adds a charming postscript to this revealing document: 'On leaving the composer of *Pelléas* I remembered his

---

[1] These references to instrumental effects in the works of Weber, which Godet attributes to Debussy, are not always clear. The *Konzertstück* is of course for piano and orchestra, and it is more likely that Debussy was referring to Weber's Concertino or one of his two Concertos for clarinet. The flute passages are (1) Act I, Scene i of *Freischütz*, or the Volkslied in Act III, and (2) Agatha's aria in Act II, 'Wie nahte mir der Schlummer', where the flutes are particularly effective in the lower register. The piccolos are strikingly used at the conclusion of the storm scene in Act II of *Freischütz* and the horn quartet occurs in the same scene. The bold writing for trombones in the overture to *Freischütz* is well known. The combination of muted and non-muted strings occurs at the very opening of the overture to *Oberon*. The 'octet' in *Euryanthe* is probably the finale of Act II where the violins play an important part in an ensemble in which four of the characters are joined by a chorus of tenors and basses. There is a subtle introduction of the tone-colour of the clarinet in the *Andante con moto* section of Act I, Scene iii of *Freischütz* before Max's aria, 'Jetzt ist wohl ihr Fenster offen'. All these examples show Weber's sensitivity to tone-colour and combinations of timbre. There may also have been literary or pictorial reasons for Debussy's attraction to Weber. A poem of Baudelaire, inspired by the paintings of Delacroix, speaks of a landscape of this painter

Où, sous un ciel chagrin, des fanfares étranges
Passent, comme un soupir étouffé de Weber.

recent meeting with a lady who tried to ingratiate herself with him by reducing the history of music to a few names reflecting the snobbishness of the moment. "Palestrina, Schumann, Moussorgsky—do you see anyone else?" To which he had answered as gravely as possible: "I will think it over." This incident returning to my mind, "Well", I said, "you have kept your word, you have thought it over." "Oh hardly. . . . All the same let us add Weber." "And Debussy?" "Since we have been fortunate enough to forget him, let us continue doing so. Besides he is falling asleep. Let us hope that the night will bring him good counsel."'

Other Romantic composers are approached from a bold, independent viewpoint. Debussy's views on Beethoven are sometimes contradictory and his admiration is often given to works such as the Ninth Symphony, which hardly seem to belong to his sphere of experience. He was repelled by the piano writing of the sonatas, particularly of the late sonatas which, he maintained, were in the form of transcriptions of orchestral works. These 'often require a third hand, which Beethoven certainly heard, at least I hope so'. The song *Adelaide* is a piece 'which the old Master must have forgotten to burn'. The realistic effects in the Pastoral Symphony, on which he wrote on two occasions, provoke sarcastic condemnation. Curiously enough, he finds this work pedantic ('*Beethoven est responsable d'une époque où l'on ne voyait la nature qu'à travers les livres*'). In the storm scene 'the fear which nature arouses in the hearts of men is lost in the folds of a romantic shroud'. The imitative bird-calls at the conclusion of the 'Scene by the Brook' were obviously calculated to shock Debussy's impressionistic conception of nature, and he unhesitatingly condemns other instrumental features of this movement, notably the slow-moving bassoon solo which convinces him that the animals who normally come to drink at the brook are cows. On the other hand, the Ninth Symphony is admired because its explosive character bursts the rigid symphonic mould. 'The lesson of Beethoven was not to retain the old forms . . . it was to open our windows on to a free sky. . . . Nothing in this enormous work is without its particular function.' Debussy must surely have been aware that the words of Schiller's *Ode to Joy* were added to music Beethoven had already written. '*Beethoven n'était pas littéraire pour deux sous*', he tauntingly remarks, and he insisted that the voices in the finale have a purely instrumental function.[1]

The literary qualities of other German Romantic composers are often found wanting. 'Schumann understood nothing at all of Heine', we read with astonishment. 'In the *Dichterliebe* Schumann misses completely Heine's fine sense of irony.' Debussy apparently mistook such poems as *Ich grolle nicht* and *Ein Jüngling liebt ein Mädchen* for German equivalents of the lighter amorous poems of Verlaine.

Debussy's artistic opinions, though dictated by an infallible instinct, were frequently mercurial. 'Il aimait un jour la musique russe, un jour pas', notes Catherine Stevens. 'Ceci faisait partie de son paradoxe.'[2] At times, also, they were almost unbelievably aggressive. Some kind of underlying apprehensiveness transformed into the most aggressive form of irony marks the article 'Open-Air Music' in which Debussy proposes that 'M. Gavioli, the famous maker of street organs, . . . should be induced to make his instruments worthy of playing the *Ring*. Did not Wagner declare again and again that he could be understood only in France? . . . The Opéra does not shrink from playing *Pagliacci*; shrink then no longer from making street organs worthy to perform the *Ring*.'[3]

It is easy to see that Wagner almost invariably created this feeling of apprehension in Debussy's mind. He heard the complete *Ring* for the first time in April 1903 at Covent Garden and sent three articles on the work to *Gil Blas* in the form of letters from London. The first dealt primarily with his impressions of London which he was visiting on this occasion for the second time;[4] the second was

---

[1] In his study, 'Contrepoint à trois voix sur le Finale de la IXe Symphonie de Beethoven' (*Contrepoints*, No. 8, 1952), F. Goldbeck shows that Debussy's ideas on Beethoven's use of the chorus in this work wholly coincided with those of Nietzsche ('Beethoven needed the persuasive colour of the human voice') and of Furtwängler ('The human voice was to be an extra instrument').

[2] Extracts from the manuscript notes of Catherine Stevens were published by Marcel Dietschy in *La Passion de Claude Debussy*. André Schaeffner similarly draws attention to this dichotomy in Debussy's nature. 'Qu'est-ce qui est *certain* chez Debussy?' he searchingly asks. 'Le plaisir de scandaliser, l'humeur du moment, le bonheur d'un mot, mais aussi certaine fantaisie imaginative . . . peuvent fausser à des degrés divers ce que dit ou écrit Debussy.' If we were to take the opinions of Monsieur Croche literally, Monsieur Schaeffner points out, it would seem that Debussy really preferred the operas of Vincent d'Indy, *Fervaal* and *L'Etranger*, to the *Ring*.

[3] M. D. Calvocoressi revealed that the new editor of *La Renaissance Latine*, for which this article was originally written, flatly refused to publish it. 'Mais c'est idiot!' he exclaimed. It later appeared in *La Revue Blanche* and *M. Croche*.

[4] His first visit, at the invitation of Messager, was from 12 July to approximately

an assessment of the cast of the *Ring*, headed by Richter, and of the standards of production and performance at Covent Garden ('Whatever are the reasons for the alleged superiority of the Anglo-Saxons, they have among other things Covent Garden'); and the third was a criticism of the *Ring* followed by a description of an evening spent at the Empire Music Hall in Leicester Square (the 'equivalent', he dutifully tells the readers of *Gil Blas*, 'of our Folies-Bergère').

Having no English, Debussy in London felt himself to be an anonymous personality, impressed, however, in the traditional manner of foreigners in London by the courtesy of policemen, by a preoccupation with 'respectability [he uses the English word] common to everyone from Joseph Chamberlain to the drunken newsvendor', and also by the great number of idlers he noticed in the streets. An earlier visitor to London, Taine, had declared that there were no idlers in London. He was entirely wrong, said Debussy; English idlers are serious-minded, he notes, and seem to have a goal in view. They do not idle, like the French *flâneurs*, for the mere pleasure of idling. He wrote his first dispatch in a building on the Embankment. He had so far only heard *Rheingold*, and was anxious lest these London letters became 'too personal'.[1]

The main article, entitled 'Impressions of the *Ring* in London', does not conceal the extent to which a musical mind can be ravaged

---

21 July 1902 when, as in 1903, he stayed at the Hotel Cecil in the Strand. *Tristan*, with Litvinne and Van Dyck, was given at Covent Garden during this period and also two English operas, Ethel Smyth's *The Forest*, sung in German, and Herbert Bunning's *Princess Osra*, sung in French, with Mary Garden in the title role. Such were the linguistic vagaries at Covent Garden at that time. With Mary Garden, on 15 July, he heard Forbes-Robertson in *Hamlet* at the Lyric Theatre. 'He seemed like a child in a trance', Mary Garden recorded. 'So profoundly was he affected that it was some time before he could speak. I have never known anyone to lose himself so completely in the spectacle of great art.' Apart from the Turners he may have seen at the National Gallery and the Tate Gallery, a private collection of Turner's pictures was on view at this time at Lawrie & Co. Mary Garden also refers to a visit of twenty-four hours she made with Debussy to London to hear Sarah Bernhardt as Pelléas and Mrs. Patrick Campbell as Mélisande. Two performances of Maeterlinck's play were given in French at the Vaudeville Theatre in London by these actresses on 1 and 18 July 1904.

[1] Debussy must have remembered that ten years earlier, in 1893, he had himself taken part in a truncated version of *Rheingold* at the Opéra, the first performance of this work in Paris. Besides Debussy's letter to Chausson of 21 May 1893 describing the false position in which he was placed, an earlier letter to him, of 7 May 1893, has since been published: 'Je demande bien pardon à Wagner d'avoir participé à tout cela, mais les temps sont proches où cet homme va prendre une jolie revanche sur les Parisiens.' Elsewhere in this letter he expresses the wish that in music he would like to be his own grandson.

by Wagner. 'It is difficult to imagine the effect made even on the toughest mind by the four evenings of the *Ring*. A quadrille of *Leitmotive* is danced in the mind in which the theme of Siegfried's horn forms a curious partnership with that of Wotan's Sword, while the "Curse" theme persists in performing a *cavalier seul*. One is more than obsessed; one is subjugated. You are no longer yourself, you are merely a *Leitmotiv* walking or wandering about in the Nibelung entourage. Normal civilized behaviour cannot henceforth prevent us from greeting our fellow-creatures with cries of the Valkyries: "*Hojotoho? Heiaha! Hoioho! Hoioho!*" Even the London newsvendor will be shrieking, "Heiaho mylord!"[1] How tiresome these helmeted figures clad in the skins of wild animals become by the end of the fourth evening!' And Debussy proceeds to sling his well-known jibe at Wagner's conception of the *Leitmotiv*: 'It suggests a harmless lunatic who, on presenting his visiting card, would declaim his name in song.' Debussy was understandably censorious of Wagnerian mythology and of the Wagnerian plots. But of the music he wrote in terms of the highest praise. 'Suddenly, effects loom up of unforgettable beauty. They are as irresistible as the sea. . . . One does not criticize a work of such magnitude as the *Ring*. . . . Its too sumptuous greatness renders futile the legitimate desire to grasp its proportions.' And he grandiloquently concludes: 'Wagner can never quite die. He will eventually feel the cruel hand with which time destroys the most beautiful things. Some splendid ruins will, however, remain, in whose shade our grandchildren will dream of the past greatness of a man who, had he been but a little more human, would have been great for all time.' In the same year, replying to a questionnaire organized by the *Mercure de France* on the German influence in France, Debussy prophetically declared: 'Wagner, if one may express oneself with some of the grandiloquence that belongs to him, was a beautiful sunset that was mistaken for a dawn.' Those are words in which Debussy was speaking from the heart. They show that, over the period from Wagner's death to the outbreak of the first World War, the seed of pessimism in Wagner's work had taken root far beyond Germany.

The evening spent at the Empire Music Hall during Debussy's

[1] Perhaps Debussy was thinking here of the satirical story *Pan et la Syrinx* by Jules Laforgue, in which characteristic features of different historical periods are combined as in a surrealist fantasy. Like the London newsvendor, the nymph Syrinx, pursued by Pan, similarly utters these *Hojotoho! Heiaha!* cries of the Valkyries.

stay in London was 'a reward for good behaviour while listening to the *Ring*'. Impressions jostle in his mind as he completes his article in the train taking him back to Paris. On the stage of the Empire a conjuror had produced out of a top hat the British and French flags. (While Debussy was in London Edward VII was in Paris to celebrate the Entente Cordiale.) The Wagnerian critic also watches a ballet and listens to music-hall songs. All these events are dutifully set down but with a certain undertone of bitterness, even terror. To his account of the four evenings spent at Covent Garden Debussy amazingly adds a laudatory criticism of the Empire Music Hall orchestra which, he says, 'would be able to play the *Ring* as well as it plays the music of its conductor, one Leopold de Wenzel'. Towards the end of his article the train passes through the Normandy countryside. The apple trees are in blossom and the overwhelming Covent Garden *Ring* is left to recede into the widening shades of Debussy's London memories.

There remain the impressions recorded of the music of Richard Strauss. After the Bayreuth experiences of *Tristan* and *Parsifal*, *Till Eulenspiegel*, heard in Paris under Nikisch twelve years later, was apparently, among orchestral works, the most profoundly disturbing of Debussy's musical experiences up to that time.

It might be called 'An hour of the new music played to lunatics' [he writes]. The clarinets form frenzied designs, the trumpets are continuously muted and the horns, awaiting a sneeze from the trumpets, retort 'God bless you!' while a big drum goes boom! boom! apparently in imitation of a kick in the pants from a clown. One wants either to scream with laughter or shriek in pain, and the amazing thing is that when the work is over all the members of the orchestra are in their right places. In the mean-time if the double-basses had blown down their bows, if the trombonists had drawn an imaginary bow across their brass tubes, or if Nikisch had perched himself on the knee of a pro-gramme-seller nothing here would have been in the least sur-prising. There is no denying that there is genius in this work, particularly in the amazing assurance of the orchestral writing and in the wild sense of movement that sweeps us along from beginning to end, compelling us to share in each of the hero's merry pranks.

Two years later, when Strauss himself conducted in Paris, Debussy reproduced this criticism almost word for word.[1] He became interested then in Strauss's ideas on programme music, his method of musical development and the pictorial and philosophical associations in his work. He 'thinks in coloured images', his music is a 'book of pictures, even moving pictures'. Elsewhere, terms somewhat difficult to assess are used by Debussy when he asserts that Strauss achieves 'un développement de couleurs rythmiques' and that he attempts to seek 'la forme directement dans la couleur'. 'Couleur', in this sense, can only mean instinct or mood.

Tod und Verklärung is held by Debussy to be the musical equivalent of a Boecklin. On the other hand, it is a work that cannot conceal the innate vulgarity of certain of Strauss's themes. A notice on this early work of the composer whom Debussy nevertheless persistently admired begins: 'In the cookery book under "Jugged Hare" will be seen this wise recommendation: "Take a hare." Richard Strauss proceeds otherwise. To write a symphonic poem he takes anything.' Elements of Berlioz and Liszt are evident in Strauss, Debussy notes, but definitely no element of Wagner ('En tout cas aucune influence de Wagner'). Whether from an objective viewpoint this is wholly true is irrelevant; the point is that this is how the music of Strauss struck Debussy in his time.

These few references to Strauss in *M. Croche* and elsewhere are instructive, but they reveal only one aspect of the æsthetic problem created by the introduction of his works in Paris. In the decade before the first World War the music of Strauss, though eagerly received in many quarters, represented nothing less than an assault on French musical sensibility. Opinions of his work in Paris were therefore confused or contradictory. In later chapters we shall attempt to reconstruct this complex impression.

[1] Elsewhere in Debussy's criticisms we find a statement he had originally made about one composer attributed to another. He wrote of a group of Danish songs by Delius in *La Revue Blanche* in 1901: 'They are very sweet and innocent songs, music to rock the convalescents of the rich neighbourhoods. There is always a note hanging over a water-lily in a lake, tired of being watched by the moon, or like a little balloon blocked by the clouds.' Two years later, in *Gil Blas*, we find the identical passage in a notice of some songs by Grieg.

4

Debussyism

L'heureux temps où je n'étais pas connu.

André Gide

We have seen that up to the time of the production of *Pelléas* in 1902 Debussy's name had hardly been known to the wider public. Indeed, until he was in his fortieth year Debussy's reputation had been that of a composer associated with the pre-Raphaelites and Mallarmé, a musician with literary leanings not to be taken too seriously in the tougher musical world where it was required that a composer should produce an important body of works, symphonic or operatic, in an uninterrupted stream. Debussy was too independent a figure to follow a conventional career of this kind. The exteriorization of an artist's ideas in the form of a completed work is a difficult and often a painful process. For Debussy it was frequently an abhorrent process, representing a compromise with his inner vision from which he instinctively recoiled.[1]

Ironically, *Pelléas* soon became the subject of an unending controversy, and Debussy himself was ruthlessly held in the lime-light. It has often happened in musical history that a movement, a

---

[1] He was particularly aware of the artist's poverty on completing a work. Writing to Louÿs in 1895 of the first version of *Pelléas*, then nearing completion, Debussy says: 'Finir une œuvre n'est-ce pas un peu comme la mort de quelqu'un qu'on aime?

> Un accord de neuvième
> Les bémols sont bleus.'

Six years after its production he stated in *Musica* in January 1908 that 'the scenic realization of a work of art, however successful it may be, is always in conflict with the inner dream of the work [*est toujours contradictoire au rêve intérieur*]'. The characters are 'like ghosts' and 'nothing remains of the old dream. Another mind divides you from it.'

vogue, or a fashion has taken its rise from a journalistic controversy, and it was a journalist who was at first responsible for the movement that became associated with Debussy's ideas. On 22 January 1904 there appeared in *Le Journal* an article by Jean Lorrain entitled *Les Pelléastres*. There was no doubt some malice in this title, but on the other hand there is no reason to doubt the accuracy of Lorrain's description of the younger members of the audience who at that time flocked to hear Debussy's Symbolist opera. Followed by other articles of this kind and reprinted in 1910 in book form,[1] this tirade provoked a new campaign for Debussy's work that was to be pursued until the first World War.

Lorrain started out by making legitimate artistic and musical comparisons.

The legendary public that used to attend the first nights of the productions of Lugné-Poe [i.e. of the plays of Ibsen and Maeterlinck at the Théâtre de l'Œuvre] is now to be found at the Salle Favart [the familiar name of the Opéra-Comique] at every production of *Pelléas et Mélisande*. Consisting of fervent admirers of *Peer Gynt* and of the clever orchestration of *Fervaal* [the opera of Vincent d'Indy], this public has agreed to adopt the music of M. Claude Debussy. Sent into raptures by the sunny pizzicati in the little masterpiece *L'Après-midi d'un faune*, they have decreed that they are to be sent into a swoon by the deliberate dissonances in the lengthy recitatives of *Pelléas*. The enervating effect of long-sustained chords, the titillations at first sensuous, then exasperating but ultimately cruel, inflicted on the ears of the public by an upward-rising phrase cut off a hundred times and which never comes to an end—this whole limbo-like work, made up of little sensations, so artistic and oh! so quintessential, so bewildering, was calculated to receive the support of the snobs and the poseurs.

[1] The title of the book is *Pelléastres*. Jean Lorrain (whose real name was Paul Duval) is frequently referred to in the correspondence between Debussy and Louÿs. His work and personality, illustrating the least appealing aspects of the *fin-de-siècle*, are analysed in detail by Mario Praz. 'A being of feminine sensibility, a hysterical with homosexual tendencies', he dyed his hair red, frequented the underworld, and 'gave himself the airs of a murderer'. It is curious to see how this *'fumiste* of deplorable taste' was drawn to many of the artists, including Gustave Moreau and the Pre-Raphaelites, and even particular works of art, such as Botticelli's *Primavera*, admired by Debussy.

He then branched out, as gossip-writers were often inclined to do at that time, into a description of the audience.

Thanks to these ladies and gentlemen M. Claude Debussy has become the leader of a new religion, and at every performance of *Pelléas* the Opéra-Comique came more and more to look like a sanctuary. Everyone now became grave, knowing winks were exchanged and also certain looks. The interludes were listened to in a religious silence and the initiated would greet each other in the corridors with finger on lips. Strange handshakes were hastily given in the dim light of a box. Faces took on a tortured expression, eyes a far-away look.

A familiar theme was now taken up, the substitution of the artistic for the religious experience and the nature of the cult of Wagner as opposed to the new cult of Debussy.

Music is the latest religion of this faithless century. Performances at the Théâtre du Châtelet of *Tristan* and *Parsifal* fill the upper galleries with an ardent, hypnotized public resembling the early Christians huddled together in catacombs. But at any rate the adepts of Wagner are sincere; they come from all classes of society and their simple ordinary clothes, the often sublime ugliness of their drawn features is proof of the fervour and intensity of their faith. The religion of M. Claude Debussy is more elegant. His neophytes are to be found in the orchestra stalls and the first-tier boxes. Surrounding that blonde girl, so frail, so pale and so fair, obviously got up to look like Mlle Garden, and indolently turning over the pages of a score on the edge of a box, is a whole group of good-looking young men (nearly all the Debussyists are young).

Lorrain proceeds to poke fun at the preciosity of the audience, particularly in regard to their clothes.

Their long hair is effectively parted down the middle, they are plump in face, of mat complexion and they have deep-set eyes. They wear velvet-collared coats with puffed sleeves, or frock-coats rather too tight at the waist, large silk ties hunched up round the neck or a flowing lavallière tie. On the little fingers of their beautiful hands they wear an Egyptian or a Byzantine ring, a turquoise scarab or a jewel in green gold.

Finally, as a writer long practised in the reporting of society morals, Lorrain was unable to refrain from making a rather obvious pun.

The neophytes of Debussy are always to be found in pairs like Orestes and Pylades, they talk to each other as if each were the character of Pelléas, or as if they were exemplary sons, young men with lowered eyelids, accompanying their mothers! . . . They have some kind of visionary look in their eyes and in moments of intense feeling they whisper in each other's ears the soulful words, *Les Pelléastres*!

Fictitious English characters, 'Sir Reginald Asthom', 'Lord Chapman', and 'Sir Edward Ytter, son of the great English painter William Ytter', were associated with these neophytes, the last 'having the score of *Pelléas*, signed and dedicated, prominently displayed on his Erard piano'.[1]

Wounded and incensed by these almost libellous statements, Debussy immediately wired Louÿs and proposed challenging Jean Lorrain to a duel. His feelings may be judged by the conciliatory letter sent to him by Pierre Louÿs on 22 January 1904:

What does this article amount to? A story running to two columns which doesn't concern you—with a very unpleasant

[1] Lorrain may have been prompted to write this article by the article of Willy entitled 'Bayreuth et l'Homosexualité' which appeared in *La Revue Blanche* of 15 March 1896, followed by a lively discussion in the following two numbers (1 and 15 April). Willy refutes a German writer, who, he declared, outrageously suggested that there were homosexual aspects of *Parsifal*: 'If Kundry had not arrived Parsifal would have lost his virginity. . . . Between the second and third acts he could have married.' And he asserts that 'in 1882 Wagner ravenously kissed a flower maiden in the wings'. In the following number an anonymous writer supported the contention that Parsifal's relationship with the knights of the Grail was 'un régal de pédérastes'. Elsewhere he suggested that Tannhäuser and Lohengrin, like Parsifal, certainly required a great deal of persuading; also that in *Tristan* the masculine figure was Isolda. These were ideas similar to the Wagnerian satires of Jules Laforgue, a writer whom Debussy particularly admired. Closely associated with *La Revue Blanche*, of which he was later the music critic, Debussy is likely to have seen the articles of Willy, and to have compared their wit and agility with the ponderous manner of Jean Lorrain.

introduction about a section of your public and five or six violent lines on your music. Nothing about you personally. If you challenge him to a duel you will merely receive a statement to the effect that nothing injurious has been said about yourself. And the entire press will have something to say about this article on which it is best to keep quiet. As for replying to him, a hundred times no! Reply to a musical criticism written by Reyer or d'Indy. But don't discuss such a matter with a journalist. An artist simply doesn't do such a thing. . . . Your best reply will be your book.[1]

The sting of Lorrain's satire did, however, persist, with the result that Debussy's works inspired a controversy almost as fierce as that which, a generation earlier, had been set aflame in Paris by Wagner. The following year, in the *Mercure Musical* of 15 November 1905, Emile Vuillermoz took up the matter of Debussy's influence in the form of an imaginary conversation, entitled *Une tasse de thé*, between society people and a fashionable composer. 'You must confess that of all our contemporaries Debussy is the most troublesome', declares the hostess. 'He has divided society, the musical public is in a state of confusion, the reviews set out to demolish each other and the most feared of our musical scribblers are at each other's throats!' 'Music has now its Dreyfus affair!' retorts the baron. 'Henceforth France will be divided by the Debussy affair!' A distinguished Egyptologist and a retired general point out that Alfred Dreyfus and Achille Debussy have in fact the same initials, and that future generations may well have some difficulty in distinguishing between these two great moral and æsthetic conflicts that clouded the opening years of the twentieth century. Confusion may arise and future studies of ancient history may even go so far as to state that 'a conductor of military music, one Achille Dreyfussy, was accused of high treason by an expert in harmony who had examined his writing. . . . Given to dissonance, he was accused of forgery and as a punishment was compelled to sit for the Prix de Rome examination at the Conservatoire of Devil's Island.'[2] 'Where he wrote *The Devil in the Belfry*', interjected

[1] As we saw in Chapter 3, Debussy had apparently intended at this period bringing out in book form a collection of his articles in *Gil Blas* and *La Revue Blanche*.

[2] The allusion is to the opera on Poe's tale *The Devil in the Belfry* on which Debussy was known to be engaged at this time. Dreyfus was imprisoned on Devil's Island in

another guest. 'And *L'Après-midi d'un faux*', added the general. Asked for his opinion on this disturbing music, the fashionable composer ironically stated that as a musician his views on music were considered worthless. He may criticize a picture of Monet or a sonnet of Mallarmé but not a symphony or a quartet.[1] The company proceed to upbraid both Camille Mauclair, who had written an article entitled *La Debussyte* which amounted to 'a re-edition of Jean Lorrain's *Pelléastres* in a more professional and therefore a more dangerous form'[2] and Debussy's secretive friend, jealous of his protégé, Louis Laloy. Agreement is eventually reached on the fact that if Debussy's harmony is not in itself novel his use of it is.

Nothing constructive emerged from these satires unless they

1894. Debussy's attitude to the Dreyfus affair is recorded in the first edition of René Peter's *Claude Debussy: vues prises de l'intimité* (1931) but was suppressed, no doubt for political reasons, in the enlarged second edition published during the war (1944). Debussy, Peter states, 'appeared at first to take only a mild interest in the matter. He instinctively took the side of the nationalists who believed that Dreyfus had been rightly condemned.' Among his friends Louÿs, an ardent nationalist, and René Peter, an equally ardent Dreyfusard, found themselves at loggerheads. Peter took Debussy to meetings in Montparnasse where he heard speeches in favour of Dreyfus given by Anatole France, Jean Jaurès, and others but he remained persistently neutral. The one personality in the Dreyfus affair to whom Debussy was drawn was Lieut.-Colonel Picquard, the well-known amateur of music who was a friend of Paul Clemenceau and Gustav Mahler and who had been imprisoned for his belief in Dreyfus's innocence. Quoting the phrase from *Pelléas*, 'Mais la joie on n'en a pas tous les jours' Debussy, in a letter of 1898 to Louÿs, ironically ascribes it to both Golaud and the staunch champion of Dreyfus.

[1] This was an unfortunate but a true state of affairs. Ravel similarly deplored a statement made by Gaston Carraud, critic of the *Revue S.I.M.*, that Debussy's later works were admired not by musicians but by painters and writers. 'Vous avez bien compris, vous, qui, bêtement, vous laissez aller au charme éclatant, à la fraîcheur exquise des *Rondes de Printemps*', Ravel wrote of the reception of Debussy's orchestral *Images*; and sardonically he added: 'Vous n'êtes qu'un littérateur ou un peintre; . . . Moi aussi, je ne suis qu'un littérateur ou un peintre. (M. Ravel, 'A propos des *Images* de Claude Debussy', *Cahiers d'aujourd'hui*, No. 3, February 1913).

[2] Camille Mauclair's article appeared in the *Courrier Musical* of 15 September 1905. The theme of this lampoon was that excessive adulation of a composer's work tended to deprive his admirers of their critical sense. The audience that came away from *Pelléas et Mélisande* 'appear to have been listening to a revolutionary hymn. They have a sniff of blood and gunpowder about them'. At other times 'they go into a sort of trance' or they 'work themselves up into a state of feverish mysticism'. Twelve years earlier, when Debussy himself took part in a performance of fragments of *Rheingold* at the Opéra, similar terms were used to describe the excessive claims of the Wagnerites. In 1893 a wit writing under the name of Dr. Cuniculus published the pamphlet *Les Maladies wagnériennes et leur traitement*. The various diseases, he specified, were 'Wagneromania, Wagneralgia, and Wagneritis'. Remedies 'for the daily abuse of the *Ring* Elixir and the deadly Parsifaline' included 'a diet of Rossini macaroni together with a glass of Auber mousseux'. In serious cases 'frictions are advised of the balm of Bach and Handel'.

succeeded in exposing the snobbery and the sham invariably associated with novel fashions. Debussy, who was revolted by fashions ('Heureusement nous ne sommes pas modernes', he wrote to Robert Godet), was himself becoming a victim of the very fashion which, unwittingly, he had created. Four years later, in 1909, the polemics were renewed when *La Revue du Temps Présent*, which had published a series of articles entitled 'Claude Debussy et le snobisme contemporain', set up an enquiry pretentiously called *Le Cas Debussy*. Writers, painters, composers, and critics were asked to reply to a questionnaire. 'What is the importance of Debussy and what is his part in musical evolution? Is his individuality an original or is it merely an accidental phenomenon? Can he or should he form a school?'

At the age of twenty-six Ernest Ansermet stated emphatically that there was nothing accidental in either the harmony or the melody of Debussy and that 'not since Beethoven had there been a composer with such a sense of, or indeed with such a need for tonal unity'. By his inner nature 'Debussy belongs to the spiritual family of Mozart and Schumann'. His work is 'the most important musical phenomenon since Wagner and the Russians and it clearly represents a continuation of their achievements'. Debussy's technical innovations 'have had an effect on nearly all contemporary composers. I will not speak of Mahler whose work I do not know sufficiently well; but almost every page of *Elektra* provides proof of this contention.'[1] The philosopher Albert Bazaillas drew attention to 'the supple, fleeting and indefinite ['*imprécis*'] qualities' in Debussy's work which, he maintained, expressed the anxieties of the modern sensibility. Romain Rolland sent in a reply signed 'Jean-Christophe'. 'I don't like all your modern French music very much and I am not mad about your M. Debussy. But what I can't understand is that, being so poor in artists, you have to quarrel about the greatest one you have. As for the question of whether he is the leader of a school, and what this school will be worth, one can simply say that every great artist has a school and that all schools are evil.

[1] Fifty years later in his philosophical study, *Les Fondements de la musique dans la conscience humaine* (Lausanne, 1961) Ansermet restated and enlarged upon his belief in the essentially tonal qualities of Debussy's harmony. Writing of *La Mer*, he observes: 'Il y a toujours chez Debussy une tonalité fondamentale, mais on n'y est presque jamais.' The secret of *L'Après-midi d'un faune* is to be found 'dans la conduite tonale signifiée par le mouvement de la basse et engendrée par celui de la fondamentale des perspective tonales enchaînées'.

It might then be better if there were no great artists?' The complex
role played by Romain Rolland in the music of his time will be
discussed later; for the moment one notes the apparent distaste of
this idealist for polemics. Joseph Péladan, whose lascivious imagination led him to write a novel, *La Vertu suprême*, containing a
monstrous parody of *Parsifal*, stated that Debussy's music made him
physically uncomfortable. Péladan was an incorrigible poseur with
very little sense of fitness. He described Debussy as 'the musician of
the Autumn Salon, someone comparable to Matisse'. More to the
point, Jean d'Udine declared that Debussy 'had disturbed the entire
musical organism of his time and his significance was evident enough
from the fact that every scribbler of music now produces examples
of Hypodebussy if not of Hyperdebussy'.

Le Cas Debussy was published in 1910. In August of the same
year Louis Laloy made much bolder claims. His long study
'Debussy et le Debussysme' was published first in the special
number of *La Revue S.I.M.* devoted to the festival of French music
at Munich, and the following year, in a German translation, in the
Viennese journal *Der Merker*. Since this study was the work of a
distinguished critic who was Debussy's personal friend and his first
French biographer, the claims put forward, namely, that Debussy's
significance in musical history was comparable to that of Monteverdi and that Debussyism was the equivalent in music of Impressionism in painting and Symbolism in poetry, were accepted as
statements *ex cathedra*.[1] It is, however, essential to be reminded of
the fact that Laloy wrote this study not so much for French readers
as for the musicians in Munich and Vienna who were about to hear

[1] Louis Laloy (1874–1944), historian of music and playwright, was closely associated
with Debussy from 1902 onwards. Their friendship was based on the views which they
shared of the music of oriental civilizations, of ancient Greece, and on Laloy's social
influence. Laloy introduced Debussy to the wealthy society figures, the Princesse de
Cystria and the Comtesse de Greffühle. Encouraged by Romain Rolland, whom he
replaced as lecturer on musical history at the Sorbonne, Laloy undertook a study of
Aristoxenus, the early Greek authority on musical theory who held that the relationship
of notes in a scale was to be judged not by mathematics but by the ear, and later published a study of Chinese music. Appropriately, Debussy dedicated to him the piano
piece, from the *Images*, *Et la Lune descend sur le temple qui fut*, a title reminiscent of
Chinese poetry. In another sphere of musicology Laloy's work on Rameau (1908)
helped to promote the revival of Rameau's operas by which Debussy was deeply
affected. His biography and æsthetic study of Debussy (1909, revised 1944) was the
first large-scale study of this kind to be published and is particularly valuable since the
views expressed were approved by Debussy. Eighty-two letters of Debussy to Laloy,
dealing among other subjects with their relationship with Diaghilev, were published in
La Revue de Musicologie (1962).

for the first time not only *Pelléas et Mélisande* and the orchestral works of Debussy but the Eighth Symphony of Mahler and the early works of Schoenberg. In the years before the first World War the French viewpoint was perhaps unconsciously over-stressed. Not all of Laloy's views are valid today; indeed, in many of them the emphasis seems to us to be misplaced. But his study, if we read between the lines, illuminates many aspects of the growing conflict between the two great musical civilizations of Europe.

'It is in France that the latest stage in the development of music has been reached', Laloy asserts. This came about not in the manner of the reforms of Gluck and Wagner but 'solely as the result of the impact made by the works of Debussy'. Whatever opinion one may have of these works they establish a date in history 'at least as important as that of the early Florentine operas which allowed song to express passion and harmony to take its rise from counterpoint'. The works of Debussy similarly 'enriched both the emotional and technical aspects of music'.[1]

Debussy's contribution to music 'can be expressed by a single word, now frequently used, by some in mockery, by others with pride: Debussyism'. This development in music 'corresponds to Symbolism in poetry and Impressionism in painting'. Laloy goes on to state that verbal symbolism 'is a mystical doctrine', since it has often allegorical associations, and that it leads directly, like Impressionism, to the 'apotheosis of sensation'.[2] Music, he argues, 'is concerned only with sensation; sounds used in music have no meaning nor can they represent an object'. Music, therefore, among all the arts 'must originally have been the one which is essentially symbolist and impressionist'. Non-European musicians, the Chinese, the Indians, and the Senegalese, 'are Impressionists and Symbolists without being aware of it; they hear, they are moved and they dream'. But the Westerner is by his nature a reasoning individual; sounds must be classified. The invention of scales 'reaches back to the Greeks and has lasted until our time'. Thus the sound 'ceases being a sound to become a *note*, that is to say a number in a

[1] The comparison with the operas of the early seventeenth-century Florentine composers is far-fetched. The aim of these composers, which they failed to achieve, was to resuscitate the musical declamation of ancient Greek tragedy. No comparable aim was envisaged in *Pelléas*.

[2] In this section of his study Laloy uses philosophical terms in the manner of Schopenhauer: 'Pour les adeptes du symbolisme il n'est point de matière sans pensée, ni de pensée sans matière.'

certain order'. No particular impression is created by one note or another, but 'a note is recognized as the first, third or sixth of a certain scale'.[1]

Laloy then proceeds to restate a familiar argument at that period: the classical composers maintained 'rules', while the romantics challenged them. With Wagner 'the struggle assumes epic proportions but the fortress [of tonality] is unshakeable and resists'. Deliverance came only with Debussy. It came 'suddenly and effortlessly. . . . As if touched with a wand the ramparts of the fortress of tonality disappeared into thin air'. The principle of the new music, Laloy informed his German and Austrian readers, is that one note may be attracted to another without suggesting the underlying order of a scale. 'Everything is connected but nothing is preordained.' It is 'music which obeys no precept, only the laws of sensation. Music is entirely a matter of hearing, as Impressionist painting is entirely a visual experience'. Frequently its melodies 'use only the notes of the major scale and chords appear to belong to a specified tonality'. This comes about 'not in accordance with some preconceived system but simply because a tonal scheme happens to express the composer's feelings at that point'. One seems to hear 'echoes of ancient modes associated with Gregorian chant or Greek music, Chinese scales without semitones, or chromatic scales entirely in semitones, whole-tone scales, and still others with accidentals hitherto unused on the fourth, fifth and seventh degrees of the scale'. But this is all an illusion. In truth this music which seems to use so many different scales 'does not really use any of them. It is not built on scales; it is built only on melodies.'[2]

Similarly, Debussy's harmony does not follow pre-ordained successions. It 'knows only consonance and is in no way concerned with dissonance'. A dissonant chord 'is an unstable, provisional chord, which requires resolution into a consonance'. And Laloy made the astounding statement in 1910 that 'we are arriving at a period when any chord, however built and even if it cannot be broken down into component harmonics, can count as a consonance'. A chord 'need no longer be legitimate'. It is 'a sonority

[1] To support this view Laloy in *La Musique retrouvée* offers a discussion of the theories of Pythagoras and of the treatises of Rameau and Helmholtz.

[2] If, as we may assume, this statement was made with Debussy's approval the overbold statement made by Ferdinand Löwe, at a public reception to him in Vienna, to the effect that Debussy had 'abolished melody' was indeed unfortunate.

which if properly used will give the ear full satisfaction'. Combinations of sound will contribute 'to another, over-all sound, in the same way that juxtapositions of colour will create the impression of another, different colour'.

All of this signified a new 'system' of composing. The trouble was that Debussy was radically opposed to any such idea. Nevertheless, the controversy raged on all sides, among the journalists, the critics, the historians. People were aware of a vast upheaval on many different planes. Not only technical matters were discussed. Psychological and æsthetic matters were raised; and so were national and moral problems. Writing in 1910 to Jean-Aubry of Mallarmé's opinion of *L'Après-midi d'un faune,* Debussy says that the lines Mallarmé had written on his copy of the poem were his 'best recollection of a period when I wasn't yet continuously bothered with Debussyism'. He was in fact almost tortured by his admirers. 'Tu sais, Claude, les Debussystes m'agacent', René Peter confided to him at their last meeting, before the war. 'Moi, ils me tuent!' came the heartfelt retort. Debussy's inner development undoubtedly suffered from exposure to these polemics. Yet in the wider European scene there had been a deep-seated change of emphasis. Shortly after *Pelléas* the German historian Hugo Riemann wrote to Paul Landormy: 'I must tell you that at the present moment the German hegemony in musical composition seems to be somewhat in danger of being usurped, possibly rather by the French than by the Slavs.'[1] Before long xenophobia set in and Pfitzner in Germany sourly complained that the national spirit of his works prevented them from achieving wider recognition.

There remains one other view of the Paris scene to complete our survey, the dispassionate view given by Romain Rolland in his ten-volume novel *Jean-Christophe.* It would be wrong, however, to extract Rolland's judgements on Debussy from his vast picture of the Paris scene of those years for the reason that in Rolland's view the achievement of Debussy was part of a much bigger European movement which he attempted to interpret from many different angles. Rolland's original and idealistic views have nowadays been largely forgotten. But it is essential to revive them and to examine them afresh. For one thing they offer a contemporary view of

[1] Paul Landormy, 'L'Etat actuel de la musique française', *La Revue Bleue,* 2 April 1904.

Debussy entirely different from any of the views we have so far considered. Also, it will be instructive to contrast Rolland's views with those of another writer who was coming into prominence in this period and who was undoubtedly more finely attuned to the sensibility of Debussy, Marcel Proust. These, however, are matters which branch out into problems too wide to be dealt with in the framework of this chapter. We must therefore be content, for the moment, to have recorded the main aspects of the 'Debussyist' movement in France and to investigate later, when dealing with Debussy's numerous journeys, the impressions made by his works abroad.

Maud Allan

Loïe Fuller, by Steinlen

Strauss conducting *Salomé* with Gabriel Astruc, by Daniel de Losques

Gabriele d'Annunzio as a native of the Abruzzi mountains, by Cesare Pascarella

5
Romain Rolland and Marcel Proust

[John Christopher] breaks down the frontier between France
and Germany. If one frontier is broken, all are broken.

Gilbert Cannan, Introduction to
John-Christopher

[Madame de Cambremer] maintained not merely that music
progressed, but that it progressed along one straight line, and
that Debussy was in a sense a super-Wagner, slightly more
advanced again than Wagner.

Marcel Proust

At this point in our survey of Debussy's development a change of
focus is desirable. A broader view of the French musical scene
should eventually enable us to see Debussy's ideas and achievement
in sharper relief. But we must first look into the new image of the
composer that, at the beginning of the twentieth century, was being
drawn. Romain Rolland in *Jean-Christophe* and Marcel Proust in
Jean Santeuil presented the new type of idealistic composer aware
of the fact that music was able to reach deeper layers of the mind
than the literary or pictorial arts with which it was associated.
Thomas Mann's Adrian Leverkühn was another idealistic musician
of this kind. These literary fantasies will help us to understand
many of the problems associated with Debussy. In each of them,
in fact, the figure of Debussy, or a semblance of him, is introduced.

A musical historian, a pantheist, and in his novels a pacifist,
Romain Rolland was also a political humanitarian whose romantic
dream of a musical United States of Europe was shattered by the
first World War. In the view of this French idealist, who was

among the first to break the bonds of nationalism, Germany was to command this European musical community, an imaginary Germany symbolized by John-Christopher whose surname, Kraft (the German word for energy), discloses the uncontrollable element of aggression in every pacifist. John-Christopher was not himself a pacifist but Rolland was; and even for a pacifist, Rolland was extremely aggressive. In France he attacked ingrown preciosity, in Germany the decay of romanticism. He also held up for ridicule all aspects of what we should nowadays call provincialism in both French and German musical life. This was his crusade, and it was a healthy crusade. But there was no goal at which Rolland himself was aiming. Though he proclaimed the limitations of both Debussy and Richard Strauss—to a republican idealist in search of a new Beethoven they both represented decadence—it is easy to see to which figure he was drawn. There was an impulsive sensualist in Rolland, unsatisfied by the poetry of Debussy but excited and ravished by the music of Strauss. This pacifist, who was also a Germanophile, adored the display of force, even brute force. 'Power in music is what you cherish above all', he wrote to Strauss. 'And it is what I cherish above all, too.' [1]

In Rolland's view of the contemporary musical world Debussy was a minor figure, 'the only creator of beauty in the music of our time', he conceded. 'But what will remain of him?' In *Jean-Christophe* 'the young barbarian who was Christopher' hears *Pelléas et Mélisande* at the Opéra-Comique, the work of a musician recoiling from the fear of pain, doubtfully endowed with 'the genius of taste' except at those moments, Rolland ironically adds, when 'the spirit of Massenet slumbering in the hearts of all Frenchmen awakens to inspire a lyrical passage'. This was Rolland's dis-

---

[1] Rolland went to endless trouble in helping Strauss to bring out a French edition of *Salomé*, demonstrating to him the subtleties of French prosody, chiefly by reference to Debussy's *Pelléas et Mélisande*. It was Strauss's intention to use a translation as near as possible to the original French text of Oscar Wilde, and though he was grateful to Rolland for his detailed analyses of peculiarities in the French language of rhythm and accentuation, he apparently failed to grasp many of the essential points which Rolland so patiently illustrated. 'Do you find the eternal, monotonous rhythm of triplets always *on the same note* beautiful and poetic?' he naïvely asks about *Pelléas*. 'To my German way of thinking it is an example of how language can be distorted by a musician.' It is not surprising that earlier Rolland, in a friendly spirit, had exclaimed to Strauss: 'You Germans are too arrogant.' On the other hand, one cannot help regretting that Strauss and Rolland did not collaborate on a stage work. After hearing *Till Eulenspiegel* Rolland made the excellent suggestion of a version of Rabelais's *Pantagruel*.

dainful view of what he held was an over-refined epoch in French civilization.[1]

As an historian of the first decade of the twentieth century, Rolland was concerned with the most vital European problem of the day, the relationship between France and Germany, not only on the moral and social planes, but on what he believed were the more important literary and musical planes. In his idealized form John-Christopher is Beethoven, but in the key provided by Rolland's friend, Stefan Zweig, to the characters whom he embodies John-Christopher has also features of Handel, Wilhelm Friedemann Bach, the youthful Mozart, Gluck, Wagner (whose *Ein deutscher Musiker in Paris* is drawn upon), Hugo Wolf, Gustav Mahler, and César Franck. In opposition to John-Christopher, the man of action, is Rolland himself, the man of thought, portrayed as Olivier. Grazia, the only important female figure in the novel, expresses an ideal of spiritual love.[2]

John-Christopher is a pantheist, but a pantheist whose passion admits no element of pleasure. Nor does Grazia ever really come to life. Rolland seems in his heart to despise the conception of womanhood she embodies.[3] I will not go so far as to say that if Rolland had been attuned to the sensibility of the Impressionists and the Symbolists, *Jean-Christophe* would have succeeded in becoming the great novel of the tragedy of our European musical civilization. Yet this is its root theme. Both in the arts and in psychology Rolland's eyes were closed to the new provinces of the mind opened up in his time. The approach to the unconscious of Bergson interested him,

[1] Despite his strong German sympathies, Rolland was similarly apprehensive of developments associated in the early years of the century with Strauss. 'You have triumphed over the Europe of our time', he writes to Strauss in 1907. 'Now leave Europe and rise above her. In the European world of today there is a frantic drive towards decadence and suicide; it takes different forms in Germany and France. Beware lest your cause be identified with it. Let that which is destined to die, die—and live.' This was not a lightly held opinion. After hearing Strauss conduct *Zarathustra* in 1898 Rolland had noted in his diary: 'Well, well! I have the impression that Germany will not long remain the all-powerful country. Nietzsche, Richard Strauss, Wilhelm II—there is something of Nero in the air.'
[2] Rolland's correspondence with Sofia Bertolini Guerrieri-Gonzaga, who inspired the character of Grazia, is discussed in Chapter 7.
[3] As, for instance, when he writes: 'To a true Latin woman, art is of worth only in proportion as it leads back to life, to life and love. . . . What has she to do with the tragic meditation, the tormented symphonies, the intellectual passions of the North? She must have music in which her hidden desires can unfold with the minimum of effort, an opera, which is passionate life without the fatigue of the passions, a sentimental, sensual, lazy art.'

but that of Mallarmé not at all—he reproached him with making music and not ideas of words. He happened to be among the first to proclaim the stature of Renoir, though he amazingly compared him to Leonardo da Vinci.

Jean-Christophe should now be read in conjunction with Rolland's correspondence with Mawilda von Meysenbug. A friend of Wagner and Nietzsche, she was also associated with several other rebels and idealists, often regardless of their creed. She was seventy when Rolland as a student met her in Rome, and she quickly became a powerful influence on the young French historian. 'I was created by Mawilda', Rolland later confessed. From their correspondence it is clear that it was Mawilda von Meysenbug who planted the far-flung conception of *Jean-Christophe* in his mind. In later years Rolland wrote to her of Vincent d'Indy (whom he hoped would be a John-Christopher in real life), of Gabriel Fauré (whom he describes as a 'half-Wagnerian'), but not of Debussy. 'Away with your chord factories', says John-Christopher in Paris, obviously in reference to Debussy. 'Not all the twaddle of the harmonic kitchens would ever help to find a new harmony that was alive and not a monstrous birth.' Then comes Christopher's visit, accompanied by two Paris critics (impersonated by Théophile Goujart and Sylvain Kohn), to the Opéra-Comique to hear *Pelléas et Mélisande*:

Christopher first heard the famous work which the French had so extravagantly praised, while some of them were announcing the coming of the greatest revolution of the last ten centuries. (It was easy for them to talk about centuries: they knew hardly anything of any except their own.)

Théophile Goujart and Sylvain Kohn . . . were proud to display the opera to him—as proud as though they had written it themselves. They gave Christopher to understand that it would be the road to Damascus for him. And they went on eulogizing it even after the piece had begun. Christopher shut them up and listened intently. After the first act he turned to Sylvain Kohn, who asked him, with glittering eyes:

'Well, old man, what do you think of it?'

And he said:

'Is it like that all through?'

'Yes.'

'But it's nothing.'

Kohn protested roundly and called him a philistine.

'Nothing at all,' said Christopher. 'No music. No development. No sequence. No cohesion. Very nice harmony. Quite good orchestral effects, quite good. But it's nothing—nothing at all. . . .'[1]

Christopher's evening at *Pelléas* is, in fact, a reconstruction of an historical event, and the occasion is described in illuminating detail in extracts from Rolland's personal diary accompanying this correspondence. At a performance at the Opéra-Comique in 1907, those present were Romain Rolland, the critics Jean Marnold and Lionel de la Laurencie, Ravel, and Strauss. Rolland had earlier dined with Marnold and Ravel. The conversation turned on Strauss's *Salomé*, which Ravel declared to be the greatest work, with *Pelléas*, of the last fifteen years. Marnold went so far as to make derogatory reflections on French music. 'There are times when after having heard *Salomé* one finds all French music, even *Pelléas*, too finicky. Strauss has a force, a drive which we may reasonably envy.' On which Rolland comments: 'These were my own ideas put forward by the one who had up till now been my staunchest opponent.' The violent hostility in Paris to *Salomé* was discussed and Ravel revealed the intention of one of its adversaries: 'I should like to crack my stick across the face of those who admire *Salomé*.' Ravel went on to express his admiration for Mendelssohn and Gounod (which Rolland finds 'plucky in such an ultra-modern musician'), also for Bizet's *Carmen*, and spoke of his quarrel with Debussy. 'It is obvious', Rolland comments, 'that it all comes from Debussy who has, I know, a violent antipathy for the music (or the success) of Ravel. Ravel speaks of him with great dignity and modesty, replying to Marnold, who held there must be an element of jealousy on Debussy's part, that Debussy really had no reason for jealousy and that there was nothing in his (Ravel's) success that need worry him.'

After dinner the company joined Strauss in a box at the Opéra-

[1] From the correspondence of Strauss and Rolland it is clear that to the line of composers from Gluck to Mahler embodied in the character of John-Christopher we must now add the figure of Richard Strauss. In a letter to Strauss of 21 February 1909, referring to this account, we read: 'I am sending you *La Foire sur la place*, one of a collection of novels entitled *Jean-Christophe*, so that you should see that I am not afraid of saying what I think of the Parisians. You will find some recollections of an evening spent together at a performance of *Pelléas et Mélisande*.'

Comique. Strauss had so far known *Pelléas* only from the score. Rolland's version in his diary of this evening is in certain respects radically different from the romanticized version in *Jean-Christophe*. In the novel the belittlement of Debussy was part of the picture he was building up of an effete French world which the Teutonic John-Christopher beheld with contempt. In the more truthful account in the diary there is an element of national tragedy. Rolland is overcome by the thought of two great civilizations thus set against each other, not only musically but socially and politically:

Strauss arrived at the end of the first scene and seated himself between Ravel and myself. Jean Marnold and Lionel de la Laurencie sat behind. In the audience were Nikisch and several other foreign musicians who had come to hear *Salomé* or the concerts of Russian music.[1] In his usual uninhibited manner with no regard for conventional courtesy, Strauss hardly speaks to anyone but myself, confiding his impressions of *Pelléas* to me in a whisper. (Since all the gossip in the papers he has become distrustful.) He listens with the greatest attention and, with his opera-glasses up to his eyes, follows everything on the stage and in the orchestra. But he understands nothing. After the first act (the first three scenes), he says, 'Is it like this all the time?' 'Yes.' 'Nothing more? There's nothing in it. No music. It has nothing consecutive. No musical phrases. No development.' Marnold tries to bring himself into the conversation and says in his usual heavy manner, 'There are musical phrases, but they are not brought out or underlined in a way that the ordinary listener would appreciate.' Strauss, rather put out but very dignified, replies, 'But I am a musician and I hear nothing.' We go on with our conversation in whispers. I try to make Strauss see the quiet restraint of this art, all in half shades, this delicate and poetic Impressionism of contrasted colours, discreet and vibrant. He says, 'I am first and foremost a musician. If there is music in a work, I want it to dominate, it must not be subordinated to any other claim. It's too humble. I am not saying that poetry is inferior to music. But the real poetic dramas, those of Schiller,

[1] These were the concerts of Russian music organized by Diaghilev at the Paris Opéra in May 1907 (see Chapter 6, p. 99 *et seq.*) where Rolland gives his own and Strauss's impressions of *Pelléas* to Sofia Gonzaga.

Goethe and Shakespeare, are complete in themselves; they have no need of music. . . . There's not enough music in this work. Delicate harmonies, excellent orchestral effects in very good taste. But it amounts to nothing, nothing at all. You might as well be listening to the play of Maeterlinck as it was, without music.' He goes on listening, very conscientiously, and goes out of his way to tell me what he admires in the work, as much from a sincere desire to understand it as from consideration for me. But I feel that his attitude is motivated by politeness rather than by a real appreciation of the work. The novelty in the work escapes him. On the other hand he doesn't let a single instance of Wagnerian imitation go by without pointing it out, though not in admiration. 'But all that is *Parsifal*', he says at a certain passage. However, the scene of the tower, the prelude to the grotto scene and the following scene give him a certain pleasure. In the whole score these are obviously what he likes best. But he constantly comes back to his rather disdainful expression of praise, 'It's very refined.'

Rolland demands from Strauss an appreciation of the interior values of *Pelléas*. Its restraint, he tells him, is the restraint of Racine, a point completely lost on the triumphant composer of *Salomé*, who ingenuously retorts that, given the subject of *Pelléas*, a completely different kind of music would have occurred to him. 'I cannot after all set myself up as the champion of an art', Rolland goes on, 'the limitations of which I see more clearly than anyone else in France.'

I say, 'You see, Debussy for me is a very great artist, a greater artist than a musician.' He takes hold of my hand: 'There you are; that's exactly what I think. In very good taste, very subtle, very well written and artistic and some lovely colours.' 'A poetic feeling, too,' I add. 'All right, I'll agree to that, a poetic feeling. That's as far as I'm prepared to go. We agree.' We are rather less in agreement than he is prepared to believe. For what completely escapes him, and this was only to be expected, is the root nature of this art: the truth of its recitative, sparing yet supple, the truth of its musical speech, its expressive inflections striking deep at the heart. The farewell scene, the lovers' scene and the death of

Pelléas seem to him to misfire. What he was obviously waiting for was the big scene, and he doesn't see why Debussy didn't write it; he doesn't see that Debussy's originality consists precisely in the fact that he didn't write it.

In this account may be seen the root nature of Rolland's forked allegiances.[1] Rolland suggests to Strauss that *Pelléas* is a reaction against the exaggerated declamatory style in opera.

He grants that it may be a reaction. 'Against Massenet and Gounod,' he says. Not only against Massenet and Gounod. Against Wagner too. Also against Strauss. This I can't say to him. (Perhaps in his heart he senses something of the sort.) But he sees the work conceived only from an intellectual viewpoint; musical development and spontaneous expression seem to him to be cut short by an obsession with simplicity. What is even more surprising is that the last scene means nothing to him at all. My own feeling is that the work here reaches a lofty plane. Not since Monteverdi has music of such intensity been written with such sparing resources. . . . Strauss says that there is not enough music in it. I say to him, in a phrase that is just the opposite of the reply of Mozart after *Don Giovanni*: 'A single note more and it would be spoilt.' He turns round, looks at me and shakes his head. 'No, no', he declares.

Nor could Rolland obtain from Strauss a deeper expression of admiration for *Pelléas* in the discussion that went on after the performance at the Taverne Pousset. At most Strauss would rub his fingers together in an expressive gesture to convey the work's commendable subtlety.[2] The modern French opera particularly admired by Strauss was Charpentier's *Louise*, the work which, as we have seen, was held by Debussy to be particularly crude and altogether meretricious. In all sincerity Rolland is obliged to record his dis-

[1] It was a duality of mind shared by other French musicians of this time. Edouard Colonne, who was present at the rehearsal of *Salomé* in 1907, remarked to Rolland of Debussy and Strauss: 'Comme c'est curieux que la décadence des deux peuples, France et Allemagne, se soit incarnée en deux hommes, qui la représentent, l'un avec son raffinement efféminé, l'autre avec sa brutalité!'

[2] Rolland, writing in French and German, gives a valuable glimpse here of Strauss's limited understanding of *Pelléas*: 'Strauss dit: "C'est très fin, très . . . (il fait des gestes avec les doigts) très *gekünstet*, mais ce n'est jamais spontané; cela manque de *Schwung*." '

illusionment with Strauss. Before going to the Opéra-Comique to hear *Louise* Strauss had over-eaten:

> He speaks of this like a child, pulls pitiful faces and holds up his stomach. But as soon as the music begins he forgets all this and follows it with delight, looking through his opera-glasses. He is especially interested in the fourth act, from the beginning of the duet (when Paris, lit up, is seen below Montmartre) to the beginning of the procession of the Muse; he leans forward, cups his hand behind his ear, speaks to himself in German, looks at me and talks, laughs happily like a child, and when it comes to the good things in the score, interesting points of orchestration or modulation, he gently puts his tongue out as if to lick his lips at the taste of something good.

To Rolland's objection that *Louise* is showy and rhetorical, Strauss replies, 'But, my dear friend, that's Montmartre. The French are like that. Great gestures, fine words, exaggeration and rhetoric. This is the picture we have of you in Germany; and very good and very true it is too. Every people has its faults. These are yours. You seem not to like the work.'

At Strauss's request *Louise* was given in Berlin, a fact duly noted in the *Journal* and followed by a thumbnail caricature in illuminating contrast to Rolland's earlier portrait of Strauss as 'the artist of the new German Empire with his Nietzschean contempt for the feeble'. Strauss's host is now left with a vision of the great composer very much diminished. Having gorged on cheap music and French food 'he seemed to be quaking at the knees as he hurried off to his hotel in his skimpy frock-coat hunched up at the back. Not an heroic figure—very far from it!' And Rolland nostalgically continues, 'I'm afraid I may never see him as an heroic figure again.'[1]

The musicians who inspired Rolland's *Jean-Christophe*—Beethoven, Strauss, and the other figures mentioned by Zweig—are radically opposed to the composers, imaginary or real, who were at

[1] The first World War was calculated to shatter the conception of a European soul personified in John-Christopher. At the end of his life, during the second World War, Rolland wrote a work on another idealistic figure, Charles Péguy, the Catholic philosopher and poet with whom Rolland had been associated at the time of the latter's *Vie de Beethoven*. Concerned almost exclusively with religious and political affairs, Péguy nevertheless had some dealings with Debussy at the time of the controversy aroused by *Le Martyre de Saint-Sébastien*.

the back of the mind of Marcel Proust when he wrote *Jean Santeuil* and *A la Recherche du temps perdu*. Rolland had lost his heart to the romantic Germany of the early nineteenth century, that is to say to Beethoven and to Goethe. Consequently, his orientation was anti-Wagner, anti-Nietzsche, and anti-Debussy. In Proust's works we are back again in the artistic world of Paris dominated by Wagner, or rather by the spirit of Wagner, transformed and fructified by a wide variety of French influences.

A la Recherche is a great psychological exploration, but it is also another attempt, like the earlier work of Mallarmé, to bring about the Wagnerian ideal of the fusion of the arts. Memories and sensations are analysed by Bergotte, the writer, Elstir, the painter, and above all by Vinteuil, the musician, and this twelve-volume *roman-fleuve* thus becomes a Wagnerian pendant to *Jean-Christophe* which, as we have seen, was concerned not with subjective memories and sensations but with abstract ideals, with positive actions and with what Rolland believed was an impregnable philosophy. Time has moved against Rolland's monument of musical idealism to favour Proust's descriptions and analyses of sensations.[1] As a musically inspired work, that is to say inspired, even though unconsciously, by the Wagnerian technique of the *Leitmotiv*,[2] *A la Recherche* is the last and perhaps the greatest of the French literary works which have their roots in the Wagnerian movement. It is, moreover, a work of the first importance for an assessment of the art of Debussy. For Proust, like Debussy, was concerned to throw into relief and to enrich the present moment. All the literary and musical analyses of Proust and Wagner, all their psychology, ultimately recognize, and in fact derive from, the supremacy of pleasure in the present moment, and an expression of this pleasure. The pleasure of sensa-

[1] As early as 1931 Denis Saurat, one of the most profound critics of Proust, stated that as a result of Proust's influence 'man is no longer his own master. He does not control himself; he no longer knows who he is.' This, he implies, is not necessarily a disaster. The moderns, he wrote at that time, 'are suspicious . . . of romantic passion which they accuse of charlatanism. Whoever claims to love for a lifetime and then everlastingly is essentially lying. What is real then? Sensation is real; what the senses perceive, what the being feels at the moment he feels it.' As a positive contribution Saurat nevertheless allowed that Proust's followers 'have brought to literature two qualities at a level hitherto unattained: total sincerity and total courage'. (Translation by Jeffrey J. Carre.)

[2] Writing of the recurrence and the transformation of sensations associated with 'the little phrase' of Vinteuil in *A la Recherche*, André Coeuroy goes so far as to say: 'Il n'y a pas, dans toute l'œuvre de Wagner, de leitmotiv employé avec plus de conséquence et plus d'habileté que cette petite phrase de Vinteuil.'

tion in the work of Debussy is similarly supreme. And so it came about that the spirit of Wagner, which had united Mallarmé with Debussy in *L'Après-midi d'un faune*, was also to unite Proust with Debussy as the composer who, having resisted the Wagnerian invasion, was able to profit from his revolutionary musical and psychological ideas.

It is certain that music was one of the great inspiring forces in Proust's work. 'Music has been one of the great passions of my life', he told Benoist-Méchin. 'I say "has been" because at present I have hardly an opportunity to hear music in any other way than by my recollections of it. It has brought me joys and reassurances which cannot be expressed, and it has also given me proof that something else exists besides emptiness which, elsewhere, I have been brought up against on all sides. It is a guide through the labyrinth of my entire work.'[1] Many attempts have been made to trace the origins of Proust's musical ideas and to define his musical allegiances, notably in regard to the associations of 'the little phrase'. Proustians have long tried to discover the work or works that generated the idea of 'the little phrase'. Proust himself gave two versions, to Jacques de Lacretelle and to Prince Antoine Bibesco. Besides works of Schubert, Saint-Saëns, Franck, and Wagner (*Lohengrin* and the Good Friday music from *Parsifal*), both include works by Fauré, the Ballade and 'some ravishing piano pieces'. I do not believe these two versions tell us everything. Whether Proust mentions them or not we must take into account other works he heard before or during his work on *A la Recherche*. One of them was the Quartet of Debussy which was played to him in private by the Capet Quartet under curious conditions. Proust was in the habit of deliberately seeking and creating for himself the impressions he needed.

On one occasion [writes André Maurois] he had the Capet Quartet come and play for him, and for him alone, during the night at the rue Hamelin [other accounts say in Proust's corklined bedroom in the Boulevard Haussmann]. He wanted to hear the Quartet of Debussy which would help him in an indirect way to complete his account of the Septet of Vinteuil. He had hesitated to invite other people, saying to Céleste: 'If there were other

[1] See Jacques Benoist-Méchin, *Retour à Marcel Proust* (1957).

listeners I should be obliged to be polite and should not listen to it attentively. For my book I need impressions in their original state.' While the musicians played he reclined, with eyes closed, on a couch seeking some mystical association with the music.[1]

We are concerned here not so much with Proust's knowledge of the music of Debussy, which was obviously extensive,[2] nor with the inspiration Proust derived from Debussy's work, but with a certain similarity of outlook between the writer and the musician, and also with an aspect of Proust's work which we may reasonably call Debussyan. When Debussy recalled, while staying in the hills of Burgundy, his childhood visions of the sea at Cannes and the fact that his father had wished him to be a sailor, he was himself indulging in a Proustian reconstruction of time. At that time Debussy was writing La Mer of which, he said, he had 'many memories', adding that these 'were worth more than reality'.[3]

Passages suggesting the music of Debussy abound in A la Recherche, particularly where Proust speaks of the sea, 'the plaintive ancestress of the earth pursuing, as in the days when no living creature existed, its lunatic immemorial agitation'. Elsewhere, in the decorative tradition of Debussy, he speaks of 'little plumed triangles of an unmoving spray delineated with the delicacy of a feather or a downy breath from Pisanello's pencil and fixed in that

[1] In the second volume of his Marcel Proust George D. Painter reveals that Proust had also engaged the Poulet Quartet to play at his house the quartets of César Franck, Fauré, Mozart, and Ravel.

[2] Proust heard Pelléas in 1911 on the 'Théatrephone', a curious forerunner of the outside broadcast. By means of a mechanical device performances at the Opéra, the Opéra-Comique, and other theatres, as well as public concerts, were relayed over one's private telephone. Proust wrote at length of Pelléas to his bosom friend Reynaldo Hahn, but with great circumspection, for it was common knowledge that Hahn and Debussy were unable to tolerate each other. Nevertheless, Proust succeeds in conveying his immense admiration for Pelléas which, like Debussy's Quartet, prompted the inspiration of several passages in A la Recherche.

[3] Though he does not mention the important parallel of La Mer, Georges Piroué indicates a similar connexion when he writes of the underlying spirit in Proust's work: 'The product of his recollections is sensation, retained and compressed by the mind, the type of sensation which Debussy attempts to reconstruct in sounds and the Impressionists in colour. The revolution which Debussy brought about in music, Proust brought about, too, in literature, and more successfully.' Besides René Peter, who had introduced Debussy to Proust, the composer and the writer shared many common friends, among them Robert de Montesquiou, who was approached by Debussy for a private production of Pelléas, Gabriel Mourey, and Pierre Louÿs, with whom both Proust and Debussy corresponded, and Jacques-Emile Blanche. Among the musicians, besides Reynaldo Hahn, Proust was particularly friendly with Fauré. (See E. Lockspeiser, 'Gabriel Fauré and Marcel Proust' in The Listener, 1 June 1961.)

white unalterable creamy enamel which is used to depict fallen snow in Gallé's glass'. In such passages he was determined to drain impressions of their last associations ('*aller jusqu'au bout de son impression*') somewhat in the manner that Debussy was determined to cut away all inessentials in order to reach 'the naked flesh of feeling [*la chaire nue de l'émotion*]'. Proust and Debussy were also united in their musical preferences, chief among them Chopin and Wagner, and they were united, finally, in their conception of the dream-nature of music. *Images, Estampes,* the Preludes—almost any of the musical evocations of Debussy might have inspired this description by Proust of the Septet of Vinteuil: 'This music seemed to me to be something truer than all the books that I knew. Sometimes I thought that this was due to the fact that what we feel in life, not being felt in the form of ideas, its literary (that is to say an intellectual) translation in giving an account of it explains it, analyses it, but does not recompose it as does music. . . . In Vinteuil's music there were thus some of those visions which it is impossible to express and almost forbidden to record since when at the moment of falling asleep we receive the caress of their unreal enchantment at that very moment . . . our eyes are already sealed . . . and we are asleep.'

6

Strauss and Mahler

If a person has no delicacy he has you in his power.
William Hazlitt

During the decade before the first World War Paris became the artistic and intellectual centre of the world. French artists led the way in painting and literature and many artists of other countries were drawn to Paris, either to live there or to seek approval from the French public. The French were also prominent in other spheres, among them the development of the cinema, and in scientific and mechanical inventions, notably of the aeroplane and the automobile. Something in the nature of a renaissance on all intellectual levels took place in Paris at this time. Musically, too, Paris during this period became the most important European centre. French musicians have sometimes been accused of insularity or chauvinism. In the early years of the century the contrary is true. At no other city could one hear such a profusion of Russian and Italian music—Tchaikovsky's Pathetic Symphony was on one occasion conducted in Paris by Mascagni—of the works of Wagner, and of Scandinavian and Spanish works. The two principal German and Austrian composers of this period, Strauss and Mahler, both of whom Debussy knew personally, were frequent visitors to Paris. The impressions which their works made in France require investigation from several viewpoints. It is instructive to see how the critical French minds of those days judged the novel Germanic styles of their works; and an assessment of their reception in Paris, though not directly connected with the ideas of Debussy, must for this reason serve to throw the æsthetic of Debussy into bolder relief.[1]

The impact made by Richard Strauss on French musical life during the first decade of the century was almost as powerful and as disturbing as that made by Wagner a generation earlier. It is true that, apart from Romain Rolland and the conductors Gabriel Pierné and Edouard Colonne, Strauss had fewer whole-hearted admirers in France than Wagner had had, and it is also true that his work had nothing of Wagner's wide-ranging influence among painters and poets. Nevertheless, together with the visits of Rimsky-Korsakov and other Russian musicians, Strauss's frequent appearances in Paris as a conductor of his works were the principal events contributed to the Paris scene during this period by a foreign musician.

This French vogue for Richard Strauss reached its height in June 1907 when Strauss himself conducted six performances of *Salomé* at the Théâtre du Châtelet. It was given in German with Emmy Destinn as Salomé and was the first of Strauss's operas to be heard in Paris. It was also the only opera by Strauss known to Debussy.[2] He had received the score in the very month of its first performance in Dresden[3] and, according to Louis Laloy, lost no time in distinguishing between its sensuous and its meretricious aspects. 'Debussy admitted the skill with which it was written,' Laloy writes, 'a skill which was sometimes that of a filcher rather than an artist. Also he had no illusions on the matter of the treacherous vulgarity of ideas which pretended to have dignity, such as the

[1] The social and political background of the Paris musical scene at this period should also be borne in mind, particularly in regard to certain hostile statements by Debussy which have often been misinterpreted as chauvinistic. From 1906 onwards the threat of war from Germany, which was carrying on a pin-pricking campaign against France in Morocco, became increasingly real. At the turn of the century no one had seriously thought of war with Germany. Reciprocal visits were arranged between French and German orchestras and in 1899, at the time of Strauss's first Paris visit, a Franco-German musical entente, based on a common acknowledgement of the genius of Wagner, seemed highly desirable. Unfortunately, by the time that Strauss's *Salomé* and Mahler's Second Symphony were given in Paris, repeated German provocations in Morocco, together with the annexation of Bosnia-Hercegovina by Austria-Hungary, were beginning to cause the gravest anxiety to the least politically minded of French observers.

[2] Later operas by Strauss, though produced in Germany in Debussy's lifetime, were not given in France until long after this. *Rosenkavalier* was not given at the Paris Opéra until 1927. *Elektra* was first given in Paris in 1932 and *Ariadne auf Naxos* in 1937.

[3] *Salomé* was first given at Dresden on 9 December 1905. Sending the score to Durand on 31 December, Debussy writes: 'Voulez-vous commencer l'année avec "*Salomé* ou le manque de cordialité dans tous les accords"?'

music of Jokanaan, nor on the composer's wretched intention of physically hurting the listener. "Sometimes he gives us chalk for cheese," was his comment, "thinking that we shan't know the difference; alternatively he grates until blood is drawn and he even grates into blood."' Though we cannot be sure that Debussy attended one of Strauss's performances of *Salomé* at the Châtelet the references to Strauss in Debussy's correspondence at this time certainly suggest that he did. Writing a few weeks later to Paul-Jean Toulet from a dull seaside town on the Normandy coast, he says: 'To be back in Paris I would willingly give the nine symphonies of Beethoven bound in the skin of Richard Strauss.'

The first impressions created by *Salomé*, now an accepted work in the operatic repertory of all countries, provide an illuminating view of the changing æsthetic values in the early years of the twentieth century and more particularly of the root nature of the conflict on musical and artistic matters between France and Germany.[1] In his usual manner, devastating but glinting with irony, Willy in the *Mercure de France* wrote of Wilde's distortion of an episode from the New Testament as 'une énorme éléphantaisie biblique d'après St. Mathieu, St. Jean, and St. Gustave Flaubert'— the reference is to Flaubert's tale *Hérodias*—and he added: '*Salomé* is welcomed in France because it comes from Germany and in Germany because the play of Oscar Wilde has some pretension to deriving from the *Psychopathia sexualis*.' In the same journal Camille Bellaigue, Debussy's friend from his Conservatoire days, confessed that the incessant developments, variations, and metamorphoses of themes in *Salomé* reminded him of 'a weasel, a whale, and a camel'. (A weasel normally ruins an egg by sucking out its contents; *chameau*, the French word for camel, also means a foxy scoundrel.) To underline the affront to his standards of civilized moderation Bellaigue, with much elegance, went on to compare aspects of Strauss's insatiable Salomé with observations on excess by classical

---

[1] In his discussion of the character of Salomé in French and English literature Mario Praz draws attention to the fact that in Germany Wilde's play 'has held the boards for a longer period than any other English play, including the plays of Shakespeare'. By comparison with the Salomés of Flaubert, Laforgue, and Mallarmé and with the paintings of Salomé by Gustave Moreau, much admired by Debussy, Wilde's *Salomé* is rightly said by Praz to be 'a specious second-hand document'. Alternatively, its rather childish dialogue may have been conceived by Wilde as a parody of the style of Maeterlinck. One of the reasons the opera aroused so much hostility in France is that Strauss rode rough-shod over all the traditions of irony and parody in the French treatment of this sadistic figure.

Debussy and Stravinsky

Debussy and Erik Satie

Debussy in 1913, by Ivan Thiele
Madame Emma Debussy

and contemporary authors. According to La Harpe, Bellaigue says, one may say that a man is charming, but one hardly speaks of his charms. Salomé proceeds otherwise: 'Quelle nomenclature! Quelle analyse! . . . Ta bouche! Je veux baiser ta bouche! Donne-moi ta bouche à baiser!' In Renan's *Vie de Jésus*, he points out, 'Salomé executes a character dance considered not unsuitable in Syria to a distinguished young person.' In Strauss's opera this scene becomes 'an unbearable horror'. The opera is 'a neurotic work combining erotomania and blasphemy in a manner which can only be described in the words of the Abbé Taconet, "Tout cela c'est des grandes saletés." '[1]

It is a curious fact that this musical treatment of *Salomé*, a subject so lovingly and so variedly treated in French literature, should have been considered by many of the French artists as unbelievably gross. As opposed to the reticence of Debussy, Strauss, to these people of discernment, displayed a vulgarity which they found wholly intolerable. Or was it that the unashamed vulgarity of Strauss's music was by its nature too revelatory? In his *Journal* André Gide stated that *Salomé* contained music 'so execrable and so rhetorical as to make one long for Bellini'. Its 'flagrant insincerity' and its continuous mobilization of all resources made of it a work that was 'fundamentally inartistic'. '*Cet art-là,*' he concludes, '*c'est vraiment l'ennemi.*'[2]

The impresario Gabriel Astruc who had brought Strauss to conduct at the Châtelet had also promoted, a few weeks earlier, a series of five concerts of Russian music at the Opéra, organized by Serge Diaghilev. Rimsky-Korsakov conducted suites from his *Snow Maiden*, *Mlada*, and *Christmas Night*, Chaliapin sang excerpts

---

[1] Toussaint Gaspard Taconet was a librettist of eighteenth-century opéras-comiques given at the Théâtre de la Foire in Paris, among them *Le Baiser donné et le Baiser rendu* (1770).

[2] *Salomé* was not to be given in London until 1910, but an English estimate of Strauss, by Arthur Symons, was in the meantime published in the *Mercure Musical* of 15 November 1907. Strauss, Symons reassuringly told his French readers, 'is the only decadent in music, and he has attempted to corrupt music as Stuck tried to corrupt painting and Klinger sculpture'. We may form some idea of these forgotten artists from the fact that Franz von Stuck played an important part in the propagation of the *Jugendstyl*. The sculptor Max Klinger created polychrome sculptures of Beethoven and other composers. The great champion of Strauss in England was Bernard Shaw, who in 1910 expressed an opinion that might have originated from Romain Rolland: 'I have often said, when asked to state the case against the fools and the money-changers who are trying to drive us into a war with Germany, that the case consists of the single word, Beethoven. Today I should say, with equal confidence, Strauss.'

from *Prince Igor* and *Boris Godounov*, and these gala programmes also included symphonies by Tchaikovsky and Scriabin and excerpts from *Khovanshchina*. Meanwhile *Pelléas* had been revived at the Opéra-Comique with the original cast, including Mary Garden. Once again our trusted historian here is Romain Rolland. In a letter of 31 May 1907 to his Italian friend Sofia Bertolini Guerrieri-Gonzaga[1] Rolland assesses the Russian, French, and German aspirants in this musical scene from a broad, unprejudiced viewpoint:

> Over the last weeks we have had an almost uninterrupted succession of concerts, gala performances, musical evenings, and dinners. Never in Paris has there been such an eventful season. The principal Russian and German composers and conductors have all been here together: Richard Strauss, Rimsky-Korsakov, Glazounov, Rachmaninov, Scriabin, Nikisch, Blumenfeld, etc. I have seen a great deal of them, particularly Strauss with whom I am quite intimate; and I was extremely interested to talk to them and to observe in real life the feelings, the thoughts and the weaknesses of these great artists who, together with certain French figures, are the greatest musicians of today. The ironic situation which emerges—and it is also a little comic and rather sad—is that not one of them understands the others. I took Strauss to hear Debussy's *Pelléas et Mélisande* which is the masterpiece of our contemporary French music; he listened with touching concentration and then said to me: 'I don't understand it at all.' The same evening Rimsky-Korsakov listened to the same production and understood nothing of it either.[2] Korsakov also loathes Strauss and hissed his *Salomé*. And Strauss said to me of Rimsky and the Russians: 'Not one of them is worth anything.' You realize that Strauss, Debussy, and Rimsky are three artists of the first order, altogether superior to other musicians in Europe. But what pitiful figures! For whom do they write?

[1] Sofia Gonzaga, whom Rolland had met in his youth in Rome, inspired the character of Grazia in *Jean-Christophe*. By contrast with the Teutonic fierceness of John-Christopher and the logical clarity of Olivier, it was intended that Grazia, *la linda* (the limpid), should convey the gentleness of the Italian spirit. Rolland's correspondence with Sofia (1901–8) dates from the time he was engaged upon *Jean-Christophe*.

[2] Judging from his injunction to his pupil Stravinsky, 'Better not listen to it or you may get used to it and eventually get to like it', Rimsky-Korsakov was apparently not entirely impervious to the attractions of Debussy's works.

They are not understood by the public at large. Their equals in the sister arts have no understanding of them either. Who then remains? A handful of people, a few 'odd' people like myself. You can soon count them.[1]

Of the three Rimsky writes the most tranquil, collected music: no ideas, no feelings, but he produces charming fairy-tales, clear in texture, exquisitely rich in colour, but altogether childish. Debussy produces the most perfected art: he is the poet of a refined and ancient civilization in whom we see the genius of taste[2] and the religion of beauty. Strauss is a Shakespearean barbarian: his art is torrential, producing at one and the same time, gold, sand, stone, and rubbish: he has almost no taste at all, but a violence of feelings which borders on madness. Of the three he is, despite all his faults, the one I love the most because he is the most vital. And he himself is greater than his works: sincere, loyal, and absolutely open. He is a good judge of himself and he has a regard and a friendship for me because I have never spared him criticism. Unfortunately he has a terrible wife who has done him great harm here. She is the daughter of a general and a woman in a sick state of nerves. In Germany her transports of anger are well known; in France people don't greatly care for these displays of hers. Would you believe that this foolish woman went about saying in Paris society that there was only one way of getting the French to do something, and that was with fixed bayonets![3] Strauss himself has shown a deplorable clumsiness of speech, slinging abuse at the Republic and bitterly criticizing Paris. In a word people have come to hate them. The Germans have lost their sense; it would seem that they have made a point of getting

[1] Two years earlier when writing of the Strasbourg festival of French and German music of 1905, Rolland took an entirely different view. He pointed then to 'the greatest danger which threatens music in Germany: There is too much music in Germany. . . . As in the *Sorcerer's Apprentice* musical Germany is being drowned in a musical flood.'

[2] Rolland's use here of the term 'taste' (*le génie du goût*) is slightly pejorative. Rolland probably did not know Edward Fitzgerald's saying 'Taste is the feminine of genius', but he would surely have agreed with it if he had. One is almost tempted to think that Strauss assumed the stature of a genius for Rolland not despite the fact that 'he almost has no taste at all' but because of this alarming lack.

[3] In his *Journal* Gide quotes Madame Strauss as saying 'Allons il est temps de revenir ici avec les baïonettes.' The fact is that at the rehearsals of *Salomé* Strauss had been understandably angered by the custom of deputies replacing prominent instrumentalists. This rendered earlier rehearsals useless. The story is not, as Gide suggests, apocryphal, though the amusing retort of Jean Cocteau, 'Non, Madame, les rasoirs suffisent', probably is. *Rasoir* is slang for a bore.

other people to loathe them. And yet what fine and beautiful qualities they possess. Having said so much bad about them, how much, at heart, I love them.[1]

Apart from the mingled excitement, adoration, and hostility created by the performances under the composer's direction of *Salomé*[2] much controversy was aroused by several other new works of Strauss given in Paris in the first decade of the century. Between 1899 and 1911 Strauss himself conducted in Paris seven times.[3] Debussy's published criticisms show that many of the earlier symphonic poems were known to him. Apparently, however, he missed Strauss's first appearance in Paris. In a letter to Debussy of 23 January 1899, Pierre Louÿs describes the distinguished gathering, including Fauré and Jacques-Emile Blanche, who had come to hear Strauss conduct *Also Sprach Zarathustra* at the Concerts Lamoureux. Debussy, he says, was not among them.

> What we heard [he reports] was something like a fantasy of Vincent d'Indy on an opera of Meyerbeer's and which weighed 120,000 tons. The composer wrote a programme guide to the work which I recommend to you as a piece of philosophy and literature: it is Nietzsche seen through the eyes of Charles Grandmougin—I hope you see my point.[4] Which is to say that

[1] Rolland continued to be haunted by the many conflicts, æsthetic, moral, and political, between France and Germany. Referring to the annexation in October 1908 of Bosnia-Herzegovina by Austria Hungary, thus aggravating the tension between France and Germany, he wrote to Sofia on 6 November 1908: 'Once again a grave conflict has arisen between France and Germany, that is to say between one part of Europe and another. Since my childhood there have perhaps not been two years without a threat of war from Germany.'

[2] After the fourth performance the Russian dancer Trouhanova, who had doubled Emmy Destinn in the Dance of the Seven Veils, refused to appear, having been told by Strauss that since dancing was 'an inferior art' she was not to take a curtain. 'I told Strauss', Trouhanova writes, 'that if anything is inferior it is the third-rate play-acting of a man of talent, or of a man who believes he has talent, who comes on to the stage every night to bow to an audience which has not asked him to appear.'

[3] The works of Strauss conducted by the composer in Paris were *Also Sprach Zarathustra*, 1899; *Don Quixote* and *Heldenleben* (two concerts), 1900; *Heldenleben*, *Aus Italien*, love scene from *Feuersnot*, 1903; *Sinfonia Domestica*, 1906—some of the crude, realistic scenes in this work, supposedly inspired by domestic harmony, were contrasted with a delightful satire of mid-nineteenth century morals, *Monsieur, Madame, et Bébé* by Gustave Droz; Prelude to *Guntram*, *Tod und Verklärung*, *Sinfonia Domestica*, 1908; and *Zarathustra* and *Tod und Verklärung*, 1911.

[4] Charles Grandmougin (1850–1930), a Parnassian poet of minor gifts who wrote librettos for operas by César Franck, Benjamin Godard, and Massenet and who, in an ostentatious manner, gave public readings of his poems in provincial towns in France and Switzerland.

there wasn't a moment of boredom [. . .] You must really hurry
up and reform music because things really can't go on as they have
been for the last fifteen years. We have got to the point where a
chord cannot be resolved without pretending to resolve some
problem of God himself! And one plunges into the depths of
mystery to the extent that yesterday no less than twelve double-
basses had to come to our rescue. During the first fifty bars they
played alone.[1] The public were delighted. They are well trained,
this public of ours, and a good thing too! And all this with themes
so childish, so unbelievably childish [*avec des thèmes d'un coco, mais
d'un coco!*].[2]

In 1906, the year when Strauss conducted his *Sinfonia Domestica*
in Paris, Debussy and Strauss had lunch at the home of the publisher
Jacques Durand. This meeting between the two foremost composers of France and Germany, perhaps the last great composers of
these countries, was an historic occasion, though not of the romantic
kind associated in the popular imagination with meetings between
great men. Proposed by Strauss, it was a meeting convened not to
discuss artistic matters, but to promote certain practical and financial
interests.

We must pause here to consider certain facts which may at first
seem to be entirely prosaic but which, if we look beneath the
surface, disclose perhaps the most fundamental difference in the
psychology and the musical character of the two composers. In his
memoirs Jacques Durand states that Strauss had consulted his father
on the organization of a French society formed to ensure the proper
distribution of royalties. No society with such powers existed in
Germany though Strauss himself had recently formed a smaller
organization of this kind. At lunch 'Strauss spoke unceasingly
about this society to Debussy who, being entirely ignorant of the
workings of the French society, took little pleasure in this conversation which he judged to be too commercially-minded. As matters
turned out Debussy managed to extricate himself from an em-
barrassing situation by thinking of other things, by appearing to be

---

[1] In the last twelve bars of the introduction of *Zarathustra* the double-basses are
prominent, but nothing more. This episode has hardly the importance which Louÿs
ascribes to it.
[2] Willy was similarly driven to use this expression of themes in *Salomé*: 'Musique . . .
chiquée en ses triturations toujours prestigieuses de thèmes souvent coco.'

lost in his dreams. The lunch thus took place to the accompaniment of an active conversation provided by Strauss while Debussy maintained a stubborn silence.' And Durand laconically concludes: 'I do not think that the meeting sought by the composer of *Salomé* wholly met his expectations.'

That Strauss and Debussy at this single encounter should have spoken entirely of money matters—or rather that Strauss should have delivered a monologue on this subject while Debussy turned a deaf ear—goes deeper than an immediate concern with material matters; it allows us to measure certain psychological and æsthetic values associated with wealth and poverty. Strauss was by his nature practical-minded. His revenues from his compositions were large. At one time it was said that he had become a millionaire from his music and it was suggested, with some justification, that his ornate music itself exhibited the lavish taste of a millionaire. Strauss may not have realized that Debussy had spent the whole of the early part of his life in abject poverty and that at the time of their meeting, when he was living in apparent ease with his wife and daughter, he had sunk more heavily in debt than ever. To Debussy, struggling almost for his life, a conversation with his renowned German contemporary on the subject of royalties must have seemed grotesque. As we saw earlier Debussy's financial difficulties became particularly acute after the death of Emma Debussy's uncle, the wealthy financier Osiris, in February 1907. Apparently Osiris, from whom Emma Debussy had expected a legacy, had looked askance at his niece's relationship with a composer who, unlike Strauss, was unable to support himself, let alone his wife and daughter; and the will of Osiris came as a severe blow. Most of his huge fortune was left to charities: twenty-five million francs to the Pasteur Institute and a substantial sum for a cause not more worthy than a memorial at Lausanne to William Tell. Thereafter Debussy, though stricken with cancer and temperamentally unsuited to compete for engagements and performances, plunged into the full stream of professional music-making, travelling widely and accepting whatever engagements were offered to him. The efforts he made in the last decade of his life to establish a practical financial basis for the day-to-day needs of his small family were enormous and amounted to a revolution in his economic outlook. But whether it was that, after his vagabond years with Gabrielle

Dupont and Rosalie Texier, his standard of living was now too high, or whether he was to remain unable, whatever the circumstances, to break the bonds of financial dependence, his debts mounted incessantly, almost overwhelming him in his race to fulfil his commitments and often driving him to serious thoughts of suicide.[1]

In broad terms if Debussy was poor, apprehensive, sensitive, and dependent, Strauss was rich, ruthless, gross, and overpowering. The French composer, exploratory and idealistic, penetrated far into the unconscious dream-world. His German contemporary, 'almost a genius' as Debussy admitted, was brazen, even vulgar. Money, therefore—the complicated feelings arising from the longing for money, the possession of it or the contempt for it—did seem to have more than a material significance in their guarded artistic relationship. For Debussy, who was never able to acquire money of his own, it was that which was possessed by others, the symbol of an independence which he never achieved. For Strauss, for whom everything turned to gold, it threatened to become the greedy possession of the dominating superman.[2]

[1] Referring to material difficulties in an undated letter to Durand he says: 'I assure you if it weren't for my little Chouchou I would blow my brains out, in spite of the cowardly and ridiculous nature of such an act.' In 1914 he writes to Godet 'of passing hours which can hardly bring anything but suicide'. Referring in 1916 to a court appeal in connexion with alimony for his first wife, he writes: 'I ought not to be abandoned and left with no other way out except suicide.' The many references to debts which occur in Debussy's letters from 1910 onwards, often in regard to small sums which he is unable to repay, reveal the terrible economic anxieties of his existence. In 1910, pressed by the impresario Henry Russell for repayment of a debt, he is far from being able to procure 5,000 francs. In the same year he asks a Monsieur Bertault for the loan of 6,000 francs. A letter to Laloy in 1911 or 1912 asks urgently for a loan of 20,000 francs 'from Marnold or anyone else'. In 1914 he is glad to accept 4,800 francs from Monsieur Bertault. An anonymous correspondent, related to a banker, declared that the commercial term 'affaire' represented a nightmare for Debussy. 5,000 francs 'or at any rate the half' is begged for from this benefactor in 1916. In the same year when his doctor orders his wife and daughter to rest in the country he tells Godet that this is utterly impossible since 'there is often only just enough not to die of hunger at home'. In the meantime advances on royalties were increasing, according to Vallas, at an alarming rate. Before the war he was humiliated to the extent of pledging all his forthcoming royalties to the curiously named insurance company, 'L'Avenir du Prolétariat'.

[2] If not commercially minded Strauss certainly possessed outstanding money-making gifts. Dr. Mosco Carner has kindly told me of an illuminating incident related to these gifts, which took place at a rehearsal of Elektra conducted by Strauss at Vienna about 1925. Strauss's gestures as a conductor were economic; to spare himself unnecessary effort when conducting he sometimes went so far as to prop up his forearm on the conductor's desk. His stockbroker, who had come to the Opera House with some important financial advice, perceived Strauss conducting in this manner and had no hesitation in interrupting the rehearsal by tapping the master on the shoulder. Undismayed, Strauss readily stopped the orchestra in order to conclude what he no doubt hoped would be a profitable financial deal.

The early works of Strauss made a powerful impact in Paris in the decade before the first World War, and so, during this same period, did certain of the symphonies of Mahler. We have seen that Romain Rolland was the principal French supporter of Strauss and that Strauss's French reputation reached its height with the performance of *Salomé* in 1907. Mahler similarly won a band of French admirers, chief of whom were Paul Clemenceau, the younger brother of Georges Clemenceau, the famous 'Tiger' of the first World War, and the Swiss critic William Ritter. In April 1910, three years after Strauss's performance of *Salomé* at the Châtelet, Mahler conducted the first Paris performance of his Second Symphony at the Trocadéro. Debussy was present at this concert which, curiously enough, was organized by the Comtesse Greffühle, the most distinguished lady in Paris society and the model for the Duchesse de Guermantes in Proust's *A la Recherche du temps perdu*.[1] The worlds of Gustav Mahler and Marcel Proust, fundamentally opposed from every æsthetic and psychological viewpoint, were thus, at this Paris concert, momentarily brought together.

In order to assess Debussy's feelings about Mahler at this time we must not only try to reconstruct the impressions made by Mahler on his several visits to Paris; we must also attempt to interpret contemporary French criticisms of his work. One of the most fervent of Mahler's early admirers, the French-speaking critic William Ritter, was a native of Neuchâtel and able to comprehend, therefore, the French and the German viewpoints. Ritter had heard Mahler's Fourth Symphony in Munich in 1901. Writing in a style not inappropriate to the music of Mahler, he says of this work in his *Etudes d'art étranger*, published in Paris in 1906, 'The mountebanks are in the temple, the circus is in the cathedral. . . . [The Fourth Symphony] brings out, cajoles and enlivens the latent streak of sensuality in us all; the winds of a contagious folly blow through the score and almost make us roar with laughter. A constant merry-making and a lumpishness is made out of some enticing theme, and this by all sorts of means, great and small. It veers from the sublime to the ridiculous in an effort to embrace us all, the high-minded

[1] Under the presidency of the Comtesse Greffühle a concert-giving organization, the *Société des Grandes Auditions Musicales*, had been formed to introduce works of particular interest.

and the wretched. . . . The sacrilegious buffooneries of this Nietz-schean Jew defy our Christian spirit; our loyalties to the past are affronted by the capitulation of all our artistic principles. The work of a creator, yes, but a work magnifying the ironies of Heine, a hundredfold, a caricature and a parody of the holiest of ideals.' Elsewhere, Ritter describes Mahler's Fifth, Sixth, and Seventh Symphonies as representing a 'Laocoön' succession, or a vision from Dante. And intent on driving home his message to his Paris readers, he grandiloquently concludes: 'I am captivated by Mahler as Heine was by the haunting Elizabeth. . . .[1] I lay down my arms before the work of this Nietzschean Jewish magician. . . . I await him in Paris!'

Before conducting his Second Symphony at the Trocadéro Mahler had frequently visited Paris. During the World Exhibition of 1900 he conducted concerts with the Vienna Philharmonic Orchestra at the Théâtre du Châtelet and the Trocadéro. His pro-grammes on this occasion included the *Symphonie Fantastique* of Berlioz and the Scherzo from Bruckner's Fourth Symphony, one of the first performances of Bruckner's music outside Germany or Austria. In 1905 three of the *Lieder eines fahrenden Gesellen* were sung by Madame Faliero-Dalcroze at the Concerts Lamoureux. In 1909 Mahler's First Symphony was given at the Salle Gaveau by a visiting orchestra from Munich, and in the same year the bust of Mahler was sculptured in Paris by Rodin.[2] The Fifth Symphony, which had earlier been given at the Franco-German festival at Strasbourg, was first performed in Paris in 1911. A substantial part of Mahler's work was therefore known in Paris during the latter part of his life.[3]

Mahler's knowledge of the French music of his time was, how-ever, patchy. Though he frequently conducted French operas in

[1] The reference is to Elise Krinitz, '*La Mouche*', who inspired Heine's finest poems, written in Paris at the end of his life.

[2] According to Alma Mahler, Rodin said Mahler's head was a mixture of Franklin's, Frederick the Great's, and Mozart's. After Mahler's death Rodin did a head in marble from memory, which, he pointed out to Frau Mahler, resembled Mozart. The Rodin Museum in Paris has three busts or heads of Mahler by Rodin, in marble (listed as a head of Mozart), in bronze, and in plaster.

[3] Apart from William Ritter, who frequently wrote on Mahler in *La Revue S.I.M.*, other supporters of Mahler in Paris included Alfredo Casella, known at the time of the production of Stravinsky's *L'Oiseau de Feu* as *L'Oiseau de Mahler*, and Lazare Pon-nelle, critic of the *Journal des Débats*, whose book *A Munich* (1913) contained substantial studies of Mahler, Strauss, and Busoni.

Vienna and gave the first performances there of *Louise* and *Samson and Delilah*, he appears to have had no knowledge of the music of Debussy, Ravel, or Fauré. In Hamburg in 1892 he had conducted *Le Rêve*, the first of a series of operas by Alfred Bruneau on the novels of Zola, the success or failure of which, in Paris, was largely determined by factions of the Dreyfus case to which Zola was either allied or opposed. Mahler's activities in France were similarly promoted by figures associated with the Dreyfus case. These included Paul Clemenceau and his Austrian wife Sophie, a future Prime Minister, Paul Painlevé, the War Minister, General Picquard, and General L'Allemand who was a friend of Ernest Chausson.[1] Musicians did not normally belong to the circle of Mahler's Paris friends. When he heard *Tristan* in Paris in 1909 it was in the company of the French War Minister and the Chief of Police. Alfred Bruneau was the only prominent French composer he seems to have met until his visit to Paris in 1910. On this occasion, Gabriel Pierné gave a dinner-party in his honour to which were invited Alfred Bruneau, Paul and Sophie Clemenceau, Fauré, Dukas, and Debussy. 'Mahler was not happy or at ease that evening', Frau Mahler states, adding somewhat enigmatically, 'and he had good reason.' Then came the performance of the Mahler symphony at the Trocadéro which involved an extraordinary incident. 'I suddenly saw Debussy, Dukas, and Pierné get up and go out in the middle of the second movement', Frau Mahler states. This left nothing to be said, she goes on, 'but they said afterwards that it was too Schubertian for them, and even Schubert they found too foreign, too Viennese—too Slav.'

Obviously, this can only be a superficial account, and we must await further evidence, possibly in the correspondence of Debussy and Dukas, to form a judgement of what actually occurred. In the meantime it is impossible to believe that any French musician could have described Schubert as 'too Slav'. But it does seem that Mahler

---

[1] Paul and Sophie Clemenceau (née Szeps) actively promoted Franco-Austrian musical relations. The 'Dreyfus Quartet' or the 'Paris Mahlerites', as they are referred to in the memoirs of Berta Szeps, 'were present at nearly every concert Mahler gave, and often followed him about on his tours'. As a result of this interchange between Paris and Vienna, Ravel, whose *La Valse* was originally to have been entitled *Wien*, was a guest in Vienna, shortly after the first World War, of Frau Mahler. The widow of the composer of *Das Lied von der Erde* found Ravel 'a narcissist' who 'came to breakfast rouged and perfumed' and who 'related all things to his bodily and facial charms'.

met with something like a calculated rebuff on this occasion. Frau
Mahler's comment on this episode is: 'The success he had with the
public was no consolation for the bitterness of being so misunder-
stood, and indeed condemned by the foremost French composers.'

The facts are that the main impression created by Mahler's
Second Symphony was that it was a work in the tradition not of
Wagner but of Berlioz, a composer who at this period, and indeed
during his lifetime, was far more widely appreciated in Germany
than in his native country.[1] It thus came about that Mahler's music
in Paris revived in a new guise the former clash between the
interests of Berlioz and Wagner, but with the roles reversed so to
speak—that is to say with the Latin Debussy as the Wagnerian and
with Mahler, the 'Nietzschean Jew', as the Berliozian. The nature
of this clash was made even clearer when in September 1910,
shortly after the Paris performance of the Second Symphony,
Mahler's Eighth Symphony was first performed in Munich, followed a few days later by a five-day festival of French music
there. The works performed included Berlioz's *Benvenuto Cellini*,
the Requiem of Fauré, and orchestral works of Dukas, Debussy, and
Ravel. Mahler, who was a member of the festival committee,
apparently did not stay for the performances. Debussy was similarly
absent. 'The German press, still overcome by Mahler,' dryly states a
report in *La Revue S.I.M.*, 'was half curious, half sympathetic.'
Dukas's *L'Apprenti Sorcier* was appreciated, but not Debussy's
Nocturnes. 'The horizon of Debussy is small', declared the critic
Eduard Wahl after hearing Mahler's Symphony of a Thousand.
If Paris was turning its back on Berlioz, Munich was reluctant to
gaze upon the final glories of the Wagnerian sunset.

Debussy and his ideals may seem somewhat remote from these
musical events which took place in the Paris musical world of his
time. But, as it was pointed out at the beginning of this chapter,
it is precisely because Strauss and Mahler, each representing values
foreign to Debussy, made such wide and disturbing impressions
that an account of these impressions will help us to see the ideals of
Debussy in clearer relief. Debussy refused to attend the Munich
festival, and he set out his reasons for declining the invitation

---

[1] A detailed and penetrating study of Mahler's Second Symphony by Amadée
Boutarel, published in *Le Ménestrel* of 23 August 1910, convincingly demonstrates
that this work is 'an enlarged, amplified and exaggerated *Symphonie Fantastique*'. See
the chapter on Bayreuth (Vol. I, p. 94) for Alfredo Casella's opinion of Mahler.

clearly enough: 'It is obvious that we have been more than gracious towards German musicians', he wrote.

In fifty years' time we shall see what remains of our present enthusiasms. We have a way of loving everything that comes from abroad. Like children we gleefully clap our hands when we hear a work from afar—from Scandinavia, the Germanic, or the Latin countries—without assessing the real value or substance of such a work, without wondering whether we are able to experience the true thrill of delight in the marriage of a foreign soul to our own. We are very fortunate if we manage to avoid clumsily imitating what is said better by these artists in their own language; if we do not become infatuated with pseudo-Italianism in music, with pseudo-Ibsenism in literature, or if we do not make ourselves look ridiculous by imitating some exotic fashion. The Germans need not trouble to understand us, any more than we should attempt to absorb their thoughts and ideas. Moreover though Munich, as *Le Figaro* says, may be an appropriate choice from a political viewpoint, it is a town which has remained indifferent to our art. Concerts of modern music are attended there only by a few amateurs. Of course German audiences will listen to French music out of courtesy; and given their patronizing manner, it will seem that our music has created a good impression. But I am convinced that nothing will be achieved by performances of our works in Germany. It will be suggested, of course, that a closer understanding will result from these performances. The answer to this is that music is not written for such purposes. And the time is badly chosen.

These are not the words of an insular or a chauvinistic musician. The previous year, 1909, the weak and incompetent Bethmann Hollweg had succeeded Prince von Bülow as German Chancellor. This marked a turn for the worse in Franco-German relations since it allowed the impulsiveness of Wilhelm II a freer rein, an impulsiveness which contributed before long to the outbreak of the first World War. In the meantime armaments were piling up between the countries of the Triple Alliance (Germany, Austria-Hungary, and Italy) and those of the Triple Entente (France, Russia, and Great

Britain). The French were developing a war-like spirit too, but of a different kind. It was about this time that a professor at the Ecole de Guerre declared that entire faith should be placed in the French 75 mm. gun. As a weapon of war, he said, it was 'the Father, the Son, and the Holy Ghost'. In July of the following year, 1911, war again seemed imminent when a German gunboat was sent to Agadir in Morocco 'to protect German interests'. Debussy's refusal to attend the French festival at Munich was not therefore motivated by any kind of pique; he rightly felt that Munich could hardly offer a sympathetic response to the values which he represented. At the last moment Fauré declined to attend the Munich festival, possibly for the same reason. His place was taken by Alfred Cortot. Under the growing threat of European war two composers, in a last pathetic attempt to bridge the Franco-German gulf, gave an un-official concert at Munich consisting of carefree waltzes. The waltz is a dance-form belonging to the nineteenth, not to the twentieth century, and these composers similarly belonged in spirit to the nineteenth century. They were Saint-Saëns, who played his *Valse Mignonne*, and Richard Strauss, who played and sang the waltzes which he had completed only a few days earlier from his *Rosenkavalier*.

PART II

The Later Years

1908-1918

7
Travels Abroad

Car nous sommes où nous ne sommes pas.
Pierre-Jean Jouve

In his youth Debussy had been a great traveller. He was stimulated
by new places and peoples, and in his travels as in his work he was
driven on by a restless exploratory spirit. By the time he was thirty
he had travelled extensively in his own country, he had been twice
to Italy, Germany, and Russia, and had even made plans to go to
America. We cannot be sure of all his movements in the last decade
of the nineteenth century, but it seems likely that he was at any rate
occasionally abroad during this period too.[1] In the latter part of his
life he again became a restless traveller, but for different and rather
sadder reasons. Throughout the first World War, when he was
fighting a losing battle against disease, he was glad to find some
peace of mind for a month or two in a country villa or hotel, and
these war years were accordingly spent moving from one part of
France to another. Before that he was obliged to travel abroad to
earn fees conducting his works, and at any rate from 1907 onwards
he was obliged to sacrifice some of his idealism to financial considerations. Commissions had to be accepted for works which
otherwise would certainly not have been written. Engagements
as a conductor in foreign towns had to be sought out. There was
nothing harmful here, of course; Debussy was not a hothouse plant
unable to withstand the rougher worldly shocks. The trouble was
that all the contemporary evidence shows that he had no gifts as a
conductor. There was nothing of the extrovert in his nature and he

[1] A poem of Pierre Louÿs addressed to Debussy and beginning 'Doux maître qui
revient des terres étrangères' is presumed to refer to a journey to Mercin in 1898, but
may be taken to refer literally to a foreign land.

consequently abhorred appearing in public. Also, from the time of his first London appearance, in January 1908, he was always likely to be ill, often seriously.

It is indeed pathetic that these foreign engagements were calculated to devour more and more of the time which remained to him. They moreover frustrated him in his creative work and caused additional physical suffering. The following list of journeys from 1902 onwards, undertaken for personal and professional reasons shows the extent of his travels. (After the death of Osiris, that is from 1908 onwards, all the journeys were made to fulfil conducting engagements.)

July	1902	London
May–June	1903	London
July	1904	London, Jersey
July–August	1905	Eastbourne
January	1907	Brussels
January	1908	London
February	1909	London
May	1909	London
November	1910	Vienna, Budapest
June	1911	Turin
December	1913	Moscow, St. Petersburg
February	1914	Rome
February–March	1914	The Hague, Amsterdam
April	1914	Brussels
July	1914	London

In assessing contemporary criticisms of Debussy's work outside his own country one is struck by the wide range of associations it evoked. In England, where a resemblance to Rossetti was observed, his work was said to reflect the æsthetic principles of Poe, Mallarmé, and Walter Pater. In Vienna, where he appeared when Schoenberg's paintings had become known, comparisons were made between his work and that of the German Art-Nouveau painter Gustav Klimt. The Italians, after giving a hostile reception to *Pelléas et Mélisande*, welcomed him like the English, as an antidote to Richard Strauss. In Russia he was held to be 'the spiritual heir of Moussorgsky and Rimsky-Korsakov'. It is clear from all this that Debussy's journeys stirred up great controversies. But he himself remained severely aloof. Polemical discussions meant nothing to him: they merely made the artist's mission more difficult since they attempted to define his work and thereby to limit it.

We are able to draw upon many contemporary records of these journeys, but Debussy himself seems to have written few letters when he was abroad and his own impressions are therefore lacking. The intimate letters to Emma Debussy and his daughter Chouchou written on these journeys are at first sight puzzling. Their main theme was that foreign travel was boring and tiring. In at least two cities, London and Turin, Debussy's lack of experience as a conductor proved to be disastrous and his one desire was to return to his wife and daughter in Paris. But perhaps one need not look too far into these letters written from the heart.[1] Undoubtedly the hard-driven composer was sick, dejected, and lonely. He seems also to have been curiously anxious. On his short journeys in 1914 to Holland and Belgium telegrams were sent to Emma Debussy every few hours merely to re-assert the extent of his despair or to anticipate the pleasure of seeing her again.

Debussy's first appearance as a conductor in London was on 1 February 1908 at the Queen's Hall where he performed *L'Après-midi d'un faune* and *La Mer*. He had been invited by Sir Edgar Speyer, the wealthy patron of music who had formed a syndicate to take over the Queen's Hall Orchestra. Speyer had asked Henry Wood to go to Paris to negotiate Debussy's visit to London at the substantial fee at that time of one hundred guineas. This must have been by far the largest sum Debussy had ever been offered for a professional appearance. The negotiations were carried on through Madame Debussy, and as a result Wood was obliged to report that Debussy had refused Speyer's generous offer. 'What, a hundred guineas for *me*!' he is said to have exclaimed. 'And yet you pay Caruso four hundred guineas.' Having corrected this false impression, Wood received Speyer's agreement to conclude for two hundred guineas.[2] 'A crowded audience was present to give him a

---

[1] The letter from Moscow of 4 December 1913 to Emma Debussy is typical of the many passionate outbursts in this correspondence: 'J'en ai tellement gros sur le cœur, que je ne sais pas par où commencer. . . . Tâchons de mettre de l'ordre dans mes regrets, qui peuvent être contenus en un seul: le regret de toi, chère petite Mienne à moi. Je me sens affreusement dépareillé et, si je veux m'appuyer sur le "côté cœur", c'est là la pire douleur, puisque c'est en toi qu'il trouve son appui; on dirait, romantisme à part, que l'on marche sur mon âme.'

[2] On his last visit to London, in July 1914, when he was being hunted by his creditors, Debussy seems still to have been obsessed by the magnitude of the fees paid to

real English welcome', Wood writes of Debussy's first London appearance. 'I recall most vividly my first impressions of that dark, bearded Frenchman: his deep, soulful eyes; his quiet rather grating voice; most of all, his enormous head. I have never seen such a head on a man of his stature; it reminded me of the heads of early Egyptians. Debussy seemed delighted—almost like a child—because he thought that we in London appreciated his music more than his countrymen. . . . Not even Strauss had received a warmer welcome.'

Before dealing with this London reception of Debussy we must record a triumphant event in his public career. In fact, his concert with the Queen's Hall Orchestra was only the third time he had conducted. A few days earlier, on 19 and 26 January 1908, he had conducted La Mer with the Orchestre Colonne at the Théâtre du Châtelet in Paris. 'My heart began to beat loudly when yesterday morning I mounted the rostrum for the first rehearsal', Debussy wrote to Victor Segalen on 15 January. 'It is the first time in my life that I have played the game of being a conductor and you may believe that my utter lack of experience must disarm these curious beings called orchestral musicians, good-hearted as they are. . . . One of my main impressions is that I really reached the heart of my own music. Also, when everything was effectively coordinated I had the feeling of being myself an instrument of many different sonorities, animated, so to speak, by movements of the little stick. If this interests you at all I'll tell you more about it all some day.'[1]

The two performances which Debussy gave of La Mer in Paris achieved a spectacular success. Not since the production of Pelléas had he been seen at one of the Paris symphony concerts. 'To let everyone behold the sight of his pale, bloated appearance, his ink-black hair and his bulging forehead, chock full of chords of the ninth, he was biding his time', wrote Willy in his 'Lettre de l'Ouvreuse'

Caruso: 'I am going to London for a few days', he then wrote to Jacques Durand, 'to take part in an evening given by Lady Speyer. Caruso would ask what I am receiving for his accompanist. Anyhow, it is a drop of water in the desert of the awful summer months.'

[1] This sense of an identification with instruments is expressed also in a letter to André Caplet of 15 August 1911: 'And what a joy it is to listen to music in a state of complete relaxation; to feel oneself immersed in a constantly heightened state of happiness until one no longer knows whether one really exists, or whether one has not actually become that agonizing drum-roll or that harmonic on the cello. Enough, enough!'

in *Comoedia* on 20 January 1908. It is important to remember that this performance of *La Mer* had been rehearsed in close co-operation with the conductor Edouard Colonne and its success was therefore largely due to Colonne's preparatory work. 'Never had my ears heard a din like this outburst of enthusiasm', Willy reported. 'What we heard were wild yells of joy, the cracking sounds of hands clapped together, calls for the composer and de-mented shouts. Debussy picked his way ten times through the forest of the music desks in order, it seemed, to confide his gratitude to the prompter's box. Now and again a piercing, violent whistle, as if a guard were signalling the departure of a train, set off the triumphant reception afresh and had the effect of redoubling the zeal of tired muscles and sore hands. To appease these delirious melomaniacs the conquering hero, who had rushed away down a staircase, had to be brought back once again, this time in his over-coat and his bowler hat which in our modern costume takes the place of the ancient laurel wreath.' Almost incredibly, the applause continued even when Colonne and Jacques Thibaud had deter-mined to go on with the programme by playing Lalo's *Symphonie espagnole*. They were obliged to stop and start again.

Debussy was not greatly affected by this show of enthusiasm. 'It was very kind of you to think of me during the hard times of Sunday last', he wrote to Segalen on 22 January. 'What a feverish atmosphere and what lunatic screaming! It wasn't at all funny. I felt like a freak showman or an acrobat who has carried off some perilous jump. And Sunday next it's to start again. Music sometimes leads one into strange paths.'[1]

The first performance of *La Mer* in London did not create the sensation of its Paris performance though it made a deep impression. Besides Wood and Sir Edgar Speyer, Debussy's friends in London included Louise Liebich, who in 1908 published the first biography of Debussy, Georges Jean-Aubry, who with T. J. Guéritte was active in promoting the interests of French musicians in England, Edwin Evans, who became Debussy's most powerful English advo-cate, and Arthur Symons, the English authority on Symbolist

[1] A letter of the same date to Paul-Jean Toulet records similar impressions: 'Since I saw you I have made my début in the career of a conductor. . . . It's amusing so long as you are able to pick out the colour you want from the end of the little stick, but afterwards it's like an exhibition in which the applause which greets you is like that given to a freak showman or an acrobat at the completion of a dangerous act.'

literature who was also at this time music critic of the *Saturday Review*.

The early impressions made by Debussy's music in England revive the worlds of Pater and Beardsley. The Symbolist movement, which had taken its rise in Paris, soon became known in London, particularly in literary circles, and in the early years of the century Debussy's music became as fully understood in London as it had been in Paris among the followers of Mallarmé. In 1908 Arthur Symons declared that a performance of Debussy's Quartet enabled him 'at last to enter into the somewhat dark and secret shadows' of what he called 'the wood'. He recognized in it 'a new kind of music . . . filled with an instinctive quality of beauty which can pass from mood to mood, surprise us, lead us astray but end by leading us to the enchantment in the heart of what I have called the wood.' Unfortunately Symons was not to hear *Pelléas et Mélisande*, given in London in 1909, but he had heard sufficient works of Debussy to be able to state that 'words, however vague, are too precise for this music, which suggests nothing but music'. It was 'an achievement of a new kind' not to be found, he believed, in Fauré or Ravel: 'This genuine quality is not in them, or only here and there by accident.' Debussy's Verlaine settings, on the other hand, disappointed him. *Mandoline*, however, suggests a vision of the Art Nouveau. It is music which 'is echoed like a bird answering a bird, the tinkle in the music is the same tinkle as in the verse. . . . An insect's web has been woven across a flower; it glitters a little, and at a breath it evaporates; and the flower and its perfume remain.'

The following year, after Debussy's appearance at the Queen's Hall, Symons attempted to assess Debussy's achievement in the light of his inspiration from both Verlaine and Mallarmé. Debussy, he maintained, 'is the Mallarmé of music, not because he has set *L'Après-midi d'un faune* to sound, but because the music has all the qualities of the poem and none, for instance, of Verlaine. . . . Mallarmé has a beauty of his own, calculated, new, alluring; and Debussy is not less original, aloof, deliberately an artist.' *L'Après-midi d'un faune* 'has precisely the same beauty as the poem, and it is in no sense programme music. It matches the poem because the art of making is the same in poet and musician.' Disappointed by the first movement of *La Mer* ('on a first hearing it left no impression

except that of unsuccessful effort') Symons found a 'new gaiety' in
Jeux de vagues, and in the last movement 'a drama of elements'
that 'convinced the mind as well as the senses; it had a deeper meaning than anything of Debussy's music which I have heard'. It was
not easy, he maintained, nor indeed profitable, to compare the
work of Debussy with other contemporary or even earlier music.
It 'has the conscious and lovely eccentricities of Poe,[1] the secret
glitter in the jewels of Mallarmé'. Like other observers in England,
Symons was impressed by Debussy's appearance. 'The face of Debussy has a singular likeness to the later portraits of Rossetti; there
is the same brooding meditation in eyes and forehead.' And he goes
on: 'A certain heaviness of aspect is characteristic of most artists of
extreme delicacy: Gautier, Renan, Pater, Maeterlinck, among
writers. Languor was part of their genius, and Debussy's music is
defined beforehand in the first four lines of Verlaine's *Langueur*:

> Je suis l'Empire à la fin de la décadence,
> Qui regarde passer les grands Barbares blancs
> En composant des acrostiches indolents
> D'un style d'or où la langueur du soleil danse.'

Debussy is Merlin, Symons suggested, solitarily living in a wood
with his phantoms and 'no Vivien has taught him to be human! . . .
The phantoms have unearthly voices; they express neither love nor
hate, hardly desire; but for the most part dreams that have no outset
nor conclusion, and when they are awake they play indolently at
acrostics. Beardsley would have recognized his perverse elegance in
these wandering outlines, in which sound plays pranks in the brain.
He would have collected them in visible outlines, he would have
shown them to us in fancy-dress, playing indolently at acrostics.'[2]
A return visit of Debussy to England was planned for 1909 when

---

[1] Arthur Symons' American contemporary James Huneker similarly drew a comparison between Debussy and Poe (see Vol. I, p. 213). In his study 'Mélisande and
Debussy' in *Bedouins* (New York, 1920) Huneker states that *Pelléas et Mélisande* 'has
the dream-drugged atmosphere of Edgar Allan Poe; the Poe of the dark tarn of Auber,
of Ligeia, of Ellenora, of Berenice and Helen, those frail apparitions from claustral
solitudes and the Valley of the Many-Coloured Grass all as exotic as they are incor-
poreal'.

[2] The reference to sound which plays 'pranks in the brain' may be indicative of the
insanity of which Symons was shortly to be a victim. Published on 8 February 1908,
Symons' study of Debussy was one of the last articles he wrote before his mental
collapse. In November of the same year he was certified insane and sent to Brooke
House, Clapton.

he was to have appeared in London and also in Manchester and Edinburgh. These plans were upset by the beginnings of a grave malady. In January of this year the first signs were declared of an illness which later developed into cancer of the rectum. The following month he suffered almost daily from hæmorrhages for which he was obliged to take morphine and cocaine. He arrived in England at the end of February, ill and dejected. 'Forgive me for having left you without news', he wrote to Durand on 27 February 1909, the day of his concert at the Queen's Hall. 'Arrived here on Thursday, have been ill all the time and have consequently been obliged to cancel my journeys to Edinburgh and Manchester. The concert today went off admirably. *Fêtes* was encored and it only depended on me to secure an encore for *L'Après-midi d'un faune*, but I could hardly stand up—a very bad posture for conducting anything.'

Wood's account of what actually happened throws a rather different light on Debussy's anxieties at this concert. Out of consideration for the fact that the composer was by no means an experienced conductor, and apparently unaware of the gravity of his illness, Wood had rehearsed the orchestra 'until there was practically nothing for Debussy to do'. The rehearsal went off smoothly, Wood writes,

but at the concert there was a peculiar accident. I do not remember ever witnessing anything like it. In the second of the *Nocturnes* (*Fêtes*) the time changes a good deal. To the surprise of us all Debussy (who quite candidly was not a good conductor even of his own works) suddenly lost his head, and his beat! Realizing what he had done, he evidently felt the best thing was to stop and begin the movement again. He tapped the desk, and tapped again. Then the most extraordinary thing happened. The orchestra refused to stop. . . . They obviously did not intend to stop: they knew that the audience would think the fault was theirs. Moreover, the work (which they liked immensely) was going beautifully and they meant to give a first-rate performance of it. . . . The audience by no means missed the fact that something had gone wrong. . . . At the end, in truly English fashion, they recorded their appreciation to such an extent that he was compelled to repeat the movement.

In the evening Debussy was due to attend a reception at the Aeolian Hall of which an account is given in the memoirs of Arnold Bax. 'Tonight I have to attend a reception organized by the society of English composers', Debussy wrote to Durand. 'What sort of figure shall I cut? Something like a man condemned to death. It appears that I cannot get out of it because of the Entente Cordiale and other such sentimental ideas invented to hasten the death of others.' The society referred to was in fact the 'Music Club',[1] and Debussy was the first of four eminent musicians—the others being d'Indy, Sibelius, and Schoenberg—invited to be present at a concert of their works. 'Of the four guests,' Bax writes, 'Debussy's torments were certainly the most excrutiating.' The concert of songs, sung by an American singer accompanied by Bax, and instrumental works was preceded by an address given in guttural and almost unintelligible French by Alfred Kalisch. 'The great composer,' Bax writes, 'an inordinately shy man, was planted in a chair in the exact centre of the platform facing the audience. He was clearly utterly nonplussed and could only attempt to solve his problems by rising and making a stiff little bow whenever he recognized his own name amid Kalisch's guttural mumblings. This part of his ordeal over, he was permitted to shamble dazedly to the rear of the hall, where he confided to Edwin Evans that he would rather write a symphony to order than go through such an experience again.' Like other people who met Debussy at this time, Bax was impressed by his almost oriental appearance. 'Never shall I forget the impression made upon me by that thick-set clumsy figure, the huge greenish, almost Moorish face beneath the dense thicket of black hair, and the obscure dreaming eyes that seemed to be peering through me at some object behind my back. As he lumbered vaguely forward, extending a cushioned hand, he looked like some

[1] In his *Farewell, my Youth* Sir Arnold Bax gives an arresting picture of the meetings of this club: 'In 1908 or thereabouts was founded the "Music Club", a dressy concert-cum-supper affair presided over by Alfred Kalisch, critic of *The Star* and a pious thurifer before the altar of Richard Strauss. Kalisch was a lovable little man: in person, with his barrel-like trunk, thick colourless skin, squat features and habitual cigar, suggesting the gentleman constructed entirely of motor tyres who used at one time to figure in M. Michelin's advertisement. The club members were mostly elderly, and notable for wealth, paunchiness and stertorous breathing. Bulging pinkish bosoms straining at expensive decolletages, redundant dewlaps, and mountainous backs were generously displayed by the ladies, whilst among the men ruddy double-chins, overflowing their collars at the back of the neck, and boiled eyes were rife. The assemblage indeed was ever inclined to bring to mind Beardsley's famous drawing, "The Wagnerites".'

Triton arisen from "the glaucous caverns of Old Ocean". "A mythological survival!" I said to myself.'¹

Arthur Symons had been prominent among the early English admirers of Debussy and his two articles in *The Saturday Review* appraised the æsthetic of Debussy in terms related to ideas in the contemporary literary movement. His successor on *The Saturday Review*, Filson Young, similarly took a radical view of Debussy's work though he kept severely to musical considerations. Having heard the concerts devoted in 1909 to Debussy's works in London at the Queen's Hall, the Aeolian Hall, and the Bechstein Hall (the last organized by the Society of French Concerts), Filson Young boldly stated: 'It is most important that those who care for music as a living art should come to their critical bearings about Debussy. He is a discoverer; he has wandered into a new world of tonality, and what for want of a better term we must call musical colour; he speaks to us in a new language, which we are obliged to learn before we can form any judgement of his work.' Young was left in two minds by several of the works he had heard. Nevertheless, he accurately measured the break-through made by the new music. Debussy's work, he concluded,

helps to make obsolete many forms which should have been obsolete long ago; forms in which the great composers of the past wrote great music, but in which no modern composer can write any but feeble music. It makes it a little more absurd for us to go on flogging those dead donkeys, the oratorio and the cantata; it makes experiment respectable, and even fashionable, where yesterday it was deemed disgraceful. It helps in the real appreciation of the great composers of the past, and will help to send us back to Bach for our fugues, Handel for our oratorios (if we really want oratorios), Schumann for our romance, Brahms for our musical philosophy; it will help us to discriminate between what was and what was not inspired in the works of the great, instead of accepting everything as pure gospel which bears the name of Mozart, Beethoven, Rameau,

¹ The quotation is from Shelley's *Prometheus Uubound* (Act II, scene i). Bax was one of the first to note that as early as February 1909 Debussy's appearance suggested the illness which, nine years later, brought about his death: 'Recalling that morbidly sallow complexion of his, I must conjecture that even so early the malignant foe, destined to bring about his death in his early fifties, was already prowling within his body.'

Bach, Palestrina. It will do this because whatever its faults and failures, it appeals boldly on the single ground of beauty, and not of erudition, imitation or conservatism. It claims every licence, and stands or falls by its justification of that licence.[1]

In May 1909 Debussy was again in London to superintend the rehearsals of *Pelléas et Mélisande* given at Covent Garden on 21 May under Cleofonte Campanini who the previous year, on 19 February, had first conducted the opera in America, at the Metropolitan Opera House. Rose Féart took the part of Mélisande and Warnery was the Pelléas. Debussy became enraged by the producer's irrelevant ideas ('I've seldom had a stronger desire to kill someone') and felt that the work was being too hurriedly mounted. He attended the dress rehearsal but on the night of the first performance stayed at his Kensington hotel.

The work was enthusiastically received. In *The Musical Standard* Louise Liebich, who had become acquainted with *Pelléas* through Louis Laloy and Debussy himself, wondered whether in the larger framework of Covent Garden the intimate character of the opera would suffer. Never before, she declared, had it been heard under such favourable conditions. 'Space enhanced the beauty of detail and prolonged the fine-spun harmonies.' Mrs. Liebich also maintained that far from producing purely 'atmospheric' effects Debussy conveyed 'the true Celtic feeling for Nature', illustrated also, she believed, in the work of the German philosopher Fechner.[2] 'It is not only atmosphere that he reproduces; it is the Earth-Soul.'

---

[1] Filson Young perceived that Debussy foreshadowed the revolt against the whole heritage of Romantic music which took place after the first World War. In 1921 Diaghilev, according to Ernest Newman, had declared Beethoven to be 'a mummy', Brahms 'a putrefying corpse', Schumann 'a home-sick dog howling at the moon'. Diaghilev's iconoclasm was reflected by Hindemith, who at about this time proclaimed Beethoven to be at the root of all the Romantic evils ('Mit Beethoven fängt die Schweinerei an'), and also by Arthur Bliss who in 1921 declared himself to be bitterly opposed to 'the pseudo-intellectuality of the Brahms camp-followers with their classical sonatas and concertos and variations and other stock-in-trade'. This attempt to revolutionize the whole pattern of concert giving, though unsuccessful, represented a genuine impulse to break away from what seemed to be the paralysing weight of tradition, and to set standards valid in themselves, for their time alone, unencumbered by past associations.

[2] Gustav Theodor Fechner (1801–87) did valuable pioneer work in psychophysics and in the measurement of sensations which later proved useful to researchers in vision and hearing. He provided psychology with methods that could be expressed in terms of mathematics. His philosophy was based on an animistic concept of the world in which even plants and the stars were believed to be animated.

Possibly on evidence supplied by the composer, Mrs. Liebich went on to predict that 'M. Debussy's next opera will perhaps contain further suggestions of that Earth-Soul. For the owner of the "House of Usher" is made by Poe to believe in "the sentience of all vegetable things".'

These early views of Debussy furthered his cause in one way or another but the most penetrating assessment of his work was given in a lecture on *Pelléas* by Edwin Evans at the Royal Academy of Music on 25 May 1909. After relating Debussy's conception of opera to the Wagnerian theories, and also to the theories of Camille Mauclair expressed in his essay 'L'Identité et la fusion des arts', Evans asserted that though the music of *Pelléas* was avowedly anti-Wagnerian 'it constitutes a more advanced step towards the complete realization of Wagner's theories than any step taken by Wagner himself. Wagner dreamed of an art work where drama and music should be indissolubly joined, but his music dramas are crowded with scenes that are equally effective in the concert-room, separated from all the trappings of drama. The music of *Pelléas*, on the contrary, cannot be separated from the drama without losing its purpose. And conversely, after one has heard Debussy's musical setting, one actually finds it difficult to imagine Maeterlinck's drama without Debussy's music, so closely are the two knit together.'[1] Elsewhere in this lecture Evans suggested that the æsthetic of Debussy derived from the following theory of Walter Pater: 'Art is always striving to be independent of the mere intelligence, to become a matter of pure perception, to get rid of its responsibilities to its subject or material; the ideal examples of poetry and composition being those in which the constituent elements of the composition are so welded together that the material or subject no longer strikes the intellect only; nor the form, the eye or ear only; but form and matter, in their union or identity, present one single effect to the imaginative reason, that complex faculty for which every thought and feeling is twin-born with its sensible analogue or symbol.'

[1] Evans endorses here the opinion on *Pelléas* of the American critic Lawrence Gilman, which he quotes: 'What the Camerata, and their successors, could not accomplish for lack of adequate musical means, what Gluck fell short of compassing for want of boldness and reach of vision, what Wagner might have effected but for too great a preoccupation with one phase of the problem, a Frenchman of today has quietly and perfectly achieved.'

This quotation is from the essay entitled 'The School of Giorgione' in Pater's *The Renaissance*, the interesting point here being that it was in this essay, first published in 1877, that Pater developed his theory that 'all art constantly aspires towards the condition of music', thus anticipating the later theories of the Symbolists and Impressionists.[1] Evans met Debussy in London and may well have mentioned Pater's *Renaissance* to him. He was at any rate to hear of this work from another source. In January 1918, shortly before Debussy's death, Robert Godet wrote to him: 'I wanted to tell you of a book which you will perhaps be pleased to read—the French translation of *The Renaissance* by Walter Pater, a very perceptive English essayist who has both a mind and a feeling for constructive criticism rather similar to that of Wilde; moreover, he carries his knowledge lightly and never makes a show of erudition. What he leaves unsaid is nearly always as valuable as what he says and his implications find their way into his prose, or rather emanate from it, in a most musical fashion.' Godet goes on to say that in this respect Pater reminds him of Keats's *Ode on a Grecian Urn* which, he suggests, 'is implicitly dedicated to you (did not the late Le Mercier [the translator of Keats who were their common friend] suspect this?)' and of which he sends Debussy a French translation:

Douces sont les mélodies qu'on entend; mais celles qu'on n'entend pas
    Sont plus douces; sonnez donc, délicats pipeaux,
Non pas à l'oreille sensuelle, mais plus délectables
    Sonnez à l'esprit des chansons de nul nom.

After London, Vienna and Budapest. Debussy's works began to be known in Germany and Austria at the beginning of the century but they had made little impression. Busoni's performance of *L'Après-midi d'un faune* in Berlin passed almost unnoticed. The first performance of *Pelléas* in German was given at Frankfurt on 19 April 1907. In the Berlin journal *Die Musik* Hans Pfeilschmidt referred to Debussy as one of the '*Neutöner* [new soundmakers] who use their art to deepen and colour poetry but who make no

---

[1] Pater's argument was to some extent ill-founded. It was partly based on the subject of the picture in the Pitti Palace, *The Concert*, which Pater too readily attributed to Giorgione. But the whole of the latter part of his study in which he discerns an association in Giorgione's mind between the sensuousness of sound and the presence of water anticipated later ideas, notably those in Gaston Bachelard's psychological study of Symbolist poetry, *L'Eau et les rêves* (see Appendix F).

attempt to create absolute music.' Germany was the country of absolute music, he implied, and the subordination of music to poetry was a foreign conception, even though it had originated with Wagner. Pfeilschmidt found the vocal writing too consistently declamatory and several scenes monotonous. This was a common impression of listeners not attuned to the gradations of expression in the work. The harmonic liberties seldom went beyond those in the third act of *Tristan*, Pfeilschmidt maintained, and he made a curious comparison between *Pelléas* and the score written by Liszt to accompany a dramatic declamation of Lenau's Ballade *Der traurige Mönch*.[1]

The journey to Vienna in November 1910 marks the beginning of the correspondence between Debussy and his second wife. Earlier journeys had been undertaken together, but Debussy's material situation was becoming increasingly acute and it became imperative for him to accept whatever engagements were offered. 'You realize', he wrote to Emma Debussy from Vienna, 'that I have undertaken this journey for us, because of our persistent poverty without which I shouldn't be so far away from you, so deprived of your caresses.' He had hoped to pass away the time on the journey to Vienna by reading Chateaubriand's *Mémoires d'outre-tombe* but he fell to reflections on his home in Paris: 'It was with much difficulty that I kept myself from weeping.' In his hotel room, while unpacking, he is overcome by the fact that he is desperately alone. 'Everything annoys me. My nerves are on edge and I find that a composer of music is required to excel in those qualities of toughness possessed by a travelling salesman.' After rehearsing *Ibéria* with the Vienna orchestra he was filled with anxiety. If only he could hurl abuse at someone. 'No, I must devour myself in silence [*il faut que je me mange en silence*] . . . bitterly and as an unfortunate exile.' But he is usually able to laugh at himself at the right moment: 'If only you could see my expression—something like the mask of Beethoven or that of Dante on his return from Hell.'

On the day of the concert he tells Emma that he will have to think fervently of her 'in order not to appear hopelessly bored and

[1] This comparison was prompted by the fact that this work of Liszt, a short 'melo-drama' for speaker and piano, opens with an ascending figure, several times repeated, in the whole-tone scale. Against a piano accompaniment the verses of Lenau are not sung but spoken. There is no evidence that Debussy knew *Der traurige Mönch*.

even disgusted'. And with much self-knowledge he goes on: 'We expect to procure the approval of a public of which the greater part consists of idiots; this is a rather ridiculous situation and most ironic and contradictory. Let us hope that I shall have enough nervous strength to overcome this state of mind which results in my being my own worst enemy.'[1]

An illuminating account of Debussy's impression on the audience of the Konzertverein in Vienna was given by Richard Specht in *Der Merker*. Specht imagined that he was going to see a tall, elegant Frenchman like a character, he says, from *L'Aile bleue*, a well-known picture at that time by the contemporary Belgian painter Fernand Khnopff, whose portraits, strongly influenced by the Pre-Raphaelites, were usually of people who were idealistically handsome or angelic.[2] Debussy, Specht found, was the opposite of angelic. He was 'thick-set with small abrupt movements, a sort of gnome in tails'. He also made the impression of 'a black-and-white sketch of Beardsley', or perhaps he had been 'carved out of a hefty black radish'.[3] As a conductor he appeared only approximately to indicate the tempos and entries, 'making a colourless impression' quite the opposite, Specht was bound to declare, of his music 'which is all colour and painting'. On the technical plane he was said to have 'gradually eliminated the thematic element in music and the importance of the motive'.[4] Specht freely admitted 'that one must constantly refer to the art of painting to describe his art'. Whistler and Böcklin are among the painters whose work Debussy evoked, but more than anyone he suggested the work of Gustav Klimt.[5]

[1] In his *Journal*, Gide, in 1908, records a conversation about Debussy which goes some way towards explaining the tone of this correspondence: '"He is so affectionate", said Madame X. "Oh no, Madame! He is so wheedling [*câlin*]", retorted Madame Debussy.'

[2] A forgotten figure of the period, Fernand Khnopff (1858–1921) was associated not only with the Pre-Raphaelites but with Maeterlinck and Verhaeren. His best-known work was an oil-painting characteristically entitled *En écoutant du Schumann*.

[3] A forbidding caricature of Debussy by Rudolf Herrmann which appeared in *Der Merker* of May 1911 and which is reproduced facing p. 50, was presumably inspired by Specht's description.

[4] Nearly all forward-looking composers have been taunted with the fact that they have forsaken melody, and this was apparently the impression made by Debussy's music in Vienna. In the course of his visit he met Ferdinand Löwe, conductor of the Konzertverein orchestra and disciple of Bruckner. Correlation of the letters to Caplet and Godet suggests that it was Löwe who, having publicly congratulated Debussy on having abolished melody, received from him the outraged retort: 'Mais voyons, Monsieur, toute ma musique aspire à n'être que mélodie!'

[5] Gustav Klimt (1862–1918) was one of the principal artists of the Viennese *Jugendstyl* movement, the Teutonic counterpart of *Art Nouveau*. His work was noted

The following year, in June 1911, Specht wrote a further article on Debussy in *Der Merker* following Bruno Walter's performance at the Hofoper of *Pelléas et Mélisande*.[1] It so happened that in Vienna during the spring months of 1911 the rival claims of Debussy, Mahler, and Schoenberg were first put forward. The preceding number of *Der Merker* had contained an obituary of Mahler, who had died in Vienna on 18 May, but was otherwise entirely devoted to detailed, serious studies of contemporary French music. This publication was no doubt a reflection of the Franco-Austrian musical entente promoted in Paris by Paul Clemenceau, the younger brother of the French Prime Minister, on the occasion of Mahler's visit to Paris in April 1910. In *Der Merker* Egon Wellesz and Theodor Tagger wrote on the new French works they had heard, but the main study in this number, *Claude Debussy und der Debussysmus*, a translation of the article that had appeared in *La Revue S.I.M.* the previous year, was by Louis Laloy. Two points were principally developed by Laloy in the image of Debussy thus presented to the Viennese: he was an artist of 'innocence and purity', in the category, he suggested, of Josquin des Prés and Mozart; and he was an artist who was constantly exploring and evolving. He was said to be unsuited, therefore, by his temperament to become a *chef d'école*, revered for theories and systems.

Specht's review of *Pelléas* was perspicacious. 'It recedes to a state of pre-music, to the moment before music takes on being and form.' It is curious to read that it was on his performance of Debussy's score that Bruno Walter was judged to be 'the true heir of Mahler, the only one in whom something of the spirit and power of the unforgettable one remains'—curious since Walter never became known as a conductor of the works of Debussy.[2] It is also interesting to see that Specht's laudatory review of *Pelléas* appeared in a Schoen-

---

for its rich barbaric reds and gleaming jewel-like enamels. In describing Debussy as 'der Klimt der Musik' Specht was probably thinking of *Ibéria* in which the orchestration is exceptionally vivid. The works of both Klimt and Khnopff (see p. 131, note 1) are illustrated in *The Sources of Modern Art* by J. Cassou, E. Langui, and N. Pevsner (London, 1962).

[1] Professor W. Austin of Cornell University has kindly informed me that Alban Berg was present at this performance but not Schoenberg. The subject of Schoenberg's early symphonic poem, *Pelleas und Melisande*, had been suggested to him by Richard Strauss.

[2] This first performance of *Pelléas* in Vienna would surely have been conducted by Mahler had he lived. In the last years of his life Mahler had introduced to Vienna the operas of Charpentier, Camille Erlanger, and Saint-Saëns.

berg number of *Der Merker* where, together with a study of
Schoenberg by Specht, extracts were published from the *Har-
monielehre* and the libretto of *Die glückliche Hand*. This number also
contained reproductions of a selection of Schoenberg's paintings
seen that year at the first exhibition of the 'Blaue Reiter' in Munich.[1]
By contrast with his reviews of Debussy, Specht's article on
Schoenberg was guarded. Reasonably enough, he saw the young
revolutionary composer as belonging to the group of exploratory
figures in Vienna including Mahler, Gustav Klimt, and Kokosch-
ka, but in 1911 he confessed to being more baffled by the latest
works of Schoenberg[2] than by those which he had recently heard of
Debussy.

From Vienna Debussy went to Budapest to take part in a chamber
concert on 5 December 1910 with Rose Féart and the Waldbauer
Quartet. He played the *Estampes* and *Children's Corner* in a programme which also included the String Quartet and the *Proses
lyriques*. There was something wrong, he felt, in playing the intimate pieces forming *Children's Corner*, written for his daughter, to
an audience of no less than fifteen hundred people.

Debussy did not meet either Bartók or Kodály in Hungary.
Having tried to meet Debussy in Paris,[3] Bartók also missed him in
Budapest. At the time of Debussy's visit there Bartók was devoting
himself to research in folk music. His lasting impression of Budapest
was of the Tzigane violinist, Radics, who appears to have played in
a highly evocative manner. One imagines that Bartók would
similarly have been impressed by the spontaneous sincerity of this

---

[1] They received praise from Kandinsky and other Expressionist artists. In *The Sources
of Modern Art*, Emile Langui points out that in the first decade of the twentieth century
Vienna had little sympathy for the Expressionist movement, despite the fact that Freud,
Mahler, and Schoenberg were living there. The dominant styles were those of the
Jugendstyl and Klimt. On the other hand, Schoenberg's music is said by Langui to have
impressed the painter Richard Gerstl.

[2] These were the first Chamber Symphony, op. 9, the second String Quartet with
soprano voice, op. 10, first given in Vienna in 1908 with Maria Gutheil-Schoder, who
took the part of Mélisande in the Viennese première of *Pelléas*, and *Das Buch der
hängenden Gärten*. It is, however, unlikely that any of these works were known to
Debussy. In a letter of 1911 to Robert Godet he wrote rather contemptuously of the
charms of Vienna, mentioning composers far removed from Schoenberg: 'Vieille
ville fardée où l'on abuse de la musique de Brahms, de Puccini, d'officiers aux poitrines
de femmes, et de femmes aux poitrines d'officiers.'

[3] A meeting was sought, according to Halsey Stevens, through the pianist Isidore
Philippe. 'Do you not know that Debussy has the reputation of being extremely
rude?' Philippe said. 'Do you want to be insulted by Debussy?' 'Yes, certainly', Bartók
replied.

gipsy violinist. 'The best thing the Hungarians have', Debussy wrote to Robert Godet, 'is a Tzigane named Radics who has an infinitely greater love for music than many celebrated musicians. He plays in an ordinary, common café, but you imagine that he is playing to himself in some dark forest, and he manages to extract from the depths of his soul some kind of melancholy that we are seldom able to glimpse. He could wrench secrets out of an iron safe.' Writing to his host in Budapest, the impresario Monsieur Barczy, Debussy said that he hoped to return to Budapest 'simply to listen to Radics until the end of my life'.[1] On his return to Paris Debussy received from Barczy some editions of Hungarian folk music which disappointed him. In a letter to Barczy of 19 December 1910 he sets out his views on the matter of folk-song editions in a manner wholly in keeping with the independent spirit of Bartók:

I have received the Hungarian music and thank you for it. But how different it is from the impression left on me by Radics! This music is like a beautiful butterfly under glass. The wings are brilliant but they are not alive and their rich colours have become dulled. I do not think that you Hungarians can judge this music as it really is. It's something that really belongs to your life. It is so familiar to you that you fail to see its great artistic importance. Remember what happened when this music was arranged by Liszt! Although Liszt was a genius he tamed it; it loses its freedom and its innate sense of the infinite. When you listen to Radics you are transported. You actually inhale the scent of forests; you hear the sound of running brooks; and he expresses the secrets of a heart that suffers and laughs almost at the same time. In my view this music must never be changed. As far as possible it must be kept away from the clumsiness of professionals.

[1] The Hungarian gipsy violinists continued to make an overwhelming impression on visitors to Budapest long after Debussy's death. Referring in his *Foreign Faces* (1964) to certain Hungarian gipsy musicians who obviously belong to the same artistic family as Radics, V. S. Pritchett eloquently says that they 'know how slowly to fill every molecule of the air with their smoky, sullen chords that rumble like fire shut up in a furnace, a sound that slurs and slumps, breaks off and picks up again with wicked suddenness and passes to the tricky clipping of the strings, rises to ferocity, then clouds away and falls into a blank carnal sadness. It is the music of the sexual act.' Debussy's enthusiastic remarks concerning Radics are in striking contrast to the acrimonious tone of his letters to the famous Hungarian violinist Jenö Hubay, with whom he had a serious misunderstanding regarding the organization of his Hungarian visit. Debussy's unpublished letters to Hubay are in the Library of Congress, Washington, and at the Eastman School of Music, Rochester, N.Y.

What I wish to say is that your Tziganes should be treated with more respect. Don't think of them as mere entertainers who give colour to a party and help in the consumption of champagne. The truth is that their music is as beautiful as your old embroideries and lace. Why, then, do you not treat it with the same respect and love? Your young musicians could profitably be inspired by this music, not by copying it but by finding the equivalent of its freedom, its qualities of evocation and suffering and by using some of its rhythmic features. The lessons of Wagner were harmful to music in many ways and to the national interests of music. The folk music of one's country should be used only as a fundamental inspiration, never as a model. This is particularly true of your folk music. Love it passionately, but don't attempt to dress it up in some scholarly way.

Forgive me for going into matters that do not perhaps concern me. It's simply that I have a great love for music—not only French music—and that I dislike seeing the riches of music squandered, or its real meaning, its national meaning, deformed. In France we have too long suffered, and suffer still, from the German influence. Don't fall into our error and be deceived by pretentious profundities or by the detestable German 'Modern-style'.

It would be interesting to know which composers were believed by Debussy to write in the 'detestable "modern-style"'. Surely not Strauss, many aspects of whose work he admired, nor Mahler who could not possibly be accused of having in any way been influenced by the *Jugendstyl*? Debussy was not a rabid nationalist, but in his contribution to the wider European scene he did most fervently wish to re-assert distinctive French qualities. On his next journey, to Italy, we find him battling against the traditions of Verdi and Puccini.

On the occasion of the Industrial Exhibition held at Turin in 1911 several prominent musicians were asked to take part in concerts there. Vittorio Gui, the young conductor of the Turin orchestra, had invited Elgar, Kajanus, d'Indy and Pierné, and also Debussy who, on 25 June 1911, conducted *L'Après-midi d'un faune* and *Ibéria*. We are fortunate in having a detailed account of this Italian journey. It was a sad and a humiliating episode. Possibly for physical reasons Debussy was now hardly able to assert authority

DEBUSSY: HIS LIFE AND MIND

over the orchestra. In a memoir written some twenty years after Debussy's visit Vittorio Gui, with exquisite courtesy, makes it clear that had it not been for his assistance at rehearsals the concert could not have taken place. Debussy had at first refused this assistance, Gui states, declaring that 'conducting had always been an old, unsatisfied passion for him'. From his first contact with the orchestra, however, 'it was evident that he was no conductor. . . . Not one of the qualities required from a conductor was in his nature. His gestures were uncertain, his eyes remained glued to the score (and it was his own music), he was unable to control either the players or himself, and several times he actually turned over the pages of the score with the same right hand that held the baton, thus missing a beat and throwing the orchestra into confusion.' Under the pretext of translating Debussy's directions from French into Italian, Gui approached the orchestra and was at any rate able to restore some sense of discipline. So far only *L'Après-midi d'un faune* had been rehearsed, but when it came to the complicated score of *Ibéria* things became very much worse. 'The confusion was such that Debussy felt that nothing of his score was understood; he was himself becoming nervous and, losing himself in what appeared to be a chaos of sounds and rhythms, he hastened to concede the ten-minute break and retired in an anxious mood to the artists' room.' He now willingly accepted the proposal that Gui should take charge of the rehearsals while he himself would appear only at the concert, put back a couple of days in order to allow adequate time for its preparation. When it eventually came to the concert Debussy reluctantly took up his baton 'with an almost childish fear'. 'Here was a new experience for me', Gui charmingly confides. 'For the first time I felt fear for another, a paternal fear as if in some strange way the roles were reversed and as if he, not I, were the younger of the two.' At the concert Debussy conducted 'as well as could be expected, correctly but without inspiring either the orchestra or the audience which, in one of the most poetic passages of *Parfums de la nuit*, was further put off by a shower of rain beating down on the glass roof of the hall, causing them to wonder how they were to reach home without their umbrellas.'

The account given of this event in a letter of 24 June 1911 from Debussy to André Caplet presents a different picture. Debussy had been too humiliated to tell his friend the truth: 'Where are you,

André Caplet?' he exclaims. 'Or rather why aren't you with me to help me persuade this Turin orchestra that music is not played with one's hands in one's pockets! What a job! Six hours' rehearsal every day. You will agree that for one with so little practice it's hard. . . . I am a pitiful sight, worn out and meeting precisely the description of the "thinking reed" given by Pascal.'[1] Apparently motivated by the same desire to conceal the near-disaster with the Italian orchestra he wrote from Turin to Durand: 'If only you knew how it is to feel that beneath it all the music of Claude Debussy means nothing to them and that at the first expedient they will go back to their Puccini, Verdi, and what-have-you in the Italian language.'[2]

Two years were to pass before he travelled abroad again. At the invitation of Koussevitzky he spent the first fortnight of December 1913 conducting concerts of his works in Moscow and St. Petersburg.[3] Recalling his impressions in *La Revue Musicale*, Rimsky-Korsakov's pupil Lazare Saminsky stated that 'for the young Petrograd composers Debussy was in a way the spiritual son of Moussorgsky and of Rimsky-Korsakov, forming a link between Russia of the East and France of the West.' In fact, though Debussy's works had been played in Russia by Siloti and Koussevitzky, few of the composers in Russia at that time responded to Debussy's work. César Cui had written a parody of Debussy's music entitled *L'Après-midi d'un faune qui lit son journal* and Rimsky-Korsakov, who had died five years earlier, had been bitterly censorious of Debussy's work in the same way and for the same reason as Saint-Saëns; they resented the undermining of musical form and of the principles of tonality. Among the composers he met in Russia was Prokofiev who, at a reception given by the magazine *Apollon*, played to him his *Legend* and his early Studies. Prokofiev's exuberant

[1] The reference is to this passage in the *Pensées* of Pascal: 'L'homme n'est qu'un roseau, le plus faible de la nature; mais c'est un roseau pensant. Il ne faut pas que l'univers entier s'arme pour l'écraser: une vapeur, une goutte d'eau suffit pour le tuer. Mais quand l'univers l'écraserait, l'homme serait encore plus noble que ce qui le tue, parce qu'il sait qu'il meurt, et l'avantage que l'univers a sur lui, l'univers n'en sait rien.'

[2] Italian opera of the Romantic period was outside the range of experience not only of Debussy but of nearly all other French composers of his generation. In 1905 Fauré, in Cologne, happened to hear a performance of Bellini's *Norma* which struck him merely as a mummified relic.

[3] Koussevitzky's letter of 1 November 1913 to Debussy, in the Library of Congress, states that he is 'awaited with great impatience by the whole musical world of Moscow and St. Petersburg. . . . Should I send someone to meet you at the frontier? We will do everything we can for you not to feel lonely in Russia.'

musical nature was, however, more naturally drawn to Ravel than to Debussy.

Debussy's letters to his wife and the charming postcards to his daughter[1] convey only superficial impressions of his stay in Russia, which he had not visited since he was engaged there in his youth by Madame von Meck. One of his friends from those early days, Sonia von Meck, now a middle-aged woman, was present at one of the receptions. One or two new works hold his attention. We find him reading the score of Busoni's Piano Concerto, which he finds 'boggy music containing the worst faults of Richard Strauss'; he dines at Koussevitzky's home in Moscow with Diaghilev, who amuses him with an account of the Russian Ballet's visit to South America; and he spends a pleasant evening hearing for the first time Moussorgsky's *Sorotchinsky Fair*. Otherwise, this last Russian journey was a grim ordeal. One gathers from the intimate letters to Emma Debussy that throughout this short but strenuous tour he was much more of a sick man than he knew. Everything was an effort for the reason that he suffered continuously from insomnia, a symptom of the type of cancer of which he was a victim.[2]

The contemporary Russian composer with whom there might have been a bond of sympathy was surely Scriabin. Though there is no mention of Scriabin in Debussy's writings or correspondence I do not think there can be any doubt that the work of this composer of such a heightened, feverish sensibility was known to him. Scriabin, who had given recitals in Paris, had been closely associated with Koussevitzky, and in 1910 accompanied him on the first of his famous tours of the Volga.[3] One imagines that Debussy would

---

[1] From St. Petersburg he sent Chouchou a series of postcards containing the jingles:

Près la perspective Newsky
Habite Monsieur Debussy

and

Ce sont bien des tramways électriques
Bien que cela paraisse excentrique.

Earlier, from Vienna, he had sent her a story in instalments, spread out over five postcards, entitled 'Les Mémoires d'outre-Croche' and signed 'Le Papadechouchou'.

[2] His account of his first night in Moscow was typical: 'I went to sleep broken-hearted. . . . After an hour, not being able to sleep, I got up and walked about like a demented one, from one room to another. . . . I drop into an armchair, fall off to sleep and am awakened by the cold. . . . I lie down again and try to get to sleep by doing the silliest things such as counting to a thousand forwards and backwards. Then someone comes in to ask what I want for breakfast.' By the end of his stay his insomnia had become acute: 'If ever I do get to sleep I wake up a moment afterwards.'

[3] On these tours Koussevitzky took his symphony orchestra on a chartered steamer to outlying provincial towns that had never before heard orchestral music. The

have criticized a certain manufactured crudeness in Scriabin, but he would surely have been interested in Scriabin's theories of music and colour. Writing of a meeting between Rimsky-Korsakov and Scriabin in Paris, Gerald Abraham states: 'These two, the tall pillar of moral and musical respectability and common sense and the amoral little mystic, meeting in the Café de la Paix after a rehearsal, found themselves in agreement on one point, the definite association of musical keys with certain colours.' One cannot help regretting that Debussy was not present at this meeting.[1]

On his return from Russia Debussy was only to stay in Paris about two months. At the end of February he made the fourth and last of his Italian journeys, to conduct the orchestra of the Augusteo in Rome on 22 February 1914. The works given were *La Mer*, *Rondes de Printemps*, and *L'Après-midi d'un faune*. By this time his reputation among the young composers in Italy, Malipiero, Respighi, and Casella, was at its height and despite some hostile demonstrations the critic of *Tribuna* spoke of the 'delirium' of the audience.[2]

No musical matters enter the anxious correspondence with Emma Debussy who in Paris was left to deal with the claims of creditors. Telegrams and letters which Debussy sent her from Dijon, Pisa, and Rome express a mounting concern. He describes a state of 'dreadful anguish'. Separation, he declares, is intolerable. In the course of a sleepless night 'I was convinced I was going to die and decided to give up conducting concerts throughout Europe. I

---

greater part of Debussy's 'Lettre de Russie', published in *La Revue S.I.M.*, January 1914, is devoted not to the reception of his works in Russia nor to his impressions of Russian music but to a description of Koussevitzky's Volga tours. Debussy was struck by the fact that the appreciative peasant audiences at these concerts were so moved by the music they heard that they hardly dared to applaud.

[1] One wonders whether either of the two composers was aware of the programme of a Scriabin–Debussy recital given during their lifetime, in 1910, by the pianist Ohtaguro in Tokio. The programme was exhibited at the Debussy Exhibition, Bibliothèque Nationale, Paris, 1962.

[2] The first performance of *Pelléas* in Italy, at La Scala under Toscanini in 1908, was enthusiastically received by forward-looking musical minds but met with a hostile reception from the regular Italian opera public. In the *Rivista Musicale Italiana* (No. 2, 1908) Ildebrando Pizzetti, recalling the principles of the early Italian operas of Peri and Caccini, proclaimed *Pelléas* as one of the first examples of an opera in a Latin country in which there was a true union between music and drama. The audience at La Scala, however, were either hostile or indifferent. At the conclusion most of them hurried away without either approving or condemning the work, and the cast embarrassingly appeared before a mere handful of people whom Toscanini himself applauded with the encouraging words, 'Molto intelligente, molto intelligente!'

hardly dare write this down but I confess my terrible fear of losing your love.'

On his return to Paris he was to leave almost immediately for Amsterdam and The Hague. At least six telegrams were exchanged with Emma Debussy in the course of this short journey, that is to say at every stop, Antwerp, Brussels, Rosendaal, and Amsterdam. At the end of February and the beginning of March Debussy conducted his works at two concerts of the Concertgebouw Orchestra and also played three of his Preludes. His old friend Gustave Doret, who had given the first performance of *L'Après-midi d'un faune* in Paris, was in charge of the Dutch orchestra, and at the second of the two concerts also conducted works by Saint-Saëns. Not having met Debussy for six years, Doret was struck by 'his depressed mood and his inability to make a decision'. At a reception at Amsterdam speeches were made in his honour but he found it impossible even to acknowledge what had been said in a few words. Under the table Doret received a kick on the shin. 'Impossible!' Debussy muttered. 'Répondez pour moi.' Doret made a short formal speech on his behalf, applause followed and glasses were clinked. 'Awkwardly and with his features now painfully drawn, Debussy finally stood up. "Merci, Messieurs", he muttered and sat down again as if he had gone through the worst ordeal.'

There remained the journeys in 1914 to Brussels at the end of April and, at the invitation of Lady Speyer, to London in July. Debussy stayed with the Speyers at their home in Grosvenor Street where, on 17 July, he took part in a private concert of his works including the Dances for harp and *Children's Corner*. It was his last journey abroad. He returned, however, in a restless, frustrated mood, undoubtedly also in a low state of health and anxious, despite his protestations of fatigue and boredom in travelling, to leave again as soon as possible. 'Paris is becoming more and more hateful to me', he tells Durand at the end of July, 'and I should like to be able to leave for a while; I am literally at the end of my tether.' In the few days that remained before the outbreak of war he was able to complete three of the *Epigraphes antiques*, an arrangement for piano duet of pieces he had written years earlier for a recitation of *Les Chansons de Bilitis*.

8
Edgar Allan Poe

To the few who love me and whom I love—to those who
feel rather than to those who think—to the dreamers and
those who put faith in dreams as the only realities . . .

E. A. Poe, Dedication of Eureka

In addition to his completed works Debussy, like most composers, entertained a large number of projects, some of them ephemeral, others throwing a valuable light on his development in one way or another. Of outstanding interest among these unfinished or projected works of Debussy are the two operas on tales by Edgar Allan Poe. Not all the manuscript sketches of these unfinished operas have been brought together, but I think it is safe to assume that those which still remain inaccessible will not greatly alter the size of this legacy which, apart from the libretto for *La Chute de la Maison Usher*, is remarkably small. We are not, however, principally concerned in this chapter with the manuscripts of these Poe operas themselves. Debussy was fascinated throughout his life by Poe's ideas and the nature of this fascination, which he shared with many of his contemporaries, will enable us to see aspects of several of his other works in a new light.

The projects for two short operas on Poe's tales, *The Fall of the House of Usher* and *The Devil in the Belfry*, occupied Debussy during the whole of the latter part of his life. We have seen that Debussy's attraction to Poe dates from 1889 when, according to a letter from André Suarès to Romain Rolland, he was engaged on a 'symphony on psychologically developed themes based on the *House of Usher*'. We have seen that *Pelléas* itself, both the play of

Maeterlinck and Debussy's score, has many associations with Poe, notably with the imagery and the symbolism of Poe's tale of incestuous love; and we have dealt briefly with the French interpretations of both Poe and Swinburne in regard to Debussy's artistic evolution.

In his study *Edgar Allan Poe and France* T. S. Eliot investigates the far-reaching influence of Poe on the French literary mind and states, 'there are aspects of Poe which English and American critics failed to perceive.' Poe was in fact almost entirely a creation of the French.[1] None of the writers in the rich generation from Baudelaire to Paul Valéry, including Gide and Marcel Proust, escaped his fascination, and the aspect of Poe to which they were drawn was the rising to the surface of unconscious fantasies. 'His most vivid imaginative realizations', Eliot states, 'are the realization of the dream.' Nearly all Poe's tales with their dark symbolism of corridors and underground passages, stagnant water and enveloping whirlpools, haunted also by fantasies of incest, cruelty, and death, are in essence dream tales, and although Eliot, like most other English critics, is censorious of Poe as a stylist, he readily concedes that the Symbolist figures in French literature, from Baudelaire onwards, saw in Poe an expression of the new sensibility that they were themselves seeking and that they were thus able to interpret Poe for English writers in his true light.

Belonging entirely, in spirit and outlook, to his generation, Debussy was similarly profoundly affected by Poe. Indeed, the dream-like symbolism in Poe's tales became together with the Wagnerian influence one of the most stimulating factors in Debussy's imagination.[2] In his correspondence, Debussy frequently

---

[1] By far the finest of the many translations of Poe's prose works are those of Baudelaire on which he was engaged during seventeen years of his life and which in volume constitute almost half of the poet's output. Baudelaire, who began this enormous task with only a rudimentary knowledge of English, dedicated his translations to Maria Clemm, Poe's foster-mother and the central figure in his life. They were re-edited by Y. G. le Dantec in 1951. A selection of the poems was published by Mallarmé in 1888 with illustrations by Manet, but the translation of the complete poems was the work of Debussy's friend Gabriel Mourey.

[2] It was Thomas Mann who first instinctively saw the impact that Poe was bound to make on music. Writing in 1933 on the fiftieth anniversary of the death of Wagner, Thomas Mann suggested that the inspiration derived by Baudelaire from Wagner was of the same nature and intensity as that which he had derived from Poe. 'Wagner and Poe—what an extraordinary juxtaposition!' he comments. 'Immediately we see the work of Wagner in a new light. We see a deeper colour in his work, a world haunted by death and beauty, a pessimistic world, intoxicated by sensuous refinement.' Mann

says so in as many words. He speaks of the 'tyranny', the 'obsession' which Poe exerted over him. As we have seen, earlier critics of Debussy, Arthur Symons and James Huneker, drew attention to Debussy's affinity with Poe. Yet though they were able to make pertinent comparisons they had not quite the understanding of Poe's significance that we have now acquired. They were themselves part of the movement that had sprung from this French influence of Poe. And they were therefore unable to see, as we are today, that the fantasies to which Debussy gave a musical expression were almost Surrealist fantasies, the chaotic fantasies of dreams, such as those illustrated in the scene of the vaults in *Pelléas*.

The impact made by Poe on Debussy needs to be assessed in two distinct spheres: the practical sphere where far-reaching plans were made for the use of two of Poe's tales as librettos for operas; and the imaginative sphere where Poe's ideas are seen to be associated with the mood or sensibility of one or other of Debussy's works. We may follow the plans for operas on tales of Poe in Debussy's correspondence. The contract for the production of *La Chute de la Maison Usher* and *Le Diable dans le Beffroi* was in the form of a letter, together with a receipt, dated 5 July 1908 from Debussy to Giulio Gatti-Casazza, director of the Metropolitan Opera, New York. In consideration of the sum of ten thousand francs (two thousand francs paid on signature) Debussy gave the Metropolitan priority for the production of *La Chute de la Maison Usher* and *Le Diable dans le Beffroi* on condition that both these works were played at the same performance and that no other work of another composer appeared in the same programme. He also gave the Metropolitan an option on his subsequent works, notably *La Légende de Tristan*. In his memoirs Gatti-Casazza states that Debussy was reluctant to accept this offer. 'It is a piece of bad business you are doing', he told the American impresario. 'I have some remorse in taking these few dollars. I do not believe I will ever finish any part of all this.' And he added significantly, 'I write for myself alone and do not trouble myself at all about the impatience of others.' If we bear in mind that Debussy considered these settings of

---

knew nothing of Debussy's life-long attachment to Poe, and obviously this conception of an art deriving from both Wagner and Poe corresponds only vaguely to the spirit of Debussy's libretto and sketches for an opera on *The Fall of the House of Usher*. He had foreseen, however, the appeal which Poe's mind was likely to make to a musician.

The House of Usher and *The Devil in the Belfry* as among the few projects during his later years on which his heart was set, as opposed to the numerous works commissioned for one material reason or another, then some of the underlying reasons for this hesitation in completing these long-cherished projects become apparent. Not only was he frequently side-tracked into fulfilling commissions at short notice, but, as we now see, the nature of his adaptations of these two works of Poe was bold, and one has the impression that he preferred to let these experimental ideas simmer in the mind rather than bring them to too hasty a conclusion. However this may be, the letters addressed to Durand, Godet, Caplet, and Laloy, extending over eight years, reveal that his feelings were more deeply engaged in *Usher* and *Le Diable dans le Beffroi* than in *Le Martyre de Saint-Sébastien*, even than in the orchestral *Images* and *Jeux*. Often, too, these letters disclose a network of associations illuminating not only the impact made by Poe's tales on his imagination but some of the more subtle processes of artistic creation.

On 18 June 1908, shortly before signing the contract with the Metropolitan, Debussy had written to Durand: 'These last days I have done much work on *La Chute de la Maison Usher*. It is an excellent means of strengthening one's nerves against any kind of fear.[1] Nevertheless there are times when I no longer see the world around me [*où je perds le sentiment des choses environnantes*], and if the sister of Roderick Usher were suddenly to appear I shouldn't be extremely surprised.' The following month, on 18 July, he tells Durand: 'I have been wanting to write to you these last days but the heir of the Usher family has hardly left me in peace. I am constantly being rude and the outside world hardly exists for me [*le monde extérieur n'existe presque plus pour moi*]. This is a delightful state of mind which, however, has the disadvantage of being unsuited to our twentieth century.' This retreat into oneself is entirely typical of the solipsism of Poe's characters and particularly of Roderick Usher. On 26 June 1909 Debussy again writes to Durand: 'These last days I have been working on *La Chute de la Maison Usher* and have almost finished

---

[1] '*Contre toute espèce de terreur*'. The reference is to the observation made of Usher by his friend, 'To an anomalous species of terror I found him a bounden slave', and to Usher's confession: 'I have no abhorrence of danger, except in its absolute effect—in terror. In this unnerved—in this pitiable condition—I feel that the period will sooner or later arrive when I must abandon life and reason together in some struggle with the grim phantasm, FEAR.'

a long monologue for poor Roderick. It is sad enough to make the stones weep and as it happens there is a question of the influence of stones on the state of mind of neurasthenics.[1] The music has an attractive mustiness obtained by mixing the low notes of the oboe with harmonics of the violin. Don't speak of this to anyone for I am rather proud of it.' The following month, having apparently been pressed by his publisher to deliver the score of the orchestral *Images*, he writes: 'I must confess that I have put them aside on account of Edgar Allan Poe. I have so much to do on these works that you will excuse me, I hope. You need have no doubt that I will return to the *Images* and complete them to your satisfaction.' And on 14 August: 'I live almost exclusively in the work which you know and never cease conversing with E. A. Poe.' Of the same period we have a curious letter, dated 25 August 1909, to André Caplet: 'No, it is not neurasthenia, nor is it hypochondria. It is the delicious malady which springs from the idea of being able to choose any idea, dear André Caplet.[2] I have recently been living in the House of Usher which is not exactly the place where one can look after one's nerves—just the opposite. One develops the curious habit of listening to the stones as if they were in conversation with each other and of expecting houses to crumble to pieces as if this were not only natural but inevitable. Moreover, if you were to press me I should confess that I like these people more than many others—not to name them.[3] I have no confidence in the normal, well-

[1] Poe writes of 'an effect which the *physique* of the grey walls and turrets, and of the dim tarn into which they all looked down, had at length brought about upon the *morale* of his [Roderick Usher's] existence.' Later, referring to 'the sentience of all vegetable things', Poe discerns the 'silent yet importunate and terrible influence' of 'the grey stones of the home of his forefathers . . . the order of their arrangement, as well as in that of the many *fungi* which overspread them, and of the decayed trees which stood around. . . .'

[2] 'C'est le délicieux mal de l'idée à choisir entre toutes, cher André Caplet.' This must be one of the first expressions in twentieth-century music of the despair experienced by a composer in face of a disorganized musical language. It is the feeling expressed also by Stravinsky in his Harvard lectures *Poetics of Music*, translated by A. Knodel and I. Dahl (London, 1947): 'As for myself, I experience a sort of terror when, at the moment of setting to work and finding myself before the infinitude of possibilities that present themselves, I have the feeling that everything is permissible to me. If everything is permissible to me, the best and the worst, if nothing offers me any resistance, then any effort is inconceivable, and I cannot use anything as a basis, and consequently every undertaking becomes futile.'

[3] The following year, in a letter of 24 August to Louis Laloy, Debussy identifies himself with the Usher family in a similar manner: 'I am in a hateful mood, taking no pleasure in anything unless it be the pleasure of every day destroying myself a little more. . . . There is something of the Usher family in this situation, although this explanation may not bear too close a scrutiny, for they are the best family I have.'

balanced type of person.' And he goes on to make an unexpected comparison: 'There was a great moralist, Carlyle, who was a Scot and something of a Calvinist and who preached moral ideas to all his contemporaries. This was the man who made his wife very unhappy and walked five miles a day to declare his passionate romantic love to another woman who made light of it all in accordance with other, probably superior, standards of morality. I speak to you of Carlyle because reading his works is part of the treatment I am obliged to follow every day.'[1]

The letters to Durand at this period show the same exclusive pre-occupation. 'I must rely on your friendship to forgive my having neglected the *Images* recently', opens a letter of 21 September 1909. 'I have allowed myself to be concerned with hardly anything other than *Roderick Usher* and *Le Diable dans le Beffroi*. I go to sleep with them, and on waking find either the sombre melancholy of the one or the derisive laughter of the other. You rightly draw my attention to other obligations, and I shall put my puppets aside so as not to keep you waiting too long.' A letter of the same date to Caplet gives an even franker account of his exclusive concern with his settings of Poe at this time: 'I cannot hide from you that I have got to the point of having entirely sacrificed the *Images* to Monsieur E. A. Poe. Although dead this figure exercises an almost agonizing tyranny over me. I forget the normal rules of courtesy and close myself up like a brute beast in the house of Usher unless I am keeping company with the devil in the belfry.' The following year he has hardly the time to glance at one of his new publications. 'I have received the scenario of *Masques et Bergamasques*', he tells Durand on 2 June 1910, 'but I haven't had time to re-read it. Your letter found me in the *House of Usher*. Allow me to return.' The following month, on 8 July 1910, he expresses the hope that he 'may be able to reach the inexpressible'. *The House of Usher* is to be 'a progressive expression of anguish. . . . If I manage to bring it off as I wish, I believe I shall have served music well and also my publisher and friend Jacques Durand.'

[1] This ironic attack on Carlyle was based on the view, commonly held of him at the time, of a selfish, irascible man, cruel or indifferent to his clever wife—the antithesis, as Debussy saw him, of Roderick Usher. Debussy's allusion is apparently to the numerous journeys made by Carlyle on foot from his house in Cheyne Walk, Chelsea, to the home in Piccadilly of Lady Harriet Baring. Jane Carlyle was greatly disturbed by her husband's relationship with Lady Harriet even though it was known to be purely platonic.

This 'progressive expression of anguish', culminating in the violent deaths of both Roderick and his twin-sister Lady Madeline, is indeed the underlying theme of Poe's tale, but there is reason to suspect that Debussy felt himself too deeply involved in its emotional significance to be able to deal with the libretto he had devised from an objective viewpoint. Nor, apparently, did he discover the ideal musical expression of the subject that he was pursuing. A different picture of his progress, not only on *Usher* but also on *Le Diable dans le Beffroi*, is given to Robert Godet. After explaining that he had been obliged to work on *Khamma* and *Sébastian*, he writes to his trusted old friend on 6 February 1911: 'The two tales of Poe have thus had to be postponed until I don't know when. Writing to you, I will admit that I am not very sorry since there are many points of expression [*accents*] with which I am not yet satisfied. Also a scheme which is not sufficiently clear in my mind [*une mise en place insuffisamment rigoureuse*] notably in regard to *Le Diable dans le Beffroi* where I would like to achieve an extremely supple and at the same time an extremely fluid manner of choral writing.'

We may profitably pause to consider here this twin project of an opera on *The Devil in the Belfry*. In *Usher* Debussy was manifestly concerned with new orchestral effects and a type of harrowing declamation. In *Le Diable dans le Beffroi* he was experimenting with new choral effects. 'Understand me correctly,' he insists in this same letter to Godet, 'the clear-cut choral writing in *Boris* does not meet my requirements any more than the persistent counterpoint in the second act of *Meistersinger*. Something else is surely to be discovered—some kind of inspired aural deception. It's the devil! And then there is this ridiculous custom to be overcome of separating the men and the women of a chorus as if they were in a bathing establishment. In the end you will see that terrifyingly big words will be used to describe a very simple matter.' In a statement said by Léon Vallas to have been made to Pierre Lalo—it is quoted by him without indication of date or place—Debussy outlines this same conception of choral writing in greater detail: 'The people in *Boris* do not form a real crowd. Sometimes one group sings, sometimes another—but not a third, each in turn—and generally they sing in unison. As for the crowd in *Meistersinger* they are not a crowd either, they are an army solidly organized in the German manner, marching in rows. What I should like to achieve is something more scattered and split up, something both more nimble and intangible, something apparently inorganic, and yet with an underlying control—a real human crowd in which each voice is free and in which all the voices combined nevertheless produce the impression of an ensemble.'

In this novel conception of opera only the crowd, thus split up, were to sing. The principal character, the Devil himself, was only to whistle. The irony of *Le Diable dans le Beffroi* would thus have formed an admirable foil for the lugubrious character of *Usher*, and it is characteristic of Debussy's dual nature that he should have been attracted to these two works simultaneously. Poe's ironic story is built in fact around the single character of the Devil who at midday in the Dutch village of Vondervotteimittiss ('I wonder what time it is') maliciously strikes the bell in the belfry thirteen times. The sketches of the libretto for this opera, dating from 1903, consist of two tableaux and show that the tale was to be very freely adapted. The first tableau, set in Holland, introduces children, a bell-ringer and his son, and the mayor and his daughter ('shy as a tulip'). A romance develops between the bell-ringer's son and the mayor's daughter. When the thirteenth chime is struck at midday a jovial good-natured Devil descends from the belfry to amuse the crowd.[1] The chimes are struck again, this time producing odd cracked sounds which the Devil proceeds to parody on his violin by altering the rhythm and also the melody. We further read about 'a fantastic jig' built up by means of powerful rhythms and a crescendo 'in which the Devil's violin is pitted against the trombones'. The crowd begin to dance heavily and clumsily. But the jig mercilessly continues, compelling the crowd to follow the Devil, who goes off in the direction of the canal and jumps into it. The mesmerized crowd wish to follow him but he lifts up his violin bow, using it as a conductor cutting off a chord with his baton at the end of a movement, and the curtain falls.

The *Gigues* from the *Images* for orchestra, inspired by a poem of Verlaine, come to mind here; at any rate we may note that André Caplet, who completed the orchestration of *Gigues*, declared that a

[1] Writing to Messager in 1902 of his conception of this tale Debussy states: 'The Devil is much more ironic and cruel than the traditional sort of red clown. I want to destroy the idea of the devil as the spirit of evil. He is rather the spirit of contradiction.'

Debussy and 'Chouchou' at Le Mouleau, 1916

Chopin, by Delacroix

Debussy, by Steinlen

section of the work represented 'the angular gesticulations of a grotesque marionette'. Poe's Devil might well have been in Debussy's mind here. His sketches and correspondence show that in the first tableau of *Le Diable dans le Beffroi* the orchestra was to contain a prominent part for the cimbalom. In this first tableau the orchestra was to be the centre of interest; in the second the 'nimble and intangible' chorus. The Dutch village of the first tableau becomes in the second an Italian village and the scenario introduces episodes which have no connexion whatever with Poe's tale. The two young lovers and the Devil find themselves in an imbroglio in which the Devil is outwitted. Eventually, when the chimes ring in the accustomed manner, the Devil is subdued and ultimately disappears. It is a scenario that looks forward to Stravinsky's *Histoire du Soldat* and also to his *Pulcinella*. The many accounts given by Debussy of his aims and ideas in these two works force us to the conclusion that none of Debussy's projects, nor even his completed works, illustrates more strikingly than *Usher* and *Le Diable dans le Beffroi* the two aspects of his imaginative mind: the ruminating, introspective poet, a reflection of Roderick Usher, and the caustic ironist.[1]

In June 1911 Stravinsky's *Petrouchka* was given in Paris. Praising the early scores of Stravinsky and particularly their *mise-en-place* (form and texture), Debussy, in a letter to Godet of 18 December, confides in him his anxieties regarding his Poe operas. 'On the matter of form and texture, I have not yet managed to find those I want for the two little dramas adapted from Poe. The further I proceed the more horror I have of this deliberate disorder, which is only an aural deception, and also of certain bizarre and amusing harmonies which have only a snobbish value [*qui ne sont que jeux de société*]. How much has to be discovered and then discarded before arriving at the naked flesh of feeling. One should trust one's instinct to beware of mere texture and colour.'[2] A few days later, on

---

[1] The only known manuscript of *Le Diable dans le Beffroi* is the sketch of the libretto with three pages of music dated 25 August 1903. Since Debussy worked on this score at least until 1912 the manuscript of 1903 cannot represent all that was left of the work. In his memoirs Henri Büsser mentions a visit paid to Debussy on 31 March 1912: 'He spoke to me of his projects . . . *Le Diable dans le Beffroi* of Edgar Poe for which he has written many sketches. He played me on the piano some very picturesque and amusing fragments in a manner entirely different from his usual style.'

[2] Debussy's expressions here recall Baudelaire's *Mon cœur mis à nu* which itself had been inspired by Poe's *My heart laid bare*. His knowledge of these works is discussed in Vol. I, Appdx. D, 'Swinburne and Poe in France', p. 214.

22 December, Debussy enlarges on these ideas in a letter to André Caplet:

> I haven't yet managed to finish the two little operas of Poe. Everything strikes me as being so deadly dull [*tout m'en parait ennuyeux comme une cave*]. For a single bar that I write that may be free and alive, there are twenty stifled by the weight of what is known as tradition, the influence of which I consider to be hypocritical and despicable. Observe, if you please, that I am little concerned about the fact that it may be my own tradition we are talking about. It is nevertheless a matter of trickery by which you merely see yourself in different guises. One must put aside everything that devours the best part of one's thoughts and bring oneself to a state in which one concentrates relentlessly on oneself alone. What happens, of course, is just the opposite: there is in the first place the family to reckon with which stands in the way either through kindness or simply because they are blind to facts. And then there are the Mistress temptations, *the* Mistress temptation, I should say, which one hasn't even reckoned with, so ready is she to give herself until everything is abandoned. . . . And even now I haven't told you the half. . . .

He continued, however, to be preoccupied with the two works until the war. Having completed *Jeux* under great strain, he tells Durand on 12 September 1912: 'Although I am very tired I have taken up my old works again. I am sufficiently fond of them to derive new energy from them. At least that is what I am hoping.'[1] In September 1916, some eight months after undergoing an operation, he finally completed the libretto of *Usher*. It was among his last works. In September 1916, writing for the last time of the work to Godet, from his house in the Avenue du Bois de Boulogne, he says: 'This house has a curious resemblance to the house of Usher. Although I haven't the mind troubles of Roderick, nor his passion

[1] The last mention of these works before the first World War is in a letter from Victor Segalen to his wife of 5 September 1913: 'Lunched this morning with Debussy, more open and confiding than ever. He is writing, almost to order, things that annoy him: *Khamma*, an Egyptian ballet for Maud Allan, a nude dancer, and *Crimen Amoris* on pieces of Verlaine put together by Charles Morice. He cannot even finish for himself his two little dramas of Poe.'

for the last thought of C. M. von Weber,[1] we are alike in our super-sensitiveness. . . . On this point I could tell you things which would make your beard fall off, which would be most unpleasant not for your beard but for me who doesn't like attracting attention.' Thereafter his powers began to decline and he increasingly saw both Godet and himself as replicas of Poe's harrassed, over-refined character. Observing that what he was writing was 'always of yesterday, never of tomorrow', he desperately exclaims in one of his last letters to Godet, of 6 October 1916, 'You are my only friend, alias Roderick Usher!'

It remains to assess both the sketches and the final form of Debussy's libretto for *La Maison Usher*, adapted from the Baudelaire translation. In its original form Poe's tale is almost a monologue declaimed in the first person by the unnamed friend of Roderick Usher. In fact Roderick himself, so realistically described, speaks only four times, merely saying a few words. His twin-sister Lady Madeline[2] has a dumb role. The fourth character, the doctor of the family, appears only once, his role being of very slight importance. It was thus essential that a theatrical work based on this monologue should fill out the characters not only of Roderick but also of Lady Madeline and the Doctor. This was the solution that Debussy proposed. In the sketch for the libretto the work is divided into three scenes. In the first the characters are Lady Madeline and Roderick; in the second the Doctor and the friend; and in the third the friend and Roderick. Though the character of Roderick, obsessed by an incestuous love for his sister, is kept in the foreground, the plot is remodelled to bring into relief on the stage the final appearance of Lady Madeline. Her clothes are now covered in blood and her collapse, overwhelming her brother, is followed by the crumbling of the House of Usher. In the tale Poe gives us to believe that the supposed death of Roderick's sister occurred accidentally and she is buried alive by Roderick aided by his friend. In Debussy's sketch for the libretto it is the Doctor, built up into an extremely sinister character, who buries Lady Madeline alive

[1] The allusion is to this passage in *The Fall of the House of Usher*: 'Among other things I hold painfully in mind a certain singular perversion and amplification of the wild air of the last waltz of von Weber.'
[2] Debussy surely knew of the existence of his English cousin Lucie Madeline de Bussy, daughter of his paternal uncle Jules Alexandre, though he never met her. (See Vol. I, p. 5.)

without Roderick's knowledge.[1] The work opens with two verses of the poem 'The Haunted Palace', sung not by Roderick accompanying himself on the guitar as in the tale, but by Lady Madeline. In the final version the three scenes are reduced to two, or rather they take the form of a prologue and a single principal scene. The plot and the dialogue are substantially the same as in the sketch and the work ends, as in the tale of Poe, with the house of Usher crumbling into ruins, only reflections of its fragments being discernible in the deep dark tarn as the blood-red moon rises over the sombre landscape. It is clear that Debussy was primarily concerned with the essentially soliptic character of Roderick Usher: the enraged, self-devouring lover guilty of loving his sister. 'Celle que tu aimais tant,' he says to himself, 'celle que tu ne devais pas aimer.' Parent of the indecisive, Hamlet-like Pelléas, Roderick perishes with the rise of the same blood-red moon, we note, that appears so dramatically at the end of *Salomé* and of *Wozzeck*, symbols in these operas, as in *Usher*, of love and of murder.

The unfinished musical score of *Usher*, consisting of twenty-one pages and now in the Bibliothèque Nationale in Paris, follows the text of the final version. A performance of the entire manuscript for soprano (Lady Madeline), tenor (the friend), baritone (the Doctor), and bass (Roderick) has not yet been undertaken for the reason that too much of it is illegible or incomplete.[2]

A study of Debussy's unfinished operas on tales of Poe and of the ideas that they engendered offers an illuminating view of many subsequent musical developments. The main interest, however, of the musical manuscript of *Usher*, which does not noticeably transcend the recitative style of *Pelléas*, is not in its purely musical value; it is in the æsthetic theories with which these few pages are associated. The dream visions in Poe's tales, colliding as in a nightmare,

---

[1] Debussy introduces episodes of fierce jealousy between the Doctor and Roderick, both enamoured of Madeline, 'sœur trop aimée'. These episodes are nowhere to be found in Poe's tale and are entirely of Debussy's invention. Recalling his twin-sister, Debussy's Roderick speaks of 'ses lèvres qui tentent comme un fruit inconnu où ma bouche n'a jamais osé mordre!' The Doctor is 'le médecin de la mort. . . . Il nous surveille comme un vieux corbeau avide de chair morte.' He is the Raven in fact of Poe's famous poem, with its recurrent refrain 'Nevermore', which had earlier inspired Mallarmé, Manet, Gauguin, and Ravel (in *Le Gibet*).

[2] A section of Roderick's monologue was performed at the Société Française de Musicologie, Paris, in 1959. In addition to the manuscripts of *Usher* reproduced in my *Debussy et Edgar Poe* there are a musical sketch, 'Ce qui sera peut-être le prélude à *La Chute de la Maison Usher*', and an earlier version of the libretto, both shown at the Debussy Exhibition at the Bibliothèque Nationale in 1962 (Nos. 194 and 195).

were developed by several later writers, among them Villiers de l'Isle Adam, whose *Axel* had inspired Debussy and whose *Contes Cruels* were later to inspire Dallapiccola's opera *Il Prigionero*, and Henry James, whose *The Turn of the Screw* was set by Benjamin Britten. *Pelléas, La Chute de la Maison Usher, Wozzeck, Il Prigionero, The Turn of the Screw*—the line of the æsthetic development of twentieth-century opera is clear.[1]

Poe expressed some striking ideas, known to Debussy, on the nature of music. 'I know that indefiniteness is an element of true music,' Poe writes, 'a suggested indefiniteness bringing about a definiteness of vague and therefore of spiritual effect.' Commenting on this passage, Edmund Wilson, in his book *The Shores of Light*, writes:

The real significance of Poe's short stories does not lie in what they purport to relate. Many are confessedly dreams; and, as with dreams, though they seem absurd, their effect on our emotions is serious. And even those that pretend to the logic and the exactitude of actual narratives are, nevertheless, also dreams. . . . No one understood better than Poe that, in fiction and in poetry both, it is not what you say that counts, but what you make the reader feel (he always italicizes the word 'effect'); no one understood better than Poe that the deepest psychological truth may be rendered through phantasmagoria. Even the realistic stories of

[1] Not for nothing was Poe's life and work the subject of an exhaustive psychoanalytic study by Marie Bonaparte with a preface by Freud (*Edgar Poe: Etude Psychanalytique*, 2 vol., 1933; English translation by John Rodker, London, 1949). In the literary sphere Poe was almost a precursor of Freud. Undoubtedly it was his power of analysis that fascinated Baudelaire. Fifty years before Freud, Baudelaire, writing in his second preface to Poe's works 'of the fervour with which he was able to throw himself into the grotesque for the love of the grotesque and into the horrifying for the love of the horrifying' drew the conclusion: 'I have already observed that this fervour was often the result of a vast, vital energy left idle, sometimes of a stubborn chastity and also of a profound, repressed sensibility.' It is instructive to compare Debussy's version of *The Fall of the House of Usher* with the analysis of the tale by Marie Bonaparte; one has the impression that, since Debussy laid such stress on the incestuous aspects of Roderick's relationship with his sister, he might have endorsed certain of Madame Bonaparte's interpretations. On the other hand, Baudelaire's amazing statement, 'Love plays no part in Poe's writings', must surely have been unacceptable to him. ('When sexual manifestations are so deeply buried in the unconscious', Madame Bonaparte comments, 'they seem to the layman to be non-existent.') A later writer, D. H. Lawrence, saw these manifestations clearly enough and interpreted *The House of Usher* from a viewpoint nearer the approach taken by Debussy: 'The Ushers, brother and sister . . . would love, love, love, without resistance. They would love, they would merge, they would be as one thing. So they dragged each other down into death.' (*Studies in Classic American Literature*, London, 1924.)

Poe are, in fact, only phantasmagoria of a more circumstantial kind. . . . Poe's mentality was a rare synthesis.

And he concludes with a statement that shows at once the lasting appeal of Poe for Debussy: 'He had elements in him that corresponded with the indefiniteness of music and the exactitude of mathematics.' And Edmund Wilson asks: 'Is not this what modern literature is tending toward?' The indefiniteness of music and the exactitude of mathematics—these are also, as we know, the ideals of much later developments in twentieth-century art, rooted in these unfinished works of Debussy.

9
Maud Allan and Gabriele d'Annunzio

J'aime les situations extrêmes.
Debussy

At the beginning of February 1911, shortly after his return from Vienna and Budapest, Debussy informed Robert Godet that he was obliged to put aside his operas on the tales of Poe in order to fulfil two commissions:

> Back in Paris I have begun working on a ballet for Miss Maud Allan, who is an English girl to her fingertips. By way of compensation the ballet is Egyptian; the plot is childishly simple and, rightly, presents no interest in itself. The reasons that have encouraged me to write this work are another matter, and there are also economic reasons. At the very same time Gabriele d'Annunzio appeared on the scene with *Le Martyre de Saint-Sébastien* for which I agreed to write the incidental music. This is a much more lavish proposition than the wretched little Anglo-Egyptian ballet. I needn't tell you that the worship of Adonis is mingled in this work with the worship of Christ; that it is assuredly very beautiful; and that if I were given the necessary time some rather lovely ideas could be discovered.

The circumstances which led Debussy to accept these two commissions, deflecting him, as he says, from his work on the Poe operas, need investigation, particularly since neither the ballet *Khamma*, commissioned by Maud Allan, nor the incidental music for d'Annunzio's mystery play were, in the manner in which they were eventually presented, successful. There have been several attempts to revive the *Saint-Sébastien* music, and in many different forms. *Khamma*, on the other hand, though completed in 1913, was not even played in Debussy's lifetime, and it is still the least known of Debussy's later works. It is hardly ever heard and none of the studies on Debussy give even a summary of it. Yet there are reasons to believe that its failure was not altogether warranted.

In the revised as in the earlier edition of his *Debussy et son temps*, Vallas persists in stating that '*Khamma* was a piece of hack work . . . a short music-hall number . . . written for a certain English dancer Maud Allan.' In fact, though it was written for this well-known dancer, the work is described in the published score as a 'Légende dansée de W. L. Courtney et Maud Allan'. A lecturer in philosophy at Oxford and a brilliant literary and dramatic critic, W. L. Courtney, at the time of his association with Maud Allan and Debussy, was literary editor of the *Daily Telegraph*. The novel choreographic art of Maud Allan, he pointed out, contained 'something derived from music, something derived from drama, something derived also from the painter's art'.[1] Though she later appeared as a solo dancer in London at the Palladium and the Coliseum, Maud Allan was not a music-hall dancer and it was never suggested that *Khamma* should be anything in the nature of a music-hall composition. A gifted musician as well as a dancer, she had been a pupil of Busoni and had also studied painting and sculpture in Italy. Her *Vision of Salomé* with music by the Belgian composer Marcel Rémy, which she gave in London in 1908, was considered particularly poetic. It was 'not the actual dance executed before Herod and Herodias', notes Courtney, but 'a repetition of it in half-conscious memory'. Maud Allan had also undertaken serious research into the hieratic dances of Egypt and the early forms of Greek dancing.[2]

[1] In *Rosemary's Letter Book* (London, 1909) Courtney published a sonnet to Maud Allan entitled *An Arcadian Idyll*. He also compared her work to that of Isidora Duncan. Like Loïe Fuller, who devised choreographic versions of Debussy's *Nuages* and *Sirènes*, Isidora Duncan was eclipsed only by the more spectacular appeal of the dancers of the Diaghilev ballet.

[2] In *My Life and Dancing* (London, 1908) Maud Allan gives the explanation, which she discovered in a work of 1896, of the much discussed Greek title of Erik Satie's piano pieces, *Gymnopédies*, two of which Debussy orchestrated: 'The exquisite Gymnopaedia simulating an attack and defence, danced by naked boys crowned with chaplets of palm.'

The scenario of *Khamma* which, as Debussy states, is admirably uncomplicated, is worth summarizing if only because this work has hitherto been unfortunately misrepresented. The action takes place in the inner temple of the ancient Egyptian sun-god Amon-Ra. The Prelude suggests the rumble of a distant revolt with approaching trumpet calls.[1] In the surrounded temple the High Priest and other worshippers pray to the image of Amon-Ra for the delivery of the town. The stone image is able to respond with no reassuring gesture and the High Priest prepares to leave. He has, however, an intuition concerning the secret of victory. In the second scene the veiled figure of Khamma the dancer appears. She wishes to escape and her apprehension is expressed in the ensuing section, *La Peur de Khamma*. Presently the temple is flooded with moonlight and Khamma prostrates herself before the statue. She then performs three dances in the hope of delivering the country from the invaders. At the conclusion of the third dance she perceives that the head and shoulders of the statue begin to move. The hands of the stone god rise from the knees, the palms turned upwards. Delivered from fear, Khamma performs a fourth dance, an ecstatic dance of joy, but at the climax, marked by a flash of lightning and a thunder clap, she suddenly falls to the ground and dies. The third scene opens on the scene of the temple at dawn. The victorious crowd approaches and the door of the temple is thrown open to them. The final celebration scene is cut short when the crowd perceive the body of Khamma, who has sacrificed her life, and the work ends with a solemn blessing bestowed upon her by the High Priest.

It is true that Debussy was loath to accept a commission to compose a ballet on this subject, and it is also true that he agreed to do so principally for material reasons. The same is true, however, not only of *Saint-Sébastien* but also of *Jeux* and, in varying degrees, of several other works of his later years. Rather unwillingly, Debussy was being drawn at this time into the world of the ballet and the theatre. This was not surprising. It was in this domain that, before the age of film music, a composer could hope to procure the most lucrative engagements. In his uncertain state of health and with his

---

[1] This was no doubt intended to be an allusion to the religious revolution against Amon-Ra launched by the Pharaoh Ikhnaton, held to have been one of the most remarkable idealists of the ancient world before the Hebrews.

growing liabilities towards his wife and daughter, Debussy threw himself into the composition of these commissioned works, overcoming as best he could many personal and artistic aversions. Out of deference to Maud Allan, who was then alive, many of the references to her were deleted from the published correspondence between Debussy and his publisher Durand. He rather contemptuously refers to her as 'la girl anglaise', and it is clear that she angered Debussy by her request to be allowed to use the score as she wished. We have also to take into account another reason for the acid remarks the sick and impecunious composer was inclined to make about Maud Allan. As with other works of this period, Debussy lacked either the time or the physical strength to complete them unaided. Between 1911 and 1913 André Caplet, who had served Debussy as amanuensis in *Gigues* and *Saint-Sébastien*, was often in Boston and London. Charles Koechlin, a composer less well known to Debussy, was thus called upon to assist with *Khamma*. The piano score was written by Debussy, but he orchestrated only the first few bars; the remainder he entrusted to Koechlin under his supervision. In his book on Debussy, Koechlin promised to make known one day a remark which the harassed composer had made to him about *Khamma* and which he had up till then withheld. On his last visit to London Koechlin kindly supplied me with the text of this remark, an amazing remark in whatever context it was made, and which understandably left Debussy's young associate nonplussed. It was: 'Write *Khamma* yourself and I will sign it.'

Despite misgivings and his reluctance to undertake the work, Debussy by no means belittled the value of the score ultimately provided for this ballet of Courtney and Allan. To Durand on 1 February 1912 he writes: 'When will you come and hear the new version of this curious ballet—with its trumpet calls which suggest the revolt and the fire and which send a shiver down your back? I should very much like to dedicate *Khamma* to Madame Jacques Durand.' We gather from this text (as opposed to a truncated version of it from which Vallas concluded that Debussy's reference to *Khamma* was contemptuous) that he was sufficiently interested in the work to have written a second version, and that in this form he held it to be worthy of dedication to the wife of his publisher. Though completed in 1913 it was not published until 1916. A concert performance was not given until 1924 and it was performed as a ballet only in 1947, at the Opéra-Comique with choreography by Jean-Jacques Etcheverry.[1]

We may now return to the ambitious scheme of Gabriele d'Annunzio for a theatrical work in five acts, reconstructing the legend of the martyrdom of St. Sebastian in its most masochistic aspect, in which the orchestral and choral music of Debussy was to be combined with speech, also with mime and dancing devised by Fokine, the whole of this grandiose spectacle to be enhanced by the blues, golds, and emerald-greens of the costumes and scenery of the Russian painter Léon Bakst. It is impossible to believe that for this gaudy work Debussy could have agreed to supply an immense score for any other than material reasons. 'This is a much more lavish proposition than the wretched little Anglo-Egyptian ballet', he had told Godet. Behind this laconic remark is the fact that the composition of *Saint-Sébastien* involved a much larger sum of money.

In 1910 Gabriele d'Annunzio, the mystical Italian poet, soldier, and patriot, known today chiefly for his spectacular raid on Fiume in 1919 and for his later association with Mussolini, had been chased by the bailiffs from his luxurious villa in Florence and fled to Paris, where he lived under several different pseudonyms. Here he continued his life of unbelievable luxury, possessing a hundred suits, mixing scents, of which he used a pint a day, and indulging in unmentionable vices. It was said that in Italy his horses had slept on Persian rugs. It is essential to include this vignette of d'Annunzio, seemingly the last person to be associated with the retiring figure of Debussy, in order to see his attraction to the subject of Sebastian's martyrdom. He was seized by this subject partly as an historian of the pagan cultures preceding the Christian era, but even more

[1] The fact that this ballet was not performed until almost thirty years after Debussy's death is due to circumstances which have not hitherto been made known. In July 1916, at the time of the publication of the ballet, Maud Allan, who had commissioned the work, stated in *The Dancing Times* that she was devising the choreography for it. No doubt it would have been produced by her in London at the end of the war or shortly afterwards had her career not in the meantime been compromised. In June 1918 she lost her case in the criminal court against Noel Pemberton Billing who, with the intention of revealing widespread corruption and pro-Germanism in influential circles associated with Allan's performances, had accused her of indecency in her characteriza-tion of Wilde's Salomé. Though the scandalous nature of the trial overshadowed any moral objection to Allan's art as a dancer, the fact that she lost her case, which in the end became an issue of national importance, reflected on her unfavourably, with the result that she was no longer able to pursue her career.

as one of the last and certainly as one of the most florid and blatant of the 'decadents'.[1]

We are fortunate in being well documented on the personal and artistic relationship between d'Annunzio and Debussy. What appears to be the entire correspondence between them has been published, and we may also draw upon the correspondence on the matter of *Saint-Sébastien* with Emma Debussy and with André Caplet. D'Annunzio boldly introduces himself in a letter written from Arcachon on 25 November 1910:

My dear Master,

Far in the past, on the hill at Settignano, the native province of the most lyrical of Tuscan sculptors [Desiderio da Settignano, a follower of Donatello] Gabriel Mourey[2] spoke to me of you and of *Tristan* in moving terms. I already knew and loved your work. I used to frequent a little Florentine group where a few earnest artists had developed a cult for your work and enthusiastically upheld your 'reform'. Then, as today, I suffered from not being able to write the music for my tragedies. And I wondered when I might possibly meet you. This summer, as I was sketching out a Mystery play which I had long been thinking about, a friend would sing to me your most beautiful songs with that inner sense of poetry they require. The play on which I was working was sometimes deeply affected by them. But I hardly dared to hope for your co-operation.

Do you love my poetry? In Paris two weeks ago I was impelled to go and knock at your door. I was told that you were not at home. Now I can no longer withhold my request. I ask if you

---

[1] It is curious to read an opinion of d'Annunzio by André Gide who, like Debussy, upheld the French ideals of moderation and was therefore revolted by the excessively flamboyant manner of d'Annunzio: 'In Italy a fierce campaign has been launched against him based on proof that he copies and plagiarises Maeterlinck, Shelley and Flaubert. It is rather absurd that despite this his reputation is largely a French matter. . . . It may seem rather silly, after what I have said, to confess that *nevertheless* I admire him very much.' (Letter to Marcel Drouin of 1898.) Debussy would probably have agreed with Gide's view of d'Annunzio, expressed in the same letter, as an Italian counterpart of their old friend Pierre Louÿs.

[2] Debussy's life-long friend Gabriel Mourey had been associated, as we have seen, with earlier projects of Debussy. The subject of the martyrdom of St. Sebastian, as dealt with by d'Annunzio, has many affinities with the earlier occultist works of Mourey and Jules Bois in which Debussy had been interested in the 1890s. The whole matter of Debussy's occultist tendencies, as they affect the music he wrote for *Saint-Sébastien*, is dealt with in a study by Léon Guichard (see Appendix E).

will kindly see me and listen to what I wish to tell you of this work and this dream. Send me word straight away. I am shortly leaving. I shall at least have the pleasure of conveying to you my gratitude for the beautiful thoughts that you have been able to arouse in my restless spirit.

Debussy's reply, written from the Hotel Krantz in Vienna, was sent without delay:

30 November 1910

My dear Master,
    Your letter reached me here where I am regretfully spending some time. Forgive me for not having been able to tell you immediately of my joy on receiving it. How could I possibly not love your poetry? The mere thought of working with you sets up some sort of feverish excitement.[1] I shall return to Paris about 20 December. Need I tell you how happy I shall be to receive you? Believe, my dear Master, in my heartfelt admiration.

A statement made by Debussy almost immediately after the dispatch of this letter offers a very different view of his proposed collaboration with d'Annunzio. From Budapest on 3 December he writes to Emma Debussy: 'I wrote to d'Annunzio from Vienna. . . . This proposal means nothing to me of any worth [*Cette histoire ne me dit rien qui vaille*]. Also, I should seem to be running a line for dancers.' And half ironically, half cajolingly, in view of the fact that he had already accepted one such commission, he adds, 'We mustn't forget Miss Maud Allan.' Letters later written by d'Annunzio and the impresario Gabriel Astruc to Madame Debussy indicate that d'Annunzio's offer was ultimately accepted only as a result of considerable persuasive efforts on Emma Debussy's part.[2] Influences of one kind or another were brought to bear on Debussy by both the renowned Russian-Jewish dancer Ida Rubinstein, who

---

[1] One wonders which poems or other works of d'Annunzio Debussy could have known at this period. He may well have seen *La Città morta* in a French version with Bernhardt in 1898. Three volumes of d'Annunzio's poems were published in 1903 and 1904 in Italian.
[2] 'You helped to promote great undertakings', Astruc writes to Madame Debussy in the course of the negotiations. 'Your gracious manner and your shrewdness have given d'Annunzio and myself confidence in ultimate success.'

was to take the part of the Saint, and the Comte Robert de Montesquiou, the model of Marcel Proust's Baron de Charlus, who had
been the first to support d'Annunzio's venture. Their first choice
of a collaborator for d'Annunzio had been Roger-Ducasse, who had
refused, and no time was lost in concluding the bargain with
Debussy. Having returned from Central Europe earlier than he had
expected, Debussy received from d'Annunzio, on 10 December, a
telegram so grandiloquently worded as to appear a caricature in the
worst Italian taste: 'Je reçois la grande nouvelle, ô Claude roi!'
Debussy, who throughout his life had refused to give himself airs
of any kind and who was quick to spot the artificial element of
play-acting in an artist's character, must have been horrified by
this regal attribution.[1] He had, in any case, accepted the commission
without having seen a word of d'Annunzio's play.

It was not until February of the following year, however, that
work was begun on the score. Since the play was to be produced in
May, only two months were left for the composition of a score
which, as Debussy told his friends, would normally have taken him
two years. On 14 February 1911 he tells André Caplet that d'Annunzio 'is a kind of irresistible whirlwind', and goes on: 'The whole
thing will be called Le Martyre de Saint-Sébastien. Of course I
have very little time to write a great deal of music—you know how
much this pleases me! So there is not a minute to lose in deciding.
In the yield of a mine there is a type of coal known as unsorted coal.
This applies to me precisely. I have nevertheless accepted because it
is worth risking; and also because I am perhaps still not too old to
act irrationally—and even to do the wrong thing.[2] Some of our
good friends whom you know are honouring me by betting with
each other on my slender chances of succeeding in such a perilous
undertaking. I can say nothing definite for the moment, but I
think that there will be something interesting in this matter for you
later on.'

[1] It was d'Annunzio who pompously attributed to Debussy the name 'Claude de
France', as opposed, presumably, to his Italian namesake Claudio Monteverdi. Another
composer with whom d'Annunzio collaborated, Pizzetti, was proclaimed in the same
ostentatious manner 'Ildebrando da Parma'.

[2] To d'Annunzio on 29 January Debussy had given a different view of his misgivings: 'I have reached the point where all music seems to me useless by comparison
with the constantly renewed splendours of your imagination. It is thus not without
some terror that I foresee the moment when I shall have to make up my mind to write.
Will I be able to? Will I be able to find what I want? Fear of this kind is perhaps a
salutory sign for one cannot enter into mystery armed with vanity and pride.'

Caplet was in fact called upon to assist Debussy in several ways, and the extent of his contribution to the hurriedly written score of *Saint-Sébastien* will be discussed presently. For the moment we must examine the significance for Debussy of d'Annunzio's curious text. In offering the dedication of this work to the French nationalist figure Maurice Barrès, d'Annunzio appears to have been embarrassed at having dared to write this half-pagan mystery play in a language other than his own. More than this, he told Barrès that it was his intention, when the work was finished, to take the manuscript to Chartres Cathedral and, as an act of self-accusation, to place it next to the statue of the ass playing the hurdy-gurdy. This indicates that the over-bold poet was keenly aware of sacrilegious elements in his *Saint-Sébastien*. Indeed, Barrès was in two minds about accepting the dedication of a work in which Christian values appeared to be alternately upheld and undermined.

Despite the rhetorical effusions of d'Annunzio's *Saint-Sébastien*, it is a work which tells us much about the spirit of the time. The scenarios of Stravinsky's *Sacre du Printemps* and Ravel's *Daphnis et Chloé*, given only two years later, were similarly inspired by pagan subjects. This interest in pre-Christian subjects was not a passing fashion. The pagan cults of the *fin-de-siècle*, which had flourished in narrow bohemian circles, were an inspiration now to great artists, and some historians have held that it was this same spirit which, having affected social and moral values on a wide scale, found its most terrifying expression in the brutalities of the first World War.[1]

Writing shortly after the Paris production of *Saint-Sébastien* in 1911, Professor Gustave Cohen, the authority on Roman and early Christian literature, pointed out that the disintegration of religious values in Europe at that time corresponded to the disintegration of moral values at an early period of Roman history when the paganism of the Orient and of Greece was confused with the new values of Christian morality. D'Annunzio, he maintained, saw Christianity

---

[1] Critics and other observers in the years preceding the first World War were quick to identify the growing feverishness in the music of many different composers with an impending disaster. Referring in his *Journal des années de guerre* to a concert of Russian music, including Stravinsky's *Petrouchka* which he had heard in Paris in January 1914, Romain Rolland declared that 'les sursauts de violence et d'ivresse frénétiques, l'hystérie disloquée, furieuse et burlesque de Stravinsky, me semblent s'accorder assez bien avec la grande folie de l'époque actuelle, et, somme toute, l'annonçaient. . . . Cette ivresse du rhythme, c'est bien aussi la même qui entraîne ces peuples d'Europe à mourir et à tuer.' When Rolland wrote those words he had heard *Le Sacre du Printemps*.

in its most primitive aspect, emphasizing the masochistic nature of St. Sebastian, and introducing, as in Klingsor's garden, miracles and elements of magic. In recent years these episodes have frequently been interpreted in the light of contemporary psychology. The instruments of torture prepared in the first act for the Christian twins Mark and Marcellian, the dance which Sebastian steels himself to perform on the burning embers, and his final exhortation to the archers to pierce him with their arrows so that, in pain, their love for him may be exquisitely revived—all these episodes in *Saint-Sébastien*, often conceived in crude taste, foreshadow not only the cruelty and ruthlessness that rose to the surface in the first World War but the similar ruthlessness of the social philosophies that developed in the post-war years.[1]

The first performance of *Le Martyre de Saint-Sébastien* at the Théâtre du Châtelet on 22 May 1911 was an important historical event. But no one has ever tried to obscure the fact that, despite many splendid qualities of the music, the production was a failure, or that it represented for Debussy anything but a severe set-back at the very moment when he had made an almost superhuman effort to establish his material life on a secure footing. 'With *Le Martyre de Saint-Sébastien* begins the martyrdom of Claude Debussy', observes Marcel Dietschy. A jibe was prompted by the fact that the work had lasted over five hours: 'Ça Saint-Sébastien? C'est la Sainte-Barbe!' When the last attempt was made to revive the work in a dramatic form, in 1957 at the Paris Opéra, Emile Vuillermoz, who had been assistant chorus-master in the original production, still could not conceal its defects. 'This strange work in which an element of magic is introduced in the rotation of planets',[2] he then wrote, 'was born forty-six years ago under an unlucky star.

[1] Noting in his study of d'Annunzio that manifestations of cruelty are particularly relished by the extremely civilized and the extremely barbarous, Anthony Rhodes shows that d'Annunzio was himself both a decadent and a barbarian. 'This explains', he writes, 'why he was later to prove himself a warrior. Most people expect a voluptuary, an intellectual, and a decadent to be a poor soldier with unreliable nerves. This was far from the case with d'Annunzio.' The author of *Saint-Sébastien* served with distinction in the first World War and showed remarkable physical courage. Having temporarily lost the sight of an eye as the result of a wound during the war, he declared that the music of Debussy was his 'only consolation'. In later years when he lived in luxury under the Fascist régime ('A bad tooth you either pull out or fill with gold', Mussolini said of him) he retained his love for the music of Debussy, which continued to epitomize for him the cruel and exquisite *fin-de-siècle* pleasures.

[2] The reference is to the second act of *Saint-Sébastien*, *La Chambre Magique*, the occult chamber of the Chaldean fortune-tellers who are portrayed gazing at the planets.

Wagner, by Renoir

Ida Rubinstein,
by Antoine de la Gadara

Paul-Jean Toulet

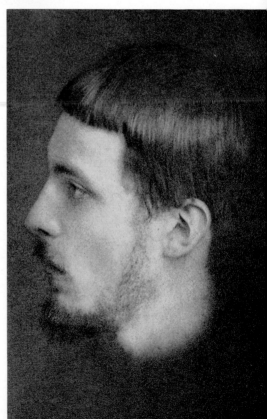

A gathering of wicked fairies was apparently assembled at its cradle to mark out its unfortunate future.'[1]

In the latest publication of Vuillermoz certain facts are disclosed which were not perhaps unsuspected. On learning that the score was to be delivered in two months, Debussy was 'appalled'. Not only did he set to work on his heavy task 'unwillingly' but 'his health was already giving some anxiety and the work he was required to do became a strenuous drudge'. He was obliged to rely on his faithful friend André Caplet to help him 'in the material aspects of his professional work'. In the same account we read: 'Rehearsals of the work were well advanced at the Théâtre du Châtelet but the score was far from complete. [Debussy] had to be satisfied with noting briefly the substance of certain pages and entrusting Caplet—whose writing was exactly the same as his—with completing, according to his exact indications, the orchestration and the harmonization of such and such a passage clearly settled in his mind.' Vuillermoz is obviously not sure here to what extent the score of *Le Martyre de Saint-Sébastien* is the work of Debussy or the work of his amanuensis André Caplet who conducted the first performance. The letters to Caplet contain no precise information on this important matter. The two (incomplete) full scores at the Bibliothèque de l'Opéra are written partly by Caplet, partly by Debussy. Another score, in Debussy's hand, was said to be in the possession of the publisher Durand.[2] A short manuscript note, regarding the harp and cymbal parts sent by Debussy to Caplet and reproduced in the letters to Caplet, suggests an improvement Debussy wished to make, possibly after a rehearsal. On the other hand, according to an account which has not been contradicted, the final chorus, missing from the two manuscripts at the Bibliothèque de l'Opéra, was held to be entirely the work of Caplet. On 4 June 1911 a

---

[1] In later years Jean Cocteau used maliciously to imitate the bitter disappointment expressed by the shrewd impresario Gabriel Astruc, usually successful, at the failure of one of his most ambitious ventures: 'Je n'y comprends rien! J'ai réuni le plus grand musicien, le plus grand poète, le plus grand décorateur, le plus grand chorégraphe. . . . Et c'est mauvais!'

[2] Of these three scores I have been able to consult only the two at the Bibliothèque de l'Opéra. The catalogue entry at this library gives a detailed analysis of the handwriting in these two scores. I have collated this analysis with the manuscripts and am satisfied that in the larger of these two scores the pages written by Caplet are more numerous than those written by Debussy. This, however, does not necessarily mean that the pages in Caplet's handwriting were orchestrated by him; he may have been copying from Debussy's sketches. Some of the vocal parts are written in a third hand.

dispatch from Paris to the Italian journal *Il Tirso* stated: 'There is a persistent rumour in Paris art circles that the chorus of the fifth act in Paradise—the musical section least admired by the public and the critics—was not the work of the illustrious master. People who maintain that they are well informed state that Debussy . . . invited one of his most faithful disciples to compose the chorus of the fifth act.' This rumour was neither confirmed nor contradicted. It is doubtful whether further correspondence or other evidence can enlighten us on this matter, and it is therefore unlikely that we shall ever be certain of the extent of Caplet's participation in *Saint-Sébastien*.[1]

A series of unfortunate events seriously prejudiced the success of the widely advertised work. The Archbishop of Paris, having learnt that the character of a saint was to be impersonated on the stage by a dancer, forbade Catholics to attend performances under penalty of excommunication,[2] and the whole of d'Annunzio's works were put on the Index. On the morning of the public dress rehearsal, on 21 May, the Minister of War was killed in an aeroplane accident. Official mourning was declared and this important social event was cancelled. At the first performance the following day confusion reigned among the choristers. Bakst had taken it upon

---

[1] D. E. Inghelbrecht, the chorus-master under Caplet at the first performance, gives this account of Debussy's strenuous efforts: 'He composed day and night, shut up at his home, sending off the pages of the score one by one, to the printer. "I am labouring like a piece-worker", he declared, "with never a look back".' A letter to his publisher was signed 'Votre bien ensébastianisé'. The last pages, sent in April, were accompanied by the message: 'Here, if you agree, is the last appeal of St. Sebastian and I confess that I am not displeased with it. As I have told you several times already, I am at the end of my tether.' Debussy's friendship with André Caplet, which dates from 1907, led to their co-operation on several other projects, among them the orchestration, by Caplet, of *Children's Corner* and *Pagodes*, the re-casting of the orchestration of *Jet d'eau* and the completion of the orchestration of *Gigues* and *La Boîte à joujoux*. Other orchestral works of Debussy were arranged by Caplet for two (*Ibéria*) and three (*La Mer*) pianos. Born at Le Havre in 1878, Caplet was particularly admired by Debussy as a conductor. From 1910 to 1914 he was conductor of the Boston Symphony Orchestra and in 1912 conducted *Pelléas* at Covent Garden. Through his intimate friendship with the English singer Nina Russell, wife of the impresario Henry Russell, an important series of letters addressed to him by Debussy between 1908 and 1914 remained in England and was published in 1957.

[2] The censure was dictated not so much by the fact that St. Sebastian was portrayed on the stage but by the fact that the saint was impersonated by a woman dancer making a powerful sexual appeal. It was all very well for d'Annunzio to protest to the Archbishop that Ida Rubinstein was 'as pure as a Perugino painting, in a sense asexual, an androgyne'. His telegram to Ida Rubinstein before the performance, which he signed Sanae, the name of one of the archers who killed the saint, read (according to Anthony Rhodes), 'Play finished. I kiss your bleeding legs.' The Archbishop's reply to d'Annunzio was uncompromising: 'Today a sacred drama no longer has a mystic religious meaning, it is given simply to divert and delight the spectators.'

himself to place together slaves, warriors, and archers, motivated simply by the contrasts of colours offered by their costumes and with no regard whatever for the choral groups to which they happened to belong. Dressed up in enormous coloured cloaks with lowered hoods, the assistant chorus-masters Chadeigne and Vuillermoz mingled with the hopelessly dispersed choristers on the stage, whispering a note into their ears or singing a part that one or other of them was unable to maintain.

Many passages in the score reminded critics of *Parsifal*. Shortly after Debussy's death, in 1921, Vuillermoz urged that the work should be resuscitated: '*Saint-Sébastien* is to be rediscovered. Debussy in *Saint-Sébastien* wrote his *Parsifal*. But it is a *Parsifal* that awaits its Bayreuth.'[1] Marcel Proust, who was not averse to labyrinthine explorations and who was normally enamoured of Debussy's music, was able to commend d'Annunzio for his command of the French language but spent most of his time at the performance staring at the beautiful legs of Ida Rubinstein. He wrote to Reynaldo Hahn: 'All the foreign elements in d'Annunzio were transferred to Ida Rubinstein. On the matter of style how could one believe that d'Annunzio is a foreigner? How many Frenchmen can write with this precision?[2] And, as I always come round to

[1] The later versions of *Saint-Sébastien* took many different forms. Ida Rubinstein appeared in several revivals of the work in its original form, notably at La Scala in 1926 under Toscanini. Concert versions in the form of a symphonic suite or an oratorio, with one or more narrators reciting an abridged version of d'Annunzio's play, were made by André Caplet, D. E. Inghelbrecht, and Roland Manuel. The most successful of the later versions was an open-air performance given by the actress Véra Korène in co-operation with Victor de Sabata, at the Théâtre Antique de Fourvière in 1952. The length of the spectacle was reduced from five to two hours. The merits of these various versions are discussed by Raphael Cuttoli in the special number of *La Revue Musicale* devoted to *Saint-Sébastien* (1957). In 1914 Debussy and d'Annunzio went so far as to discuss a film version of the work. The latest version, in which d'Annunzio's text is entirely deleted, was given by André Souris in Brussels in 1964.

[2] Proust, who must have been aware that Robert de Montesquiou was one of several French writers to whom d'Annunzio had submitted the text of *Saint-Sébastien*, had heard the moving references to Debussy in the introductory scene. One wonders whether Montesquiou himself had a hand in the composition of the lines:

> Mais l'autre est Claude Debussy
> qui sonne frais comme les feuilles
> neuves sous l'averse nouvelle
> dans un verger de l'Ile-de-France . ..

or:

> Marie lui jette sa ceinture
> qui devient une mélodie.
> Or c'est Claude qui la recueille
> sur la flûte de sept roseaux . . .

your view in the end, I found the legs of Mme Rubinstein (like those of both Clomenil and Maurice de Rothschild) sublime. For me this was everything. But I found the play very boring despite certain moments, the music pleasing but very slender and insufficient, and it was moreover completely overwhelmed by the style of the work, the publicity, not to speak of the huge size of the orchestra for these few squeaks [*ces quelques pets*].[1] In the temple of the third act I was convinced that they were playing the music from *Les Petits Joyeux*. But at the very end, under the steady rays of the sun after the death of St. Sebastian, there is a beautiful joyous effect.' All the same, says Proust, 'it was a complete flop for both the poet and the musician . . .'.

One more opinion of this work, which contains the seed of many of the religious conflicts of later years, must be given, that of Charles Péguy. A warrior like d'Annunzio and a Christian too, he was, however, a much more ardent religious spirit than the spectacular Italian whom he nevertheless resembled in ferocity and ruthlessness. Perhaps it was this very resemblance which prompted Péguy to write with lurid undertones appropriate to the subject of St. Sebastian: 'The experience of twenty centuries has shown me that once the tooth of Christianity bites into the heart it never gives up the flesh of the heart. Thus I shall never again speak to your pagan soul. This tooth is like the fanged hook of a halberd, the bite of which cannot be reversed. It is a tooth which enters but which cannot be withdrawn. The bite is sharp-edged, starting at the outside and going right into the inside. . . . It is a barbed arrow which cannot relinquish its target, and it is thus that St. Sebastian is the protector of everyone in the world—except d'Annunzio.' The attack on d'Annunzio was fierce and unrelenting. Out of respect for Debussy, perhaps also from a feeling of regret that he had been associated with this doubtful Christian in this venture,[2] Péguy addressed to the musician of *Saint-Sébastien* shortly before the first

[1] If Proust was disappointed with the alleged meagreness of Debussy's score for *Saint-Sébastien*, the opulent Richard Strauss, it was rumoured in German and Italian papers, was now to write a score for a stage work of d'Annunzio. This was indeed nothing but a rumour. Yet one cannot help thinking that Strauss and d'Annunzio would have formed an harmonious partnership. The *Mondo Artistico* went so far as to state that Strauss had specified the subject required from d'Annunzio. It was 'The Night of a Courtesan in Montmartre'.

[2] In 1914 Debussy and d'Annunzio were hoping to collaborate on another stage work, seemingly on an Indian subject. Debussy left a few unpublished bars for a work entitled *Bouddha*.

performance of d'Annunzio's mystery play a collection of his own works bearing the laconic inscription:

A monsieur Claude Debussy
musicien,
Charles Péguy,
écrivain.

The association of Debussy with d'Annunzio was indeed strange, but this singular encounter with Péguy, the ardent Christian soldier, was stranger still. Péguy was in fact wrong about dissociating himself from the pagan spirit. *Saint-Sébastien* shows that in the turbulent unsettled spirit of those years and under the threat of impending war the pagan and the Christian had in fact, if only for a moment, formed an alliance and had become united.

10

Diaghilev and Stravinsky

Quand les cimes de notre ciel se rejoindront
Ma maison aura un toit.

Paul Eluard

The enthusiasm for Wagner in both literary and musical spheres was still being maintained in Paris at a high level, when another attempt at a synthesis of the arts was launched. Diaghilev's Russian ballet similarly proposed to unite the arts of painting, dancing, and music. Today we think of the æsthetic of the Russian ballet as opposed to that of the earlier Wagnerian movement, as having in fact been conceived as a reaction to it. This was not at all the view of Diaghilev's early contemporaries. Critics in the years preceding the first World War were quick to see a resemblance between the aims of the Symbolist movements, which had evolved under the influence of Wagner, and those of Diaghilev. Looking back now on the many cross-currents in the arts at this period one can see a similar assault on the senses. In his study 'Karsavina et Mallarmé' Camille Mauclair went farther. He showed how the Wagnerian ideals which first took root in the world of drama at the Théâtre d'Art of Lugné-Poe were eventually to find their complete expression in the Diaghilev Ballet.[1]

Debussy first became acquainted with Diaghilev in 1909, that

---

[1] 'Le culte de Wagner nous avait révélé la fusion des arts', Mauclair writes in this study. 'Nous façonnions avec une ingénuité de pauvres la grossière idole qu'embellissaient nos illusions. Cette idole est devenue la déesse rayonnante du ballet russe: le bouquet de génie composé par Léon Bakst, Alexandre Benois, Michel Fokine, Nijinsky et Tamara Karsavina, c'est sur l'humble autel de notre symbolisme de jeunesse qu'il se pose.'

[168]

is in the year of Diaghilev's first Paris season. In May and June of that year Diaghilev presented at the Théâtre du Châtelet five rather conventional ballets with choreography by Fokine. Though his later productions, particularly those in which he was associated with Stravinsky and Picasso, were indeed revolutionary Diaghilev's early reputation in Paris was that of an organizer of exhibitions, concerts, and ballets sponsored by prominent society figures and calculated to make their full effect in fashionable circles.[1]

The first project entertained by Debussy and Diaghilev was a Venetian ballet, *Masques et Bergamasques*, with a scenario by Louis Laloy. Debussy was Diaghilev's first choice among the composers in Paris who co-operated with him, and *Masques et Bergamasques* was to have been the first of Diaghilev's French ballets. Curiously enough Debussy, usually dilatory in the fulfilment of commissions, was on this occasion over-enthusiastic to the extent of finding himself in the odd position of having to apologize to his collaborator for having, in an impulsive moment, written the scenario himself. At any rate this is the explanation given by Debussy himself. 'I humbly confess', he wrote to Laloy, 'that I was prompted and impelled to act so suddenly by what I recognize to be an unfortunate character trait of mine: a sudden burst of enthusiasm which soon gives way to an unpleasant return to the starting-point.'[2] Debts or other financial considerations no doubt helped to motivate this unilateral decision; and indeed before this decision was announced to Laloy, Debussy had told his publisher that he was looking forward to the advance on royalties on delivery of the piano score. Plans were apparently well advanced for the production of the ballet in Rome and Moscow as well as in Paris, and Nijinsky and Karsavina were to take the principal parts. 'I shall not expect

[1] Diaghilev first became known in Paris in 1906 when he organized an exhibition of Russian paintings at the Salon d'Automne under the patronage of the Comtesse de Greffühle. Not surprisingly the works of Bakst, Benois, Larionov, and Roerich made little impression, and Paul Jamot in the *Gazette des Beaux-Arts* noted that they contrasted sadly with the standards of English and French painting. In the musical sphere Diaghilev's early efforts were more successful. The following year he organized the series of concerts of Russian music conducted by Nikisch and others, and in 1908 triumphantly presented Chaliapin in *Boris Godounov*.

[2] Embarrassed at being obliged to give this explanation, Debussy tells Laloy in this letter that he is keeping a warm place in his heart for their project of a work based on the *Oresteia* of Aeschylus: 'We shall be our own masters, we shall have all the time we need, and we shall not allow ourselves to be worried either by the Russians or by our publishers.' No further mention is made of this most ambitious scheme. A summary of Debussy's scenario for *Masques et Bergamasques* appears in Appendix C.

the legs of Nijinsky to express symbols of one kind or another, nor the smile of Karsavina to explain the doctrine of Kant', Debussy flauntingly wrote to Laloy in reference to the pretentious theories that were at this time being bandied about on the ballet. He had foreseen *Masques et Bergamasques* as a light work in the form of a divertimento similar in character to his sketches for *Le Diable dans le Beffroi* and to the scenario for Stravinsky's *Pulcinella*. But not a note of the score was written.

The reason was surely that Debussy and Diaghilev were each, in their different ways, too imaginative and egocentric to allow any kind of co-operation between them. Soon after Diaghilev's first Paris season a rupture occurred with Debussy that was never to be completely healed. In August 1909, when the scheme for *Masques et Bergamasques* was abruptly brushed aside, Debussy wrote bitterly to Laloy. 'Kipling maintained that the Russian is a charming fellow until he tucks in his shirt. The Russian whom we both know imagines that the best way to deal with his fellow men is first of all to lie to them. This perhaps requires more talent than I possess, and in any case in friendship I have no desire to play any game of this kind. The essential point is that between ourselves there should be no misunderstanding and that we place ourselves above Diaghilev together with his treacherous Cossack regiment.'[1]

Diaghilev next conceived a ballet on Debussy's score of *L'Après-midi d'un faune*. According to Serge Grigoriev, Diaghilev was influenced in his conception of this ballet by the Swiss composer Emile Jaques-Dalcroze. Diaghilev had met Dalcroze about 1911 and became greatly interested in his theories of musical training through rhythm, known as Eurhythmics. It is curious that this purely educational system of inculcating a sense of rhythm should have had such a far-reaching influence on Diaghilev's ideas. In fact, the adventurous Russian impresario was to remain strongly drawn to this rather dry Swiss pedagogue until the war years. In 1912 when the Russian ballet visited Dresden Diaghilev renewed his acquaintance with Dalcroze at his school at Hellerau and arranged

[1] In later years Debussy's attitude to Diaghilev was less hostile. His correspondence with Diaghilev, in the possession of Serge Lifar, includes a letter of 20 May 1917, written after the production in Paris of Satie's *Parade*. Referring to a line in Mallarmé's *L'Après-midi d'un faune*, he writes: 'Il faut que vous sachiez ma joie d'avoir retrouvé la beauté particulière des ballets russes: "C'est du rêve ancien qui recommence", et c'est très mélancolique parce que trop d'horreurs ont bouleversé ma vie.'

for his famous protégé Nijinsky to pay daily visits there in order that he should apply the methods of Dalcroze to the choreography of *L'Après-midi d'un faune*. This was the first ballet for which Nijinsky devised the choreography and it was intended that the application on the stage of the theories of Dalcroze should help to evoke something of the pagan character of the work. Alas, this over-bold ballet of Nijinsky was an unfortunate failure. 'The choreography was not choreography as we understood the term', writes Gregoriev of Nijinsky's efforts. 'The dancers merely moved rhythmically to the music and then stopped in attitudes, which they held. Nijinsky's aim was, as it were, to set in motion an archaic Greek bas-relief, and to produce this effect he made the dancers move with bent knees and feet placed flat on the ground heel first (thereby reversing the classical rule). They had also to keep their heads in profile while still making their bodies face the audience, and to hold their arms rigid in various angular positions.'

We are concerned here with an obscure episode in the history of the Diaghilev ballet though it has a considerable bearing on Debussy's own ideas of the ballet. Debussy's consent for the use of his score of *L'Après-midi d'un faune* for a ballet production was given unwillingly and his co-operation was not in any way sought, either by Diaghilev or Nijinsky. It is known that he attended the dress rehearsal where it appears that he viewed the arbitrary nature of Nijinsky's choreography with distaste. So much we gather from his enraged comment on Nijinsky's personification of the faun: 'Vous êtes laid, allez-vous-en!' The extent to which Dalcroze's theories were incorporated in the frieze-like choreography of *L'Après-midi d'un faune* is difficult to ascertain,[1] but there is no doubt that in *Jeux*, the succeeding ballet of Debussy for which Nijinsky devised the choreography, the Dalcrozian recommendations for the movements of arms and feet were strictly adhered to. In his authoritative account of the Jaques-Dalcroze method Percy B. Ingham shows how movements of arms and feet were somewhat artificially co-ordinated: 'Time is shown by movements of the arms, and time-values, i.e. note-duration, by movements of the feet and body. In

---

[1] Probably not to a great extent since Dalcroze himself was censorious of Nijinsky's production. 'What shocked me', he writes, 'was the lack of connexion, of sequence in the attitudes, the absence of that continued movement which should be noticeable in every expression of life animated by continued thought' (quoted in *The Eurhythmics of Jaques-Dalcroze* by J. W. Harvey, London, 1917).

the early stages of the training this principle is clearly observed. Later it may be varied in many ingenious ways, for instance, in what is known as plastic counterpoint, where the actual notes played are represented by movements of the arms, while the counterpoint in crotchets, quavers or semiquavers, is given by the feet.'

Whatever the educational value of this theory, it was obviously madness to attempt to apply it to the choreography of ballet. Understandably, the Dalcrozian theories were condemned by Debussy in the strongest terms. Writing to Godet in June 1913, shortly after seeing Nijinsky's choreography for *Jeux*, he deplores the fact that Nijinsky 'has given an odd mathematical twist to his perverse genius'. 'This fellow adds up demi-semi-quavers with his feet,' he graphically reports, 'proves the result with his arms and then, as if suddenly struck with paralysis of one side, listens for a while to the music disapprovingly. This, it appears, is to be called "the stylisation of gesture". How awful! It is in fact Dalcrozian, and this is to tell you that I hold Monsieur Dalcroze to be one of the worst enemies of music! You can imagine what havoc his method has caused in the soul of this wild young Nijinsky!'[1]

Though the choreography of *L'Après-midi* was severely criticized the ballet nevertheless enjoyed the doubtful reputation of a *succès de scandale*. Indeed, the first performance of this ballet, which had at last exteriorized Mallarmé's erotic theme, initiated the series of riots associated with Diaghilev's productions, the most notorious of which was that provoked by *Le Sacre du Printemps* the following year. The music of *L'Après-midi d'un faune* was of course by this time well known and there was no question of any hostility to the composer. The trouble arose from the fact that in the representation of Mallarmé's poem a moral issue was raised. At the end of the ballet the faun, in a far-fetched interpretation, reclines on the veil of one of the nymphs in a gesture of amorous ecstasy. No doubt the significance of this gesture was exaggerated for it seems incredible that frequenters of the ballet in Paris should have been shocked by such a harmless symbolical act. However this may be, half of the

[1] Dalcroze's unfortunate influence on the Russian ballet continued until the period of Stravinsky's *Les Noces*. The calamitous choreography of Nijinsky for *Le Sacre du Printemps* was similarly inspired by the theories of Dalcroze. In the course of rehearsals for this work Diaghilev appealed to Dalcroze for help from one of his pupils. Stravinsky had himself met Dalcroze, and Diaghilev mentions a project of Dalcroze in a letter to Stravinsky written as late as 1915.

audience angrily protested while the other half gleefully applauded. Diaghilev quickly saw his advantage and seized on this divided manifestation to order a repeat performance.

The ensuing controversy in the press has frequently been described. Nijinsky's principal supporters were the aged sculptor Auguste Rodin and Debussy's friend Odilon Redon, who had felt unable to accept Diaghilev's invitation to undertake the décor. Rodin's long article in *Le Matin* in praise of Nijinsky's work brought reiterated counter-attacks providing the ballet with the type of crude publicity which Debussy, as a disciple of Mallarmé, must have abhorred. 'The spirit of Mallarmé is among us this evening', Redon told Diaghilev at the first performance. His spirit must surely have withered in the limelight in which, subsequently, it was so mercilessly held. Debussy, who was ultimately at the root of this controversy, took no part in it. Only when *Jeux* was given the following year was he persuaded to publish his opinion of Nijinsky. Defining the limitations of Nijinsky's art, Debussy's article, which also appeared in *Le Matin*, forms a sober contrast to the panegyric of Rodin.[1]

The circumstances which led to the commission by Diaghilev of the ballet *Jeux* appear in the memoirs of Jacques-Emile Blanche and in the *Diary* of Nijinsky. Snatches of conversation and of letters are set out in both these publications with many overtones of gossip and scandal, and without corroborative evidence one is reluctant to accept them as authentic. Nevertheless, with our knowledge of the complexity of Debussy's material and emotional problems at this period[2] and in view also of the fact that, though written independently, the accounts of Blanche and Nijinsky largely coincide, we are at any rate required to assess them from an unprejudiced viewpoint. In his *Portraits of a Lifetime* Jacques-Emile Blanche says that the idea of *Jeux* was proposed by Nijinsky in the course of a luncheon with Diaghilev and Bakst on an unspecified date at the

[1] Nijinsky, whose knowledge of French was rudimentary, had in fact never heard of Mallarmé's poem. It is doubtful whether one can trust more than a fraction of the salacious gossip which appears in his published *Diary* on the origin of his two ballets on the scores of Debussy. The articles on Nijinsky by Rodin and Debussy appear in Appendix C.

[2] On 13 January 1912 he writes to Durand: 'Je suis dans la fièvre de trouver tout ce qui me manque et dans l'angoisse de finir n'importe quoi à tout prix.' In the course of the year it became a matter of great urgency for him to borrow at short notice twenty thousand francs. A few months later, on 18 January 1913, he tells Godet, 'Je suis hanté par le Médiocre et j'ai peur.'

Savoy Hotel in London. Nijinsky sketched out on the tablecloth designs for a ballet scenario for which Debussy was to write the music. 'There should be no *corps de ballet*,' Blanche was told, 'no ensembles, no variations, no *pas de deux*, only boys and girls in flannels and rhythmic movements. A group at a certain stage was to depict a fountain, and a game of tennis was to be interrupted by the crashing of an aeroplane.' Blanche naturally declared this to be a most childish idea. But he was nevertheless required to wire the scheme to Debussy who, according to the same account, replied: 'No, it's idiotic and unmusical. I should not dream of writing a score for this work.' Following a discussion between the Russians and Blanche, Debussy was sent a second wire stating that 'his fee was to be doubled'.[1]

Whatever the fee finally paid to Debussy this purely financial consideration was apparently the deciding factor in his accepting Diaghilev's commission. He was surely not attracted to this trivial subject. Even Nijinsky, who was eventually persuaded to eliminate the absurd aeroplane episode, became disillusioned with the subject of his scenario. Yet he, too, makes it clear that Debussy was lured into the scheme by the high figure Diaghilev was prepared to offer. Describing the homosexual aspects of the scenario in terms of his attachment to Diaghilev, Nijinsky, writing in 1918, says, 'I wanted people to feel as disgusted with the idea of evil love as I did, but I could not finish the ballet [presumably meaning that he could not finish it in the way he wished it to be concluded]. Debussy did not like the subject either, but he was paid ten thousand gold francs for this ballet and therefore had to finish it.'

He did not, however, enter into the contract unwillingly. Once the decision was made Debussy wrote the complicated score of *Jeux* at great speed, seemingly within the first three weeks of August 1912. (The manuscript bears a series of dates, marking its conclusion, from 23 August to 2 September 1912; there is no

[1] J. E. Blanche gives a different version, emphasizing the cynical attitude of Diaghilev, in *La Pêche aux Souvenirs* (1949). This version cannot be valid since there is a hopeless confusion of dates. Debussy was married to Madame Bardac in 1908, three years before the conversation he reports could have taken place: '"Debussy has not yet married Mme Bardac", Diaghilev exclaimed. "He will not have the millions of Osiris until later. The five hundred thousand francs which Durand will pay him for the score and the two thousand pounds which I will add will bring his decision." Debussy replied by telegram saying, "The subject of *Jeux* is idiotic. Cannot be done. Propose another subject to Nijinsky".'

question of the work in his earlier correspondence of this year.) At the end of July 1912 he apologized to Robert Godet for his long silence, due, he says, to a period of severe depression: 'I have had to grapple with one of these too frequent crises in which I fall into a vacuum of stupidity; I then devour the best part of my energy fighting and destroying myself. It is a ridiculous and also a dangerous game in which one becomes depressed as after a bout of drunkenness.' Three weeks later, on 25 August, he tells André Caplet that despite his impecunious state the composition of *Jeux*, probably the final draft, is completed. 'How was I able to forget the cares of this world', he excitedly exclaims, 'and manage to write music that is nevertheless joyous and alive with droll rhythms? Nature, so absurdly harsh, sometimes takes pity, it seems, on her children.' And he goes on to point out that, as in certain effects in *Parsifal*, the texture of the orchestration will have to be 'illuminated as from behind'; or it must be almost aerial (*'un orchestre sans pied'*). To satisfy Diaghilev—'the Russians are like Persian cats', he tells Durand—the final pages were altered in order to convey 'a rather risqué situation'. Fine points of this kind, however, did not easily cross the footlights of the Russian Ballet. Moreover, the presentation of Nijinsky's choreography was not achieved without frequent quarrels with his partner Karsavina, who invariably failed to understand what Diaghilev's young favourite was driving at. On the first night, on 15 May 1913, which inaugurated the Russian Ballet season at the newly opened Théâtre des Champs-Elysées, Debussy became repelled by Nijinsky's choreography to the extent that before the performance was over he had left his box to smoke a cigarette at the night porter's lodge.

As a ballet *Jeux* had a poor reception and it was hardly more successful when it was given the following year in concert form, conducted by Gabriel Pierné. In a warm letter of thanks to Pierné, Debussy wondered whether the orchestra of the Concerts Colonne had shown any real feeling for the work. The performance, he maintained, lacked a sense of unity. 'A connecting link between the various episodes does exist,' he pointed out, 'a subtle link perhaps, but it is nevertheless there.'[1]

[1] This is one of the few occasions when Debussy refers to the form of his works. The thematic episodes in *Jeux* are analysed by Herbert Eimert in his penetrating study of the work which appeared in *Die Reihe*. Though it is difficult to subscribe to Eimert's interpretation of *Jeux* as illustrating 'Debussy's principle of endless variation' (Debussy

Jeux, performed exactly a fortnight before the historic first performance of *Le Sacre du Printemps*, marks the end of Debussy's association with Diaghilev. It had lasted merely a few years.[1] During this period the most remarkable productions of the Diaghilev company were the three ballets of Stravinsky, *L'Oiseau de feu* (Opéra, 1910), *Petrouchka* (Théâtre du Châtelet, 1911), and *Le Sacre du Printemps* (Théâtre des Champs-Elysées, 1913). Debussy had in the meantime formed a close friendship with Stravinsky, his junior by twenty years, based on certain musical ideas which they shared and also on the fact that they were both sought after by Diaghilev, as indeed was Ravel, whose *Daphnis et Chloé* was given shortly after Nijinsky's ballet on *L'Après-midi d'un faune*, in 1912. Debussy's artistic and personal relationship with Stravinsky is one of the most important matters we have to deal with in his later years, but before investigating the nature of this relationship we must take into account the ideas that Debussy himself had formed of the ballet.

They did not always coincide with those of Diaghilev, still less with those of Stravinsky. While watching a music-hall ballet at the Empire Music Hall in London in 1903, Debussy had allowed his thoughts to wander on the nature of an ideal ballet. Conventional ideas on choreography or mime were to be distrusted: 'The action must never be defined except by the mysterious symbolism inherent in the movements of the danseuse or the rhythm of her body.' Emotional intensity should be conveyed in a purely physical manner: 'Love or hate can be more effectively expressed in the agitated movements of a dancer's feet than by conventional gestures.' Especially significant are Debussy's ideas on the scenery of the ballet. 'A dreamy imprecision [*l'imprécision rêveuse*]' is desirable 'with changing effects of lighting rather than clear-cut lines'. These changing effects of lighting, recalling the methods of the Impressionist painters, were used to great effect by Loïe Fuller who, in May 1913, presented at the Théâtre des Champs-Elysées

---

abhorred the variation form; 'c'est un moyen de faire beaucoup avec très peu', he caustically remarked) the writer clearly defines twenty-three different motifs or themes announced in the course of the fifteen-minute work which, as Debussy maintained, are subtly inter-related.

[1] Diaghilev was to give only one more season in Paris before the first World War, in May 1914 when he presented Stravinsky's *Nightingale* at the Opéra. After this Debussy saw the Diaghilev ballet once again, in 1917, on its single visit to Paris during the war. Debussy's letter quoted on page 170 was written on this occasion.

choreographic versions of two movements from Debussy's *Noc-turnes*.[1] In 1912 Diaghilev had himself planned to present a choreographic version of *Fêtes*, but it did not materialize, possibly because the tendency towards mime in the Russian Ballet, encouraged by Stravinsky in *Petrouchka*, was beginning to underline a serious divergence between Debussy and Diaghilev. An idea of the ballet he wished to write was firmly established, however, in Debussy's mind, though, like several other of his most cherished projects, it was not realized. Confided to Jacques-Emile Blanche, this scheme was a most revolutionary conception. 'He spoke to me insistently', Blanche writes, 'of a rather nebulous project and even begged me to supply him with a sketch for it. He imagined a cosmogonical drama without words or action in which the singers, consisting of a chorus and soloists and who would be invisible, would utter onomatopoeic sounds whilst the stage would come to life by the play of light effects. The performers, forming part of the scenery, were to represent symbolical forms of clouds, of winds and of the sea.'[2]

On another plane Debussy was interested in a children's ballet, *La Boîte à joujoux*, the scenario of which was devised by André Hellé, a painter who specialized in children's books and who later supplied the imaginative cover for Ravel's *L'Enfant et les Sortilèges*. Hellé had come to an agreement for this ballet with Debussy in 1913, before the production of *Jeux*, and by October of the same year the piano score of the work was completed. The orchestral score, sketched out in view of a production by April of the following

[1] See the references to the connexions between the art of Loïe Fuller and the Art Nouveau in Vol. I, pp. 117 and 224. In *La Danse au Théâtre* (1924) André Levinson describes the combined effects of light and veils used by Loïe Fuller in her famous Serpentine Dance in a manner which suggests an entirely abstract art: 'Les légers tissus qu'elle manie s'incurvent en spirales, en volutes, en trombes. . . . C'est la lumière encore qui, réverbérée par le verre, sature cette envolée frémissante de voiles d'une vie colorée, insaisissable et passionante.' In a letter of 5 May 1913 (not 1909 as it appears in the published edition) Debussy invites André Caplet to see her: 'If you have nothing else to do come to the Théâtre des Champs-Elysées this evening. You will see your old friend Loïe Fuller in her exercises.'

[2] The idea for this ballet, apparently may have the origin of the universe, may have originated from Debussy's knowledge of Poe's *Eureka*, rightly described by Valéry as a *poème cosmogénique moderne*. This 'essay on the material and spiritual universe', as Poe describes it, 'dedicated to those who feel rather than to those who think', puts forward many imaginative theories of astronomy, particularly in regard to the origin and formation of the Milky Way. The repeated references to the stars Aldebaran and Sirius in Debussy's writings, in *M. Croche*, and in his letters to Stravinsky, Godet, Jean-Aubry, and Walter Rummel, show a persistent interest in astronomical matters, suggesting that the subject of this 'cosmogonical drama' long lingered in his mind.

year, was put aside during the war years. In November 1917, when a production was again proposed, Debussy reported that the orchestral score was 'nearing completion'. It was in fact completed by André Caplet after Debussy's death, and first produced at the Théâtre de Vaudeville on 10 December 1919.

This was a minor, unpretentious work aspiring to none of the sophistication of the children's opera of Ravel and Colette. It is a companion piece to the earlier suite *Children's Corner* of which there are several reminiscences, notably of the 'Golliwog's Cakewalk' in the music accompanying the entrance of an English soldier. Letters and other references make it clear, however, that *La Boîte à joujoux*, which some writers have persisted in comparing to *Petrouchka*, was thrown off as a musical work for a children's party. It is merely a 'pantomime', Debussy announced in 1914, 'on music which I have written for Christmas and New Year albums for children—a work to amuse children, nothing more'. Primarily intended for Debussy's daughter, Chouchou, the work has as its subject a triangular love-story among marionettes who inhabit a large old-fashioned toy-box.[1] Musical-box effects are introduced, also folk-songs, including 'Il pleut bergère'. Mendelssohn's Wedding March and themes from *Carmen* and *Faust* are good-humouredly guyed, and there is a miniature battle scene in which the ammunition of the warring punchinellos consists of nothing more dangerous than dried peas. 'I have tried to be clear and even amusing without any kind of pose', he told Durand. At first he thought the little work should be given as a marionette play. Later he agreed with Hellé that the characters should be played by children.

It is with this knowledge of Debussy's many abortive attempts to establish himself in the new world of the ballet that we must judge his reception of the three ballets of Stravinsky, who had

[1] The catalogue of the sale of Debussy's manuscripts (Andrieux, 1933, No. 193) contains music which he wrote on an English calendar depicting old-fashioned coaches and inns, probably in the style of the music of *La Boîte à joujoux*. Debussy remained closely attached to his daughter, of whom a portrait is outlined in Chapter 11. Two months after the completion of the piano score he wrote to her from St. Petersburg: 'Your poor father is sad indeed to be away for so many days from Chouchou, not to hear your songs and your laughter and all that noise which sometimes makes you an unbearable little person, but more often charming.' In 1915, on the eve of an operation, he tells his wife that she and Chouchou 'are the only two beings who should prevent me from disappearing altogether'. If he were not to survive 'continue to love me', he begs her, 'in our little Chouchou'.

[178]

rapidly been recognized in Paris in the immediate pre-war years as the most forward-looking and electrifying composer of his time. At first impressed, Debussy was later frankly overwhelmed by Stravinsky's genius. So much one gathers from his published letters to Stravinsky. His correspondence with other musicians presents another picture. We have also to take into account records of contemporaries and the letters from Stravinsky to Debussy which have so far remained unpublished.[1] It is not surprising that as their paths more frequently crossed elements of suspicion developed between the two composers. Recently published documents show that their admiration for each other was not as genuine as it seemed. Rivalry was inclined to distort their judgements. An uneasy ambivalence marked the relationship of the two composers on whom the public placed, in this turbulent period, their entire faith in the future of music.

Debussy first refers to Stravinsky in a letter to Durand of 8 July 1910 on *L'Oiseau de Feu*: 'It is not perfect but in many ways it is nevertheless very fine because music is not subservient to the dance, and it contains combinations of rhythm that are most unusual.' In the same letter he tells Durand that 'French dancers would never have agreed to dance to such music' and states with evident undertones of suspicion: 'So Diaghilev is a great man and Nijinsky is his prophet, unless it be Calvocoressi.' It was on this occasion that Diaghilev introduced the young Russian composer to Debussy. 'The great composer spoke kindly about the music,' Stravinsky recounts in his *Expositions and Developments*, 'ending his words with an invitation to dine with him. Some time later, when we were sitting together in his box at a performance of *Pelléas*, I asked him what he had really thought of *L'Oiseau de Feu*. He said: "Que voulez-vous, il fallait bien commencer par quelque chose." Honest, but not extremely flattering. Yet shortly after the première of *L'Oiseau de Feu* he gave me his well-known photograph in profile with a dedication: "A Igor Stravinsky en toute sympathie artistique." I was not so honest about the work we were then

---

[1] The Andrieux catalogue of Debussy's manuscripts and other possessions lists two letters and three postcards from Stravinsky. The text of one of these letters, dated 4 November 1911 from Clarens and written on receipt of a dedicated score, has been communicated to me but Mr Stravinsky has not authorized its publication. A lengthy e xtract from the second, dated 11 October 1915 from Morges, together with the text of one of the postcards, dated 13 December 1912 from Clarens, appear in the catalogue of the Collection Alfred Dupont (Nos. 276-7).

hearing. I thought *Pelléas* a great bore on the whole, in spite of many wonderful pages.'

In an earlier account of this episode, in his *Chronicle of my Life*, Stravinsky allows no suggestion of his derogatory opinion of *Pelléas*. Nor is there a suggestion of any but the most cordial feelings on the part of Stravinsky in the letter to Debussy of 4 November 1911 (referred to on p. 179, note 1). The following year, after the performance of *Petrouchka*, Debussy leaves no doubt of Stravinsky's stature. He writes to Godet of a young Russian musician living near him in Switzerland 'who has an instinctive genius for colour and rhythm'. Whatever may have been his reservations about *L'Oiseau de Feu* his enthusiasm is unbounded: 'I am sure that both he and his music will give you infinite pleasure. And what a mind he has! His music is full of feeling for the orchestra [*C'est fait en pleine pâte orchestrale*] conceived directly for the orchestral canvas and concerned only with conveying an emotional intensity. He is afraid of nothing nor is he pretentious. It is music that is child-like and untamed. Yet the layout and the co-ordination of ideas [*la mise en place*] is extremely delicate. If you have an opportunity of meeting him do not hesitate!' The same enthusiasm is freely expressed in a letter from Debussy to Stravinsky of April of the following year: 'Thanks to you I have passed an enjoyable Easter vacation in the company of Petrouchka, the terrible Moor and the delicious Ballerina. I can imagine that you spent incomparable moments with the three puppets. . . . I don't know many things of greater worth than the section you call "Tour de passe-passe" . . .'[1] There is in it a kind of sonorous magic, a mysterious transformation of mechanical souls which become human by a spell of which, until now, you seem to be the unique inventor. Finally there is an orchestral infallibility that I have found only in *Parsifal*. You will

[1] This is the scene in the first tableau where the showman, playing his flute in front of the marionette theatre, suddenly discloses the three puppets, Petrouchka, the Moor, and the Ballerina, and by a conjuring trick with his flute (*le tour de passe-passe*) brings them to life. (Full score of the 1912 edition: pp. 41–3.) The mysterious orchestration here foreshadows the tragedy of these human marionettes and produces a *frisson* not encountered elsewhere in Stravinsky's works. The writing in the opening bars for gruesome bassoons and double bassoon, leading to a texture woven of string harmonics, a feverish tremolando and celesta and harp figurations, is an example of what Debussy calls the extraordinary *mise en place* of Stravinsky's orchestration. After the nonchalant flute solo of the showman the strings take up the bassoon figure, which is now contrasted with a profusion of trills and grace-notes on the wood-wind. Trumpets and cornet finally chime in with reiterated *pp* notes to create one of the most moving effects in modern orchestration.

understand what I mean, of course. You will go much further than *Petrouchka*, it is certain, but you can be proud already of the achievement of this work.'[1]

Debussy's feelings about *Le Sacre du Printemps* were divided. A graphic description is given by Louis Laloy of the occasion when, shortly before the first performance, the two composers played the mighty, explosive work together in a piano arrangement at Laloy's home at Bellevue:

> One bright afternoon in the spring of 1913 I was walking about in my garden with Debussy; we were expecting Stravinsky. As soon as he saw us the Russian musician ran with his arms outstretched to embrace the French master who, over his shoulder, gave me an amused but compassionate look. He had brought an arrangement for four hands of his new work, *Le Sacre du Printemps*. Debussy agreed to play the bass. Stravinsky asked if he could take his collar off. His sight was not improved by his glasses, and pointing his nose to the keyboard and some-times humming a part that had been omitted from the arrange-ment, he led into a welter of sound the supple, agile hands of his friend. Debussy followed without a hitch and seemed to make light of the difficulty. When they had finished there was no question of embracing, nor even of compliments. We were dumbfounded, overwhelmed by this hurricane which had come from the depths of the ages and which had taken life by the roots.[2]

Debussy attended the rehearsal of *Le Sacre* in the spring and appears then to have formed reservations on the work. Writing to

[1] The translation of this and other extracts from Debussy's letters to Stravinsky is from *Conversations with Igor Stravinsky*, by Stravinsky and Robert Craft (London, 1959). A similar opinion of *Petrouchka* was given by Debussy to Jean-Aubry, but with undertones of something approaching alarm: 'You must hear this music, it's amazing. This wild young man has genius, and what a mind he has!' 'Several times', writes Aubry, 'he repeated to me the following phrase, clenching his teeth as he emphasized the adjective: "He has a *redoubtable* mind!"'

[2] The English edition of Stravinsky's memoirs has a letter to Stravinsky from Debussy dated 8 November 1913 in which he says: 'Our reading at the piano of *Le Sacre du Printemps* at Laloy's house is always present in my mind. It haunts me like a beautiful nightmare and I try, in vain, to reinvoke the terrific impression. That is why I wait for the stage performance like a greedy child impatient for promised sweets.' Stravinsky comments that 'Laloy incorrectly attributes [this reading] to the spring of 1913.' I think Laloy is correct. In the English edition this letter is surely incorrectly dated. Debussy could not have been looking forward in November to a stage per-formance of *Le Sacre* which had been given earlier in the year, in May. In the French edition the letter is undated.

André Caplet on the date of the first public performance he says, 'Le Sacre du Printemps is an extraordinarily savage affair. . . . If you like, it is primitive with every modern convenience.' It is certain that Debussy must have been greatly impressed by the explosiveness and the violence of Le Sacre. Shortly after the outbreak of war he confessed to Ernest Ansermet to being disturbed by this latest musical development. 'It seems to me that Stravinsky is trying to make music with non-musical means', he told him, 'in the same way as the Germans are now pretending to produce steak out of sawdust.' (This was a spurious means of overcoming the food shortage in Germany during the war.)

In the meantime further scores had been exchanged. In 1913 the score of Jeux was sent to Stravinsky and Stravinsky's cantata Le Roi des Etoiles, on words by the Russian Symbolist poet Constantine Balmont, was dedicated to Debussy. The acknowledgement reveals nothing of the enthusiasm for Petrouchka, nor even for Le Sacre du Printemps. A certain cautiousness, not to say a note of disparagement, creeps into the assessment of this work. 'The music for Le Roi des Etoiles is still extraordinary', Debussy writes. 'It is probably Plato's "harmony of the eternal spheres" (but don't ask me which page of his). And except on Sirius or Aldebaran I do not foresee performances of this "cantata for planets". As for our more modest Earth a performance would be lost in the abyss.' Le Roi des Etoiles has in fact remained one of the less often performed of Stravinsky's works. The score of Le Sacre, sent to Debussy later in the year, brought the following comment: 'For me, who descend the other slope of the hill but keep, however, an intense passion for music, it is a special satisfaction to tell you how much you have enlarged the boundaries of the permissible in the empire of sound.' And he adds: 'Forgive me for using these pompous words, but they exactly express my thought.' Music, he felt, was inevitably developing in a direction from which he felt estranged.

Here we may pause to consider certain aspects of Stravinsky's character and the nature of his musical ideas as they appeared to an unbiased observer shortly after Le Sacre. At the age of thirty-two Stravinsky was greatly affected by the outbreak of war. His nationalist feelings were powerfully aroused though he took no part in the war, spending most of his time in neutral countries,

chiefly Switzerland. Accounts of his meetings at Vevey and Inter-
laken during these years with Romain Rolland reveal a dominating,
ruthless personality. We read in Rolland's *Journal des années de
guerre* under the date 24 September 1914: 'Long visit of Igor
Stravinsky.' (The war had broken out the previous month and it
was just over a year since the first performance of *Le Sacre*.) 'We
spent three hours talking in the garden of the Hotel Mooser [at
Vevey]. Stravinsky is about thirty: short, puny-looking, ugly, a
yellowish face, thin and tired, a narrow forehead, his hair thin at the
top, the eyes behind his pince-nez wrinkled, a fleshy nose and thick
lips, the length of his face out of proportion with the size of his
forehead. He is very intelligent and simple in his manner; he speaks
fluently though he sometimes has to seek French words; and everything he says is original and carefully thought out, whether true
or not.'

The conversation first turned on political questions. It is perhaps
not surprising that Stravinsky at this time was acknowledging the
romantic attraction of force for its own sake. Stravinsky told
Rolland that Germany was not at all a barbaric state but a decrepit
and a degenerate state. He claimed for Russia 'the role of a fine,
healthy barbaric state, full of germinating ideas that will inspire
thought throughout the world'. He further told Rolland at this
early date that 'after the war a revolution, which is already being
prepared, will overthrow the dynasty and will lay the foundations
of the Slavonic United States'. His anti-German feelings in these
early days of the war were particularly violent: 'The attitude of the
German intellectuals provokes from him the most profound
contempt. Hauptmann and Strauss, he says, are nothing more than
lackeys. He praises the older Russian civilization, not known in the
West, and the artistic and literary achievements of the Russian towns
of the North and the East.'

Rolland gave Stravinsky his impressions of a concert performance of *Le Sacre du Printemps* and referred also to the disparity,
at a stage performance, between the musical ideas and the plastic
expression of them. 'He agrees that a modern theatrical presentation
of such a work must diminish the appeal of the music and also
narrow its emotional content. However, he is in favour of movement on the stage (a form of rhythmic gymnastics more artistic
than those of Dalcroze) but conceived on broad animated lines.

Scenery and costumes that are too sumptuous or too original will detract from the appeal of the music. The painter, in his view, is an enemy of the musician. The Wagnerian dream of a complete work of art in which all the arts are associated is false, he says. Where music exists it must reign! One cannot serve two masters. Colour is to be suppressed! Colour makes too powerful an appeal. It is a realm to itself, a music of its own. "Speaking for myself", says Stravinsky, "colour is an inspiration to me when writing music. But when it is written, the music is self-sufficient; it is its own colour."' Borrowing a terminology often used by Debussy, he suggested that in music one should 'think only of light (which should be used in a more varied manner than it has been and which should follow the modulations of sound), of gestures and of rhythm'.

Directly after *Le Sacre* Stravinsky began to write a suite of tiny pieces for orchestra and a single voice. They were called *Dicts*, says Rolland, 'a form of very old Russian popular poetry, consisting of a succession of words which have almost no sense and which are connected by associations of images and sounds'. These must be the *Pribaoutki* of 1914. What Stravinsky finds amusing, Rolland observes, 'is to make sudden contrasts in music between the portrayal of one subject and another completely different and unexpected subject'. Also, 'he must write every day whether he is inspired or not'. Nothing, however, is comparable to the joy of the first conception of an idea, described by Stravinsky as 'almost a sadistic pleasure'.

On music and musicians his judgements are decisive and implacable. Still drawing on the memoirs of Rolland, we discover that at this time Stravinsky 'cares for almost none of the established masters, including J. S. Bach and Beethoven'. On the other hand, he is fond of Mozart and, among the Germans [for he considers Mozart more than half Italian], he loves Weber, whose style is Italian through and through. Among his compatriots he esteems only Moussorgsky. He tells Rolland that 'in art, as in all things, he loves only the spring, the new life'. Periods of maturity in art displease him 'for they mark the beginning of a decline'.

Two years later Stravinsky still considers the war a salutary experience which 'with the help of God will eliminate the weak and preserve the strong'.[1] From Morges he wrote to Debussy in a letter of 11 October 1915 that certain current events were coldly calculated by the Germans to undermine people's morale. His own morale would not be affected, he insisted, nor, he hoped, would that of his friend. Debussy did not quite share these sentiments. 'There is something higher than brute force', he replies. 'To close the windows on beauty is against reason and destroys the true meaning of life.' When the noise of cannon has subsided, he points out, 'one must open one's eyes and ears to other sounds. The world must be rid of this bad seed. We have all to kill the microbes of false grandeur, or organized ugliness, which we did not always realize was simply weakness. You will be needed in the war against those other, and just as mortal, gases for which there are no masks.' In those words may be seen a compassionate quality conspicuously lacking in the character of Debussy's young Russian friend settled in Switzerland. 'Dear Stravinsky, you are a great artist', he nevertheless unequivocally states. 'Be with all your strength a great Russian artist.' There can be no doubt of the sincerity of this adjuration. Yet about three months earlier, on 14 October 1915, Debussy had written to Godet: 'Just now we may wonder into whose arms music may fall. The young Russian school offers us hers. But in my opinion they have become as un-Russian as possible. Stravinsky himself is dangerously leaning in the direction of Schoenberg,[2] but nevertheless remains the most wonderful orchestral technician of our time.'

After their first meeting since the outbreak of the war, at about the beginning of 1916, Debussy seems to have been noticeably disillusioned. In the summer of the previous year Debussy had

---

[1] 'Why is he not engaged in it?' asks Rolland in all amazement. 'Stravinsky is intelligent and alive', he further comments, 'but within the beam of his lighthouse; a trenchant beam of light, and beyond, complete darkness. In these times of intellectual unilateralism he is the most unilateral of all.'

[2] Debussy was no doubt thinking of Stravinsky's *Trois Poésies de la lyrique japonaise* (1913). Referring to this work in his *Expositions and Developments* Stravinsky says: 'The great event in my life then was the performance of *Pierrot Lunaire* I had heard in December 1912 in Berlin. Ravel was quickly contaminated with my enthusiasm for *Pierrot*, too, whereas Debussy, when I told him about it, merely stared at me and said nothing. Is this why Debussy later wrote his friend Godet that "Stravinsky is inclining dangerously *du côté de Schoenberg*"?' In his earlier *Chronicle of My Life* Stravinsky gives a rather different account of this Berlin performance of *Pierrot Lunaire*: 'I did not feel the slightest enthusiasm about the aesthetics of the work which appeared to me to be a retrogression to the out-of-date Beardsley cult.' In these earlier and probably more reliable memoirs Stravinsky merely stated of Schoenberg's score that 'the merits of the instrumentation are beyond dispute'.

completed his pieces for two pianos, *En blanc et noir*, the third of which he later dedicated to Stravinsky. But the old enthusiasm has gone. A distrustful, perhaps a cynical note is heard. On 4 January 1916 he writes to Godet: 'I have recently seen Stravinsky. He says, my *Oiseau de Feu*, my *Sacre*, just as a child says "My toy, my hoop." And that is exactly what he is—a spoilt child who sometimes cocks a snook at music. He is also a young barbarian who wears flashy ties and treads on women's toes as he kisses their hands. When he is old he will be unbearable, that is to say he will admit no other music [*il ne supportera aucune musique*], but for the moment he is unbelievable. He professes a friendship for me because I have helped him to mount a rung of the ladder from which he launches his squibs, not all of which explode. But once again, he is unbelievable! You have really understood him and, even better than I, have been able to understand the unrelenting workings of his mind [*son dur mécanisme*].'

Rivalry between Debussy and Stravinsky no doubt motivated or distorted the judgements they expressed of each other, but in any assessment of the æsthetic problems which to some extent they shared this matter of personal pique or resentment is not the main consideration.[1] We must brush this personal matter aside for we are primarily concerned here with the achievements of two giants on whom, as it seemed at that time, the whole future of music depended. Whatever confidential remarks were made to one or other of Debussy's friends it is certain that of all his contemporaries Stravinsky, at any rate from 1911 onwards, made the deepest impression on him. Stravinsky, similarly, was the one composer of that time who was aware of the far-reaching significance of Debussy's æsthetic and technical conquests. For a time, therefore, they were happy to travel together, and points of resemblance in their works are clear enough. Stravinsky's influence is noticeable in *Jeux*, while that of Debussy is to be seen principally in the two Verlaine songs (1910) of Stravinsky, the Prelude to the second part of *Le Sacre*, and the Prelude to *The Nightingale*.[2]

[1] In his *Conversations* Stravinsky writes: 'After reading [Debussy's] friendly and commendatory letters to me I was puzzled to find quite a different feeling concerning my music in some of his letters to his musical friends of the same period. Was it duplicity, or was he annoyed at his incapacity to digest the music of the *Sacre* when the younger generation enthusiastically voted for it? This is difficult to judge now at a distance of more than forty years.'

[2] The two works of Stravinsky dedicated to Debussy, *Zvezdoliki* (*Le Roi des Etoiles*)

There was an harmonious partnership between the two composers, but there was also a serious parting of the ways. Where did this difference arise? Plunged into the wider cosmopolitan world of music, both composers were committed to something more than explorations of their particular musical minds. Both were caught up in the new spirit that had broken through, straining to bring into a single vision an almost universal conception of music. By his use of exotic scales, among them the pentatonic and the whole-tone, Debussy enlarged the musical horizon to embrace the civilizations of the Orient. He also used the Gregorian modes and an aspect of his work thus reaches back into the Middle Ages. On the other hand, in his conception of harmony he challenged the orthodox distinctions between consonance and dissonance and his harmonic experiments thus became the basis of many new developments. On yet another plane he expressed the quintessential sensibility of the generation before the first World War, yet his later works were to look forward to the neo-classical manner of the post-war period. He was thus, at the most acute crisis of our musical civilization, a Janus-headed figure facing both the remote past which he was able to infuse with new life, and the stylistic eclecticism of later generations, an eclecticism unsure of itself yet kept alive by a spirit of constant experiment.

Stravinsky similarly became a Janus-headed figure of this kind. Little by little in his later years almost the whole history of western music was reviewed and re-interpreted in his work until in the end his very identity becomes challenged. One province, however, was to remain closed to him, the province of the revolutionary dream symbols, and of the deeper layers of the unconscious explored by Wagner in *Parsifal*, by Proust in *A la Recherche du temps perdu*, and by their precursors Poe and Baudelaire. This dream-world, from which Stravinsky excluded himself, was Debussy's stronghold. It was the world of Debussy's projected 'cosmogonical drama', and the greatest musical achievement in this sphere was the allegory of *Parsifal*. 'Je pense à cette couleur orchestrale qui semble éclairée par derrière et dont il y a de si merveilleux effets dans *Parsifal*', Debussy wrote of his final orchestral work *Jeux*. The passage which particularly appealed to him in *Petrouchka* likewise reminded him—

and the Symphony for Wind Instruments, are discussed by Robert Craft in *Avec Stravinsky* (1958).

though Stravinsky could not have been delighted by the comparison —of the ethereal orchestration of *Parsifal*.[1] It is clear that Debussy believed that music was to be kept alive by some kind of allegiance to Wagner, however hidden. Stravinsky did not. Any form of Wagnerian inspiration was to remain his declared anathema, and the ambiguous dream-world, that other world in which is buried all the pleasure in the beauty of things, became almost a bogy to him.

[1] In his *Chronicle of my Life* Stravinsky describes a performance of *Parsifal* which he heard at Bayreuth in the company of Diaghilev at the time he was writing *Le Sacre du Printemps:* 'I sat humble and motionless, but at the end of a quarter of an hour I could not bear any more. . . . I withdrew into myself, but I could think of only one thing, and that was the end of the act which would put an end to my martyrdom. . . . I managed to bear the second act. Then there were more sausages, more beer, another trumpet-blast, another period of contemplation, another act—Finis!'

I I

Portraits

Ce portrait qui n'est pas ressemblant
Qui fait roux tes cheveux noirs plutôt,
Qui fait rose ton teint brun plutôt,
Ce pastel, comme il est ressemblant!
Car il peint la beauté de ton âme . . .

Verlaine

At this point we may stop to consider some of the personal aspects of Debussy's character. The life of a creative musician takes place in the depths of his unconscious mind, and he alone can plunge into these depths. Paradoxes and other contradictory situations confront the investigator here, and although we cannot know all the inner workings of an artist's imaginative mind we may at any rate discover what it is that makes it function.

What is immediately striking in Debussy's character is not so much his sense of paradox. Contradictory in his actions and in his pronouncements he may have been, and even at loggerheads with himself. But there is something more than paradox here. Many artists, particularly those belonging to sophisticated eras, tend to replace a sustained flow of inspiration by a sense of paradox, branching out into teasing forms of deception or tantalizing riddles. In the work of such artists feeling has apparently lost its intensity; a clever mind takes over and for the time being diversion is supplied by an activity, in art, of the intellect. The emotional responses of Debussy did not diminish with advancing years; he was divided in his allegiances and found himself increasingly obliged to sacrifice time and energy to fulfilling lucrative commissions. But the underlying strength of his inspiration remained unimpaired to the end.[1] We should therefore not be justified in ascribing his many baffling and contradictory statements both on works of music and the character or behaviour of his friends to a love of paradox. We are concerned here with a deeper matter: the nature of his ambivalent character and the circumstances by which this ambivalence was maintained and even accentuated.

André Schaeffner came near to defining this problem when he pointed out that we still seem to be far from knowing what Debussy really felt about any of his contemporaries.[2] Moreover, as memoirs and other documents accumulate more, not less confusion is created, or so it seems at first sight. The mercurial nature of his opinions on Russian music, noted by his fiancée Catherine Stevens and quoted in Chapter 3, is typical. His panegyric of 1901 on Moussorgsky in *La Revue blanche*, 'Never was a more refined sensibility conveyed by such simple means', is followed by what seems to be a condemnation of the Russian composer's methods when, in 1911, there was question of applying Moussorgsky's choral technique to *Le Diable dans le Beffroi* ('The patchwork of *Boris* does not meet my requirements'). The contradictory nature of Debussy's feelings in regard to Wagner is particularly bewildering, not only in the latter part of his life when, under the influence of Stravinsky, his attitude might have become understandably modified, but in his youth. During his stay in Rome, he proclaimed, 'I was a Wagnerian to my fingertips.' Yet two years later, in 1889, a letter to his former teacher Guiraud from Bayreuth begins: 'What catch-phrases are these *Leitmotive*! *The Ring* . . . is a work of effects; they even manage to take the colour out of my beloved *Tristan*, and it grieves me to see that I am breaking away from this work.'[3]

[1] The last of the piano Studies, *Pour les Accords*, with its widespread chords hammered out over the entire range of the keyboard, is one of Debussy's most elemental and powerful works.

[2] 'On his true tastes, as on the exact extent of his knowledge, one cannot be too cautious', Schaeffner writes; and he pertinently asks: 'How much fantasy or make-believe is added to the matters he writes about?'

[3] The contradictions in Debussy's early feelings about Wagner are admirably discussed in *La Passion de Claude Debussy* by Marcel Dietschy, who publishes for the first time the manuscript notes on Debussy and Wagner by Pierre Louÿs. These include an account of an attempt by Debussy to play the three acts of *Tristan* by heart which he undertook, unsuccessfully, for a wager of one hundred francs; and the many conflicting feelings aroused in his mind by *Parsifal*, *The Ring*, and *Tristan* during the composition of *Pelléas*. Debussy had apparently conceived an article, about 1890, entitled 'De l'Inutilité du Wagnérisme'. If it was written it was certainly never pub-

An evolution of ideas and even radical changes of opinion are of course bound to occur over the years. Also, the revelations to a musician of the temperament of Debussy of the virile forms of art of Wagner, Moussorgsky, and Stravinsky were bound to produce wide and sudden fluctuations of judgements if only because of the violence of their impact. The power of the impact fairly annihilated the sensitive receiving apparatus. The radically opposed ideas with which we are thus sometimes confronted in Debussy's pronouncements must therefore be seen as an expression of an inevitable ambivalence. Nor were these fluctuations due merely to external events. In varying degrees ambivalence marked every novel impression created on Debussy, in the personal as well as the artistic sphere. As a result constancy to an ideal or, its counterpart in the personal sphere, fidelity, was seldom attained. This does not mean that Debussy drifted aimlessly; it means that he claimed an unusual degree of freedom and independence. 'The sincerity of an artist', wrote Jean Bazaine in his *Notes sur la peinture d'aujourd'hui* (1948), 'consists in allowing himself to be led he knows not where.' This is admirable in principle but it comes about that the freedom of an artist of this outlook cannot be claimed without the birth of doubt in his mind—doubt which undermines confidence but which, paradoxically, is also the necessary condition to promote enquiry or exploration. The dilemma of Debussy is that he was condemned both to doubt the nature of the problems he had opened up and at the same time to seek new territories of exploration. A letter to André Caplet of 24 July 1909 freely recognizes this dilemma: 'There is no point in denying it: I am in the state of mind in which it would be better to be a sponge at the bottom of the sea or a Japanese vase on the mantelpiece, anything rather than a man of thought, that fragile piece of mechanism which only functions when it wishes to and against which the will of man is as nothing. Orders are given to someone who does not obey you, and this someone is yourself. Since one does not wish frankly to be called an idiot,

---

lished—fortunately, perhaps, in view of the statements of Louÿs regarding Debussy's persistent attachment to Wagner: 'During and after the composition of *Pelléas* he was attached particularly to *Parsifal*.' Yet 'when I tell him that the first scene of the third act of *Parsifal* is that which most resembles *Pelléas* he seems to be upset by this comparison'. Illustrating the manner in which he chaffed his friend, Louÿs adds: 'When speaking to Debussy of Wagner I used such exaggerated expressions that I provoked contradictions.'

one goes on creating illusions in an empty circle—like abandoned wooden horses at a merry-go-round without music and with no one to ride them. Perhaps this is the punishment reserved for those who are too much addicted to thinking or who persist in following a single idea: hence the *idée fixe*, which is a prologue to madness.'[1] A letter of three years earlier, to Laloy, reveals a state of utter frustration and despair, hinting also at a suicidal element: 'Fortunately no one has genius in our time, for this would be the most shameful and ridiculous thing to happen in the world.' In 1910 he tells Laloy: 'I am in a hateful state of mind, antagonistic to any kind of joy, unless it be that of increasingly destroying myself day by day.' During the latter years of Debussy's life thoughts of suicide became increasingly frequent.

The contradictory opinions of Debussy on his contemporaries which have recently come to light and which have caused some bewilderment among his more conventional critics include those on Stravinsky, Ravel, and Fauré among composers, on G. Jean-Aubry and M. D. Calvocoressi among critics, and on Maggie Teyte and Rose Féart among singers.[2] From one viewpoint it would seem that such remarks, though conflicting with opinions expressed elsewhere by Debussy, need not indicate any kind of duplicity: they may be held to indicate the many-sidedness of Debussy's powers of observation and also the capacity, when confronted by a multiplicity of impressions, frankly to admit their conflicting nature.

[1] Debussy was no doubt thinking of a form of obsessive madness glimpsed also by Poe and by Baudelaire. Like Debussy these writers were able ultimately to control an obsessive fury by the fact of their having given expression to their fears. Describing Roderick Usher's improvisations on his guitar, Poe writes: 'They were . . . the result of that intense mental collectedness and concentration . . . observable only in particular moments of the highest artificial excitement.' This excitement, Poe declares, allowed him to perceive in Usher, as he played on his guitar, 'the tottering of his lofty reason'. A letter of Baudelaire's to his mother discloses similar turmoils: 'I asked myself how it was that I who have always had, in my nerves and in my mind, all that is needed to become mad, have never become so. For this I thanked heaven.'

[2] Debussy's censorious remarks on Ravel and Stravinsky are given on pages 37 and 186. 'Fauré est le porte-musique d'une bande de snobs', he caustically declares in an unpublished letter. After writing amiable letters to Jean-Aubry he tells Caplet in 1909: 'Les Jean-Aubry ne me tourmentent plus; ce sont de pauvres petits moustiques, ennuyeux certes! mais avec un peu d'air froid l'on s'en débarrasse.' Debussy's opinion of Calvocoressi, following his support of Ravel, appears on page 38. A surprising opinion of Maggie Teyte was expressed in 1908. 'Miss M. Teyte continues to exhibit about as much emotion as a prison door. She is a more than distant princess.' But a few weeks earlier she was said by Debussy to 'possess a charming voice and a very accurate idea of Mélisande's character'. Rose Féart, whom Robert Godet declared to be Debussy's favourite singer, 'is unspeakably ugly and lacks poetry'.

But these heightened powers of observation made him increasingly cautious of the outside world. The account, given by Pierre Lasserre, of the extreme isolation to which he was driven, possessing in his humble home no scores or a library, indeed no musical creation except his piano,[1] contains also an anecdote on his musical views, no doubt apocryphal, but disclosing an element of truth: 'He admired almost nothing which had been achieved in his own art. . . . A person who had taken part with him reading the score of *The Magic Flute* at the piano told me that in this work he allowed himself to admire only two bars; and that these two bars were in different parts of the work.' When working on *La Chute de la Maison Usher* he told his publisher that he had almost completely retreated from the outside world.

Connected with the doubts and the ambivalence of his character, also with the fact that he was constantly turned in upon himself was Debussy's compulsion, under the guise of borrowing, to acquire money. More precisely, it was a compulsion to remain impecunious so that money must be demanded and supplied forthwith. An almost continuous state of crisis thus prevailed on both the material and emotional planes of his life, and it was only when this state of crisis was maintained that the creative spirit was nourished. The rare periods of financial ease were artistically sterile. Baudelaire sensed the nature of a similar dilemma when he wrote to his mother: 'I am not sure that anger begets talent; but supposing it did, I ought to have an enormous amount of talent, for I rarely work except between a quarrel and the bailiffs, the bailiffs and a quarrel.'

We are concerned here with the perpetuation, referred to in earlier chapters, of certain aspects of child-behaviour, particularly those aspects in which spontaneous, uninhibited responses to the senses are carried over into adult life where the mature artist is able to reconstruct and convey these responses in their full elemental force. Two inter-related conditions must be fulfilled when money is acquired in this way. It must gratify a sense of luxury; and it must be supplied immediately—not next week or when convenient. On the conscious plane an urgent necessity to settle debts may be real enough, but with people of this disposition the underlying, un-conscious purpose or motive of such debts is to recreate a situation

[1] See Vol. I, p. 168, note 2. This appears in the article 'Claude Debussy', published under the pseudonym Jean Darnaudat in *Action Française*, 1 August 1915.

in which the child, throwing a tantrum or resorting to some other type of hysterical appeal, cannot be refused gratification. Running through the poignant and perceptive letters of Baudelaire to his mother is the *Leitmotiv* of this same compulsion: 'Money, money,' he exclaims, 'that is the only part of your letter which relates to my own thoughts.' Or again: 'My dear Mother, Without any discussion I must have at all costs—at all costs—you understand—*at all costs—this very day*—the sum of two hundred francs.' Wagner, whose attitude to money was a reflection of this same compulsion, confronted his friends with similar critical situations. 'I must have money', he tells Theodor Apel, 'if I am not to go mad.' These are words which must be taken literally. Apel is 'the only one' to whom he can appeal. At a later period in Wagner's life, the period of *Tristan* in Munich when his style of living brought him to the verge of ruin—the walls and even the ceiling of his music room were covered with fine satins trimmed with lace and roses—during this period when, in order to live in the most extravagant luxury, he was obliged to borrow more and more furiously, he protested in all naïvety that he 'could not live like a dog'. In the same spirit of almost unbelievable bravado Baudelaire informs his mother that unless further funds are provided he will be obliged to live 'like a beast or a drowned rat'.

The letters of Debussy frequently contain anxious demands of this kind. Louÿs, Hartmann, Laloy, Bertault, and the English impresario Henry Russell are among the recipients of letters begging for money, and as the years advanced the intensity of the compulsion seems to have increased. Several of his correspondents become 'the only one' to whom appeal can be made. He does not, it is true, suggest a contrast between his extravagant style of living and that of a dog or a drowned rat, in the manner of Wagner and Baudelaire, but, like his great predecessors, he goes to pains to impress upon his correspondents his pitiful, abject state of poverty.

The frequent expressions of self-pity in Debussy's letters, completely absent from any aspect of his music, seem in part to have been motivated by a sophisticated notion of play-acting. One of his earliest creditors, Count Joseph Primoli, recounted that in his youth Debussy had shown such remarkable talents as a play-actor that he was able at a moment's notice to release a flood of tears. One does not wish to minimize the many practical difficulties with which

Debussy at the Grand Hotel,
Eastbourne, in 1905

Debussy at Houlgate in 1911

Debussy in his garden, 1905
Debussy at Le Mouleau, 1916

he was faced, still less the misfortunes of illness. Yet it is impossible not to ascribe a large part of his material anxieties to psychological causes.

Unable to repay a relatively small debt to Henry Russell, who had merely suggested presenting for payment a banker's draft, Debussy writes to him in 1910:

I understand very well that you have lost patience with me and yet I would never have believed that you would have taken such a sudden decision. I admit that you have the right to ask for my banker's order to be honoured. But do you think this will enable me to find the necessary money? Heavens no!—and the only person who will gain from this will be the bailiff.

I would wish no one to experience my trials of the last few months. My mother has been ill; my wife has been ill; and I have been carrying on with my nose to the grindstone. I am not trying to appeal to your sense of pity; I am attempting to show you the facts which make it impossible for me to meet my commitments. Before coming to the decision you have in mind, do you not think there may be other ways of settling the matter? Would you not consent to accepting the amount of my order in several payments? I give you my word of honour that I shall never have the sum of 5,000 francs to pay you all at once. The season is starting again now and I have hopes that with new works of mine which will be given I shall receive sufficient money to settle my debts. You have given me in the past too much proof of your friendship to treat me now as if you were a common creditor! Help me now, I beg you, a little more, and I will assuredly find a way of proving to you my gratitude.

It cannot be a mere coincidence that the artists of this period, Wagner, Baudelaire, and Debussy, perpetually living in a state of acute financial anxiety and obsessed with obtaining money under duress, were those who, in *Tristan*, *Les Fleurs du Mal*, and *Pelléas*, were able to convey the most intimate aspects of sexual passion. There is of course a simple explanation for their poverty: in an increasingly materialistic age they were outcasts. But this cannot be the whole story. A realm of investigation is suggested here in

o   [195]

which the discoveries of modern psychology have a distinct bearing on æsthetic problems.[1]

In any view of the æsthetic problems which Debussy faced in his later years we have to take into account the new values that were being placed, in contemporary thought, on sincerity and irony. Snobbery too—*le snobisme*—raises its disdainful head during this period, and though it would seem to be a simple matter to differentiate between these radically opposed values, they are in fact interrelated and even confused with each other. This came about because the unsettled era which followed the break-up of the artistic traditions of the nineteenth century was not easily able to exclude elements of charlatanism. In his study *Literature and Sincerity* Henri Peyre points out that the upheaval in the arts between 1908 and 1913 was chiefly motivated by a determination to be more sincere. The artists of this period (which by contrast with the preceding period of the late romantics Monsieur Peyre calls 'The Age of Sincerity') became acutely aware of the sham of romantic emotions. 'Take hold of Eloquence and wring her neck', Verlaine had earlier proclaimed. His admonition had been followed by the Fauvists, the Cubists, by Apollinaire, Proust, and D. H. Lawrence, and certainly by Debussy and the young Stravinsky. Yet by 1932 T. S. Eliot could declare of artistic sophistication that 'the greater the elevation the finer becomes the difference between sincerity and insincerity'. In the meantime a disturbance, the effects of which are seen clearly enough today, had undermined artistic belief. But what was this disturbance? Debussy, who retained his adventurous outlook to the end,[2] had nevertheless been shocked by the futurist experiments of Marinetti and Luigi Russolo,[3] and also by the music of Schoenberg, made known to him by his friend Edgard Varèse. At first sight it would seem that he might belong to the artists who,

[1] In any such investigation the attitude to money of Verlaine, one of the most exquisite of the French poets of the senses who beggared himself to the extent of becoming a vagabond, must be of capital importance. The foetuses of his mother's miscarriages were revoltingly perpetuated by her in glass jars. 'Je ne veux pas tes bocaux!' he screamed at her, returning from one of his drunken brawls. 'Je veux tes argents!'

[2] 'Shall I ever regain my power of working?' he writes to Godet after receiving radium treatment in 1916, 'my desire always to go further and beyond which for me is the bread and wine of life?'

[3] Luigi Russolo (1885–1947) was the principal composer associated with the poet Marinetti in the Futurist movement. His aim, to create 'a revolution of music through the "Art of Noises"', anticipates the present-day principle of *musique concrète*. 'Noise instruments' used by Russolo included exploders, thunderers, and whistlers.

though forward-looking like Cézanne and Manet, have frequently
been unable to identify themselves with the ideals of a succeeding
generation. (Cézanne told Van Gogh that his painting was the work
of a madman and Manet went so far as to advise Renoir to stop
painting altogether.) Yet Debussy's doubts about the music of the
new generation were not quite of this order. When the pianist
Franz Liebich mentioned the new names in music to him he was
met only by the persistent question, 'Is he sincere?' Sincerity is of
course not itself an artistic virtue, but without it one cannot begin
to think of artistic values. Debussy came near to defining the
corroding element in contemporary music when he wrote to
Durand in 1908: 'I find the period in which we live thoroughly
ungracious in that an enormous amount of noise is made about less
than nothing. We are in no position to criticize the bluff of the
Americans whilst here we cultivate a kind of artistic bluff which,
one of these days, will redound on us—and very unpleasant it will
be for our French vanity.' He was particularly worried by disturbing
elements in the development of harmony. 'The older I become', he
wrote to Godet in 1911, 'the more I loathe this deliberate confusion which is merely deceiving us—also the bizarre or amusing
harmonies which have merely a snobbish value [*qui ne sont que jeux
de société*].' On the matter of snobbery he was uncompromising.
To André Caplet he wrote in 1913: 'Artists who have so often
jeered at snobbery have now become a victim of snobbery themselves. Indeed, artistic snobbery is even worse than social snobbery
for it is merely necessary that something should be new for people
to find it beautiful. The æsthetic of the fashion shop!'[1]

Debussy's letters become increasingly bitter at this period, but his
music tends more and more to take refuge in understatement. In
his study, *L'Ironie ou la bonne conscience*, Vladimir Jankélévitch
shows that understatement, legitimately classed as a form of irony,
is sometimes extended in music almost to the borders of silence.
'Presque rien', Debussy writes at the end of his ballet *Jeux* and of
the piano piece *Mouvement*. The same direction appears at the end

[1] A letter written three days later, on 9 June 1913 to Godet, is even more bitter in
tone: 'En ce moment c'est ce qu'on appelle "La Grande Saison". Vous n'avez pas idée
combien cela augmente le nombre d'idiots qu'on a coutume d'y rencontrer. Ces gens,
non contents d'écorcher le français, importent des esthétiques qu'ils croient nouvelles,
et qui sentent déjà la mort: un mauvais goût plus féroce que le nôtre. Et cela nous
abrutit si bien que nous n'avons plus la force de résister.'

of *Cloches à travers les feuilles* and *Brouillards*.[1] One is reminded once again of Debussy's decision to live entirely within his inner world. 'Le monde extérieur n'existe presque plus pour moi', he wrote, as we saw earlier, while working on *Usher*. The solipsist world which he had created, in which the self is the only knowable realm, was complete.

Within this isolated world it was for his vivacious young daughter Emma-Claude, called Chouchou, born out of wedlock on 30 October 1905, that he seemed to have formed the warmest attachment. The smiles of Chouchou, he told Godet, helped him to overcome periods of black depression. Although only a little girl of eight at the outbreak of the war she was well known to all Debussy's friends, who frequently mention her in their letters. Having taken piano lessons 'from a lady in black who looks like a drawing by Odilon Redon' she manages to play some of her father's Preludes, and Debussy even tells Stravinsky that 'your friend Chouchou has composed a fantasy on *Petrouchka* which would make the tigers roar. I have threatened her with torture, but she goes on, insisting that you will "find it very beautiful".' When beginning *Le Martyre de Saint-Sébastien* he informs Caplet, in bantering style, that 'Chouchou has just finished her first symphonic poem for voice, two paper-knives, and piano ad libitum. The latest title is The Elephant on the Bough. It is extremely dramatic.' There is no doubt that Debussy's affection for his daughter was a great inspiration to him amidst the worries of his later years and that it accounted for more among his later works than the production of *Children's Corner* and *La Boîte à joujoux*. The child's English governess, Miss Gibbs, was responsible for her education, with the result that at the age of three she was speaking a mixture of English and French. At six she was able to write a letter in English to Caplet in America. Toulet was particularly fond of her. 'She firmly believed in fairies the last time I saw her,' he wrote in 1914, 'perhaps when I see her next she will be a Bergsonian.' 'With her Pan-like eyes, she is the

[1] Exploring the borderlands of understatement and silence in music, Monsieur Jankélévitch has ingeniously listed the expressions of silence, extinction, and loss that occur in Debussy's works. They include 'Plus rien': *Lindaraja, De Grève, Le Faune, Colloque sentimental*; 'Estinto': *Pour les quartes*; 'A Peine': *Pour les Agréments, Pour les Notes répétées, Eventail*; 'Imperceptible': *Ibéria* (second movement); 'Pianissimo possibile': Quartet (third movement), *Pagodes, Pelléas* (Act V); 'En se perdant' and 'Perdendosi': *De Rêve, De Soir, Sirènes, Mandoline, Apparition, Fille aux cheveux de lin, Pour un Tombeau sans nom, Pelléas* (Acts II and V).

daughter of your Pan-like soul', d'Annunzio told Debussy. The moving letter she wrote on the death of her father certainly shows that she had gifts as a writer, and she was apparently also a tasteful musician. Alfred Cortot maintains that he received a valuable lesson from her in the interpretation of her father's music. Playing over some of Debussy's piano works to Madame Debussy and Chouchou shortly after Debussy's death, Cortot asked the child whether his style resembled that of her father. 'Oui, peut-être, oui,' came the hesitant reply, 'mais Papa écoutait davantage.' Chouchou died just over a year after her father, on 16 July 1919, from diphtheria.[1]

Less well-defined than the bright confident character of Chouchou is the shadowy character of Debussy himself. His portraits, those made in his youth by Henri Pinta and Marcel Baschet, and the well-known Salon portrait, exhibited in 1902, by Jacques-Emile Blanche, the last of the French portraitists, hardly bring out the mingled sensuousness and cruelty of his features. The pen-and-ink drawing of Steinlen, on the other hand, conveys in its maze of criss-crosses something of the complexity of Debussy's character, and the photos of Nadar catch the fixed, unrelenting gaze in the eyes which Colette likened to those of an animal of prey. Earlier photos of Debussy lolling in a chair or secretly opening a door, taken by Pierre Louÿs, almost appear to be stills from the cinéma-vérité. Othon Friesz was inspired to do an arresting pencil drawing of Debussy, emaciated and heavily bearded, on his death-bed, and this is the place to mention, too, the imaginative monument to Debussy at Saint-Germain-en-Laye by Maillol reproduced facing p. 210. The great sculptor's memorial to the musician of woodlands, of the sea, and of dreams, consists of a crouching nude woman listening to the sounds of nature.

It is a pity Debussy is not included in the remarkable gallery of pen-portraits of musicians by Romain Rolland. We should then have seen the figure of Debussy half in caricature, half in real life, in the manner in which Rolland was able to describe Handel, Strauss, and Stravinsky. But Rolland's friend André Suarès has left some lively impressions of Debussy as he remembered him about 1900 which, though not especially revealing, faithfully present his physical appearance:

[1] Debussy's first wife Lilly Debussy died in 1932; his second wife Emma Debussy in 1934.

At first sight there was nothing striking about him. He was not tall and appeared to be neither particularly robust nor delicate. He conveyed a certain feeling of solidity but at the same time he was somewhat languid. He was well-covered, not to say stout, all the lines of his figure merging into each other. His beard was soft and silky, his hair thick and curly. His features were full, his cheeks plump. He had a bantering manner, but beneath there was a subtle shrewdness. He was an ironic and sensual figure, melancholy and voluptuous. His complexion was of a warm amber brown. Highly strung, he was master of his nerves, though not of his emotions—which must have affected him profoundly especially as he tried to conceal them.

Writing immediately after Debussy's death, Suarès was among the first to perceive the hedonistic and the ironic elements in Debussy's character:

Irony was part of nature, as indeed was his love of pleasure; he had a mischievous sense of humour and acknowledged a love of good living. He had a barbed tongue, a certain carelessness of speech and something rather affected in his gestures; his enthusiasms were controlled, his taste unfailing, and though appearance often suggested the contrary he was very simple. Debussy was as much a Bohemian as a man of the world. In his reclusion there was something feline. With all his apparent sensuality there was no sign of brutality, though there might have been a capacity for violence. . . . The shape of his head showed great obstinacy of mind.

Debussy's timidity and his cynicism impressed Suarès and, among his features, the shape of his head and the look in his eyes:

As a young man he must have been both shy and cynical. The forehead was that of a master craftsman, a master of rhythm and of harmony. It bulged outwards, a huge convex curve in contrast to the gentler brow of the poets. Mathematicians have sometimes those prominent bumps over the eyebrows. To the close observer he was not merely a musician but a man altogether out of the ordinary. His soft but mocking eyes, sad and languid but at the

same time warm and pensive, were in a sense the eyes of a
brilliant, dominating woman, such as artists sometimes have. . . .
And the look in his eyes would sometimes assume a strange
heaviness; or it would turn into an unrelenting gaze seeking and
penetrating far into the dream world.

An admirer of Monet and associated with Mallarmé and his
circle, he cultivated an informal, almost a bohemian appearance:

Debussy did not reveal the type of man he was at first sight.
Several aspects of his art and his personality suggested a painter
or a poet as much as a musician and he himself helped to confuse
his critics. From the titles he gives his works he would seem
primarily to be a painter: he calls his compositions pictures,
sketches, prints, arabesques, studies in black and white. He takes
obvious pleasure in producing a visual music and it was thus that
he made his reputation. Moreover, this reputation was helped by
his personal appearance, particularly as over the last generation
a great vogue has been enjoyed by painters. There was nothing
tragic or violent about him, no suggestion of the appearance of a
Beethoven or a Berlioz. He did not appear to be an inspired
prophet or a caged eagle, nor was he a frock-coated preacher.[1]
    Though he was not from the south, and there is certainly
nothing southern in his music, he was not unlike some Provençal
or Italian figures. He had that shrewd look deriving from the
older civilizations but there was nevertheless freshness in his
appearance and fervour. He was in no way primitive or uncouth.

Opinions differ on Debussy's manner of speaking and the tone
of his voice. Suarès remembers it as 'veiled, very musical, something
like the tone of a muted viola'. Léon Daudet, on the other hand,
found his attractive voice 'slightly stuffy'. 'The meaning of his
sentences', notes Dr. Pasteur Vallery-Radot, 'were often clouded by
deliberate imprecisions so that the element of vagueness in an idea or
an impression should be adequately conveyed. But often his

[1] At the first concert which he conducted at the Queen's Hall in London the
musician who, to English eyes, resembled Rossetti pleasantly surprised the audience
by appearing in an informal lounge suit.

sentences would contain a single word that would suddenly shine forth, resonant and vibrant.'[1]

The striking appearance of Debussy in his youth suggested many comparisons: he was Persian, an Indian Prince, a Byzantine, even a hydrocephalic Christ. 'The enormous head bulged forwards while there seemed something missing at the back of his huge skull', wrote Alfredo Casella, who met him about 1910. By this time the cancerous growth which had obliged him to take morphine was beginning to undermine his whole physique. 'His colour was sallow,' Casella's recollections continue, 'the eyes were small and seemed half sunk in the fat face; the straight nose was of the purest classical Roman type; in the thick, jet-black hair and beard fifty years had here and there sown a silver thread. As always with artists of the finer sort, the hands were most beautiful. Debussy's voice was unprepossessing, being hoarse (and this was aggravated by the abuse of tobacco), and he spoke in an abnormal, nervous, jumpy way. His dress was scrupulously cared for in every detail. His walk was curious, like that of all men who have a weakness for wearing womanish footgear.'

This contrasts rather alarmingly with impressions of only ten years earlier. In 1917, when Debussy accompanied Gaston Poulet in his Piano Sonata and Rose Féart in his songs at his last concert in Paris, André Suarès was overwhelmed by the change in his appearance:

I was shocked not so much by his emaciated, wasted appearance as by his absent-mindedness and his lassitude. His complexion was of the colour of melted wax or of ashes. There was nothing feverish in his eyes, they seemed to reflect the shadows of some dark pool. In his gloomy smile there was not even bitterness, it merely spoke of the weariness of suffering and anguish. . . . His rather large hand, roundish, supple and plump, an episcopal hand, weighed down his arm, his arm dragged down his shoulder and his head, the seat of his unique but cruel life, hung down from his body. Speaking about him, a few people made a show of confidence and pretended that he was in better health than they

[1] These isolated words in Debussy's speech apparently made a distinctly musical impression. Recalling Debussy's reading of *Tristan* at the piano, René Peter writes of the powerful, resonant timbre which he used to emphasize certain words or syllables: 'Oh! sa façon cuivrée de prononcer "Brangäne", je l'entends encore!'

imagined he would be. Meanwhile, having sat down, he allowed his eyes, under their flickering lids, slowly to roam over the audience, like one who wishes to see but is careful to remain unseen himself. Furtive glances were stolen at people or objects he was hardly able to perceive. He was overcome by confusion, as an artist often is who both loathes and is almost ashamed of suffering. It was even said that by concealing his disease he allowed it to develop.

Several conflicting personalities emerge from these sketches. Debussy was tender-hearted, infinitely sensitive, yet also brutal; he was shy and also outspoken; confident, even impetuous, yet devoured by doubts; independent but envious. Even his appearance belied his nature: he was noble, perhaps exotic, as it was thought, yet also a bohemian; he was wealthy and extravagant, as it seemed, but in reality almost a pauper. If there is a single key to the many conflicting aspects of Debussy's nature it is his ambivalence, the sudden and unaccountable veering from one extreme to another to which an artist of sensibility is perhaps inevitably condemned. 'Les extrêmes se touchent', says the proverb. This duality is illustrated in Debussy's character even in the façade that he presented during his short life to the outside world. At a public rehearsal of *Saint-Sébastien* he was moved by his own achievement to the extent of finding release from his pent-up feelings in tears. On this one occasion, at any rate, he was demonstrative, but more often he was reticent, off-putting, even poker-faced. An honest sense of shame or of decency in regard to matters of the heart demands that emotions of an intimate nature should be obscured, even throttled, rather than vulgarly expressed. To a friend who had brought him news of the infidelity of a woman friend and who was anxiously standing by ready to support him should he break into tears he replied by skilfully turning this deeply affecting matter into a joke. In cold, cutting, and objective terms he replied: 'Kindly wait until I have finished writing this page of music and I will promptly run and throw myself into the Seine.'

12

The War

The best we can do in life is to know the forces around us and in us, acknowledge them and hold the balance. That way you can stay whole.

Euripides, The Bacchæ

When Germany declared war on France on 3 August 1914 Debussy at the age of almost fifty-two was no longer, to the larger musical public, the shadowy, withdrawn figure of earlier years. The first six months of the year had been taken up in incessant travelling and concert-giving and it looked as if the poetic recluse of the period of *Pelléas* had at last determined to plunge into the more spectacular aspects of musical life. At the end of July he returned from his seventh and last visit to London, where he had taken part in a private concert of his works at the home of Sir Edgar Speyer. This distinguished patron of music, to whom Strauss dedicated *Salomé*, had not been able to promote the interests of Debussy on the lavish scale he reserved for Strauss. Nevertheless Speyer remained one of Debussy's principal supporters. He had found support, too, in Rome, The Hague, and Amsterdam where, in February and March, he had conducted concerts. In April he was in Brussels. In the meantime he had appeared in Paris as a pianist not only in his own works but, with Arthur Hartmann, in the Violin and Piano Sonata of Grieg. The first concert performance of *Jeux* was given in February, and the following month Ninon Vallin gave the first performance of the *Trois Poèmes de Mallarmé*. Here indeed is evidence of a wide field of professional activity. And as if to prove that the idealist can also be a practical-minded artisan Debussy determined to turn to good account another of his old, forgotten scores, the incidental music which he had written for a recitation of *Les Chansons de Bilitis* at the time of his association with Pierre Louÿs and which, in the summer of 1914, he arranged as the *Epigraphes antiques* for piano duet.

This, however, is not the whole story of Debussy's activities at this time. The last weeks of peace in Europe appear to have coincided with a new burst of creative activity. So much we gather from a statement made to Vallery-Radot at the end of July 1914: 'Never have I approached work with so much verve. I have still so much to say; and there are so many musical ideas which have never been expressed.' But a letter of almost the same period, dated 14 July, to Godet speaks of 'hours in which one can hardly think of anything but suicide as a way out' and reveals an extremely depressed state of mind: 'For a long time now—I must confess it—I have been losing myself and I feel frightfully shrunken. Ah! the "magician" whom you loved in me, where is he? He is merely an unfortunate charlatan who will soon break his back in a final, unbeautiful pirouette.' The strain produced on a sick man by constant travelling, the frantic efforts to meet financial commitments, the apprehension at the deteriorating political situation, the doubts produced by the less enthusiastic reception of some of his works, were all combining to produce a moral crisis. In the weeks preceding the war Debussy's state of mind was marked by a violent swaying from exaltation to despair which denoted a measure of instability.

To most people the sudden outbreak of war made a certain romantic appeal. It brought to a head the many pent-up rivalries between France and Germany in all spheres of civilization and there was thus a certain feeling of relief. Hence, on both sides of the Rhine, the exuberant enthusiasm for what was felt to be a crusade of freedom. Later, when each of the belligerents was overwhelmed by the war, when the forces of destruction which had been unleashed were seen to be almost beyond human control, people perceived that they were not masters of their own destiny. They became increasingly apprehensive of the march of events and they began to loathe the war. But for the moment the outbreak of hostilities in France in 1914 was thought of in terms of the Franco-Prussian War; this at last was the war of revenge, a short, sharp conflict redressing the humiliations of the earlier French defeat. By Christmas the victorious campaign would be over.

Debussy's enquiring turn of mind—also, perhaps, the fact that he may have been instinctively aware of the underlying causes of the war, at least on the artistic plane—did not allow him to be carried away by the popular enthusiasm. He was by no means indifferent to the war. Apart from its material horrors it represented to him a very real æsthetic conflict, a conflict in the world of music and of ideas, in which he himself was to play a leading role. We have seen that the musical conflict between France and Germany had reached its height long before the outbreak of war, and therefore to Debussy the war itself, however frightful, was seen principally as a belated material expression of spiritual or æsthetic antagonisms. From this viewpoint the cause of Debussy in the role of *musicien français*[1] had already been won. The title-page of the three Sonatas, published in 1916 and 1917, bears this description of the composer, but by this time the use of the words *musicien français* after the composer's name was merely an elegant manifestation of patriotism. French independence from the German musical hegemony dates from the 1890s.

The immediate effect on Debussy of the war was, not surprisingly, a silencing of almost all his musical activities. He wrote to Durand on 8 August: 'You know that I have no *sang-froid* and still less anything of the army spirit—I've never even handled a rifle. My recollections of 1870 and the anxiety of my wife, whose son and son-in-law are in the army, prevent me from developing any enthusiasm. All this brings about an intense, agitated state of mind and I feel I am nothing but a mere atom crushed to pieces in this terrible cataclysm. What I am doing seems so wretchedly small. I've got to the state of envying Satie who, as a corporal, is really going to defend Paris. And so, my dear Jacques, if you have any work that you can give me, do not forget me. Forgive me for counting on you, but you are really all I have.'

Until almost the end of the year Debussy remained inactive. His friend Paul Dukas was ready to join the forces; he himself was able merely to kill time, as he put it, by sitting on a committee for the welfare of musicians' dependants. On 18 August when Liège had been occupied and the Belgian Government had been trans-

[1] This self-ascribed title was used by Debussy before the outbreak of the war. Writing to Stravinsky on 17 November 1913 on the possibility of their meeting in Moscow he says: 'Vous y rencontreriez Claude Debussy, musicien français qui vous aime bien affectueusement.'

ferred to Antwerp he wrote to Durand: 'My age and military capabilities allow me at most to guard a fence, but if, to ensure victory, they are absolutely in need of another face to be bashed in, I'll offer mine without question. . . . It is almost impossible to work. In truth one hardly dares to for the side-issues of the war are more distressing than one imagines.'

The French Government left Paris for Bordeaux at the beginning of September. The Battle of the Marne marked a successful Anglo-French offensive, but the Germans penetrated as far south as Provins, to the south-west of Paris, and Rheims Cathedral had been bombarded. Alarming rumours and the fear of air-raids compelled Debussy and his family to seek refuge at Angers in western France. He must surely have been reminded of the German occupation of Paris in his youth. He soon regretted the difficult and costly journey for it was undertaken against his better judgement. The truth is that in the opening weeks of the war there was a serious misunderstanding in France of the national psychology: the press was heavily censored and official communiqués veiled the truth to such an extent that the public became distrustful. The only gain of this journey was that in the provincial town of Angers rumours were less rife. 'We must harbour our strength for the period after the war', Debussy wrote optimistically at this early stage, 'for if we are victorious—and we must ardently hope that we shall be—artistic matters are likely to receive little attention. Art and war have never, at any period, been able to find any basis of agreement. One goes on struggling but so many blows one after another, so many revolting horrors, grip at the heart and almost grind one to extinction. I am not referring to the past two months in which I haven't written a note or touched a piano. This, needless to say, is of no importance by comparison with the events of the war. Yet I cannot help reflecting on this without sadness. At my age, time lost is lost for ever.'

The only inclination to work came in October when a *Marche héroïque* is mentioned, but 'to produce a work of heroism in safety, sheltered from bullets, seems to me absurd'. The writing of *No-ya-ti* or *Le Palais de Silence*, a ballet commissioned earlier in the year by the Alhambra Theatre in London, was postponed until the end of the war. 'I wouldn't like this music to be played', Debussy tells Durand, 'until the fate of France is decided, for she can neither laugh nor cry while so many of our people are being blown to pieces.'[1] Antwerp fell on 7 October and a week later the German armies reached the Belgian coast. Elsewhere on the western front heavy German counter-attacks brought the allied offensive to a halt. At Angers during this period Debussy heard the French soldiers practising on trumpets and drums. 'They produce trumpet calls and rhythms which irresistibly remind me of the best themes of the two Richards [i.e. Wagner and Strauss]', he is bound to confess to Durand. 'If you are inclined to draw morals', he adds laconically, 'you may certainly find one here.'

An opportunity came in November to realize a project for a patriotic march. The novelist Hall Caine, who had been a friend of Rossetti and was one of the first English translators of Maeterlinck, approached the leading artists and intellectuals in the allied countries for tributes to the King of the Belgians. Debussy was the principal contributor among French musicians. It was thus in *King Albert's Book*, published in London by the *Daily Telegraph*, that Debussy's *Berceuse héroïque* was first published. Other musical tributes were contributed by Elgar, Edward German, and Messager. The French painters were represented by Monet and the philosophers by Bergson. In this wide-ranging publication Edmund Gosse and Romain Rolland wrote on the achievements of Belgian poets and musicians. Debussy attached little importance to this patriotic war-piece. 'Approached by the *Daily Telegraph* I was obliged to write something for *King Albert's Book*', he tells Godet. 'It was very hard, particularly as *La Brabançonne* evokes no feeling of heroism in the hearts of those who were not brought up with it. The result of this digression has the title *Berceuse héroïque*. It was all I was able to achieve, having been physically affected by the proximity of hostilities not to mention my own feeling of inferiority in military matters, never having handled a rifle.'

By the middle of November, after the first Battle of Ypres, rains and floods brought the struggle on the western front to a standstill. Thereafter the grim, stationary warfare of the trenches was pursued. Towards the middle of the following month the

---

[1] A few sketches for this second English ballet of Debussy (the first was *Khamma*) appear in a private collection (see No. 304 of the Debussy Exhibition at the Bibliothèque Nationale, 1962). The only note concerning the scenario, by 'M. de Fleure', in these sketches is: 'Le Scorpion oblique et le Sagittaire rétrograde ont paru sur le ciel nocturne.'

French Government returned to Paris, and although the Opéra and other theatres remained closed and the city remained darkened as a precaution against air-raids, much of the social and artistic life was revived. On 1 January 1915 Debussy wrote to Godet:

You are probably the only man who understands that silence does not mean oblivion. Indeed, these vile times serve to show that tact is a rare and a refreshing flower. The worst horrors are eventually forgotten—one's belief in the future demands that they must be. But what will not so easily disappear is a certain foreign outlook, false and heavy, which has insinuated itself—God knows with what blind hypocrisy—into our manner of thinking, listening, even feeling. For forty-eight years [i.e. since 1871] we have sought to diminish ourselves; even in France the French were convinced that they were 'mugs' and imagined that they were hard done by. I must confess that for months I no longer knew what music was. The familiar sound of the piano became hateful. Pythagoras, who continued to work on his mathematical problems until he was struck down by a soldier, and Goethe, writing his *Elective Affinities* during the French occupation of Weimar, were admirable figures.[1] I am just not on this level and had better devote myself perhaps to mathematics.

The latter part of the year 1915 was to be one of the most fertile periods in the whole of Debussy's creative life, but in the early months of the year he was principally concerned with supplying Durand with a new edition of the works of Chopin. The German editions were no longer on sale and in return for the frequent advances he received from his publisher Debussy undertook this editorial work. The greater part of Chopin's work was thus eventually issued by Durand as 'revised' by Debussy. In his preface to the Waltzes Debussy claims to have based his edition on earlier editions which had been corrected by Chopin himself. In fact they are largely based on the edition of Ignaz Friedman, a pupil of Leschetizky, published by Breitkopf und Härtel. Only in regard to

[1] There is no historical foundation for the anecdote about Pythagoras. Goethe's novel *Die Wahlverwandtschaften*, presenting debatable ideas on love, marriage, and divorce, was written in 1809 during the occupation of Weimar by Napoleon's Grande Armée.

the Second Ballade, in F major, does Debussy claim to have consulted the original manuscript. This was lent to him by Saint-Saëns and allowed one or two minor rectifications to be made.[1]

At the completion of this editorial work he suffered a personal blow. He was profoundly affected by the death of his mother, Victorine, on 23 March. Questioning the significance of death in his letters ('Can one be sure what happens to us at this moment?'), he turned despairingly to his friends d'Annunzio, Varèse, and Durand.

In the opening months of 1915 a feeling of war-weariness had set in from which the hard-pressed public were severely jolted when poison gas was used against British and French troops in Flanders at the end of April. The following month the *Lusitania* was torpedoed. In June, however, when Durand, expecting no further compositions from the dejected composer during the war, suggested that Debussy undertake an edition of Bach, he surprisingly received an optimistic letter announcing that work was begun on a set of pieces for two pianos, *En blanc et noir*. 'Though I have not spoken to you about it, I have greatly suffered from the long drought created in my mind by the war', this letter states. 'I am now anxious to leave as soon as possible for my home has long oppressed me.' In July he was offered hospitality at 'Mon Coin', a cottage at Pourville, near Dieppe, with a garden overlooking the sea. ('It is not so well laid out as the gardens of Le Nôtre, but it is very pleasant if you do not want to play the part of Robinson Crusoe.') Within a few days he had sent Durand the three pieces forming *En blanc et noir*, originally *Caprices en blanc et noir*.

Like many of the earlier piano works they were conceived in the

[1] In 1917 Debussy completed his 'revision' of two sets of sonatas by J. S. Bach: the six sonatas for violin and clavier and the three sonatas for viola da gamba and clavier. His editorial work on Chopin was undertaken with zest; that on Bach with some misgivings. He wrote to Durand on 15 April 1917: 'Never correct the sonatas for violin and piano of Bach on a rainy Sunday afternoon. I have just finished the revision (!) of the above-named and it is as if it were raining within one's soul. When the old Saxon cantor has no ideas he starts off with anything and he is then truly merciless. In fact, he is only bearable when he is wonderful—which is certainly something, you will say. All the same if he had had a friend—perhaps a publisher?—who would have encouraged him to take a day off say once a week we might have been spared some hundreds of pages in which there are rows upon rows of joyless bars, always with that little rascal of a subject and its countersubject. Sometimes his wonderful writing, which is after all a form of gymnastics peculiar to the old master, does not manage to fill the terrible void which then appears to become all the wider by his determination to extract the maximum value from a commonplace theme.'

Monument to Debussy, by Maillol

Debussy on his death-bed, by Othon Friesz

'Le Tombeau de Debussy', by Raoul Dufy

manner of a painting. 'I must confess that I have somewhat changed the colour', he wrote to Durand during the composition of the most dramatic of these pieces. 'It was too consistently sombre, almost as tragic as one of the *Caprichos* of Goya.'[1] The second, inspired by François Villon's *Ballade contre les ennemis de France*, is dedicated to Lieut. Jacques Charlot, Durand's associate who was killed in action earlier in the year. Incorporating the chorale of Luther, and portraying also a distant rumbling of guns and trumpet calls, it was held by Debussy to be the most inspired of the set. The remaining two pieces are dedicated to Debussy's Russian friends of this time, Koussevitzky, who had invited him to Moscow, and Stravinsky, whom he was to meet on two occasions in Paris during the war.[2]

The three short months spent at 'Mon Coin' from the middle of July to the middle of October formed the last period of Debussy's creative activity. The fervour with which he worked during these last summer and autumn months on the Normandy coast was intense. Besides *En blanc et noir*, the twelve Studies for piano were crowded into this period, and also two of the three sonatas, those for cello and piano, and for flute, viola, and harp. At the beginning of October he wrote to Durand: 'I am taking advantage of these last days of liberty for Paris seems to me to be a kind of open prison where one no longer has the right to think. The walls there have terrible ears. . . . And so I am writing down all the music that passes through my head, like a madman, and rather sadly.' A similar letter was sent to Godet on 14 October: 'I have returned from a stay at the seaside. . . . There I was able once again to think in musical terms which I had not been able to do over the last year. It is certainly not essential that I write music, but it is all I am able to do more or less competently. I must humbly admit to the feeling of latent death within me. Accordingly, I write like a madman or like one who is condemned to die the next morning.'[3]

[1] Writing to Godet of these pieces the following year Debussy compares them to the work of another Spanish painter: 'Don't rack your brains about *En blanc et noir*. These pieces derive their colour and their feeling merely from the sonority of the piano; if you agree they are like the "greys" of Velasquez.'

[2] The meetings took place about the end of 1915, according to a letter from Debussy to Godet, and the middle of 1917. 'I saw him last about nine months before his death', Stravinsky writes in his memoirs. His statement that 'Debussy did not mention the piece from *En blanc et noir* he had written for me' is indeed strange, since it had been published with Stravinsky's name as the dedicatee eighteen months earlier.

[3] Debussy was certainly aware that his illness was fatal, and this last burst of creative

As the scope and the devastation of the war extended until it assumed world-wide proportions Debussy had come to realize that, silenced by the magnitude of the catastrophe, he was himself becoming a casualty. 'And now they are speaking of the intervention of Japan', he notes at the beginning of August. 'Why not the inhabitants of Mars while we are about it?'[1] 'I want to work', he writes in this letter, 'not so much for myself, but to give proof, however small it may be, that even if there were thirty million Boches [i.e. on French soil] French thought will not be destroyed.'

The letters to Durand show that the twelve studies were written between 5 August and 29 September. One of them, *Pour les Agréments*, 'gives new life to a worn-out device'; another, *Pour les Quartes*, contains 'effects you have never heard before'. He works at these difficult, complex works with 'the activity of an engine'. On 30 September he was able to write: 'Last night at midnight I copied out the last note of the Studies. Phew! The most minute Japanese print is child's play by comparison with the writing of some of the pages; but I am pleased, it is good work.' In dedicating them somewhat diffidently to the memory of Chopin, he was aware that comparisons would be made 'inevitably to my disadvantage', yet 'without false modesty I may say that they will acquire a place of their own'.

The Cello and Piano Sonata was completed by the beginning of August ('I like its proportions and its form that is almost classical, in the good sense of the word') and the Sonata for Flute, Viola (originally oboe), and Harp by the end of September. When the sketches were completed for this second of the projected set of six sonatas Debussy told Durand that his vision of it was, as he put it, almost embarrassingly beautiful. Two days before leaving 'Mon Coin' he informs his trusted publisher that 'I shall go on writing until the last minute like André Chénier writing poems before

energy accordingly took the form of a defiance of death. Fifteen years earlier another artist of Debussy's generation, Oscar Wilde, similarly poured forth his finest thoughts at the approach of death. Referring to the period preceding Wilde's death in Paris in 1900, Ernest La Jeunesse, the friend of both Wilde and Debussy, wrote: '[Wilde] is haunted by a foreboding of death which in the end will kill him. He then tells all his stories in one breath: it is the bitter yet dazzling final piece of display of superhuman fireworks.'

[1] Italy and Bulgaria joined the Allies in 1915. In the course of the next two years no less than nineteen countries were to enter the war on the allied side.

mounting the scaffold. This is a macabre comparison but there is some truth in it.'[1]

Shortly after the triumphant composer returned to Paris the disease from which he had suffered intermittently since 1909, cancer of the rectum, developed to the extent that his doctors, Crespel and Desjardins, advised an operation. This took place on 7 December. It was reasonably successful, but it was clear that the disease was fatal.[2] A few days before the operation, at the beginning of December, both the words and music were written for the charming but pathetic song, *Noël des enfants qui n'ont plus de maison*. Debussy's heart went out to the homeless refugee children in Flanders. Reverting to the manner of *Pelléas et Mélisande*, it is a little masterpiece of compassion. Two versions were made in these last fateful days of 1915, for voice and piano and for children's two-part chorus.

The first six months of 1916 dragged on in a mood of growing depression. The letters to Durand refer with impatience to the many forms of treatment that were proposed. Radium and morphine were administered. 'I have the right to ask whether this illness isn't after all incurable,' he complains, 'in which case I had better be told straight away. "Alors! Oh! Alors" as poor Golaud exclaims.' This was the year of Verdun. The tremendous German offensive launched in February by the armies of the Crown Prince was of a ferocity hitherto unknown, and indeed even the most spectacular offensives of the second World War were not again to claim casualties on this cataclysmic scale. By the summer nearly a quarter of a million French soldiers had been killed in this single battle and an even greater number seriously wounded. Even though the invading armies were halted—by the end of March they had nowhere advanced beyond four miles—the whole of France lived perpetually in anguish. It was then that the famous call went up from the French lines, 'Ils ne passeront pas!' For the first time the German generals wondered whether they could win the war.

[1] A royalist, André Chénier was guillotined in 1794. Debussy may have had in mind the fact that owing to the dramatic circumstances of Chénier's death a generation was to pass before his poetic genius was recognized.

[2] Authorities on rectal cancer state that in its early stages this disease is not particularly painful, and that pain is a symptom indicating that the disease has reached an advanced stage. Shortly before the operation Debussy wrote to Fauré: 'La journée du 26 [novembre] m'a mis plus bas que la terre, et, depuis, j'ai souffert comme un chien.' During the remaining two and a quarter years of his life Debussy used a colostomy.

Time was against them. In July the Battle of Verdun was followed by the equally ferocious counter-offensive of the allies, the Battle of the Somme, but still no issue was reached. The uninterrupted slaughter of the war produced on Debussy the effect 'of an open wound'. Though he admired the heroism of his friend Caplet, who was a liaison officer at Verdun, he became increasingly depressed by the routine acceptance of the war and by the growing hatred it engendered on all sides. In October, though rapidly wasting, he spent a short time at Le Mouleau, near Arcachon, where he managed to work on the finale of the Violin and Piano Sonata, the first two movements of which were begun earlier in the year. At first he was anxious to develop a 'cellular' theme. This last movement was, however, several times rewritten and eventually the choice of the opening subject went to 'a theme turning back on itself like a serpent biting its own tail'.[1] In May 1917 Debussy expresses great satisfaction with this last of his completed works, written with a stoic determination to overcome his disability. 'In keeping with the contradictory spirit of human nature it is full of a joyous tumult', he writes to Godet. 'Beware in future of works which appear to inhabit the skies; often they are the product of a dark, morose mind.'[2] The plan for the series of six sonatas 'for various instruments', begun at Pourville the previous year, was well established and though the series was only half completed at the time of Debussy's death the instrumentation of the remaining three sonatas had been definitely decided upon. The fourth was to have been for oboe, horn, and harpsichord. The fifth was planned for wind instruments (trumpet, clarinet, and bassoon) and piano. The sixth, apparently foreseen as the most important of the set, was to 'take the form of a *Concert* in which all the "various instruments" are combined and to which will be added a double bass'.

Later, in 1916, sketches were made for a patriotic cantata, *Ode à*

---

[1] Of the several versions of the finale which Debussy had mentioned to him, Dukas wrote: 'I am sure that of the six versions of the finale of this Sonata five of them are good and that the sixth is excellent.'

[2] This confident opinion of the Violin and Piano Sonata is in striking contrast to the condemnatory opinion Debussy was to give Godet of this work when writing to him in a depressed mood only a month later (see page 218). In a book on Debussy by his friend Émile Vuillermoz (Geneva, 1957), widely acclaimed on account of its illustrations by Turner, Monet, Sisley, and Pissarro, a highly derogatory criticism is made of the late works, based unjustifiably on Debussy's distorted opinions of them.

la France, on words by Laloy,[1] and in September the libretto was completed of *La Chute de la Maison Usher*. In this last year of Debussy's life illness compelled him to give in and he was thus prevented from realizing many far-sighted ideas. To the end he fought heroically. On the other hand, by its very nature Debussy's art, even though transformed during the war years, was doomed, as we have seen in earlier chapters, to remain incomplete. Indeed, there was an element of something incomplete or unfinished even in his greatest works, among them the *Nocturnes*, *La Mer*, and *Pelléas*, the orchestrations of which he was constantly revising. More than this, he was aware in his last years of pursuing an unattainable ideal, an ideal of music that should be more beautiful, more exquisite than anything he had written, than anything that could ever be written by a composer of music. This way lies disintegration. Despite the triumphs of certain of his later works the exploratory art of the successor of Wagner could never be wholly realized.[2]

The pre-war struggle in France for artistic independence degenerated during the war itself into a narrow chauvinistic spirit. Performances of works by contemporary or recently born composers from enemy countries were banned. This militant chauvinism was even directed against Beethoven and Wagner, the two composers whom the French, more than any other people, had taken to their hearts. Debussy would have none of this. Observing in a preface written in December 1916 for the series of essays *Pour la Musique française* edited by Paul Huvelin, that 'strange statements are to be heard about Beethoven who—Flemish or German— was a great musician and about Wagner who was a greater artist than a musician', he roundly declares: 'Everyone knows this; and in any case this is not the question.' French musicians, he believed,

[1] Two posthumous publications of this work were issued though it is impossible to know how much of it is Debussy's original music. The piano score, published in 1928, is said to be 'réalisé par Marius François Gaillard'. The orchestral score (1954) states that the work is 'orchestré par Marius François Gaillard'. The performance in 1928 of this arrangement without any indication of the sources was widely deplored.

[2] Some twenty years earlier, in 1895, Debussy had expressed to Pierre Louÿs his reluctance, which remained with him to the end of his life, to complete certain of his most cherished projects. As opposed to the dream-like incompleteness of Debussy's work the almost brutal finality of the work of Wagner was boldly defined by Ernest Newman: 'He gambled superbly with life, and he won. . . . He lived, indeed, to see himself victor everywhere, in possession of everything for which he had struggled his whole feverish life through. He completed, and saw upon the stage, every one of the great works he had planned.'

should be encouraged to revive the spirit of the eighteenth century. Gluck and Wagner led opera away from French ideals. Among nineteenth-century composers Chabrier is now singled out. 'Not everyone is able to write "la grande musique" ', he adds dispassionately, 'but everyone attempts to do so.' And he concludes: 'The war is to be won on several different planes: music is one of them.' Ravel was even more outspoken in his opposition to any form of chauvinism. 'I am little concerned about the fact that Monsieur Schoenberg is an Austrian', he challengingly announced. 'He remains a highly significant composer whose interesting discoveries have had a beneficial influence on certain composers from the allied countries and among us as well.' A thoroughly independent figure himself, Ravel was able to assess the independence of others and to rise above the feverish prejudices of the war: 'I am delighted that Messieurs Bartók, Kodály and their disciples are Hungarian and that they show it in their works with so much fervour.' Alone among the dominating figures of his time, Saint-Saëns inveighed against the persistent Wagnerian influence.

Stravinsky's *Sacre du Printemps* had been given in the year preceding the war and in the same year Luigi Russolo in Milan issued his Futurist manifesto on the 'Art of Noises'. Activities of this kind anticipated the war. But the characteristic works of the four war years were of an altogether different spirit. In 1917, at the height of the battles of Verdun and the Somme, the destructive æsthetic of the Dadaists was established. The nursery word *dada*, meaning both 'gee-gee' and 'hobby', was adopted to convey a spirit in music, as also in painting and literature, of utter nihilism. At Zürich a group of refugees from the warring world arbitrarily chose this word simply by opening a dictionary at random. It had no relevant meaning but it was appropriate, they thought, to express their anger at the holocaust brought upon them by what they believed to be lying civilizations. The same year one of the earliest mentions is made of the word jazz. (The following year it is spelt 'jaz' or 'jass'; to this day its etymological origin remains unknown.) On the other hand, the war created no great impression on the less adventurous composers in France and Germany though their music was beginning to show signs of disintegration. In 1915 Saint-Saëns visited the U.S.A. where he wrote the march *Hail, California!* and in the same year Strauss wrote his Alpine Symphony. This work, for gigantic orchestra (twelve horns off-stage), is the most literal and harshly realistic of all orchestral programme works.[1]

Debussy's style had changed during the war but it had not disintegrated. In 1917 he appeared several times as pianist and conductor, and took part in the first performance of his cello and violin sonatas. The Violin Sonata was first given on 5 May at a concert of his works with Gaston Poulet and Rose Féart. It was his last concert in Paris. A fortnight later he heard one of the most nihilistic works of the war, Satie's ballet *Parade* on a scenario by Cocteau and with décor by Picasso.[2] It was a work which provoked another of the now notorious scenes of hostility between public and performers. After the *Sacre* and the 'Futurist' music promoted by Luigi Russolo it was Debussy's harshest experience of the music of the future.

During the latter part of the war Debussy became increasingly attached to his old friend Robert Godet to whom, in long rambling letters, he poured out his feelings of apprehension and disillusionment. Five of Godet's letters to Debussy, full of tact and warmth, were recently published and offer one of the few glimpses of Debussy's friendships reflected in the letters of both correspondents. From his home in Switzerland, Godet, who had closely followed Debussy's life from his early Conservatoire days, was determined to provide him during the war years with moral support and also to prove to him his deep-seated affection. His judgements in this correspondence on Debussy's late works, however, remain objective. In a letter to Godet of 11 December 1916 Debussy timorously refers to a private performance of his Sonata for Flute, Viola, and Harp: 'The sound of it is not bad, though it is not for me to speak

[1] Far from showing any sense of austerity in this war-time work, Strauss wrote such opulent and taxing parts for the brass instruments of the Berlin orchestra that he recommended them to use the amazing Aerophor. This bizarre device consisted of a bellows worked by the foot and which, by means of a tube, maintained a pressurized air-chamber within the wind-player's cheeks.

[2] This circus ballet, said Georges Auric in 1917, illustrates the fact that in real life 'the song of the nightingale is smothered by the noise of trams'. Or, more appropriately, one would have imagined, by the noise of guns. If not a Dadaist work, *Parade* was an experiment in a bitterly anti-romantic vein. Produced by Diaghilev on his single visit to Paris during the war, it was apparently given in a modified form. In *Le Rappel à l'Ordre* Cocteau quaintly writes: 'The score of *Parade* was to be a musical background for suggestive noises, such as sirens, typewriters, airplanes, dynamos. . . . Technical difficulties and the rush at rehearsals prevented the instalment of these noises. We suppressed almost all of them, that is to say the work was presented incomplete and without its *bouquet*.'

to you of the music. I could do so, however, without embarrassment for it is the music of a Debussy whom I no longer know. It is frightfully mournful and I don't know whether one should laugh or cry—perhaps both?' Godet challenges this opinion.

I have not discovered at first sight such unfathomable depths as you say there are between the Claude Debussy of today and his Sonata for Flute, Viola, and Harp [he writes on 5 January 1917 in bold, confident terms]. Sometimes, while your forward march relentlessly progresses, something causes you to glance backwards, and it seems to me that your second 'French Sonata' represents one of these retrospective glances thanks to which the development of your genius remains all of a piece. In looking back to one's youth one does not see the familiar scene again, for the viewpoint has changed. . . . To convey the magic of Debussyan memories what happier combination of timbres could one hope to find than the one you have discovered? How modern it is and yet how aptly does it evoke the music of the past! It seems to me that the reflective viola resurrects your youth in some kind of veiled, tender manner while the flute, assuming both a languorous and a vivacious manner as if it were impersonating a melancholy version of Puck, seems to be questioning the hidden meaning of things. You combine these two voices, the one a warm, soulful voice thrown into relief by the other, rather colder voice, and their intercourse is woven together by the harp. Your work represents a subtle reflection of naïvety, if I may use this word, and indeed it is desirable to do so for it is this root naïvety that causes us to wonder, in listening to your work, whether we should smile or burst into tears.

Godet was similarly concerned to correct Debussy's deprecatory view of his Violin Sonata. In a letter of 7 June 1917 Debussy fairly fulminates against this tender work: 'You should know, my too trusting friend, that I only wrote this Sonata to be rid of the thing, spurred on as I was by my dear publisher. You, who are able to read between the staves, will see traces of The Imp of the Perverse [the story by Poe] who encourages one to choose the very subject which should be ignored. This Sonata will be interesting from a documentary viewpoint and as an example of what may be produced by a sick man in time of war.' Godet took time to reflect on this condemnation, and gave his opinion only two months later. On 16 August he wrote to his dejected friend: 'I have had time to read and re-read the Violin Sonata but not without outbursts of indignation against the severity of its composer. It may not present a three-dimensional view of the composer's subtlety and depth but it nevertheless speaks his true language, so it seems to me, in a friendly, youthful manner, simply and addressed to everyone. It is an appropriate work to appear at a time when everywhere there is a call to action. One would only be justified in criticizing it if it were not true music; which undoubtedly it is, and in a delightful way.'

Their correspondence continued in this vein until November, Debussy courageously portraying his sorrowful state in an ironic quip, Godet responding patiently and affectionately to his friend's exasperated state of mind. A few extracts from their correspondence show the nature of their finely attuned friendship.

Debussy to Godet from Chalet Habas, Saint-Jean-de-Luz, 28 July 1917:

Decidedly, fashionable resorts by the sea are not for me. But this house is charming. It is built in the Basque style, the interior decoration being English. The proprietor, Colonel A. L. Nicol, is English and of course he has been at the front since the beginning of the war. His wife is in London occupied there with—whatever you say.

It is a place in which you might come across S. Pickwick on the staircase. I am continuously haunted by the fine portrait of an old gentleman, severe and dejected. When I am late in the morning his severity increases and he even appears to be reproachful. All over the place are guns which, when they were in use, must have been terrifying; they were used against the Dahoman tribes. Also countless family groups painted by one of the earlier Nicols. The sea is not within sight. Behind the house are gentle mountains. A quarter of an hour's walk brings you to the bay where, as in all such bays, the bathers might with advantage be less unprepossessing. At sea is a collier, a useful boat no doubt but which spoils the view of the horizon. Further along the coast, at Guéthary, which is favoured by the presence of P. J. Toulet, a celebrated humorist and a confirmed alcoholic whose face resembles a sunset painted by Van Dongen,[1] the sea is most beautiful. All this would be very pleasant if I were not there to spoil everything. So nothing has up till now changed:

> Les morts
> C'est discret
> Ça dort
> Bien au frais.[2]

Your old devoted

C. D.

Godet to Debussy, 16 August 1917:

Whenever I leave you I am extremely unhappy at the thought of no longer being with you. . . . Your letter from Saint-Jean-de-Luz reached me, a short, bitterly delicious poem. . . . Let me embrace you on your fine luminous forehead. Let me wish you good work and, as far as possible, good health.

Debussy to Godet, October 1917:

Do not be angry with me if for some time I have not spoken to you of my projects. Music has completely abandoned me. If there is no reason to weep, it is at any rate a little absurd, but I can do nothing about it and I have never forced anyone to love me.

---

[1] Debussy's correspondence with Toulet at this period deals principally with their proposed version of *As You Like It* (see Appendix A). Since Toulet was now also an invalid, they were unable to meet. Referring to a drive which took him past Toulet's house at Guéthary, Debussy says: 'Yesterday we passed "Etcheberria"—you probably know? If I were George Meredith I should write twenty pages listing all the unpleasant associations of surprises; and another twenty putting the opposite point of view.'

[2] This quotation which appears in Vol. I, p. 130, is from Laforgue's *Complainte de l'oubli des morts*, a gruesome lament on the dead who are soon to be forgotten. Debussy misquotes the last line which should be 'Trop au frais'. Hidden references and quotations from the works of Jules Laforgue continued to appear in Debussy's writings throughout his life. In addition to those given in Vol. I a letter of 1899 to René Peter contains a quotation from Laforgue's *Le Concile Féerique* (see R. Peter, *Claude Debussy*, p. 210). The enigma in the dedication of vocal works addressed to Emma Debussy, 'A.l.p.M. [A la petite Mienne]' derives from the lines in Laforgue's poem, *O géraniums diaphanes*:

> O ma petite mienne, ô ma quotidienne,
> Dans mon petit intérieur,
> C'est-à-dire plus jamais ailleurs!
> O ma petite quotidienne!

Godet to Debussy, 26 November 1917:

> Allow me, dear and precious being, to suggest that you, less than anyone, have the right to be discouraged. You have the right to rest, or rather the spirit of rest has claims to make upon you. . . .[1]

From the beginning of 1918 Debussy, back in his Paris home, was confined to his room and eventually to his bed. He was to write nothing more until his death on 25 March. His features became hollowed out, the look on his face gradually grew duller. Though the war had dragged on with progressive weariness for almost four years recent events were now alarming in the extreme. In November 1917 a new spirit of confidence had been created by Clemenceau (the 'Tiger') whose government was in fact, in less than a year, to bring the country to victory. In the meantime, however, numerous set-backs were calculated to undermine the allied resistance. After the peace treaty which she signed with Russia in March 1918 Germany was able to throw her entire military strength against the west. Accordingly on 21 March, four days before Debussy's death, a great enemy offensive was opened with the object of splitting the British and French forces. It was almost successful. The British armies were primarily intent upon preserving their communications with the Channel ports while the French were concerned with covering Paris, now being bombarded by the long-range gun, 'Big Bertha'. In a defiant spirit the Opéra reopened on the very day, 21 March, of this last German offensive, with an afternoon performance of Rameau's *Castor et Pollux*. 'Bien le bon jour à Monsieur Castor', Debussy managed to say in a faint, toneless voice to Louis Laloy as he left him for this historic performance. By 24 March the military situation compelled the French Government again to make plans to leave the capital. Debussy's death the following day thus occurred at the most fateful crisis of the war. During the bombardment of Paris he had been too weak to be carried down to the cellar. The dramatic sequence of these events

---

[1] The correspondence of Debussy and Godet reveals that in the last years of his life Debussy favoured the interpretation of his piano works by the German pianist who had settled in France, Walter Rummel (1887–1953). Held by some critics to have had an insight into French piano music comparable to that of Gieseking, Rummel gave the first performance of Debussy's Studies on 14 December 1916. Debussy's letters to Rummel (1913–16) were kindly communicated to me by Mr Michael Mann.

is set out in the war diary of the pacifist and former friend of Richard Strauss, Romain Rolland:[1]

Thursday, 21 March, 1918. Coinciding with the first day of spring the great German offensive breaks out on the western front. Since December the threat of this offensive, full of anguish, has been hanging over my poor country. . . . How will the future judge the two statesmen who, after days of hideous slaughter, pronounced these words: William II: 'God has helped us magnificently'; Clemenceau: 'I am delighted, everything is going well.' (23 and 24 March 1918). In the course of the German onslaught Péronne is captured. Noyon is captured. The Allies retreat from the Somme to the Oise (25–26 March).

26 March. Death of Claude Debussy. Poor 'little perishing Greece'.[2] Over a period of two years the wretched artist has been devoured by cancer. . . . The only creator of beauty in the music of our time. He was drained by voluptuousness, success, goodliving, idleness and disillusionment. What will remain of him? A few well-fashioned vases, a few small bas-reliefs of perfected workmanship soon to be hidden under the grass of the Appian Way. Vestiges of the supreme elegance of an Athens in ruins.

Easter Thursday, Good Friday. Decisive days, perhaps, for the history of Europe. From the Somme to Verdun the struggle is marked by supreme efforts. People are oppressed. They speak, walk about, smile and admire the flowers. . . . On Good Friday, 29 March, at four in the afternoon during the service of the *Tenebrae* a German bomb fell on a church in Paris destroying the Gothic arch and claiming 165 victims (75 killed) mostly women and children. . . .[3] Clemenceau at the Chamber, surrounded by anxious deputies, said to them: 'I am going to tell you a secret. Last night I slept, I slept well. . . .'

[1] Rolland continued corresponding with Strauss during the war. In 1917 Strauss in all naïvety suggested that if Rolland were to hear *Ariadne auf Naxos* he might profitably alter his view of contemporary German music. Their correspondence apparently came to an end when Strauss made the appalling *faux pas* of inviting Rolland to Germany 'in order to receive impressions of our people at war'.

[2] The allusion is to Rolland's John-Christopher who could hear 'in the distance the rumbling of cannon, coming to batter down that worn-out civilization, that perishing little Greece!'

[3] The church was the Eglise Saint-Gervais where Debussy in his youth had been greatly inspired by the music of Palestrina and Vittoria (see Vol. I, pp. 171–2).

Several versions, purporting to be eye-witness accounts, have been given of the circumstances of Debussy's death. The most reliable is undoubtedly that of Chouchou, Debussy's thirteen-year-old daughter, in the form of a letter to her half-brother, Raoul Bardac. It is a moving document of simplicity and candour, almost a love letter. Unique among the letters of Debussy's friends and relatives, it is without parallel even among the letters addressed to Debussy in his lifetime. Possessing a severe sense of discipline, the child is anxious to avoid any demonstration of her feelings ('Tears repressed are worth tears shed') but she is nevertheless able to convey their intensity:

My dear Raoul,

Have you received the last telegram? You have, haven't you? It was I who first thought of sending it to you. I wrote it out and then, thinking that identification papers would have to be produced at the post office which I don't possess because I am a little girl, I asked Dolly[1] to have it sent to you. She came here because I asked her to on account of the completely convulsed features of my poor mother. As soon as she had left Mama was asked to see Papa for the nurse said he was 'very bad'. Two doctors were quickly called in both of whom ordered an injection to be given so that he shouldn't suffer. As you may well believe, I understood what was happening. Roger-Ducasse who was there said to me: 'Come, Chouchou, kiss your father.' So I immediately thought it was all over. When I went back into the room Papa was sleeping and breathing regularly but in short breaths. He went on sleeping in this way until ten o'clock in the evening, and at this time, sweetly, angelically, he went to sleep for ever. What happened afterwards I cannot tell you. I wanted to burst into a torrent of tears but I repressed them because of Mama. Alone throughout the night in the big bed with Mama, I was unable to sleep a minute. I developed a temperature, my dry eyes questioned the walls, I couldn't believe what had happened.

The next day far too many people came to see Mama who at the end of the day could no longer stand the strain—both she and I had then to give in. Thursday came, Thursday when he

[1] Chouchou's half-sister Dolly Bardac, later Madame D. G. de Tinan, who inspired the title of the suite *Dolly* for piano duet by Fauré.

was going to be taken away for ever! I saw him for the last time in that horrible box—on the ground. He looked happy, oh so happy! and this time I didn't have the courage to repress my tears. As I almost fell over I couldn't kiss him. At the cemetery Mama could not of course hide her feelings. As for myself I thought of nothing but one thing: 'You mustn't cry because of Mama.' And so I gathered up all my courage which came—from where? I don't know. I didn't shed a tear: tears repressed are worth tears shed, and now it is to be night for ever. Papa is dead. Those three words, I do not understand them, or rather I understand them only too well. And to be here all alone, struggling against the indescribable grief of Mama is really frightful. For some days it caused me to forget my own grief but this is now more poignant than ever. You, who are so far away, think a little of your poor little sister who would so much like to embrace you and tell you how much she loves you! Do you understand all that I feel and which cannot be written? A thousand kisses and love from your little sister,

Chouchou.

It is unbelievable. I don't know how I go on living, and I cannot believe in the horrible reality.[1]

The funeral took place on the Thursday before Easter. The procession included only a few of Debussy's older friends. Godet was in Switzerland; Satie, after *Parade*, had taken offence at Debussy; Pierre Louÿs and René Peter had become estranged from him. Neither Ravel nor Stravinsky was present. Henri de Régnier was apparently alone in representing Debussy's earlier literary friends. Other mourners included Pierné and Chevillard, Vallery-Radot, Caplet, and Gustave Samazeuilh. Debussy's brother Alfred, on leave from the trenches, joined the procession as it was setting off. Fourteen years later Louis Laloy, who attended the funeral in military uniform, recalled his impressions:

I see as in a bad dream the coffin near the piano and the musicians in their soldiers' uniform. . . . The door kept on opening and

[1] Chouchou Debussy's sudden and unexpected death the following year was believed to be the result of a wrong diagnosis.

closing and there was no more room for the flowers. The Minister of Education took his place at the head of the procession. Side by side, in front of me, the two conductors of our great philharmonic societies, Camille Chevillard and Gabriel Pierné, walked in silence. All those concerts in which they had so lovingly played his music were over. The sky was overcast. There was a rumbling in the distance. Was it a storm, the explosion of a shell or the guns at the front? Along the wide avenues the only traffic consisted of military trucks; people on the pavements pressed ahead hurriedly. But there was still a bustle in the populous uphill streets of Montmartre. The children made way and stood in a line in the gutter, staring at us. The women shopkeepers questioned each other at their doors and glanced at the streamers on the wreaths. 'Il paraît que c'était un musicien', they said.

The procession which reached the cemetery at Père-Lachaise numbered only about thirty. Other mourners who set out from the Avenue du Bois de Boulogne had made off on the way. It was held that the gravity of the military situation made funeral orations superfluous. Within earshot of the rumbling of cannon, funeral orations would indeed have been sardonic. Only one perfunctory speech was made, on behalf of the Société des Auteurs, to which Laloy, he tells us, barely listened. Thus, to the hollow comment of the Montmartre shopkeepers, disappeared, at the most fearful climax of the war, the greatest French composer of his time: 'Il paraît que c'était un musicien.'

CONCLUSION

Debussy's Musical Language

Q

CONCLUSION
Debussy's Musical Language

Rien de plus cher que la chanson grise
Où l'Indécis au Précis se joint.

Verlaine

Quand la couleur est à sa richesse la forme est à sa plénitude.

Cézanne

In any view of Debussy's style and the elements of his musical language the main problem is to define his attitude to tonality. The vagueness of Debussy's sense of tonality, compared to that of Brahms, or even of Wagner, was long a commonplace in essays on musical analysis, and indeed in so far as this vagueness was held to be a characteristic of Impressionism from which, after Debussy's death, there was a sharp reaction,[1] it was held, too, to be a reprehensible aspect of his work, suggesting in his approach a certain tentativeness or a timidity. Today this view seems to us superficial. In the first place the short-lived reaction against Debussy's work, which took place in the 1920s, now seems to have been less an æsthetic than a fashionable movement. Also, with our knowledge of some of the underlying origins of the great revolutionary movements at the end of the nineteenth century, we are compelled, in an assessment of Debussy's style, to view values of precision and imprecision in artistic expression in a different light. Precision is

---

[1] In 1919, only a year after Debussy's death, Jacques Rivière, asking Stravinsky to contribute to the *Nouvelle Revue Française*, writes to him: 'I intend to direct the attention of the magazine to the anti-impressionist, anti-symbolist, and anti-Debussy movements that are becoming more and more precise and threatening to take the form and force of a vast new current.'

not entirely virtuous; imprecision is not wholly to be condemned. The æsthetic proclaimed by Debussy required their fusion.[1]

Inseparable from the conception of tonality was not only the theory of harmony based on the interplay of relative degrees of consonance and dissonance but also the musical forms in which this interplay was extended into a musical discourse, an abstract musical argument built on dissonant tensions prepared and resolved. In this view of music, accepted in the eighteenth century as a dogma, tonality was everything: an unassailable order prevailed, like the unquestioned social order of this period, allowing digressions of one kind or another provided that in the end these digressions served not a disrupting but a unifying purpose. This was the principle of the sonata form against which, in broad terms, the whole of the nineteenth century rebelled. But it was a slow, almost an imperceptible revolt with many charming explorations of lanes and by-paths on the way. By the end of the nineteenth century, even after Wagner, the underlying harmonic principles of the age of Mozart were still admitted; they had been tested in many different ways, amplified and adapted, but they had not been challenged. Moreover, the work of Debussy, as we see it today, achieved no more, harmonically, than was to be expected from any successor of Wagner. It broke down the rigidity of the tonal order a little more effectively, but the principles of tonality were not relinquished. The Preludes of Debussy, belonging to his later years, are still in certain keys and although, in the course of these short pieces, departures from the keys in which they are conceived are frequent and extremely remote, the pieces do just manage to begin and end in these keys. A step farther and the principles of tonality are completely undermined; there is then no going back, and the boundaries between consonance and dissonance disappear.[2]

The distinctive achievement of Debussy was not so much his novel, ambiguous harmony; it was his recognition of the fact that since an advanced stage in harmonic development had been reached

[1] The characteristic dictum of the period, André Schaeffner suggests, should be 'Laissez-moi y mettre un peu d'obscurité'. 'If these were not actually the words of Mallarmé,' he says, 'everyone of the period attempted to obscure the issue in his own way.'

[2] Schoenberg's song-cycle *Das Buch der hängenden Gärten* dates from 1908, a short time before the Preludes of Debussy. In this work Schoenberg declared that he was 'conscious of breaking all barriers with æsthetics of the past'. It is the work which represents, according to H. H. Stuckenschmidt, 'the liquidation of tonality'.

the older forms of music could not be maintained. The sophisticated design of the ternary sonata form, consisting of a thesis and antithesis, development and recapitulation, could not be built out of harmonic elements that were lush and almost over-ripe. Thematic or harmonic development, in the form of a musical argument ruthlessly pursued, demands a firmer, less ambiguous harmonic structure, and it was no doubt for this reason that Debussy particularly distrusted musical development as a method of composition. As opposed to the impact of isolated, sensuous chords, varied in intensity, or of fragmentary themes pursued in improvisatory fashion, thematic development in the works of Mozart, Beethoven, and Wagner appeared to Debussy to be based on a mechanical procedure, a mere formula—or at least he said so. It was of course based on nothing of the sort; it was simply that organic development of this kind formed part of an entirely different philosophy. It came about, however, that an organic development of themes was brilliantly used by Debussy in several of his larger works (*La Mer*, second movement; *Pelléas*, the scene with Yniold; and *Rondes de Printemps*). Debussy was not exactly contradicting himself here. As often happens at critical periods in artistic development, theories were in advance of practice. Debussy was logically sound in condemning the classical forms once the validity of tonality had been challenged, but in his larger works he had not yet found the new forms demanded.[1]

Several recent studies on Debussy's harmony have tended to seek hidden rules for the nature and succession of his chords and thereby to establish plans of his musical forms of which the exploratory composer himself must surely have been unaware, even subconsciously. Debussy's technique is admittedly difficult to define, but, if only for the reason that it is largely empirical, the key to his technique is not likely to be found in abstract, technical arguments. 'The predominant feature of Debussy's instrumental works is repetition', observed the Belgian composer Paul Gilson in 1907

---

[1] A similar dilemma was faced by Schoenberg who, having ruthlessly swept aside the fundamental principles of tonality, anachronistically resorted to the forms most closely associated with tonality (the sonata form and the variation form) with redoubled severity. In his book *Debussy* written in 1913 with the composer's knowledge, if not his authority, Daniel Chennevière unequivocally states: 'Le classicisme est mort.' It was at any rate a pronouncement justified by Debussy's earlier admonition: 'Il faut noyer le ton.'

in a letter on the problems of Debussy's technique addressed to
Ernest Closson.

Incidental clauses are linked together as motives in a tapestry
but then suddenly the whole scheme is broken (for no other reason
than that a new idea is desirable) though the original motive
may be taken up later. [Gilson was probably referring here to
La Mer.] This is ornamental music in the broadest sense of the
term. It is undoubtedly true that in regard to works which are
solidly constructed the listener is at first able to grasp only certain
details. Such works have to be heard many times before the
listener is aware of their architecture (and this will really be
discovered only after *reading* the works; it is a task for the
analysts). Perhaps, then, it is a useless task to undertake, this
matter of 'constructing' and organizing a work of music as a
whole, of compelling oneself to follow a pre-conceived plan, or
of kneading and re-kneading the music so that it should assume
certain architectural proportions, since when all this is done
the listener will grasp very little of the over-all plan and he
will be affected only by the impression of the moment. The
instrumental works in question [those of Debussy] appear to
consist of a series of impressions connected by 'repeats' and their
instrumentation is accordingly the same as Debussy's harmony
itself, entirely impressionistic.[1]

Half a century later critics less finely attuned to the workings of
Debussy's mind attempted to discover a deeper significance in the
fleeting nature of his harmony. Arguing that since there is seldom
cadential harmony in Debussy's works, only chords which have an
isolated, 'monistic' value in themselves, Albert Jakobik maintains
that the form of a work of Debussy is determined by the relative

[1] Gilson's two letters of 1907 to Ernest Closson on Debussy's technique, published
in *La Revue belge de musicologie*, Vol. XVI, 1962, deal principally with matters of
chord formation. It is curious to see that Gilson, like Albert Jakobik fifty years later,
was struck by the absence of cadential harmony in Debussy's work (i.e. where a
hierarchy is established between the subdominant, the dominant and the tonic). It was
this, Gilson rightly maintained, which created the sense of vagueness: 'The absence of
the established tonal succession of the chords I V, I IV, and vice versa, which is at the
basis of classical harmony, gives the music of Debussy its vagueness and imprecision
[*Cette teinte vaporeuse, indécise, la tonalité étant indécise, qui lui est particulière*]. By tonal
imprecision I do not mean modulations (with the establishment of a new tonic) as in
Wagner. When Wagner modulates he remains at least eight times out of ten *tonal*.'

complexity of his chords. In the Prelude *Feuilles mortes* it is the
chord in bar 2,

a complex form of the chord of C sharp minor, overlaid with its
relative major, which magnetizes other chords towards it and which
is thus held to be the central pivot of the piece. Other writers have
investigated Debussy's use of the Gregorian modes and the pentatonic scales, notably Julia d'Almendra and Constantin Brailoiu,
the latter listing no less than 182 examples of the use of pentatonic
scales in the works of Debussy, ranging from the early song *Fleur
des blés* to the piano Studies. This is a most remarkable compilation
which allows Brailoiu to put forward the theory, nevertheless
debatable, that Debussy knowingly used these scales. On the other
hand, the properties of the hexaphonic or whole-tone scale must

surely have been prominently in Debussy's conscious mind. If it had not been older than the major and minor scales the whole-tone scale, used systematically in *L'Isle joyeuse* and *Voiles*, would seem to have been designed for the express purpose of blurring the precision of tonality. The oscillations of key in *Voiles*, which opens in A minor, but which immediately shifts into the relative C major while melodic fragments are pinned down on to a B flat pedal, are a model of the ambiguities in Debussy's work of key relationships. (See second example on p. 233.) Such static ambiguities of key have, of course, an entirely different function from the dynamic function of modulations. They are, as it were, modulations collapsed into a single moment, deprived of their perspective.

The trouble with technical analyses is that they are likely to degenerate into studies of musical puzzles, of interest to the practitioner of composition if he is so minded, and revealing little relationship to the æsthetic principles which we expect a composer's technique to serve. Fortunately the motives of several aspects of Debussy's technique have been clearly defined. Drawing a sharp distinction between the secret of an artist's work and its mystery— the one is connected with a technical, the other with a philosophical approach—Vladimir Jankélévitch suggests that the many dragging rhythms and pedals used by Debussy indicate a preoccupation in his work with stagnation and particularly the stagnation of water.[1] The dragging rhythm of the Prelude *Des Pas sur la neige*

[1] The most remarkable illustration of this preoccupation is the passage in *Pelléas*, Act III, Scene ii, when Golaud says: 'Eh bien, voici l'eau stagnante dont je vous parlais. Sentez-vous l'odeur de mort qui monte? ... Voyez-vous le gouffre, Pelléas ... Pelléas?'

is found in many other works, among them the song *Auprès de cette Grotte sombre* and the section of *La Boîte à joujoux* in which a Hindu chant is heard over a pedal.

Pedals designed to produce a sombre, if not a blurred effect are found in *En Sourdine* and in the series of pieces in which the tragic aspects of the Spanish scene are emphasized, *La Puerta del Vino*, *Lindaraja*, and the *Soirée dans Grenade*. A predilection for ostinato effects and for the indulgent rhythm of the habanera with its groups of three and two notes to a beat in two-four time belong to the same order of ideas. These are works which belong to the darker side of Debussy's character.

In contrast are the ecstatic, whirlwind pieces in quick tempo, in the nature of a *perpetuum mobile*, spiral-like constructions which, however, for all their animation, do not proceed towards a goal. They too are static, anticipating the hypnotic rhythms in the early works of Stravinsky but infinitely lighter and nearly always diaphanous. *Les Fées sont d'exquises danseuses*,[1] *Le Vent dans la plaine*, *Pagodes*, and *Jardins sous la pluie* belong to this type of gyratory virtuoso music. Few musicians after Wagner were able, as was Debussy, to write music that seems to plunge into space. Effects calculated to produce an impression of space and distance include the remote trumpet calls in *Khamma*, similar devices in *Feux*

[1] Paul Hooreman, in an article in *La Revue de Musicologie*, 1962, showed that this title which, alone among the titles of the Preludes, appears in inverted commas, was taken from the following passage in Chapter IV, 'Lock-out Time', of J. M. Barrie's *Peter Pan in Kensington Gardens*, 1906 (French edition, *Piter Pan: Les Jardins de Kensington*, 1907 and 1911): 'The fairies are exquisite dancers, and that is why one of the first things the baby does is to sign to you to dance to him and then to cry when you do it.' This publication contained coloured drawings by Arthur Rackham, the one illustrating the passage which inspired Debussy's Prelude showing a fairy suspended over a spider's web, dancing on gossamer to the sound of a bass viol played by a spider. Monsieur Hooreman surmises that Robert Godet had sent the Barrie-Rackham publication of *Peter Pan* to Debussy's daughter. On 3 January 1912 Debussy wrote to him: 'Très cher Godet, Chouchou, pour qui Rackham est déjà "ce vieux Rackham" a été ravie de votre envoi. Elle me prie de vous en remercier "bien gentiment" en vous souhaitant une "bonne et heureuse année". Vieille formule qui reprend toute sa grâce en passant par la bouche d'un enfant!' Rackham's drawings, which include illustrations of the operas of Wagner, were exhibited in Paris in 1912.

d'artifice and the *Berceuse héroïque*, and the passage for horns in the interlude before the last scene of Act III of *Pelléas*. This idea of a scene enacted far away, the *danse lointaine*, occurs also at the end of the *Soirée dans Grenade* and again in the central section of the final piano Study, *Pour les Accords*. Distance, space, and also light are suggested in the widely spread textures of certain of the piano works, *Brouillards*, the *Terrasse des audiences*, and the Study *Pour les Sonorités opposées* (See example on p. 236).

An illuminating comparison was made by Monsieur Jankélévitch between the character of certain of Debussy's melodic designs and a phenomenon in botany. Geotropism is the name given to the phenomenon which causes the roots of plants to gravitate towards the centre of the earth. Positive geotropism is the term used for this attraction to a centre of gravity, while negative geotropism signifies the tendency of stems to grow away from the centre of the earth. One is reminded here of the symbolical significance of the floral and plant designs of the Art Nouveau and their connexion with the flowing lines of women's hair. Many of the typical arabesque designs of Debussy appear to be propelled by a downward-moving force. Phrases such as this from *Syrinx*:

and from the opening of *Le Faune* (*Fêtes galantes*, second series):

are unquestionably a musical counterpart of the decorative designs carried over into Impressionism from the Art Nouveau. Falling snow and falling rain are of course illustrated in this same symbolical manner, by means of arpeggios or staccato figures in *Jardins sous la pluie* and *Pour remercier la Pluie au matin* and by a technique similar to that of the Pointillist painters in *Snow is dancing*. To express indolence and languor, particularly sensuous languor, Debussy uses a similar downward-moving design, evident in the opening of *Je tremble en voyant ton visage*:

and also in *En Sourdine* and the *Colloque sentimental* with their nervous triplets reminiscent of the early piano *Arabesque No. 2*:

Finally on this matter of the significance of the downward-moving phrase there are elements, in each of the following four examples, of both fear and flight.[1]

[1] In the chapter entitled *Géotropisme* in his work on Debussy M. Jankélévitch investigates several other technical aspects of Debussy's expressions of fear and flight, some of them symbolized by a descending harmonic design. 'Cette inclinaison pudique vers le bas', he concludes, 'est une des marques les plus caractéristiques de la phrase debussyste.'

In the last quarter of the nineteenth century the attraction of French composers—Satie, Duparc, Chausson, and Ravel, besides Debussy—to the chord of the dominant ninth or, without its fundamental, the diminished seventh, reveals the first tonal ambiguities taking the form of a musical counterpart of Impressionism. The particular property of the chord of the diminished seventh is that it is a pivot, modulating chord which may branch out into one of eight tonalities (four major and four minor). If, however, this chord is not used to modulate into another key but is linked to other seventh chords in the form of a succession a continuous feeling of suspense is created:

Once we recognize this use of chords of the seventh and ninth as a means of creating suspense we have a key to the function of other chords in Debussy's harmony. Jankélévitch draws attention to a feeling not exactly of suspense but to the kindred feeling of rootlessness. This is created by the juxtaposition of common chords, each belonging to a different tonality. Contrasted in this way, these chords do not represent a continuity of musical thought; they do not create a rational musical argument. They merely exist in space, or more precisely in musical time, as if drawn to each other by some kind of astrological 'influence'. A striking, and indeed an almost literal illustration of this technique occurs in *La Damoiselle élue* where a succession of common chords evoking the five servants

[240]

in heaven of the Blessed Damozel passes through no less than ten tonalities.[1]

Sometimes the rootlessness of these common chords (or variations of them) is emphasized by the direction, as in *La Cathédrale engloutie*, that they should be played 'sans nuances'. A bland, almost expressionless region is then suggested, the bleak hinterland of the imagination.

[1] They are F sharp minor, E minor, D major, F minor, D major, E major, C minor, D major, G major, and C major.

If Debussy's use of the chord of the seventh and the common chord have these functions of suspense and ambiguity his use of the interval of the second, either in chords or more often alone, is designed to convey one of the many gradations of feeling between indulgence and irony. Intervals of the second have, of course, been used in almost all forms of the harmonic language, notably in inversions of the chord of the seventh. But this traditional use in harmony of the interval of the second (that is to say as a dissonance requiring resolution) does not quite correspond to the use made of this interval by Debussy. Once again our perspicacious guide here is Monsieur Jankélévitch. He writes: 'Just as the downward moving design of the arabesque [in Debussy's works] ends by defeating itself in the form of a design of horizontal uniformity or in monotonously repeated notes, so the dissonant chord, the more it becomes contracted or drawn together, ends by becoming reduced to the interval of the second, which is the smallest possible interval and, in a sense, the negation of harmony.' If we look at it in this way 'the interval of the second marks the point where music returns to the realm of noise. . . . For what is this interval if not a single note disturbed only by its adjacent note, the smallest chord of all beyond which is the unison?'

The fact is that the interval of the second, both the major and the minor second which are inversions of the minor and major sevenths, were used by Debussy, as also by Stravinsky and Bartók, as a dissonance having a certain sonorous value in itself, regardless of its function in a three- or four-note chord and without any question of its resolution. This interval, probably first used in this way by Borodin, was the quintessential dissonance. Jankélévitch was right in suggesting that beyond the interval of the second we approach the borderland of music and noise. At what point does sound advance into music or, on the other hand, at what point does it retreat into noise? Debussy did not live to see the beginnings of *musique concrète* though certain of his harsher uses of the second, based on the principle that there are ultimately no borderlands between music and sound and noise, do in a sense foreshadow this present-day concept.

Despite these forward-looking views, Debussy regarded the dissonance of the second as relative, that is to say it was made to convey different effects of dissonance in different works. As we may see from the following examples, from a piece such as *Le Jet d'eau*, where seconds are used in a sensuous manner, to the harsh, threatening seconds in many of the later works, among them *Khamma*, *Ce qu'a vu le vent d'ouest*, and *En blanc et noir*, the variety of expression with which this particular interval is endowed is enormous.

All these functions of harmony bring us back eventually to the problems of form. For the painters form was inseparable from colour; for the musicians it was inseparable from the colour of instruments, from timbre. In earlier periods principles of form had no relation whatever to timbre. Indeed, before Debussy the word 'timbre', as opposed to 'tone-colour', had hardly entered the musical vocabulary. In Debussy's works timbre, or at any rate the nature of the instrument, does very largely determine formal procedures. In the piano works, as we have seen, a blurring, ambiguous technique was largely established by the nature of the piano overtones and the use of the pedals. Though the piano pieces seldom make use of thematic development an underlying sense of key is nevertheless maintained. In the orchestral works the tonal deformations are more complex. Drawing attention to the fact that the harmony of the first movement of *La Mer* consists almost entirely of sevenths and ninths, with the bass note omitted, Ernest Ansermet has shown that as a rule tonality is only implied in Debussy's works. Even when one can be relatively sure of the underlying tonality any kind of scheme of related tonalities, on which the symphonic form is normally founded, is seldom adhered to. The first movement of *La Mer* may be said to open in D minor while it concludes in the remote key of D flat. Following the introduction there are two episodes, each of which can be subdivided, broadly in D flat and B flat, a transitional section in A flat and the D flat coda. It is the first important example of a symphonic movement maintaining an onward drive without development. The second movement oscillates between E major and E minor and the last movement, opening in the implied key of E major, ends in D flat. Similar departures from orthodox procedure occur in the orchestral *Images* and in the sequence of episodes forming the score of the ballet *Jeux*. The difficulties of analysing a score of Debussy in any detail have been described by Pierre Boulez: 'A component section of a theme is defined as another is selected. We place them together and an outline of a theme is suggested; another phrase is added and we have the beginnings of a form. More material is added and we have a structure.' Perhaps in the end we may best summarize Debussy's method of composition in the simple definition of Cézanne: 'Je travaille sur le motif.' The *motif* is the generating design or symbol. How it proceeds to acquire a form is so much an internal matter that any kind of formal analysis is bound to be inadequate.

Yet the effort to convey the principles of Debussy's forms must be made. Once the æsthetic principles on which an artist builds his work are defined it becomes at any rate easier to decide on the type of critical approach to his work which is most likely to enrich our knowledge of it. Indeed, without a preliminary enquiry into the life and mind of an artist on the broadest possible lines we cannot begin to particularize on matters of technical procedure. The foregoing summary of some of the main elements of Debussy's technique does not pretend to offer more than an outline of a vast subject. Nor does it claim, within the modest framework of a concluding chapter, to have approached all the essential aspects of his technique. Principles of harmony and form in Debussy's work have been investigated but scholars have hardly touched upon the elusive nature of Debussy's orchestration. Elsewhere the matter of Debussy's sketches and manuscripts, particularly the numerous manuscript versions of *Pelléas et Mélisande* (listed in Vol. I, Appendix E), the corrections to both his manuscript and printed works and the nature of his unpublished or discarded works—this enquiry into the whole matter of Debussy's manuscripts is in itself a subject of the first importance. Above all, the wide span of Debussy's evolution requires assessment from this technical viewpoint. Now that the world of his ideas has been made known the technicians and the analysts have the field before them.

APPENDIX A

PROJECTS FOR 'AS YOU LIKE IT'

The two works of Debussy inspired by Shakespeare are the Prelude, *La Danse de Puck*, and the posthumously published incidental music for Antoine's production of *King Lear*. Many other works of Shakespeare were of course known to Debussy besides the plays illustrated in these small-scale compositions. He was drawn particularly to the character of Hamlet, played by Sarah Bernhardt in 1899 and whom he refers to in his correspondence as 'a kindred neurasthenic'. As we have seen, in 1902 he went to London purposely to see Forbes-Robertson in *Hamlet*. Every age gets the *Hamlet* it deserves and Debussy was aware that the Hamlet figures of his time were the indecisive Pelléas and the introspective Roderick Usher.

The French image of Shakespeare at this time had obviously a far-reaching influence on Debussy's work as a whole. Among the fleeting ideas to which he was drawn in his youth was a setting of *As You Like It* in an arrangement by the poet Maurice Vaucaire. According to Vallas, Debussy agreed to write the music for this play when he was a student in Rome. This may account for his somewhat surprising statement, in answer to a questionnaire of 1889 (reproduced in Vol. I, Appendix G), that his favourite heroine in drama at that time was Rosalind. However this may be, it was in Rome that he appears first to have become acquainted with Shakespeare, taking part with Paul Vidal and Xavier Leroux in readings of his plays. He was not indifferent to the important matter of Shakespeare translations. He had a preference, we are told, for the translations by Emile Montégut, which he considered superior to the over-romanticized translations by François Victor Hugo, son of the poet.

This early project for *As You Like It* was abandoned on Debussy's return to Paris but it was apparently kept alive in his mind for it was the first of several ideas for an opera to which he turned after *Pelléas et Mélisande*. In the summer of 1902, three months after the production of *Pelléas*, he writes to the poet and novelist Paul-Jean Toulet: 'I should like to have news of *Comme il vous plaira*. I am thinking of it incessantly and would like to think of it with you in mind.'

Debussy's plans for this Shakespeare opera are worth investigating in some detail. Before doing so, however, it will be helpful to bring into relief the shy, sensitive figure of Debussy's collaborator, not only because of his part in this project but also because the nature of their artistic relationship throws some light on certain of Debussy's ideas as he developed them in other works.

A seeker of sensation in the manner of Baudelaire, Toulet had spent part of his youth in Mauritius, where he became addicted to opium, and later travelled in Spain and the Orient. In 1899 he went to London to visit the writer influenced by occult sciences, Arthur Machen, whose *The Great God Pan* he translated.[1] Shortly afterwards he met Debussy. 'Dès le premier jour', Toulet notes, 'nous avons été amis comme cochons.' Their intimacy was based on an indulgence in literary banter, also on the sharing of personal secrets of their emotional and amorous lives, but particularly on their admiration for certain writers, notably Stendhal.[2] Some of the ideas, if not the titles, of Debussy's works may have derived from his knowledge of Toulet's writings. Toulet was strongly drawn to Dickens. Mr. Pickwick, he states, illustrated in one of the Preludes, 'is almost as widely read in Paris as in London.' In his novel *Monsieur du Paur*, partly influenced by Machen, Toulet hints at the associations of falling snowflakes in a manner which brings to mind *Snow is Dancing* from *Children's Corner*.[3] Toulet took little interest in musical affairs but his heart went out to Debussy as a victim of musical publicity. A curious 'Intervioue de M. Claude Debussy', which appeared in *Les Marges*, October 12, is in the form of a skit on the ignorance of musical journalists.

No music is known to have been written by Debussy for *As You Like It*, but his correspondence with Toulet, together with Toulet's sketches for the libretto, allows us to form a fairly clear idea of this

[1] This work, admired by Debussy and mentioned in his first published letter to Toulet, apparently opened a way to their friendship.
[2] In his *Notes de Littérature* (1926) Toulet describes the entirely fresh appeal made by Stendhal. He is not, he maintains, a stylist, nor an historian, nor even a critic. 'C'est un amoureux qui se découvre. . . . C'est la vie toute pure.' After Debussy's death it was his copy of Stendhal that Toulet repeatedly requested from Madame Debussy: 'I still want one of the books Claude was in the habit of reading. As I must point out once again, his Stendhal would be the thing. . . . You see that I am a persistent beggar.'
[3] 'Quel opium que la neige, pour exagérer notre paresse et la simplicité de nos désirs', he searchingly records. 'Et j'aurais aimé encore, avec cette petite Thérèse, maintenant perdue, rester auprès d'une fenêtre à suivre des yeux les flocons monotones. . . .'

project with which he was concerned until the end of his life. By the autumn of 1902 Toulet had submitted two sketches. 'Let us return to good Monsieur William', Debussy eagerly writes to him on 21 October:

> The second plan you sent me suits me in every way. Don't you think we might heighten the interest of the first scene by the introduction of a choir off-stage which would comment on the various incidents of Orlando's wrestle? They would have exclamations to sing such as 'He's down! No, he's not! Ah! He's no coward!' But, joking apart, I think that musically this idea could offer something quite original. And I would like to have some of the songs sung by a group of people. The duke is rich enough to have the Chanteurs de Saint-Gervais[1] and their conductor come to the Forest of Arden. In regard to the end I agree with you; let us leave these people in the forest. We must find some lovely ceremonial for the betrothal and have it end joyfully. Whenever you can replace the exact word by its lyrical counterpart don't hesitate. That doesn't mean that the tone in which the two scenes are written doesn't please me. Quite the contrary. I make this suggestion because of your fear of being too rhythmical. Be assured that it will all be brought out in the music. I have an idea which I offer to you for what it is worth. Couldn't we use the scene between Charles the wrestler and Oliver (Shakespeare, Scene i) as an introduction? Send me everything you can before you leave. I am convinced we have something really admirable.

Toulet was leaving for Tonkin with his journalist friend Maurice Sailland (known as Curnonsky) but he hastened to meet Debussy's requirements and to supply at any rate a considerable part of the libretto. He writes in reply in October:

> Here is scene i as I had begun it before your letter. The opening would have made a delightful scene as the curtain rises (Celia leaning on the balustrade on the right, and Rosalind slowly walking up towards her from the garden) which must be sacrificed if there is to be a scene before this.

[1] The choral society whose adventurous programmes, including performances of neglected works by Palestrina and Vittoria, had impressed Debussy in 1893.

It won't matter much and we may bring it in later. But I think the introduction required should be built from the dialogue of Celia and Rosalind. Actually, the conversation between Oliver and the wrestler can only emphasize Oliver's hatred of Orlando which we should perhaps rather tone down and make less melodramatic. (Note that Orlando's departure, which is an important feature, cannot be suggested in this scene since it occurs later as the result of a whim of the duke.) [His reference is to Act I, Scene ii, where Orlando says he is the son of the duke's enemy.] Therefore, since the characters of Oliver and the wrestler are subsidiary can they not be introduced later, in scenes ii and iii? At the end of scene i, between Celia and Rosalind, Oliver appears and speaks of the wrestler and the three exhausted young men [i.e. the brothers whom the wrestler had vanquished]. Then appears the wrestler himself who has just told Oliver that he, a wrestler, has been defied by his brother Orlando. It continues as in Shakespeare, but shorter and decidedly less harsh [*surtout adouci*]. The presence of the girls should not allow the scene to become hateful, Oliver not wishing to kill his brother but to see that he gets 'a good lesson'. 'A broken rib or two', he says, 'will make a man of him.' Apart from this I am most enthusiastic about the choir exclaiming off-stage during the wrestle. The girls themselves would not say a word; this will emphasize their concern while Oliver will utter a few words in his ironic manner.

There you are—please decide and reply by return. . . . As for the scene between Celia and Rosalind which I am sending you, note that a part of it, that in which they speak of their disguises and their assumed names, is transferred to the end of the tableau to a scene in which they persuade the clown [i.e. Touchstone] to go off with them. . . .

Debussy accepted this plan enthusiastically (or seemingly so; one cannot be quite sure) and wrote on 25 October:

Your arguments are better than mine and I accept them without further ado. You have met my desire to clarify the tenuous, complicated plot of *Comme il vous plaira* in a different way, and this is splendid.

You say nothing, however, about what I had said on the matter of the ceremony of the betrothals, which to my mind should make a graceful conclusion. I see it as an opportunity for a scenic spectacle in which wonderfully clothed people would enter to clearly marked rhythms leading to the entry of Orlando's Rosalind. All this intermingled with songs in an early style [à la façon antique], that is to say integrated in the action. Don't be afraid of developing the character of Touchstone—his fantastic character is altogether his own. This must surely be your opinion. I am alarmed to think that you are leaving so soon, for you have made me impatient to have every detail of this human fairy play. Don't forget me in the yellowness of Tonkin.

The details in these letters show the character of this projected work to have been light, charming, and decorous. At any rate, this is the impression conveyed by the sketches of Toulet. On the interpretation of Touchstone, half-philosopher, half-buffoon, Debussy and his kindly disposed collaborator were perhaps agreed. In regard to the other characters there was seemingly a difference of opinion. Toulet proposes that Oliver's hatred of his brother Orlando should not be emphasized, and he thereby distorts one of the central themes of the play. In Shakespeare Oliver does not hope to see Orlando emerge from the wrestling match 'with a broken rib or two'; he would not be sorry to see his attractive brother murdered by the professional wrestler. Moreover, the wrestling scene, suggested by Debussy as an introduction to the opera, is of the first dramatic importance, and one gathers that he did not entirely approve of Toulet's intention to transform it into a subsidiary episode.

On his return from the East in 1903 Toulet was beginning to suffer from the effects of opium, and it is doubtful whether he was physically capable of completing the libretto.[1] 'Some of the characters of Comme il vous plaira', he writes, 'have lain down on the grass and gone to sleep. Others have got lost in the forest and, God forgive me, were making a disreputable place of it.'

The project was, however, revived in another form in 1917 when

---

[1] 'If our terms of friendship did not forbid any painful discussions', Debussy wrote to him in August 1903, 'I would have told you long ago how sorry I am that you had taken to opium. An imagination as delicate as yours must obviously suffer under this. And now life is warning you . . . that you should have nothing to do with this sinister drug. It would be presumptuous of me to speak to you about this on a deeper level.'

Debussy saw a celebrated performance of *The Merchant of Venice* with Firmin Gémier as Shylock. This was the part in which this actor was held to have reached the height of his great reputation. 'I spoke to him of my old passion for *Comme il vous plaira*', Debussy writes to Toulet on 8 June 1917, 'and told him that if he intended to produce it I should like him to reserve for me the honour of writing the incidental music.' There was now no question of using Toulet's original sketches; a literal translation was what was required. By this time Debussy was desperately ill and Toulet was hard-pressed.[1] 'I distrust Gémier', Toulet wrote to Madame Debussy. 'I rather think that, like Antoine, he is afflicted with Shakespearitis [*chexpyrite*] and wants a severely literal translation.' Debussy implored him to see the play from Gémier's viewpoint. He wrote on 20 June 1917:

> Like poor Mélisande, 'je ne fais pas ce que je veux', which is indeed the greatest punishment. You imagine Gémier to be too much of a disciple of Shakespeare. If only you knew the translation of *The Merchant of Venice* you would be reassured. All Gémier wants is to use his gifts as a producer and to make his crowds move about. *As You Like It* will not be of much use to him for this. But he'll find some means of doing what he wants, you may be sure. If necessary he'll make the theatre attendants act or have the people in the stalls go and change places with the people in the balcony. But without any pointless jokes, I believe you could do *As You Like It*.

The last mention of the project is in a letter from Debussy to Jacques Durand of November 1917, from which it appears that Toulet and Gémier came to some agreement. But it was too late. The remaining four months of Debussy's life were spent in agony, and the plan for a musical version of *As You Like It*, spanning the whole of his life, came to nothing.

There are, however, several illuminating aspects of this project. Debussy was drawn not only to the characters of Rosalind and Touchstone and to the ceremonial aspects of the betrothal scene. He was apparently deeply moved by the introspective character of

---

[1] 'This project appeals to me for it means money', Toulet wrote to the poet and critic, Emile Henriot, 'and it will be the first time that I shall be earning money honestly.'

Jacques. This transpires from the recorded conversations of Robert Godet and Georges Jean-Aubry.[1] His preoccupation with Jacques, though not referred to in the correspondence with Toulet, suggests that Debussy was concerned with some of the deeper meanings of *As You Like It*. He might even have seen in this melancholy character a reflection of himself. 'Jacques is the only purely contemplative character in Shakespeare', Hazlitt writes. 'He thinks, and does nothing. His whole occupation is to amuse his mind, and he is totally regardless of his body and his fortunes.' Hazlitt even sees him as a kind of Monsieur Croche: 'He is the prince of philosophical idlers; his only passion is thought.'

It is likely that Debussy knew of a bold version of *As You Like It*, made earlier by George Sand, in which Jacques became the guiding spirit of the whole play and in which he was represented as madly in love with Celia. Overcome by a fit of jealousy, he is with difficulty restrained from fighting a duel with Orlando and the play ends with his marriage to Celia. Singular views of *As You Like It* were held by other French writers known to Debussy. For François Victor Hugo it was a 'lugubrious tragedy, opening with groans and ending with groans'. I am not suggesting that Debussy's awareness of some of the underlying conflicts in *As You Like It* led him to endorse a grotesque interpretation of this order. Rosalind, he said, was his favourite heroine, and we need look no farther. Thoroughly Debussyan is the impression which H. N. Hudson conveyed of Rosalind's character in 1880. 'In its irrepressible vivacity the pleasure of Rosalind waits not for occasion but runs on for ever. . . . We have a sort of faith that her dreams are made up of cunning, quirkish, graceful fancies, her wits being in a frolic even when she is asleep. . . . No sort of unhappiness can live in her company.'

[1] The relevant passage from the *Lettres à deux amis*, though the language is precious, is worth quoting for the connexion with another work of Debussy's, the Clarinet Rhapsody:

R.G.: . . . Mais saviez-vous qu'alors déjà la forêt d'*As you like it* recélait un fantôme bénéfique, et si congénial à notre ami que le projet formé par lui plus tard de composer une musique debussyste pour un "Comme il vous plaira", version Toulet, naquit de son intimité avec Jacques le Mélancolique?

G.J-A: Il dut se contenter, n'est-ce-pas, de lui offrir l'hommage de sa fidèle pensée dans sa *Rapsodie* pour clarinette?

R.G.: Dans la plus rêveuse de ses rapsodies, c'est juste, et il me fit l'honneur de joindre mon nom à celui du rêveur shakespearien sur l'envoi qu'il m'en adressa.

It remains to assess the published excerpts from Toulet's translation of *As You Like It*. The correspondence between Toulet and Debussy in 1917 suggests that a version made for the earlier project had been mislaid. 'You never entrusted me with anything of your old work and I have too much respect for your writing to have forgotten it. There is no question of my having lost it.'[1] Two publications of Toulet's translations have appeared: a few verses, presented by Henri Martineau, under the title 'En suivant Shakespeare' in *La Revue critique des idées et des livres*, July 1922; and seven short sections from the play in Martineau's edition of Toulet's unpublished poems (*Vers inédits*, Paris, 1936). These consist of free translations of Jacques' 'Seven ages of Man', 'Under the greenwood tree', Jacques' song 'What shall he have that killed the deer?' (Act IV, Scene ii), 'Blow, blow, thou winter wind' and Orlando's song 'From the East to Western Ind' (Act III, Scene ii). The translations of the songs were perhaps prompted by Debussy's letter of 1917: 'The vocal element can play a big part in *Comme il vous plaira*. I do not intend to miss any of the songs which adorn the text. I recommend them to your sense of kindness and, more than this, to your lyrical sense.' The translation of the 'Seven Ages of Man' is a curtailed version which, however, ends with lines to which Debussy, in the last months of his life, could not have been indifferent:

Le dénouement de cette histoire
C'est la seconde enfance en des langes nouveaux,
Des pas traînants qui tâtent le tombeau,
C'est un aveugle, un sourd, sans amour, sans mémoire.

Elsewhere Toulet apparently devised an original scene—for it does not appear anywhere in Shakespeare—consisting of an evocation of the four seasons spoken alternately by the huntsmen and the foresters. In the end they join forces to proclaim faith in a rebirth and in the perpetual renewal of the cycle of life.

[1] In his introduction to the correspondence of Debussy and Toulet, Henri Martineau states that 'there is a manuscript in the hand of Toulet, almost complete, in which Debussy underlined in pencil every word which he replaced by its lyrical counterpart.' This manuscript, now in the possession of Madame Cahen Martineau, is undoubtedly the one referred to.

APPENDIX B

MANUEL DE FALLA ON DEBUSSY

The most conspicuous of the non-French aspects of Debussy's work are those of Spanish origin. This is not surprising; the same is true of other composers, among them Bizet, Chabrier, and Ravel, and it is a well-known historical fact, recognized by the Spaniards themselves, that the most original and often the most authentic Spanish music has been written north of the Pyrenees. This came about partly because in France, unlike Spain, there were traditions of symphonic music, but also because the attraction of the romantic Spanish scene for French artists had a long history. The Spanish works of Debussy, who admired both *Carmen* and the folk-song collections of Pedrell, are the most powerfully inspired of all twentieth-century works using features of Spanish folk-music, as Manuel de Falla, the principal Spanish composer of this period, freely recognized. Indeed, as J. B. Trend pointed out in his study, *Manuel de Falla and Spanish Music*, 'it was Debussy who revealed things in the spirit of Andalusian music which had been hidden or not clearly discerned even by Falla, who was born and bred in Andalusia'. Beginning with *Soirée dans Grenade* Debussy wrote several 'Nights in the Gardens of Spain' before Falla's composition of this title and Professor Trend, who knew Falla well, made it clear that the turning-point in Falla's career dates from his journey to Paris and his meeting with Debussy in 1907. On the artistic connexions between the two composers he writes:

Debussy's Andalusia was an Andalusia of dreams . . . and to Debussy, Falla must have seemed like a visitor from his own dream-land. But if Debussy heard from Falla that his dreams had in a sense come true, Falla must have felt that he himself was, as it were, part of Debussy's dream—that he held the keys and knew the facts of those regions which Debussy knew only in imagination. Many of Debussy's works created a marvellous atmosphere of poetry and suggestion; to Falla these came with the force of an *evocación* of his own country and its music, and all his later works (down to *The Puppet Show* and the Harpsichord Concerto) may be regarded as an effort to convey this poetry and

[254]

suggestiveness with the conviction of one who knows that dreams can sometimes come true. So far he had been expressing the letter of Andalusian music; he began now to realize how Debussy had managed to convey the spirit.[1]

Bizet, who went no farther south than Bordeaux, refused to visit Spain. 'Ça me gênerait', he cautiously explained. Reality, Bizet felt, would too brutally disturb the vivid Spanish scene of his imagination. The Spanish evocations in Debussy's piano pieces and in *Ibéria* similarly derived from his imagination. After Debussy's death Falla's tribute to him was the noble *Homenaje* for guitar forming part of *Le Tombeau de Debussy*, published as a supplement to *La Revue Musicale* (December 1920). One of the first serious pieces written in modern times for the guitar, it incorporates reminiscences of the *Soirée dans Grenade*.[2] In the same number of this journal Falla discusses at length the technique and character of Debussy's Spanish pieces. This paper which, Professor Trend insisted, 'should be read in Falla's own words, as they were hammered out through several autumn mornings near the Alhambra', has not hitherto been made available to English readers. It is presented here in a translation from the French amplified with explanatory notes and a musical quotation.

*　　*　　*

Claude Debussy wrote Spanish music without knowing Spain, that is to say without knowing the land of Spain, which is a different matter. Debussy knew Spain from his readings, from

---

[1] On the occasion of Falla's first visit to London in May 1911, when at the Æolian Hall he played with Debussy's friend Franz Liebich an arrangement for two pianos made by André Caplet of Debussy's *Ibéria*, he was described by *The Times* of 26 May as a student of Debussy.

[2] Besides the work of Falla *Le Tombeau de Debussy* consists of works by Ravel (the Duo for violin and cello); Stravinsky (a piece of fifty-one bars entitled *Symphonies pour instruments à vent à la mémoire de C. A. Debussy*, set out for piano with no expression marks nor, apart from a metronome marking, a tempo indication, this became the Chorale of the *Symphonies d'instruments à vent* also used by Stravinsky as a Chorale to be played with the *Symphony of Psalms*); two short unnamed pieces by Goossens and Bartók; an extremely short song (twelve bars) by Erik Satie on a poem by Lamartine; a *Hommage* for piano by Malipiero; a piano piece *L'Accueil des Muses* by Roussel; and two piano pieces by Paul Dukas and Florent Schmitt inspired by mythological subjects. The cover of this publication is a lithograph by Raoul Dufy.

pictures, from songs, and from dances with songs danced by true Spanish dancers.

At the World Exhibition held on the Champ de Mars two young French musicians were to be seen going about together, listening to the exotic music of many countries. Mingling with the crowd, these young musicians abandoned themselves to the magic of this strange music and later they were able to discover new fields of expression. These two musicians were Paul Dukas and Claude Debussy.

Our knowledge of this simple fact will help us to understand many aspects of Debussy's work. His first-hand knowledge of new types of music, including Chinese and Spanish music, excited his imagination. 'I have always been an observer', he declared, 'and I have tried in my work to put my observations to good account.' Debussy's manner of conveying the essential spirit of Spanish music shows how successful he was. There were of course other factors designed to help him. His interest in liturgical music is well known. Since Spanish folk-song is largely based on modal music, it came about that even in works which Debussy wrote without any idea of Spanish associations one finds modes, cadences, chord sequences, rhythms, and even turns of phrase which clearly reveal a relationship with our spontaneous folk-music.[1]

Works showing this relationship are the songs *Fantoches* and *Mandoline*, the piano piece *Masques*, the *Danse profane* for harp and strings,[2] and the second movement of the String Quartet, the greater part of which, if only because of its texture, might well be one of the most beautiful Andalusian dances ever written. Yet when the master

---

[1] Falla is concerned here with a problem similar to that investigated by Julia d'Almendra and Constantin Brailoiu and referred to on page 233, namely whether Debussy used the techniques of earlier or exotic forms of music consciously. The studies of d'Almendra and Brailoiu are concerned with Debussy's use of the Gregorian modes and the pentatonic scales. Falla suggests that in his use of the modes Debussy was either instinctively aware of their connexion with Spanish folk-music or that he had made a technical study of this subject. On one occasion only have we evidence of the fact that Debussy went so far as to note down the liturgical chants he heard. In *L'Eglise et la Musique*, Amadée Gastoué writes: 'N'avons-nous pas vu à l'église de Saint-Gervais, Claude Debussy suivre fidèlement les offices . . . et noter sur son carnet, un crayon à la main, les tournures qui l'avaient le plus frappé parmi les chants grégoriens et les motets palestriniens?'

[2] Ernest Ansermet has disclosed that Debussy's twin piece for harp and strings, *Danse sacrée*, was based on a short piano piece by the Portuguese composer Francisco de Lacerda (1869–1934). Debussy's correspondence with Lacerda, dealing with their friendship with Erik Satie and the proposed publication of a collection of Portuguese folk-songs, appears in the catalogue of the Debussy Exhibition held in Lisbon in 1962.

was questioned on this matter he declared that no such idea was ever in his mind. The facts are that the character of the Spanish musical language had been assimilated by Debussy and this composer, who really did not know Spain, was thus able to write Spanish music spontaneously, perhaps unconsciously, at any rate in a way which was the envy of many who knew Spain only too well.

Only once did he cross the Franco-Spanish frontier, to spend a few hours at San Sebastian where he watched a bull-fight. This was hardly knowing Spain! He remembered, however, the light in the bull-ring, particularly the violent contrast between the one half of the ring flooded with sunlight and the other half deep in shade. The *Matin d'un jour de fête* from *Ibéria* is perhaps an evocation of this afternoon spent just over the French frontier. But this was not the Spain that was really his own. His dreams led him farther afield and he became spellbound by an imaginary Andalusia. We have evidence of this in *Par les Rues et par les chemins* and *Parfums de la nuit* from *Ibéria*, and in *La Puerta del Vino*, the *Sérénade interrompue*, and *Soirée dans Grenade*. It was with the last of these pieces that Debussy opened his series of works inspired by Spain; and it was a Spaniard, our Ricardo Viñes, who gave the first performance of it, in 1903 at the Société Nationale, as he did of the majority of the master's piano works.

The evocative nature of *Soirée dans Grenade* is nothing less than miraculous when one reflects on the fact that this music was written by a foreigner guided almost entirely by his visionary genius. Forgotten are the Serenades, Madrileñas, and Boleros with which the writers of so-called Spanish music used to regale us. Here we are truly confronted with Andalusia: truth without authenticity, so to speak, for not a bar is directly borrowed from Spanish folklore yet the entire piece down to the smallest detail makes one feel the character of Spain. There is a question here of great importance to which we will return in a moment.

Many technical devices are used to create the evocative spirit of the *Soirée*. The music actually evokes reflections of moonlit images in the lakes of the Alhambra. Evocative in the same way, too, are *Les Parfums de la nuit* and *La Puerta del Vino*. The latter, like the *Soirée*, is based on the rhythm of the Habanera, a sort of Andalusian tango, which Debussy uses to convey the nonchalant idleness and the charm of Andalusian evenings and afternoons. In *La Puerta del Vino* he brings to mind both the quietness and the brilliant sunshine of the hours of the siesta at Granada. This Prelude was suggested to him merely by the sight of a coloured photograph of the celebrated Alhambra. In this photograph the Alhambra, in the shade of great trees, throws into sharp relief the bright light on a road seen in depth through one of the building's arches. Debussy was so strongly impressed by this picture that he resolved to find its musical equivalent; and indeed a few days later *La Puerta del Vino* was written. Though related to the *Soirée dans Grenade* in rhythm and character, it differs from it in melodic design. In the *Soirée* the chant is syllabic, whereas in *La Puerta del Vino* the chant appears with ornamentations peculiar to the Andalusian *cante jondo*. This ornamented chant, used earlier in the *Sérénade interrompue* and in the second theme of the *Danse profane*, shows the extent to which Debussy was acquainted with the most subtle variations of our folk-song:

The *Sérénade interrompue*, which I do not hesitate to place with the works of the master inspired by Spain, differs from the three compositions of the same group mentioned earlier in that the *Sérénade* is based on a ternary rhythm while the others use exclusively a binary rhythm. The Spanish character of this Prelude is evident in the characteristic guitar figurations which precede or accompany the *copla*, the Andalusian grace of the *copla*, and the harshness of the defiant accents at each interruption. The music appears to be inspired by a type of scene frequently met with in romantic poetry: two serenaders vie with each other for the favours of a damsel who, hidden behind the flowers of her latticed window, follows every incident of their gallant contest.

Ibéria stands apart in this group and it is also the most important of Debussy's Spanish works. The thematic material is presented in a novel manner. The opening theme is subjected to many subtle transformations which, one freely admits, sometimes depart from a true Spanish feeling. I do not say this with the least disapproval; on the contrary, *Ibéria* opens up a new aspect of Debussy's work. Debussy strove at all costs never to repeat himself. 'One's technique must be constructed afresh according to the demands of each work', he truly remarked. So far as *Ibéria* is concerned he made it clear that he did not intend to write Spanish music, but rather to translate into music the associations that Spain had aroused in him. This he triumphantly achieved. A sort of *Sevillana*, the generating theme of the work, suggests village songs heard in the bright, scintillating light; the intoxicating magic of the Andalusian nights, the light-hearted holiday crowds dancing to chords struck on guitars and *bandurrias*—all these musical effects whirl in the air while the crowds, as we imagine them, approach or recede. Everything is constantly alive and extremely expressive.[1]

I have said nothing about the harmonic aspects of these works—purposely because harmonically these works must be treated as a single group. We know how much the harmony and other aspects of present-day music owe to Debussy. I am not referring to his imitators, but to effects achieved by composers who have attempted to emulate him, and also to the prejudices which Debussy's work has finally destroyed. From all of this Spain has greatly profited. One may go so far as to say that Debussy to a certain extent completed the musical and theoretical works of Felipe Pedrell who first indicated the wealth of modal music in our folklore.[2]

[1] Falla's description of *Ibéria* may be compared to that of Debussy, in a letter to Caplet of 1910: 'This morning rehearsal of *Ibéria*—it's getting on! The young Kapellmeister [Gabriel Pierné] and his orchestra are less heavy-footed and they are at last beginning to rise from the ground. You cannot imagine how naturally the transition from *Les Parfums de la nuit* to *Le Matin d'un jour de fête* is achieved. It sounds like music which has not been written down! And the whole rising feeling, the awakening of people and of nature. There is a water-melon vendor and children whistling—I see them all clearly.'

[2] Falla was apparently unaware that Debussy was well acquainted with Pedrell's

While much of the music of Spanish composers is based on original documents, the French master leaves these aside, creating music of his own based on the essential elements of folk-music. This method, entirely praiseworthy among our native Spanish composers (except in cases where original documents are bound to be used), is even more remarkable when a composer is not using his native material. One other aspect of the French composer's harmony deserves notice. Certain effects are known to us from the strummings of guitars by the people of Andalusia. Curiously enough, the Spanish musicians have neglected and even despised these effects. They considered them primitive. At most, Spanish composers were able to incorporate guitar figurations in works of conventional harmonic or melodic design. It was Debussy who showed how these guitar figurations were to be used with imagination. Results were immediately forthcoming: the twelve jewel-like piano pieces forming the set *Ibéria* by Isaac Albeniz are sufficient proof.[1]

There are of course many other things to be said about Debussy and Spain. This modest paper is only a sketch to be followed by a larger study in which I propose to deal with the influence of our country and music on all the great foreign composers, from Domenico Scarlatti, claimed by Joaquin Nin as a Spaniard, to Maurice Ravel.[2] Even so, within this modest framework I emphatically state that if Debussy used Spanish folk-music to inspire

work. Earlier, Maurice Emmanuel, a pioneer collector of French folk-songs, had vainly attempted to interest Debussy in the modal aspects of Burgundian folk-music. 'When twenty years later I reminded him of his disdain for this music', Emmanuel records, 'he smiled and without saying a word showed me a publication which he was carrying about *in his pocket*: it was Pedrell's collection of Spanish folk-songs. By a silent gesture he expressed the inspiration he had derived from them.' This collection was probably the one made by Pedrell of Catalan folk-songs, *La Cançó popular catalana* (Barcelona, 1906).

[1] Falla's chronology may be at fault here. The date of Albeniz's *Iberia* is 1906–9. Only the *Soirée dans Grenade* of 1903 could have been known to Albeniz at this time. Guitar effects occur in works of Debussy that were published in 1909 (*Ibéria*) and 1910 (*Sérénade interrompue*). From the correspondence with Louÿs we see that Debussy was well acquainted with Albeniz, who lived in Paris between 1893 and 1909. Two of Albeniz's pieces, *Cordoba* and *El Albaicin*, were particularly admired by Debussy: they reminded him 'of those Spanish evenings filled with the perfume of carnations and the alcohol fumes of *aguardiente*'.

[2] This interesting project was never realized by Falla. He did, however, produce a study of Ravel, *Notas sobre Ravel*, which appeared in the review *Isla* (Jerez de la Frontera, 1939), from which it is clear that the Spanish elements in Ravel's music affected him less profoundly than those in the work of Debussy.

some of his greatest works he has generously repaid us and it is now Spain which is indebted to him.[1]

Granada, 8 November 1920.

[1] In a post-scriptum Falla mentions that two years before his death Debussy had accepted an invitation to conduct concerts of the Sociedad Nacional in Madrid but that his illness prevented him from fulfilling this engagement. His important explorations into Spanish folk-music long influenced the Spanish composers. In 1929 Joaquin Nin published a piano piece, *Message à Claude Debussy*, bearing the moving epigraph: 'Lorsque les yeux de Debussy se fermèrent à jamais, sur la nuit de la mort, une soudaine angoisse vint répandre au cœur des musiciens d'Espagne une inapaisable nostalgie.'

RODIN, DEBUSSY, AND NIJINSKY

The unfortunate nature of Debussy's early association with Diaghilev was based, as we saw in Chapter 10, on an underlying distrust between these two figures. With an eye for effect Diaghilev had hoped that under his guidance Debussy would play the role of the astonishing new composer. ('Etonne-moi, Jean!' Diaghilev thundered to Jean Cocteau. 'Je veux que tu m'étonnes!') Recoiling from this spectacular role, Debussy was apparently not inclined to share with Diaghilev his own inner conception of the ballet. Accordingly, the published scenario, hurriedly written in 1909, for *Masques et Bergamasques*, the first of his projected ballets for Diaghilev, is little more than a conventional story in the manner of the *Commedia dell' Arte*.

It is worth glancing at this curious scenario, so unlike the intangible or nebulous schemes for stage works to which Debussy was attracted during this period of his life, if only to see the type of work he was ready to undertake as a commission. The three scenes were to be enacted on the Piazza San Marco in Venice. At the back of the stage is the sea. At the conclusion of the Prelude the curtain goes up on a group of musicians performing a serenade on guitars and viols. Barberina, daughter of a Bolognese doctor, appears dressed as a cavalier and declares that she will give herself only to two symbolical figures, 'L'Eau d'or qui danse' and 'La Pomme qui chante'. Tartaglia, Truffuldini, Scaramouche, Harlequin, and other Italian comedy actors enter. They create a disturbance by playing upon wooden trumpets, thus drowning the serenade. Suddenly Barberina flies into the arms of Harlequin. Scene 2 opens with an encounter between Captain Firibiribombo and the Bolognese doctor who, on retiring, discovers that his daughter Barberina has fled. The captain declares that he will find the doctor's daughter before dawn. Fishing boats now appear in the distance. Fishermen and their wives form a chorus, thus providing a vocal accompaniment for group and later ensemble dances. The Bolognese doctor asks the fishermen if they have seen Barberina but they merely taunt him and their dances are resumed. In Scene 3 Scaramouche, dressed as an astrologer, comes ashore from a gondola. The doctor asks him to help find Barberina, and at Scaramouche's signal Harlequin and Barberina, dressed as dancers, step out of a gondola and perform a *pas de deux*. At first the doctor does not recognize his daughter but Captain Firibiribombo does. The captain begs her to take off her mask and attempts to pursue her. But Scaramouche trips him up and now the doctor rushes towards his daughter. Scaramouche similarly obstructs the doctor and compels him to return to his gondola from which the beloved figures of Barberina, 'L'Eau d'or qui danse', and 'La Pomme qui chante' now appear. They dance separately and then together. The musicians who return with their viols and guitars are followed by Scaramouche, Tartaglia, and by other comedians who snatch off their masks. The doctor, seeing that he has been ridiculed, curses his daughter. Eventually a procession passes across the stage, consisting of Barberina, Harlequin, 'L'Eau d'or qui danse', and 'La Pomme qui chante'. The latter begs the doctor to forgive Barberina whereupon the captain dances a Forlane with her in which the entire company join.[1] Harlequin and Barberina return to the gondola while Scaramouche and his fellow actors resume their din on wooden trumpets.

By the time of the production of the Nijinsky ballets on scores of Debussy, *L'Après-midi d'un faune* (1912) and *Jeux* (1913), the scenario of this Italian ballet of Debussy's had been forgotten. Debussy now found himself drawn into the orbit of Diaghilev and he was aware that though Diaghilev's ideal was a union of the arts, a reflection in a sense of the Wagnerian ideal, the choreography of Diaghilev's early ballets was inclined to take precedence over the music. Debussy, like Stravinsky and other composers at this time, feared a development of the ballet on these lines. Hence their distrust of the great virtuoso dancer Nijinsky. We do not yet know all the underlying reasons for the bitter controversy provoked by the Nijinsky ballets on scores of Debussy but we are able to illuminate part of the background of this controversy by the publication of Debussy's own opinion of Nijinsky as a choreographer.

There is no doubt that the choreography of Nijinsky, though condemned by Debussy for artistic reasons of his own, marked an important departure, and that the articles and letters that appeared

[1] The idea of a dance presented at first by two solo dancers and gradually copied by the entire company occurs also in the scenario of *Le Diable dans le Beffroi*. Debussy planned in this work 'une gigue fantastique dont la puissance rhythmique et sonore ira en s'amplifiant'.

in the Paris press at the time of the production of his ballets on Debussy's scores, notably in *Le Figaro* and *Le Matin*, are important documents in the early history of the Diaghilev ballet. This history is, of course, not mainly our concern. Reading between the lines of these articles and letters, however, we discover that Debussy's works were beginning to be considered in a new light. On the eve of the production of *L'Après-midi d'un faune*, on 29 May 1912, Jacques-Emile Blanche published in *Le Figaro* an article entitled 'L'Antiquité en 1912', in which Debussy's score is re-appraised in curious terms. This work 'is the daughter', he says, 'of *Les Erinnyes* of Massenet, that is to say very similar to a work which we had imagined was completely opposed to it'. Remote echoes of Massenet there may be in Debussy's score, notably in the central section, but time has not endorsed this odd opinion. The fact is that Blanche was concerned to extol Nijinsky's choreography at the expense of the music. Nijinsky's pagan choreography, he declares, would have met with the approval of Mallarmé. The sudden laugh of Nijinsky in the role of the faun 'produces the impression of a dog that suddenly begins to grin. . . . For a few seconds mythology comes to life.'

Feelings were obviously running high. The following day, on 30 May 1912, *Le Matin* published a panegyric by Rodin entitled 'The Revival of the Dance: Loïe Fuller, Isadora Duncan, Nijinsky' in which, again in contrast to Debussy's cautious attitude, Nijinsky's evocative art is lifted on to the highest artistic plane. Tracing ideas common to Nijinsky and his American and English precursors, Rodin writes:

> Over the last twenty years the dance seems to have aimed at teaching us again the principles of the physical beauty of the body and of its movements. First of all Loïe Fuller, rightly hailed as the figure who 'revived the modern dance', came to us from abroad. She was followed by Isadora Duncan, whose wonderful illusions were the product of both knowledge and taste. Their follower today is the gifted Nijinsky. The nature and the abundance of his ideas border on genius.
>
> In the art of the dance, as in sculpture and painting, inspiration and progress were shackled by routine, prejudice and by the lack of a revitalizing spirit. One's admiration for Loïe Fuller, Isadora

Duncan, and Nijinsky is based on the fact that they acknowledge both the freedom of instinct and a tradition which has an inner respect for Nature. They are thus able to express all the underlying turbulence in the human soul. The last in this line, Nijinsky, has the added advantage of physical perfection and he has also the extraordinary capacity to give expression to a wide range of feelings. One recalls his mime of pain in *Petrouchka* and his final leap in the *Spectre de la Rose*, in which he creates the illusion of taking off into the infinite. But no role has shown Nijinsky in such an extraordinary light as his last creation, *L'Après-midi d'un faune*. Here are no leaps or jumps, only attitudes and gestures with half-conscious associations from the animal world. Nijinsky stretches himself out, leans on his elbow, walks in a crouching position, stands erect again, advances, withdraws, and all this in movements that are sometimes slow, sometimes jerky, nervous, or angular. Now he is keenly pursuing, his arms stiffen, his hand is held wide open with fingers touching; his head suddenly turns aside with a covetous, a deliberately clumsy glance but which, in the way it is performed, seems perfectly natural.

Perfect agreement, also, is achieved between the mimed and the plastic arts. The whole body performs at the command of the mind, and it is made to convey completely the underlying idea of the ballet. Nijinsky's figure has the beauty of ancient frescos and sculptures—an ideal model for a draughtsman or a sculptor. When the curtain rises Nijinsky, completely stretched out on the ground with pipes at lips and one leg folded, appears to be a statue. One can imagine nothing more arresting than his impulsive gesture at the conclusion of the ballet when he again stretches himself out, his face turned downwards on the stolen veil which he now embraces and grasps with voluptuous fervour.

The plastic aspects of Nijinsky's art alone offer a remarkable lesson in taste. One is not surprised to find an eclogue by a contemporary poet enacted in ancient Greece. Archaic gestures acquire a new significance in this ballet. I should like to see this noble effort wholly appreciated. Besides these gala performances the Théâtre du Châtelet should organize others which all artists should attend in order to commune with the presence of beauty.

As we have seen, much hostility had been provoked by Nijinsky's choreography, chiefly on moral grounds. In Nijinsky's defence Diaghilev, on 31 May 1912, wrote to *Le Figaro* quoting a letter sent to him by Odilon Redon. This reads:

Joy is often accompanied by sorrow. To the pleasure which you have given me this evening must be added the regret not to have had among us my illustrious friend Stéphane Mallarmé. He, more than anyone, would have responded to this admirable realization of his ideas. I do not think that his ideal could have been more adequately conveyed.

I remember that Mallarmé constantly referred to choreography and mime. With what joy he would have beheld the dream of his faun brought to life in the living frieze which we have just seen translated into music by Debussy, into plastic art by Nijinsky, and into vivid colours by Bakst! The spirit of Mallarmé was among us this evening.

The anti-Nijinsky faction was led by Gaston Calmette, editor of *Le Figaro*. Calmette attempted to censure not only the erotic aspects of the art of Nijinsky but also those of Rodin. The controversy died down after the production of *L'Après-midi*, but it was revived the following year when Nijinsky produced the choreography for *Jeux*. On this occasion Debussy publicly made known his opinions on the art of his collaborator. In this ballet, as in Ravel's *Daphnis et Chloé*, and Stravinsky's *Le Sacre du Printemps*, Diaghilev was unable to hold the balance between the rival claims of the dance and of music. Perhaps Debussy sensed Diaghilev's dilemma when, quoting Nietzsche's statement in *Zarathustra*, 'In all good things there is laughter', he caustically wrote to *Le Matin* on 15 May 1913:

I am not a man of knowledge and I am thus ill-fitted to speak of the dance since today nothing can be said about this frivolous subject without assuming the airs of a learned doctor. Before writing a ballet I did not know what a choreographer was, but now I know. A choreographer is a person with a superior command of arithmetic. I may not be extremely erudite but I have not forgotten some of my lessons, among them, for instance, this one: one, two, three; one, two, three; one, two, three, four, five; one, two, three, four, five, six; one, two, three; one, two, three—now a little more quickly, and all these are then added up. There may be nothing in it, but it is most moving, especially when this arithmetical problem is set by the incomparable Nijinsky. Why then did I launch myself, being by nature reserved, into an undertaking of which one simply does not know the outcome? Because at lunchtime one has to eat, and because one day I happened to lunch with Serge Diaghilev, a terrifying but irresistible man able to instil the spirit of the dance into lifeless stones. Diaghilev spoke to me of a scenario devised by Nijinsky, consisting of some kind of subtle transparency, the basis, I agreed, of a ballet. In this scenario there is a park, a tennis court, there is the chance meeting of two girls and a young man seeking a lost ball, a nocturnal mysterious landscape, and together with this a suggestion of something sinister in the darkening shadows of night. Elevations, turns, certain unforeseen, capricious steps of the dancers—everything calculated to bring alive rhythm in music is here.

I must confess that since the evenings of the Russian ballet have so often delighted me in an unexpected way, and since I have so often been moved by Nijinsky's spontaneity, innate or acquired, I am now awaiting like an excited child who has been promised a visit to the theatre, the production of *Jeux* at the Theatre in the Avenue Montaigne, now to be called the Theatre of Music.[1]

It seems to me that in our dull classroom of music, presided over by a severe schoolmaster, the Russians have opened a window which looks out on to the open countryside. Also, for one who admires Tamara Karsavina as I do, how delightful it is to have this sweetly drooping flower as an interpreter and to watch her with the exquisite Ludmilla Schollar playing with the approaching shadows of night.

The lesson to be derived from this last venture of Debussy and

[1] The Théâtre des Champs-Elysées was built in 1913 by the impresario of Central European origin Gabriel Astruc, who dedicated it, as he said, 'to the glory of Bourdelle [who executed reliefs for the theatre] and to Debussy'. Though it opened with a festival of French music, conducted by Debussy and others, Astruc was known to be particularly cosmopolitan in his tastes and the Théâtre des Champs-Elysées had been maliciously named the *Astruckisches Musikhaus*.

Diaghilev is that the ballet as a form of 'the union of the arts' (the *Gesamtkunstwerk*) could not survive. Subsequent ballet productions of *Jeux*, by Jean Borlin in Paris in 1920 and William Dollar in New York in 1950, were similarly unsuccessful.

PUCCINI AND DEBUSSY

Puccini heard *Pelléas et Mélisande* when it was revived at the Opéra-Comique in October 1903. Earlier in the month André Messager, the conductor of *Pelléas*, had given at the same theatre the first French performance of Puccini's *Tosca*, and *La Bohème* had been revived there the previous month. These operas of Debussy and Puccini were thus made known to the Paris opera public at the same time. Puccini was enthusiastically fêted on his visit to Paris, but chiefly in social circles. In musical circles national feelings still ran high and most French musicians were inclined to be distrustful of the dramatic and sharply exteriorized style of Italian opera after Verdi. In his diary Henri Büsser records his grudging impression of the dress rehearsal of *Tosca*: 'Messager conducted the work without any great conviction; he cannot like music like this after *Pelléas*.' Earlier Debussy, having found little to admire in *La Traviata*, the only opera of Verdi about which he happened to write, nevertheless considered it more satisfying than the so-called realistic operas of Puccini, Leoncavallo, and Mascagni.[1]

Puccini, on the other hand, was a sincere admirer of Debussy's work and, as most critics are agreed, was greatly influenced, particularly in *La Fanciulla del West*, by Debussy's harmony and orchestration. Büsser records a meeting between the two composers on the occasion of the *Pelléas* revival. 'Puccini, who was in the audience, was greatly moved. He came over to Debussy to tell him so.' Nevertheless, Büsser adds, 'he tells Messager that he was very surprised at the complete absence of pieces of vocal effect'. This was of course the expected impression. Puccini admired particularly, we are told, the texture of Debussy's orchestration.

It is worth recalling that Puccini had himself intended to set *Pelléas* and had gone so far as to approach Maeterlinck. He had obviously set his heart on this project and the fact that Debussy had

---

[1] In an article of 1913 Debussy was bitterly sarcastic on the subject of contemporary Italian opera: 'Inspired by scenes in the realistic cinema, the characters throw themselves at each other and appear to wrench melodies from each other's mouths. A whole life is packed into a single act: birth, marriage, and an assassination thrown in. In these one-act operas very little music need be written for the reason that there is hardly time to hear much.'

earlier secured Maeterlinck's authorization must have been a disappointment to him. By comparison, however, with the cantankerousness of Richard Strauss at a performance of *Pelléas* ('I would have written an entirely different kind of music for this play'), Puccini's whole-hearted recognition of the qualities of a very different composer from himself shows at the least an enquiring turn of mind and great humility. Puccini retained this admiration for Debussy. On 5 April 1918, shortly after Debussy's death, he wrote a moving letter to a journalist on the *Giornale d'Italia* about his contemporary's status and achievement:

> Claude Debussy had the soul of an artist shot through with a genuine and subtle sensibility. To express this sensibility he discovered a new type of harmony which at first seemed to open wide new horizons on to the future of music.
>
> When today I hear people speak of Debussyism as if it were a system to follow or not to follow I should like to tell these young musicians of the doubts which, as I can attest from my personal knowledge, assailed the great artist in his later years. His harmonic procedures which, when they were first made known, appeared so surprising and full of a new beauty, became less and less so in the course of time until ultimately they surprised no one. Even to the composer himself they appeared to represent a restricted field of experiment and, I repeat, I know how much he attempted, in vain, to escape from this field. A fervent admirer of Debussy, I was anxiously waiting to see how Debussy himself proposed to revolt against Debussyism. Now the great artist is dead, and we cannot know the manner, possibly very beneficial, in which he would have carried out this revolt.
>
> Giacomo Puccini.[1]

We see from this letter that Puccini was aware that Debussy, like himself, took a view of the technique of composition that was constantly exploratory. Analysing in technical detail the phases of Puccini's harmonic technique, Dr. Mosco Carner writes: 'He began with the simple chromatic "alterations" and the secondary sevenths and ninths of pre-Wagnerian romantic harmony (*Le Villi* and

---

[1] This letter appeared in French in *Comœdia* of 2 March 1925 and in English in *The Musical Times* of July 1918. The above translation is made from the *Comœdia* version. The original Italian version has not been traced.

Edgar); turned to *Tristan* harmonies in *Manon Lescaut*, in which he also ventured passages in parallel fifths before Debussy; and under the subsequent influence of the French Impressionists he cultivated, often to surfeit, parallel organum-like progressions (of common chords, secondary sevenths and chords of the added sixth), unresolved discords and augmented triads. From the early 1900s he began to make increased use of the whole-tone scale (*Tosca* and *La Fanciulla*); and later he experimented with bitonality, chords of the fourth and naked, harsh dissonances (*Turandot*).' And Dr. Carner conjectures: 'Had he lived longer it is certain he would have availed himself of dodecaphony and quarter tones.' One is left with the impression that Puccini, anxious to see 'how Debussy himself proposed to revolt against Debussyism', had imagined in his work an harmonic evolution on these lines.

Puccini had been frustrated in his desire to set *Pelléas*. But there was to be a curious sequel to his association with the world of Debussy. One of Puccini's principal projects about 1907 was an opera entitled *Conchita*, based on a libretto adapted by Maurice Vaucaire from the novel of Pierre Louÿs, *La Femme et le Pantin*. The sadistic Conchita, a cross between the great operatic characters of Carmen and Turandot, seems to have been a most appropriate subject for treatment by Puccini. Moreover Louÿs, whose many projected stage-works with Debussy had come to nothing, was extremely anxious to collaborate with Puccini.[1] Why, then, did nothing come of this daring dramatic subject? Many rational reasons were given by Puccini. Conchita was a despicable Spanish slut; the libretto had become too stylized. Dr. Carner suggests a deeper reason, namely that by his nature Puccini was inclined to shrink from the supreme demands made on his genius. It may well be that, as with several of the later projects of Debussy, Puccini's ill-fated venture with Louÿs indicates in these artists of sensibility just that lack of conviction necessary to carry through their many-sided work to the end.

[1] Louÿs, whose name is pronounced without sounding the final 's', is amusingly referred to in Puccini's letters as 'Inouï'. 'Inouï called this evening, very *épatant*', he writes in 1906. 'He returned to the subject of *Conchita* for a change; he won't let me alone—not a bit of it. He's a sticker, that fellow!' When Puccini, much to his publisher's distress, finally declined to set this libretto, Louÿs threatened to claim damages from him. *Conchita* was eventually set by Zandonai and produced in Milan in 1911.

APPENDIX E

DEBUSSY AND OCCULTISM

It has been shown that Debussy's attraction to the lurid subject of *Le Martyre de Saint-Sébastien* derived to some extent from his earlier interest in the occult practices in Paris in the 1890s. These practices are referred to in Vol. I, p. 109. According to a fragment of an unpublished letter, which was the only evidence then available, Debussy in 1892 had been interested in writing the incidental music for the esoteric play of Jules Bois *Les Noces de Sathan*, but had finally refused to do so. Further information on this subject has now come to light. Dr. Pasteur Vallery-Radot has generously supplied me with the complete text of Debussy's letter to Jules Bois, and Monsieur Léon Guichard, the author of several important studies on the period, kindly sent me an unpublished article of his consisting of a valuable piece of research on Debussy's knowledge of the works of Jules Bois and other esoteric writers and painters of his circle. These two documents supplement my own research in this field. Gradually, the whole matter of Debussy's early connexions with the occultists of the 1890s became clearer. As a result *La Damoiselle élue*, seemingly an innocent Pre-Raphaelite work, acquired a rather deeper and a slightly sinister significance, and the line of development from this early work to *Le Martyre de Saint-Sébastien*, which earlier critics had always sensed, now seemed unmistakable. Whatever were the immediate material reasons for writing the incidental music for d'Annunzio's play, this work must have revived many early memories. Moreover, as Monsieur Guichard shows, d'Annunzio's *Saint-Sébastien* and Jules Bois' *Noces de Sathan* have many occult features in common.

The letter from Debussy to Jules Bois, published here for the first time, together with Monsieur Guichard's study, 'Debussy and the Occultists', which is printed with his kind permission, allow us to see much more closely this strange streak in Debussy's musical character which persisted over many years.

Tuesday evening [end of March 1892]
42 rue de Londres

I have made up my mind, my dear Bois: whatever it may cost to
our friendship I have not the necessary confidence to write the
music I had promised for Les Noces de Sathan. It is clear to me
that the orchestra exists only on a scrap of paper; and when it
comes to knowing the names of the players or where they come
from one is told nothing except by a Monsieur Burger who pays
repeated calls but who cannot undertake everything himself.
Forgive me and above all do not think there is any ill will on
my part. It would all be too much like a venture into the Unknown and would take on the character of a 'mauvaise aventure'.
Let me express to you my affectionate thoughts quite simply,
without drums or trumpets.

C.D.

DEBUSSY AND THE OCCULTISTS

A minor discovery I recently made concerns a great musician
and has some importance. As I was looking through the Symbolist
reviews in the course of my research on the Wagnerian influence
in France, I stopped short at the following notice published in Le
Saint-Graal of 8 March 1892, a review founded that year by
Emmanuel Signoret[1]:

Théâtre d'art. The third evening of the season of the Théâtre
d'art will take place in the second fortnight of March at the
Théâtre Montparnasse, and the fourth one week later. At the
first evening will be given:

1. Two scenes from the Chants de Maldoror by the Comte de
Lautréamont.

[1] This review appeared in Paris intermittently between 1892 and 1899. In the first
number Verlaine enthusiastically wrote to the editor: 'Bien, très bien, Le Saint-Graal,
quel mot, quel nom! Double signification: faîte de l'art moderne, sommet du Vrai
éternel. Saint-Graal, Sang Réel, Le Sang du Christ dans l'or incandescent: Saint-
Graal, Lohengrin, Parsifal, la manifestation triomphale et triomphant de la plus sublime
musique, de l'effort poétique peut-être définitif de ces temps-ci.'

2. Two scenes from *Vercingétorix*, a play in verse by Edouard Schuré with scenery by Odilon Redon.

3. *Les Noces de Sathan*, esoteric play in verse in one act by Jules Bois. Music by Debussy. Scenery and costumes by Henry Colas. (This is the first initiatory play to be produced.)¹

4. The first book of Homer's *Iliad*. Theatrical version in four tableaux . . . Symphonic score by Gabriel Fabré.

'Music by Debussy'! This was a discovery indeed. Debussy had thus written, it seemed, in 1892 a score unknown to every one of his biographers and performed at the Théâtre d'Art! The Théâtre d'Art was directed at this time by the poet Paul Fort. Marlowe's *Faust* had been performed there and programmes also included a recitation of Rimbaud's *Bateau Ivre*. Productions were by Lugné-Poe. Jules Bois, Camille Mauclair, and Charles-Henry Hirsch lectured on Esotericism, Maeterlinck, Maurice Denis, and Henry de Groux.²

Debussy thus knew Jules Bois, the writer from Marseilles, nine years his junior, who in 1891 at the age of twenty had already published *Il ne faut pas mourir*, a poem in dialogue based on the

¹ 'La première pièce initiatique mise en scène.' Presumably this play was connected with the prevalent cult of 'Le Satanisme' described in Jules Bois' *Les Petites Religions de Paris*.

² Debussy may or may not have heard these lectures at the Théâtre d'Art but he remained closely connected with each of these subjects or personalities. Writing to Ernest Chausson in 1893 he says that music 'should have been an hermetic science' to be understood only 'by means of texts the interpretation of which would be long and difficult. . . . Instead of diffusing art I propose the foundation of a "Society of Musical Esotericism".' Debussy was of course among Maeterlinck's earliest admirers. Maurice Denis was associated with him in the publication of *La Damoiselle élue* and he admired the works of the Belgian painter Henry de Groux until the end of his life. Writing to Godet of de Groux's exhibition of painting and sculpture at the Salon d'Automne in 1911, he says: 'Yesterday I plunged back into the past. What an admirable exhibition! A figure of Napoleon leading the retreat from Russia and which freezes you more profoundly than all the snows of the landscape. . . . A Tolstoy in bronze . . . more beautiful than the clever mutilations of Rodin. And a portrait of Wagner with the face of an old cynical magician.' De Groux 'still looks like a genius of a clown and in his eyes are all the dreams of the world'. Years earlier Debussy and Godet had seen together de Groux's revolutionary picture 'Christ insulted'. This was followed by another striking picture of his, 'Zola insulted'. 'He is a fine example of moral courage', Debussy commented. 'His lesson is that one must not be disdainful of censers, and if necessary one must even spit in them.' Another member of this defiant Franco-Belgian circle which Debussy frequented was the Belgian Symbolist poet Georges Rodenbach, whose *Bruges-la-Morte* appeared in 1892. Debussy's correspondence with Rodenbach is in the private collection of Madame Marcelle Rodenbach but has remained unpublished.

ideas of one of the new religious cults. How or through whom did Debussy know him? Did he frequent at this time one of the quasi-religious gatherings described by Bois? *Les Noces de Sathan* was first published in 1890. After the performance announced in *Le Saint-Graal* it was republished by Chamuel, who specialized in esoteric publications, with a drawing by Henry Colas, but without any music. On the other hand, another esoteric play by Jules Bois, *La Porte héroïque du ciel*, appeared in 1894, illustrated by two drawings by Antoine de la Rochefoucauld, organiser of Rosicrucian meetings and containing a Prelude by Erik Satie. Satie, one of the musicians, together with Benedictus of the Rose-Croix, had composed in 1892 three Preludes in the form of incidental music to the play *Le Fils des étoiles*, by Joseph Péladan.

Satie's connexions with the Rose-Croix are well known, and so is his friendship with Debussy. It seems likely that it was through Satie that Debussy came to know Jules Bois and was commissioned to compose the musical score for *Les Noces de Sathan*. 1892 is the year of the beginning of the *Prélude à l'Après-midi d'un faune*, the poem of which is referred to in Bois' preface: *Le Symbolisme des Noces de Sathan et le drame ésotérique*.[1]

But the meeting might have taken place elsewhere, at the bookshop *L'Art Indépendant* belonging to the publisher Edmond Bailly. Memoirs relating to this bookshop do not mention the name of Jules Bois, though two works of his were published by Bailly. It was, moreover, Bailly who published Debussy's *La Damoiselle élue*, and the *Chansons de Bilitis* of Pierre Louÿs. Poets and writers who formed part of Bailly's circle included Villiers de l'Isle Adam, Mallarmé, Huysmans, Louis Ménard, Pierre Louÿs, and Jean de Tinan. Toulouse-Lautrec and Odilon Redon were other members of this circle and so was the astrologer Ely Star. Bailly was interested in music to the extent of publishing a journal entitled *La Musique Populaire*, and Debussy was one of his regular visitors. 'Almost every day', notes V. E. Michelet in *Les Compagnons de la hiérophanie*, 'towards the end of the afternoon he would come either alone or with his faithful Erik Satie.' And he adds: 'Debussy allowed himself to become strongly impressed by current theories

---

[1] At one point in the play Bois required an effect comparable to that of 'the dances of Ramayana performed in Cambodia by dancing priestesses'. During these dances 'a reciter declaims the poem in the manner foreseen by Mallarmé for *L'Après-midi d'un faune*'.

of Hermetic literature.'[1] It is not surprising, therefore, to find him collaborating with Jules Bois. Plans must have been far advanced since Debussy's name appeared in an announcement of the programme only ten days before the performance of *Les Noces de Sathan* on 31 March.

The characters in this esoteric drama consist of Satan, Psyche, Ennoia, the Elohim, stercoraceous demons, Incubi and Succubi, Adam, Eve, Cain, Mephistopheles, Faust, the Hetaerae witches, and the Ineffable Voice. Reading it through, I was reminded of the great poems of Vigny, Hugo, and Goethe, and also of *Le Martyre de Saint-Sébastien* which almost twenty years later inspired Debussy to write one of his most moving works. Like d'Annunzio's drama, Jules Bois' play conveys the same atmosphere of sensuality, the same ambiguous mysticism, and the same excessive preoccupation with detail. The stage directions require the representation of purple lilies and other exotic flowers and refer to the 'dark blue hair of the Hermaphrodite Satan' which provides him with a 'halo suggesting a stormy sky'. The subject of the play, influenced by the plays of Edouard Schuré and also by the writings of St. John, Plato, and Pythagoras, is Salvation achieved through the action of Woman and by Intuition. Satan, symbolizing the wicked aspects of human nature, grows weary of the idea of evil. By his union with the good figure Psyche he becomes a redeemer.

At which points in this play was music to be introduced? It was no doubt required for atmospheric effects and there were probably to be musical interludes. Possibly music was to be performed before the chant of the Elohim, recited by Marthe Mellot in her beautiful song-like voice, or before the entrance of Cain or the Hetaerae, or preceding the final scene.

Apparently only one critic, Pierre Valin, in the *Revue d'art dramatique*, referred to the music in *Les Noces de Sathan*. He criticized the fact that the music did not seem to be co-ordinated with the delivery of the actors nor with the rhythm of the poetry, and he also noted that the actors' voices were drowned by the instruments. 'In plays for amateurs', he rightly observed, 'such as those at the Théâtre d'Art, music obviously plays an important part. It induces in the public the atmosphere of a light or a serious style. It enables the feelings of the actors to reach the audience and it helps to create

[1] The literature on astrology, magic, and alchemy attributed to Hermes Trisnegistus.

a dream atmosphere. It also encourages the audience to listen more attentively, and by playing upon sensations, it brings to the listener that which is too subtle or too vague to be expressed in language.' This was a clear enunciation of the Symbolist musical æsthetic.

The censorious remarks of this critic would indeed surprise us if the music of *Les Noces de Sathan* had ultimately been composed by Debussy. No music could be more skilfully combined with words; no music could more effectively throw the words into relief while at the same time conveying their inner meaning. Alas, the music of *Les Noces de Sathan* was eventually written by Henry Quittard, a pupil of César Franck.

Why did Debussy at the last minute not write the music for this play? In the present state of our knowledge we cannot say. Nor is it really a question of great importance. The interesting point about this project is that it reveals to us the milieu in which Debussy moved and his attraction to an esoteric world. An element of mystery runs through the whole of the art of Debussy, as we are made aware from the study of Vladimir Jankélévitch, *Debussy et le Mystère*. 'His attraction to the mysterious', writes this author, 'derived from the occult ideas of the Rosicrucians in Paris in the 1880s [rather the 1890s], from the frequenters of the Chat Noir, and from the Sar Péladan in whose entourage mysticism would sometimes degenerate into hypocrisy or a mere hoax. Debussy became intoxicated with the Eleusinian mysteries of the *fin-de-siècle* but neither more nor less than Ravel or Satie.' It would perhaps be truer to say 'more than Ravel and less than Satie'. However this may be, the abortive collaboration with Jules Bois adds greatly to our evidence of Debussy's leanings in this direction.

Léon Guichard, 1958.

APPENDIX F

THE THEORIES OF GASTON BACHELARD

It has become a commonplace, in the criticism of Symbolist poetry and music, to invoke the line, 'De la musique avant toute chose', from Verlaine's *Art Poétique*. In fact Verlaine believed not so much that music should take precedence over other forms of artistic thought but that it was inherent in other artistic forms. 'De la musique en toute chose' was more accurately his ideal. Many of Verlaine's recommendations were adopted by Debussy, and indeed the texture of Debussy's works, particularly the aerial texture of his orchestral works, is clearly suggested in Verlaine's lines insisting that a poetic image should be

> Plus vague et plus soluble dans l'air
> Sans rien en lui qui pèse ou qui pose.

Elsewhere in this miniature poetic treatise of Verlaine the dream state is invoked. Suggestion rather than eloquence is the ideal, and nuance rather than colour:

> Oh! la nuance seule fiance
> Le rêve au rêve et la flûte au cor.

In his study written shortly after Debussy's death Robert Godet draws several analogies between the æsthetics of Debussy and Verlaine.[1] Maintaining that they shared a similar concept of the dream, he emphasizes the many associations of water in their works. Debussy, he says, has been likened to an island, 'surrounded by water on all sides', and he proceeds to list some of the associations of both running and stagnant water in his works. In *Le Promenoir des deux amants* water lies dormant in the sombre grotto, it trickles over drooping reeds, or it sparkles in the hollow of beloved hands. In *Clair de lune* a slender spray of water darts up from among marble statues, uttering a sigh to the heavens. In the setting of Baudelaire's *Le Jet d'eau* it falls upon the ground in the form of a shower of tears. Elsewhere in the Verlaine settings the heart weeps

[1] 'Claude Debussy', *La Semaine littéraire*, Geneva, 13–27 April 1918.

as rain falls on the town, hopes are drowned in the misty stream, and disturbing memories are aroused by the sight of water swirling over the stones of a river-bed. Contentment is associated with the impressionistic vision of rain in *Jardins sous la pluie*, also with the ruminations of *Reflets dans l'eau*. On another, more sombre, plane, water is symbolically associated with the funereal mood of *La Cathédrale engloutie* while in *Pelléas*, in the scene of the vaults, we are made aware of the stench of stagnant water. *Pelléas* presents a variety of dream associations of this kind. Stagnant water is associated with death in the vaults scene, but Mélisande's wedding-ring falls into clear fountain water. Finally, there are the seascapes of Debussy, sketched out in the *Trois Mélodies* of Verlaine ('La Mer est plus belle') and the *Proses Lyriques* ('De Grève'), developed in the *Nocturnes* and the sea music of *Pelléas*, and brought to their final expression in *La Mer*.

In associating the imagery of water in Debussy's works with Verlaine's *Art Poétique* Godet was anticipating a novel study on the nature of the poetic imagination, *L'Eau et les Rêves*, by Gaston Bachelard. The first of a series of studies showing connexions between the poetic imagination and the elements of Nature,[1] this work investigates the borderlands of the unconscious mind where, according to Bachelard, poetic images have their origin in images of the natural elements of fire, air, earth, and water. Music is hardly ever mentioned in this novel approach to the workings of the imaginative mind, but it is clear that many of Bachelard's conclusions apply to music as well as to poetry. At any rate a field is open here for the application of these theories to the nature of the musical imagination.

Fugitive and often superficial images, associated primarily with clear, running water, are investigated in the first place. Minor poets abound here, inspired by narcissistic themes, though Bachelard shows that the nature of narcissism demands a re-interpretation in the light of modern psychology. The function of mirrors and reflections is described in the work of a friend of Debussy, Georges

[1] First published in 1942, *L'Eau et les Rêves* was followed between 1943 and 1948 by *L'Air et les Songes*, *La Terre et les Rêveries du Repos*, and *La Terre et les Rêveries de la Volonté*. Bachelard's most recent work, summarizing a lifetime's research, is *La Poétique de la Rêverie*. Born in 1885, Gaston Bachelard started his career as a professor of chemistry and physics and produced several technical works, among them *Le Nouvel Esprit scientifique*, before applying his scientific training to an investigation in literature of the nature of the dream.

Rodenbach: 'All the mirrors in the works of Rodenbach are veiled. They have a grey life of their own like the waters in the canals of his native Bruges.' The symbolical significance of the swan is described afresh under the heading, 'Les Eaux claires; Les Eaux amoureuses', and reference is made to the symbolism of the swan in the works of Pierre Louÿs and Gabriele d'Annunzio.

Deeper waters and particularly stagnant waters ('Les Eaux dormantes; Les Eaux mortes') are associated with contemplation and thus lead rapidly, if one is attuned to this mode of thinking, to fantasies of the unconscious. In a chapter entitled 'L'Eau lourde dans la rêverie d'Edgar Poe', largely based on the interpretations of Marie Bonaparte, dream aspects of the work of Poe are presented in a manner which frequently corresponds with the ideas of Debussy. 'In the works of Poe', Bachelard observes, 'clear water inevitably darkens. Water, originally sparkling and alive, runs more slowly and gradually becomes sluggish. The idle watching of running water signifies the passing of time; the personality disintegrates and eventually faces death.' A key work in Bachelard's view of this type of poetic expression is Poe's poem *Al Aaraaf* (quoted in the translation by Gabriel Mourey) with its curious image of the 'star-isle'. Sky and water become one in Poe's view, the star-isle being a reflection of a star from the heavens in the depths of water. 'Where is reality, in the sky or in the depths of water?' Bachelard asks on the matter of the meaning of this poem. 'One cannot over-emphasize the importance of the double image, such as that of the star-isle, in the psychology of the imagination. . . . The dream endows water with a conception of a remote country, of a celestial country.'

This approach to poetry is a counterpart of the approach of certain musicologists to the problems of composition. As opposed to Bergson, the philosopher of the preceding generation who believed that the dream was a disintegrating force allied to madness, Bachelard holds that the unreal world of the dream represents the only point of departure for any artistic or indeed scientific thought. He is thus concerned to illuminate the workings of the unconscious mind at the level where poetic images are produced. Students of the processes of musical composition are concerned with a similar problem. If ever we are able to define the symbolism of the musical language with the precision that literary critics have brought to the symbolism of the poetic language, Bachelard's works will certainly be drawn upon by historians of musical Impressionism.[1]

[1] An earlier work on the dream and the poetic imagination, Albert Béguin's *L'Ame romantique et le Rêve* (1939), explores the dream world of Schumann. It is worth noting that the evolution from Schumann to Debussy, in regard to an expression of the dream, was apparently sensed by Furtwängler who, in his *Ton und Wort* (Wiesbaden, 1954), describes Debussy as 'a Schumann who might have been French and who might have been modern'. Possibly because he was aware of some hidden link between the dream worlds of Debussy and Schumann, Furtwängler showed a keener understanding of the art of Debussy than certain of his contemporaries, notably Schoenberg and Schnabel, who saw in Debussy a composer of no greater stature than Gounod or Chaminade.

APPENDIX G

DEBUSSY'S CRITICAL ARTICLES

As we observed in Chapter 3 (pages 52–3), the selection of Debussy's articles in *M. Croche antidilettante*, many of them curtailed, hardly does justice to the wide variety of Debussy's critical work, even though several of his articles have only an ephemeral value and not all of them would need to be included in an edition of his writings. The following list, indicating the articles in an abridged or altered form in *M. Croche*, is a guide to Debussy's entire critical work.

LA REVUE BLANCHE, 1901

1 April	Music (*Croche* I); Schumann's *Faust* at the Concerts Colonne; Overture to *Le Roi Lear* by Augustin Savard; Symphony of Georges-Martin Witkowski and 'Poèmes Danois' of Delius at the Société Nationale.
15 April	*The Nursery* by Moussorgsky (*Croche* IV); Piano Sonata of Paul Dukas (*Croche* V); German conductors (*Croche* VI).
1 May	J. S. Bach (*Croche* VI); Beethoven's Ninth Symphony (*Croche* III).
15 May	The Opera (*Croche* VII); *Le Roi de Paris* by Georges Hüe; *L'Ouragan* by Alfred Bruneau.
1 June	The Nikisch Concerts (*Croche* VIII); Open-air Music (*Croche* X);[1] other concerts.
1 July	Monsieur Croche the Dilettante-Hater (*Croche* I).
15 November	M. Croche and *Les Barbares* by Saint-Saëns (*Croche* II).
1 December	The works of Massenet from *Eve* to *Grisélidis* (*Croche* IX).

[1] The original proof of this article, written for *La Renaissance Latine* and kindly communicated to me by Cecil Hopkinson, bears the editorial direction, 'à détruire'. See note 3 on page 66.

GIL BLAS, 1903

12 January	Vincent d'Indy's *L'Etranger* (*Croche* XXI).
19 January	Open-air Music[1] (*Croche* X); *Namouna* by Lalo; Berlioz's *Damnation of Faust*; extract from d'Indy's *L'Etranger*; Piano Concerto by Léon Moreau. Prince Ludwig of Bavaria.
21 and 26 January	*Titania* by Georges Hüe and Weber (*Croche* XI).
2 February	*Castor et Pollux* by Rameau (*Croche* XII).
16 February	Weingartner's performances of Beethoven's *Pastoral Symphony* and Liszt's *Mazeppa* (*Croche* XIII); *La Traviata* at the Opéra-Comique.
23 February	An open letter to Gluck (*Croche* XXV); Works of Louis Vierne and Chausson at the Société Nationale; Symphony of Guy Ropartz at the Concerts Lamoureux.
2 March	The People's Theatre (*Croche* XIV); Siegfried Wagner at the Concerts Lamoureux (*Croche* XVII).
9 March	Opera and Music. Works by Paul de Wailly, Fauré and Rhené-Baton at the Société Nationale. Death of Albert Cahen.
16 March	Saint-Saëns at the Concerts Colonne (*Croche* II). Works of Rimsky-Korsakov and Grieg at the Concerts Lamoureux.
19 March	*Muguette* by Edmond Missa at the Opéra-Comique.
23 March	Meyerbeer's *Les Huguenots*. Works of Mendelssohn, Alfred Bruneau, and Saint-Saëns at the Concerts Lamoureux.
30 March	A child prodigy. Works of Gustave Samazeuilh, Ernest Chausson, and Paul Dukas at the Société Nationale. Richard Strauss (*Croche* XV).
6 April	*Parsifal* (*Croche* XVI); Centenary of the French Academy in Rome.

[1] See the similar article in *La Revue Blanche*, 1 June 1901.

13 April	Concert performance of *Rheingold*. *Les Béatitudes* by César Franck (*Croche* XVIII); Alessandro Scarlatti (*Croche* XIX). Jean de Reszke.
20 April	Grieg at the Concerts Colonne (*Croche* XX). J. P. Souza.
27 April	*Le Sire de Vergy* by Claude Terrasse. Massenet's *Werther*.
5 May	The *Ring* in London (*Croche* XXII).
8 May	Berlioz: a stage performance of the *Damnation of Faust* (*Croche* XXIII).
19 May	*Henry VIII* by Saint-Saëns.
1 June	The *Ring* in London (*Croche* XXII).
6 June	*La Petite Maison* by William Chaumet.
10 June	Recollections of a holder of the Prix de Rome (*Croche* II).
28 June	Music in 1903.

MUSICA

October 1902	Musical Taste.
May 1903	Some musical considerations on the Prix de Rome.[1]
July 1906	Charles Gounod (*Croche* XXIV).
January 1908	Mary Garden.
March 1911	Connexions between Poetry and Music.

LE FIGARO

16 May 1902	The Criticisms of *Pelléas* (interview).
8 May 1908	*Hippolyte et Aricie*.
14 February 1909	The Future of the Conservatoire (interview).

COMŒDIA

4 November 1909	The Music of Today and Tomorrow (interview).

[1] The papers of M. D. Calvocoressi, kindly lent to me by Dr. Gerald Abraham, show that this article was also published in *L'Art Moderne*, 9 October 1904. Reproduced in the special number of *La Revue de Musicologie* devoted to Debussy (1962), it is entirely different from the article of 10 June 1903 on the same subject in *Gil Blas*, which appears in *M. Croche*.

31 January 1910	Modern Italian Music (interview).
26 January 1911	The Decentralisation of Music (interview).
?	Why I wrote *Pelléas*.

LA REVUE MUSICALE DE LYON

16 October 1910	The French Festival in Munich (interview).
8 January 1911	Debussy seen by himself (interview).
22 January 1911	Music (interview).
15 May 1911	*Le Martyre de Saint-Sébastien* (interview).[1]

EXCELSIOR

9 March 1911	Russian Music and French composers.
11 February 1911	*Le Martyre de Saint-Sébastien* (interview).

LA REVUE S.I.M.

November 1912	The Crisis in French Music. Works of Beethoven, Berlioz, and Charpentier.[2]
December 1912	Respect in art. Works of Pierné, Strauss, and Beethoven.
15 January 1913	Music at the end of the year. Works of Chausson, Ropartz, and Bach.
15 February 1913	On Taste. The Concerts Colonne.
15 March 1913	A Precursor: William Rust. The Music of Ernest Fanelli.
15 May 1913	The Present State of Music. Music at the Théâtre des Champs-Elysées.
November 1913	Music and Nature. The Concerts Colonne and the Théâtre des Champs-Elysées.
December 1913	Spanish music. *Faust et Hélène* by Lili Boulanger.
January 1914	Letter from Russia.
February 1914	*Parsifal*.
March 1914	Fashion and taste. Works of Gabriel Grovlez and André Gédalge.

[1] These interviews had earlier appeared in other unidentified papers.
[2] Except for the articles of 15 May 1913 and November 1913 all works reviewed in *La Revue S.I.M.* were given at the Concerts Colonne.

MISCELLANEOUS WRITINGS

Reply to an enquiry on the German influence (interview), *Mercure de France*, January 1903.

Reply to an enquiry on the present state of French music, *La Revue Bleue*, 2 April 1904.

A rebirth of the classical ideal (interview), *Paris-Journal*, 20 May 1910.

The influence of Wagner. Interview of February 1908 with a journalist of *L'Eclair*, not published by this journal but reproduced in *Le Cas Debussy* by C. F. Caillard and J. de Bérys (1910).

The Death of Massenet (1912) in *Massenet* by Alfred Bruneau (1935).

Article on Rameau (1912). Unpublished in Debussy's lifetime, this appears in *Lettres inédites à André Caplet* (1957).

Jeux, Le Matin, 15 May 1913.

Preface to Durand's edition of the works of Chopin (in the volume of the Waltzes), 1915.

Letter in the form of a preface to Paul Huvelin's edition of a series of lectures, *Pour la musique française*, 1916.

APPENDIX H

CATALOGUE OF WORKS

It was intended, as stated in Volume I, to present here a *catalogue raisonné* of Debussy's works. This was to have been based on a publication planned in association with other scholars, but which has unfortunately not yet appeared. I have therefore limited myself in the following list to setting out the works of Debussy according to categories. On the question of the origin and the changes of the titles of Debussy's works referred to earlier the available information has been incorporated in the text. The section listing the unpublished works, though not exhaustive, nevertheless presents as complete a compilation as can be made in the present state of our knowledge.

UNPUBLISHED WORKS

SONGS

1876 (?)   Ballade à la lune (Alfred de Musset); Fleur des eaux (Maurice Bouchor).

1880–4   L'Archet (Charles Cros); Séguedille (J. L. Vauthier); Les Roses; Chanson espagnole (for two voices); Rondel chinois.
            Three songs on poems of Paul Bourget: Regret; Romance d'Ariel; Musique.
            Six songs on poems of Théodore de Banville: Caprice; Aimons-nous; O floraison divine des lilas; Souhait; Sérénade; Fête galante.
            Three songs on poems of Leconte de Lisle: La Fille aux cheveux de lin; Jane; Eclogue (for soprano and tenor).
            Il dort encore (from Banville's *Hymnis*); Coquetterie posthume (Théophile Gautier); Flots, palmes, sables (Armand Renaud).

CHAMBER WORKS

1880   Trio in G major for piano, violin, and cello.
1900   Chansons de Bilitis. Incidental music for the poems of Pierre Louÿs for 2 flutes, 2 harps, and celesta.

CHORAL, DRAMATIC AND LITERARY WORKS

1880	Hymnis (Théodore de Banville). Unfinished cantata.
1880–4	Daniel (Emile Cécile). Cantata.
1883	Le Gladiateur (Emile Moreau). Cantata.
1884	Printemps (Jules Barbier). Chorus.
1884–6	Diane au bois (Théodore de Banville). Unfinished cantata.
1889	Axel (Villiers de l'Isle Adam). One scene.
1890–2	Rodrigue et Chimène (Catulle Mendès). Unfinished opera in three acts.
1900	Esther et la maison des fous. Text for a dramatic work.
1896–1900	F.E.A. (Frères en art). Unfinished play.
1902–3	Le Diable dans le Beffroi (Poe-Debussy). Notes for the libretto and sketch for Scene i.
1908–18	La Chute de la Maison Usher (Poe-Debussy). Libretto (sketches and final version) and vocal score (incomplete).

INSTRUMENTAL AND ORCHESTRAL WORKS

1882	Scherzo for cello and piano; Intermezzo for orchestra (based on Heine's *Intermezzo*).
1883–4	Suite d'orchestre.
1898	Berceuse for piano.

PUBLISHED WORKS

SONGS

1876 (?)	Nuit d'étoiles (Théodore de Banville); Beau soir (Paul Bourget).
1877	Fleur des blés (André Girod).
1880–3	Mandoline (Paul Verlaine); La Belle au bois dormant (Vincent Hypsa); Voici que le printemps (Paul Bourget); Paysage sentimental (Paul Bourget).
1881	Zéphyr (Théodore de Banville).
1882	En Sourdine (Paul Verlaine, first version); Rondeau (Alfred de Musset).
1882–4	Pantomime (Paul Verlaine); Clair de lune (Paul Verlaine); Pierrot (Théodore de Banville); Apparition (Stéphane Mallarmé).

1887–9　Cinq Poèmes de Baudelaire: Le Balcon; Harmonie du Soir; Le Jet d'eau [piano accompaniment orchestrated by Debussy]; Recueillement; La Mort des amants.

1888　Ariettes oubliées (Paul Verlaine): C'est l'extase . . . ; Il pleure dans mon coeur . . . ; L'ombre des arbres . . . ; Chevaux de bois; Green; Spleen.

1891　Deux Romances (Paul Bourget): Romance; Les Cloches.
Les Angélus (G. le Roy); Dans le Jardin (Paul Gravolet).
Trois Mélodies (Paul Verlaine): La mer est plus belle . . . ; Le son du cor s'afflige . . . ; L'Echelonnement des haies.

1892　Fêtes galantes (Paul Verlaine), first series: En sourdine; Fantoches; Clair de lune.

1892–3　Proses lyriques (Claude Debussy): De rêve; De grève; De fleurs; De soir.

1897　Chansons de Bilitis (Pierre Louÿs): La Flûte de Pan; La Chevelure; Le Tombeau des Naïades.

1904　Fêtes galantes (Paul Verlaine), second series: Les Ingénus; Le Faune; Colloque sentimental.
Trois Chansons de France:
　　Rondel: Le temps a laissié son manteau . . . (Charles d'Orléans);
　　La Grotte (Tristan Lhermite) [This is the same song as 'Auprès de cette grotte sombre', the first of the next group.]
　　Rondel: Pour ce que plaisance est morte . . . (Charles d'Orléans).

1910　Le Promenoir des deux amants (Tristan Lhermite): Auprès de cette grotte sombre . . . ; Crois mon conseil . . . ; Je tremble en voyant ton visage.
Trois Ballades de François Villon [orchestrated by Debussy]: Ballade de Villon à s'amye; Ballade que feit Villon à la requeste de sa mère pour prier Nostre-Dame; Ballade des femmes de Paris.

1913　Trois Poèmes de Stéphane Mallarmé: Soupir; Placet futile; Eventail.

1915　Noël des enfants qui n'ont plus de maison (Claude Debussy).

The songs 'Chanson d'un fou' (Alphonse Daudet) and 'Ici-bas' (Sully Prudhomme), published under Debussy's name and attributed to the year 1882, are by Emile Pessard and the brothers Paul and Lucien Hillemacher respectively.

PIANO WORKS

(a) *Piano Solo*

1880	Danse bohémienne.
1888	Deux Arabesques.
1890	Rêverie; Ballade; Danse [orchestrated by Ravel]; Valse romantique; Nocturne.
1890–1905	Suite bergamasque: Prélude; Menuet; Clair de lune; Passepied.
1891	Mazurka.
1896–1901	Pour le piano: Prélude; Sarabande [orchestrated by Ravel]; Toccata.
1903	Estampes: Pagodes; Soirée dans Grenade; Jardins sous la pluie. D'un cahier d'esquisses.
1904	Masques; L'Isle joyeuse [orchestrated by Bernadino Molinari].
1905	Images (first series): Reflets dans l'eau; Hommage à Rameau; Mouvement.
1906–8	Children's Corner: Doctor Gradus ad Parnassum; Jimbo's Lullaby; Serenade for the Doll; Snow is dancing; The Little Shepherd; Golliwog's Cake-walk. [Orchestrated by André Caplet.]
1907–8	Images (second series): Cloches à travers les feuilles; Et la lune descend sur le temple qui fut; Poissons d'or.
1909	The Little Nigar (Le Petit Nègre); Hommage à Haydn.
1909–10	Douze Préludes, Book I: Danseuses de Delphes; Voiles; Le Vent dans la plaine; Les Sons et les parfums tournent dans l'air du soir; Les Collines d'Anacapri; Des Pas sur la neige; Ce qu'a vu le Vent d'Ouest; La Fille aux

cheveux de lin; La Sérénade interrompue; La Cathédrale engloutie; La Danse de Puck; Minstrels.

1910   La plus que lente [orchestrated by Debussy].

1910–13   Douze Préludes, Book II: Brouillards; Feuilles mortes;
La Puerta del Vino; Les Fées sont d'exquises danseuses;
Bruyères; General Lavine—eccentric; La Terrasse des
audiences du clair de lune; Ondine; Hommage à
S. Pickwick, Esq., P.P.M.P.C.; Canope; Les Tierces
alternées; Feux d'artifice.

1913   La Boîte à joujoux. Children's ballet. Scenario by
André Hellé.

1914   Berceuse héroïque pour rendre hommage à S.M. le
Roi Albert I de Belgique et à ses soldats [orchestrated
by Debussy].

1915   Douze Etudes, Book I: Pour les cinq doigts; Pour les
tierces; Pour les quartes; Pour les sixtes; Pour les
octaves; Pour les huit doigts.

             Book II: Pour les degrés chromatiques; Pour les
agréments; Pour les notes répétées; Pour les sonorités
opposées; Pour les arpèges; Pour les accords.

(b) *Piano Duet*

1880   Symphonie en si (one movement). [This and the next
work were intended to be orchestral works; only the
piano duct arrangements are known.]

1882   Triomphe de Bacchus (orchestral interlude).

1889   Petite Suite: En bateau; Cortège; Menuet; Ballet.

1891   Marche écossaise sur un thème populaire ('The Earl of
Ross March') [orchestrated by Debussy].

1900–14   Six Epigraphes antiques: Pour invoquer Pan, dieu du
vent d'été; Pour un tombeau sans nom; Pour que la
nuit soit propice; Pour la danseuse aux crotales; Pour
l'Egyptienne; Pour remercier la pluie au matin. [There
is also an arrangement of these pieces for piano solo.
They were orchestrated by Ernest Ansermet.]

(c) *Two Pianos*

1901   Lindaraja.

1915   En blanc et noir (three pieces).

CHAMBER WORKS

—	Intermezzo (for cello and piano).
1893	String Quartet.
1903–5	Rapsodie (for saxophone and piano). [The piano accompaniment orchestrated by Roger-Ducasse.]
1909–10	Première Rapsodie (for clarinet and piano) [orchestrated by Debussy].
1910	Petite pièce (for clarinet and piano) [orchestrated by Debussy].
1913	Syrinx (for unaccompanied flute).
1915	Sonata for cello and piano; Sonata for flute, viola, and harp.
1916–17	Sonata for piano and violin.

WORKS FOR SOLO INSTRUMENT AND ORCHESTRA

| 1889 | Fantaisie (for piano and orchestra). |
| 1903 | Danse sacrée and Danse profane (for harp and strings). |

ORCHESTRAL WORKS

1887	Printemps [orchestration revised by Henri Büsser].
1892–4	Prélude à l'après-midi d'un faune.
1892–9	Nocturnes: Nuages; Fêtes; Sirènes (with female chorus).
1903–5	La Mer (three symphonic sketches): De l'aube à midi sur la mer; Jeux de vagues; Dialogue du vent et de la mer.
1904	Incidental music for *King Lear* (Shakespeare): Fanfare; Sommeil de Lear. [There are a few rough notes in manuscript for six further pieces.]
1906–11	Images: Gigues [the orchestration finished by André Caplet]; Ibéria; Rondes de Printemps.

UNACCOMPANIED CHORAL WORKS

| 1898–1908 | Trois Chansons de Charles d'Orléans (for sopranos, contraltos, tenors, and basses): Dieu! qu'il fait bon regarder!; Quand j'ai ouy le tabourin . . . ; Yver, vous n'estes qu'un villain . . . |

APPENDIX H

CHORAL AND DRAMATIC WORKS

1882   Printemps (Comte de Ségur). Chorus for female
           voices.
1883   Invocation (Lamartine). Chorus for male voices. Piano
           and vocal score only.
1884   L'Enfant prodigue (Edouard Guinand). Cantata.
1887-9   La Damoiselle élue (D. G. Rossetti–G. Sarrazin).
           Cantata for solo voices, chorus, and orchestra.
1893-1902 Pelléas et Mélisande (Maurice Maeterlinck). Opera in
           five acts.
1911   Le Martyre de Saint-Sébastien. Incidental music to the
           mystery play by Gabriele d'Annunzio, for solo voices,
           chorus, and orchestra.
1912   Jeux. Ballet. Scenario and choreography by Nijinsky.
           Khamma. Ballet. Orchestrated by Charles Koechlin.
           Scenario by W. L. Courtney and Maud Allan.
1916   Ode à la France (Louis Laloy). Cantata for solo, chorus,
           and orchestra. [Completed from sketches by Marius-
           François Gaillard.]

ARRANGEMENTS AND ORCHESTRATIONS

Gluck, C. W., Caprice for piano on airs from the ballet of *Alceste*.
Raff, J., *Humoresque en forme de valse*. Arrangement for piano solo.
Saint-Saëns, C., Arrangement for piano solo of extracts from the
    opera *Etienne Marcel*.
    Introduction et Rondo capriccioso. Arrangement for two pianos.
    Second Symphony. Arrangement for two pianos.
Satie, Erik, Orchestration of *Deux Gymnopédies*.
Schumann, R., *Am Springbrunnen*. Arrangement for two pianos.
    Six Studies in canon form. Arrangement for two pianos.
Tchaikovsky, P., *The Swan Lake*. Arrangement of three dances for
    piano solo.
Wagner, R., Overture to *The Flying Dutchman*. Arrangement for
    two pianos.

[293]

CHRONOLOGY

1902[1]   Henri Büsser assumes conductorship of *Pelléas et Mélisande*, 8 May. Plans stage work on Poe's tale *The Devil in the Belfry*, June. Journey to London where at the invitation of André Messager he stays at the Hotel Cecil, 12 July. Hears Forbes-Robertson as Hamlet in London, 15 July. Stays with his parents-in-law at Bichain (Yonne), 15 September. Plans a version of *As You Like It* with Paul-Jean Toulet, October.

1903   Decorated Chevalier de la Légion d'Honneur, 1 February. Concert of Debussy's works at the Schola Cantorum, 24 April. *Danse sacrée, Danse profane* composed in the spring. Writes articles on Richter's performance of *The Ring* at Covent Garden in *Gil Blas*, 5 May and 1 June. Hears Rameau's *La Guirlande*, in Paris, 22 June. *Images* for piano (first series) begun at Bichain in the summer. *La Mer* and *Rapsodie Orientale* (for saxophone) begun there in the summer. Returns to Paris, October.

Meets Emma Bardac. Project to set Maeterlinck's *Joyselle*.

1904   *Estampes* performed by Ricardo Viñes at Société Nationale, 9 January. Accompanies his songs (*Ariettes* and *Fêtes galantes*) at a reception of Madame Colonne's, 23 June. Leaves Lilly Debussy for Madame Bardac, June. Hears Sarah Bernhardt and Mrs. Patrick Campbell in *Pelléas et Mélisande*, London, 18 July. At Jersey with Madame Bardac, July. *Masques* composed, July. At Dieppe with Madame Bardac, August–September. *L'Isle joyeuse* composed, September. Moves with Madame Bardac to 10 Avenue Alphand and later to 80 Avenue du Bois de Boulogne, Paris, September–October. Attempted suicide of Lilly Debussy, 13 October, announced in *Le Figaro* 4 November. *Danse sacrée, Danse profane* performed, 6 November.

Second set of *Fêtes Galantes* composed. *Trois Chansons de France* composed.

[1] The earlier months of 1902 are listed in Vol. I.

1905 *Masques* and *L'Isle joyeuse* performed by Ricardo Viñes at the Société Nationale, 18 February. Piano score of *La Mer* completed, 5 March. Madame Bardac divorced, 4 May. Stays at Eastbourne with Madame Bardac, July–August. Divorced from Lilly Debussy, 2 August. Exclusive contract with Durand for publication of all future works, August. Short journey to London followed by holiday at Bellevue near Paris, September. *La Mer* conducted by Camille Chevillard at the Concerts Lamoureux, 15 October. Birth of daughter, Claude-Emma ('Chouchou'), 30 October.

Images for piano, first series, completed and published. *L'Enfant prodigue* re-orchestrated. Two pieces for *Le Roi Lear* written. *Rondes de Printemps* and *Ibéria* announced for two pianos.

1906 Ricardo Viñes gives first performance of *Images* for piano, first set, at the Société Nationale, 3 March. Lunches with Jacques Durand and Richard Strauss, 25 March. Friendship with Victor Segalen, April. Receives sketch from him for the Buddhist drama *Siddharta*, 27 April. Meets Paul-Jean Toulet at the art gallery Durand-Ruel, May. Works on choral section of *Le Diable dans le Beffroi*, July. At Le Puys, near Dieppe, August.

Publication of *Sérénade à la poupée*.

1907 Goes to Brussels for first performance of *Pelléas*, 9 January. Death of Madame Bardac's uncle, the financier Osiris, in whose will she is disinherited, 4 February. *Le Jet d'eau* performed in orchestral version, February. Debussy receives study by Victor Segalen on music of the Maoris, April. First performance of *Pelléas* in Germany, at Frankfurt-on-Main, 17 April. New version of *Siddharta* received from Segalen, August. At Pourville, near Dieppe, August–September. Debussy suggests to Segalen a libretto on the subject of Orpheus, 26 August. Project for *Tristan* discussed with Gabriel Mourey, September. *Images* for piano, second set begun, October.

1908　Married to Emma Bardac in Paris (Mairie of the 16th arrondissement), 20 January. Conducts *L'Après-midi d'un faune* and *La Mer* at Queen's Hall, London, 1 February. *Pelléas* given at New York, 19 February. *Images* for piano, second set, performed by Ricardo Viñes at the Cercle Musical, 21 February. *Pelléas* given at Milan, under Toscanini, 2 April. Hears Chaliapin in *Boris Godounov* at the Paris Opéra, 17 May. Returns to *La Chute de la Maison Usher*, now conceived as an opera, June. Signs contract with G. Gatti-Casazza for productions at the Metropolitan Opera House in New York of *Usher*, *Le Diable dans le Beffroi*, and *La Légende de Tristan*, 5 July. First two acts of *Orphée Triomphant* sent by Segalen to Debussy, summer. *Children's Corner* performed in Paris by Harold Bauer, Cercle Musical, 18 December. *Ibéria* (from the orchestral *Images*) completed, 25 December.

1909　*Gigues* (piano duet version) finished, 4 January. First signs of cancer. Is obliged to take cocaine and morphine, February. Appointed member of the advisory board of the Paris Conservatoire, February. Goes to London to conduct *L'Après-midi d'un faune* and *Fêtes* at Queen's Hall, 25 February. Conducts *L'Après-midi d'un faune* at the Concerts Sechiari, Paris, 25 March. Conducts *Trois Chansons de Charles d'Orléans* at the Concerts Colonne, 9 April. *Rondes de Printemps* finished, 10 May. Debussy goes to London to superintend rehearsals of *Pelléas* given at Covent Garden, 21 May. Composes *Hommage à Haydn*, July. Writes the scenario of *Masques et Bergamasques* for Diaghilev, July. Works on scenario and music of *La Chute de la Maison Usher*, summer. Publication of the biography of Debussy by Louis Laloy, September. Begins *Rapsodie* for clarinet and orchestra, December. Writes *Danseuses de Delphes*, *Le Vent dans la plaine*, *Voiles*, *Collines d'Anacapri*, and *Des Pas sur la neige*, December.

Publication of *Le Cas Debussy*.

1910   Completes *Rapsodie* for clarinet and *Petite Pièce* for clarinet
and piano, January. Gabriel Pierné conducts *Ibéria* at Con-
certs Colonne, 20 February. Debussy conducts *Rondes de
Printemps*, Concerts Durand, Paris, 2 March. Dinner with
Mahler, 17 April. Attends performance of Mahler's Second
Symphony at the Trocadéro, April. Ravel plays Debussy's
D'un Cahier d'esquisses at first concert of the Société Musicale
Indépendante, 20 April. Publishes Preludes, Book I, May.
Projected visit to America, May. Debussy plays *Danseuses de
Delphes, Voiles, La Cathédrale engloutie,* and *Danse de Puck* at
Société Musicale Indépendante, 25 May. Hears Stravinsky's
L'Oiseau de feu in Paris, 25 June. Meeting with Stravinsky at
Bellevue at the home of Laloy, June. *La Plus que lente* com-
pleted, August. Death of Manuel Debussy, 28 October.
Rapsodie for clarinet completed, October. Ballet *Khamma*
proposed by Maud Allan, November. Journey to Vienna and
Budapest, 28 November. Gabriele d'Annunzio proposes
collaboration on *Le Martyre de Saint-Sébastien*, December.

Orchestral version by Caplet of *Children's Corner* given in
New York. Composes *Le Promenoir des deux amants* and
Trois Ballades de François Villon.

1911   First performance of three of the Preludes by Ricardo Viñes
and *Le Promenoir des deux amants* by Jane Bathori at the
Société Nationale, 14 January. *Rapsodie* for clarinet performed, Société Musicale Indépendante, 16 January. *Gigues*
(second version) finished, January. *Trois Ballades de François
Villon* first sung by Paule de l'Estang, 5 February. *Trois
Ballades de François Villon* sung by Clarke (in orchestral version conducted by Debussy) at the Concerts Sechiari, Paris,
5 March. Debussy conducts Satie's *Gymnopédies, Children's
Corner, Chansons de Charles d'Orléans* and accompanies his
songs sung by Jean Perrier and Maggie Teyte at the Cercle
Musical, 25 March. Plays four of his Preludes, *Les Sons et les
parfums, Le Vent dans la plaine, Des Pas sur la neige,* and *Minstrels,* at the Concerts Durand, Paris, 29 March. *Le Martyre de
Saint-Sébastien* performed at the Théâtre du Châtelet, Paris,
22 May. Heavily in debt, June. Conducts *L'Après-midi d'un*

faune, Children's Corner, and *Ibéria* at Turin, 25 June. At Houlgate, August.

1912 Accompanies Maggie Teyte in *Le Promenoir des deux amants* and *Fêtes galantes* at the Concerts Durand, 5 March. Plays Preludes at the Salle Gaveau, Paris, 12 March. Work advanced on *Le Diable dans le Beffroi*; plays extracts from it to Henri Büsser, 31 March. Last meeting with Pierre Louÿs, May. Diaghilev's production of *L'Après-midi d'un faune* at the Théâtre du Châtelet, 29 May. Inghelbrecht gives first concert performance of *Le Martyre de Saint-Sébastien* at the Société Musicale Indépendante, 14 June. Hears *Tristan* at the Opéra, 20 June. *Jeux* completed, August–September. Writes in *Revue S.I.M.,* November. Hundredth performance of *Pelléas et Mélisande* at Opéra-Comique, 27 December.

Writes condemnatory preface to René Lenormand's *Etude sur l'harmonie moderne.* Another project to visit America. *Khamma,* ballet for Maud Allan, begun.

1913 *Gigues,* earlier published in piano duet arrangement by André Caplet, performed in orchestral version at Concerts Colonne, 26 January. Debussy plays three of his Preludes, *Bruyères, Feuilles mortes, La Puerta del Vino,* at the Concerts Durand, March. Conducts *L'Après-midi d'un faune* at inaugural concerts at the Théâtre des Champs-Elysées, Paris, 2 April. First performance of *Les Fées sont d'exquises danseuses, La Terrasse des audiences du clair de lune,* and *Feux d'artifice* by Ricardo Viñes, Société Nationale, 5 April. Takes part in a concert of his works, end of April. Plays *Le Sacre du Printemps* with Stravinsky at the home of Louis Laloy, spring. *Jeux* produced by Diaghilev, Théâtre des Champs-Elysées, 15 May. Loïe Fuller gives choreographic version of *Nuages* and *Sirènes,* May. Debussy writes *Trois Poèmes de Mallarmé,* summer. Begins *Boîte à joujoux,* and finishes piano score, October. Conducts *Ibéria* at the Nouveaux Concerts, 15 October. Hears Chaliapin in *Boris Godounov* at the Théâtre des Champs-Elysées, 6 November. *Syrinx* given by Louis Fleury at performance of Gabriel Mourey's *Psyché,* 1 December. *Printemps* re-orchestrated by Henri Büsser; performed and conducted by C. Chevillard, 7 December. Conducts in Moscow and St. Petersburg at the invitation of Koussevitzky, December.

1914 Works on *Le Palais du Silence*, January. Accompanies A. Hartmann in the Violin and Piano Sonata of Grieg and in transcriptions of *Il pleure dans mon cœur*, *La Fille aux cheveux de lin*, and *Minstrels*, 5 February. Conducts in Rome, 22 February. Conducts at The Hague and Amsterdam, 26 February to 2 March. First concert performance of *Jeux* conducted by G. Pierné, 1 March. First performance of *Trois Poèmes de Mallarmé* given by Ninon Vallin accompanied by Debussy, who plays *Children's Corner* and some of the Preludes, 21 March. Journey to Brussels, April. Seventh and last journey to London to give concert at the home of Sir Edgar Speyer, 17 July. Arranges incidental music for *Les Chansons de Bilitis* as *Epigraphes antiques* for piano duet, summer. At Angers, August–September. Abandons *Le Palais du Silence*, October. Writes *Berceuse héroïque* for *King Albert's Book*, November. Orchestrates *Berceuse héroïque*, December.

Revision begun of *Le Martyre de Saint-Sébastien* with view to an operatic performance. Third project, made with A. Hartmann, for a tour of the United States.

1915 Prepares an edition of the works of Chopin, January–March. Death of mother, 23 March. At 'Mon Coin', Pourville, 12 July–12 October. Publishes *En blanc et noir*; begins *Six Sonates pour divers instruments* and Studies for piano; completes the Cello and Piano Sonata, summer. Studies completed, 27 September. Orchestral version of *Berceuse héroïque* conducted by Chevillard, 26 October. Sonata for Viola, Flute, and Harp completed. Writes words and music of *Noël des enfants qui n'ont plus de maison*, two versions (voice and piano and children's choir) beginning of December. Operation, 7 December.

Project for opera-ballet on Verlaine's *Fêtes galantes* (also referred to as *Crimen Amoris*).

1916 Slow recovery from operation, January–July. First performance of *Noël des enfants* given by Jane Monjovet, 9 April. Projected concert tour in the United States cancelled; edits sonatas of J. S. Bach, April. Final version of libretto of *La Chute de la Maison Usher* completed September (delivered to Durand, autumn 1917). Holiday at Le Mouleau, near Arcachon; Piano and Violin Sonata begun, 6–24 October. Private performance of Sonata for Flute, Violin, and Harp at the home of Durand, 10 December. Walter Rummel gives first performance of Studies, 14 December. Takes part in war charity concert, accompanying Rose Féart and giving first performance of *En blanc et noir* with Roger-Ducasse, 21 December. Sketches made for *Ode à la France* on a libretto by Louis Laloy, winter.

1917 First two movements of Piano and Violin Sonata completed, February. Sonata for Flute, Viola, and Harp first performed at a charity concert, 9 March. Charity concert of Debussy's vocal, piano, and chamber works, 16 March. Debussy and Joseph Salmon give first performance of Cello and Piano Sonata, 24 March. Debussy takes part in concerts of French music at the Palais de Glace with Vincent d'Indy, 25 March and 22 April. Edits J. S. Bach's violin sonatas, April. Gives first performance of Violin and Piano Sonata with Gaston Poulet and accompanies Rose Féart at the Salle Gaveau, Debussy's last concert in Paris, 5 May. Hears Satie's ballet *Parade* at the Théâtre du Châtelet, 18 May. Attends Molinari's performance of *La Mer*; plans a concert tour of England and Switzerland, June. Goes to Saint-Jean-de-Luz; plans a series of *Concerts* for piano and small orchestra, July. Plays Violin Sonata with Gaston Poulet at Saint-Jean-de-Luz, last public appearance, September. Plans incidental music for Gémier's production of *As You Like It*, November.

      Authorizes Henri Büsser to orchestrate *Soirée dans Grenade*, *La Puerta del Vino*, and *La Cathédrale engloutie*.

1918 Death at his home in the Avenue du Bois de Boulogne in Paris, 25 March. Burial at Père-Lachaise cemetery on 28 March, the eve of Good Friday when shells from the German gun 'Big Bertha' fell on the Church of Saint-Gervais.

[300]

BIBLIOGRAPHY

Much new biographical and critical material was published on the occasion of the Debussy centenary in 1962. The main publications were the special number of *La Revue de Musicologie, Claude Debussy: Textes et Documents inédits*, and the catalogue of the Debussy Exhibition held at the Bibliothèque Nationale, both edited by François Lesure (1962). The former presents for the first time the complete series of letters (1902–14) from Debussy to Louis Laloy as well as several series of letters written to Debussy by Chausson, Louÿs, Satie, Fauré, and Robert Godet. Other contents of this publication are listed in the bibliographies of the chapters to which they refer. The exhibition at the Bibliothèque Nationale similarly brought to light many new documents, manuscripts, and letters. The detailed catalogue of this exhibition should be consulted, together with the catalogue of an earlier exhibition of Debussy's manuscripts, letters, and other material, edited by Auguste Martin and held at the Opéra-Comique in 1942. The catalogue of the Debussy exhibition held in 1962 in Lisbon contains a series of unpublished letters to the Portuguese ethnologist, composer, and conductor, Francisco de Lacerda. The special number of *La Revue Musicale* devoted to Debussy (1964) contains some of Debussy's letters to his pupil Nicolas Coronio and to his publisher Arthur Hartmann. *La Revue Belge de Musicologie* (1962) has a valuable series of critical and biographical articles presented under the title *Souvenir et Présence de Debussy*. Finally, the proceedings of an international conference, *Debussy et l'Evolution de la Musique au 20e siècle*, were published in 1965. This took the form of a wide-ranging series of lectures and discussions which had been organized at the University of Paris on the occasion of the Debussy centenary under the chairmanship of Jacques Chailley. Technical and æsthetic problems are the subject of most of the papers in this publication which also contains a section devoted to Debussy's influence on later composers. An assessment of all this material as well as a discussion of certain new methods of approach to problems connected with Debussy's work is contained in François Lesure's article, 'Claude Debussy after his Centenary' in *The Musical Quarterly*, New York, July 1963.

The following detailed bibliography adheres to the plan in Volume I. The place of publication is Paris unless otherwise stated.

PRELUDE

Dietschy, Marcel, *La Passion de Claude Debussy*, Neuchâtel, 1962.

Lesure, François, *Claude Debussy, Catalogue de l'Exposition*, 1962.

Martin, Auguste, *Claude Debussy: Chronologie de sa vie et de ses œuvres*, Catalogue de l'Exposition, 1942.

Vallas, Léon, *Claude Debussy et son temps*, 1958.

CHAPTER 1

Arnoult, Léon, *Les Grands Imprécistes du 19e siècle: Turner, Wagner, Corot*, 1930.

Camacho, Mathilde D., *Judith Gautier*, 1939.

Castelfranco, Giorgio, *La Pittura Moderna*, Florence, 1934.

Clark, Sir Kenneth, 'Turner's Look at Nature', *The Sunday Times*, 25 October 1959.

Exner, Walter, *Hiroshige*, New York, 1960.

Finberg, Alexander J., *Life of J. M. W. Turner*, London, 1961.

Geffroy, Gustave, *Claude Monet*, 1922.

Goncourt, Edmond de, *Hokusaï*, 1896.

Goncourt, Edmond et Jules de, *Journal*, edited by R. Ricatte, vol. IV, 1956.

Japon Artistique, Le, 1888–96.

Kolsch, Hans Friedrich, *Der Impressionismus bei Debussy*, Düsseldorf, 1937.

Leclercq, J., 'Turner', *Gazette des Beaux-Arts*, June, 1904.

Leymarie, Jean, *Impressionisme*, 2 vol., Lausanne, 1955.

Mauclair, Camille, *Monet*, 1924; English translation by J. L. May, London, 1925.

—— 'La Peinture musicienne et la fusion des arts', *La Revue Bleue*, 6 September 1902.

—— *Turner*, 1939.

Michener, James Albert, *The Floating World*, London, 1954.

Peter, René, *Claude Debussy*, 1944.

Petit de la Villéon, Dr., 'Claude Debussy sur la Côte d'Emeraude', 'Annales de la Société d'Histoire et d'Archéologie', Saint-Malo, 1959.

Revon, Michel, *Etude sur Hokusaï*, 1896.

Rewald, John, *Post Impressionism*, New York, 1956.

Ruskin, John, *The Works of*, edited by E. T. Cook and A. Wedderburn, London, 1903–12.

Sachs, Curt, *The Commonwealth of Art*, New York, 1946.

Schuh, Willi, 'Debussy, Yvonne Lerolle, Renoir', *Neue Zürcher Zeitung*, Zürich, 19 August 1962.

Sizeranne, Robert, de la, *Ruskin and the Religion of Beauty*, London, 1899.

Souriau, Paul, 'Le Symbolisme des couleurs', *Revue de Paris*, 15 April 1895.

Stokes, Adrian, *Painting and the Inner World*, London, 1963.

Tei-San, 'Notes sur l'art japonais', *Mercure de France*, 15 October 1905.

Venturi, Lionello, *Les Archives de l'Impressionisme*, 1939.

CHAPTER 2

Bauer, Harold, 'Debussy's *Children's Corner*', *New York Times*, 21 December 1930.

Brailoiu, Constantin, 'Claude Debussy: coup d'œil historique', *Claude Debussy: Textes et Documents inédits*, *La Revue de Musicologie*, 1962.

—— 'Elargissement de la sensibilité musicale devant les musiques folkloriques et extra-occidentales', *Université radiophonique instrumentale*, 13 March 1954.

Bowen, York, *Pedalling the Modern Pianoforte*, London, 1936.

Calvocoressi, M. D., *Musicians' Gallery*, London, 1933.

Cortot, Alfred, 'La Musique pour piano de Claude Debussy', *La Revue Musicale*, 1 December 1920; English translation by V. Edgell, *The Piano Music of Debussy*, London, 1922.

Dent, Edward J., 'The Pianoforte and its Influence in Modern Music', *The Musical Quarterly*, New York, vol. 2, 1916.

Falkenberg, Georges, *Les Pédales du piano*, 1892.

Fargue, Léon-Paul, 'Ricardo Viñes', in *Portraits de famille*, 1947.

Février, Jacques, 'Les Exigences de Ravel', *Revue Internationale de Musique*, April 1939.

Gatti, Guido, 'The Piano Works of Debussy', *The Musical Quarterly*, vol. VII, 1921.

Gérar, Marcelle and Chalupt, René, editors, *Ravel au miroir de ses lettres*, 1956.

Jankélévitch, Vladimir, *Debussy et le Mystère*, Neuchâtel, 1949.

Laloy, Louis, 'Marie Jaëll', *La Revue Musicale*, May 1925.

—— *La Musique retrouvée*, 1928.

Lesure, François, ' "L'Affaire" Debussy-Ravel: Lettres inédites', *Festschrift Friedrich Blume*, Kassel, 1963.

Long, Marguerite, *Au Piano avec Claude Debussy*, 1960.

Myers, Rollo H., *Ravel: His Life and Works*, London, 1960.

Pueyo, Eduardo del, 'Autour de la méthode de Marie Jaëll', *Revue Internationale de Musique*, April 1939.

Perlemuter, Vlado, and Jourdan-Morhange, Hélène, *Ravel d'après Ravel*, Lausanne, 1953.

Schulz, H. G., *Musikalischer Impressionismus und Impressionisticher Klavierstil*, Würzburg, 1938.

CHAPTER 3

Chantavoine, Jean, 'Debussy démodé', *La Revue Musicale de Lyon*, 15 April 1911.

Debussy, Claude, *M. Croche antidilettante*, 1921; English translation, 'Monsieur Croche the Dilettante-Hater', London, 1927.

Gauthier-Villars, Henri (Willy), 'Claudine musicographe', *Mercure de France*, 15 December 1927.

Godet, Robert, 'Weber and Debussy', *The Chesterian*, London, June 1926.

Jean-Aubry, Georges, 'L'Œuvre critique de Debussy', *La Revue Musicale*, December 1920.

Pelmont, Raoul André, *Paul Valéry et les Beaux-Arts*, Cambridge, Mass., 1949.

Valéry, Paul, *Monsieur Teste*, 1948; English translation by J. Mathews, London, 1951.

—— Catalogue of Exhibition at the Bibliothèque Nationale, 1956.

Vallas, Léon, *Les Idées de Claude Debussy*, 1927; English translation by M. O'Brien, *The Theories of Debussy*, London, 1929.

CHAPTER 4

Caillard, Charles Francis, and Bérys, José de, *Le Cas Debussy*, 1910.

Cor, Raphaël, and Caillard, Charles Francis, 'Claude Debussy et le snobisme contemporain', *Revue du Temps Présent*, October–December 1909.

Laloy, Louis, 'Claude Debussy et le Debussysme', *La Revue S.I.M.*, August 1910.

Landormy, Paul, 'Claude Debussy et le progrès de l'art musical', *Courrier Musical*, 15 June 1903.

Mauclair, Camille, 'L'Etat actuel de la musique française', *La Revue Bleue*, 2 April 1904.

—— 'La Debussyte', *Courrier Musical*, 15 September 1905.

—— 'Les Chapelles musicales en France', *La Revue*, 15 November 1907.

Lorrain, Jean, *Pelléastres*, 1910.

Ravel, Maurice, 'L'Art et les Hommes', *Cahiers d'Aujourd'hui*, February 1913.

Sydow, Eckart von, *Die Kultur der Dekadenz*, Dresden, 1921.

Vuillermoz, Emile, 'Une tasse de thé', *Mercure Musical*, 15 November 1905.

—— 'Debussy et les Debussystes', *Nouvelle Presse*, 26 February 1907.

Wellesz, Egon, 'Arnold Schoenberg', *Cahiers d'Aujourd'hui*, No. 10, 1914.

CHAPTER 5

Abatangel, Louis, *Marcel Proust et la musique*, 1937.

Astruc, Gabriel, *Le Pavillon des fantômes*, 1929.

Binot, A., 'L'Audition colorée', *Revue des Deux Mondes*, 1 October 1892.

Cœuroy, André, 'La Musique dans l'œuvre de Marcel Proust', *Musique et Littérature*, 1923.

Hahn, Reynaldo, *Notes*, 1933.

—— *Journal d'un musicien*, 1949.

Montesquiou, Robert de, *Les Pas effacés*, vol. 3, 1923.

Painter, George D., *Marcel Proust*, vol. 2, 1965.

Pierhal, A., 'Sur la Composition Wagnérienne de l'œuvre de Proust', *Bibliothèque universelle et Revue de Genève*, June 1929.

Piroué, Georges, *Proust et la musique du devenir*, 1960.

Proust, Marcel, *Correspondance générale*, 6 vol., 1930–6.

—— *Lettres à Reynaldo Hahn*, 1956.

Rolland, Romain, *Journal des années de guerre*, 1952.

Rolland, Romain, *Jean-Christophe*, 10 vol., 1905–12; English translation by Gilbert Cannan, *John Christopher*, 4 vol., London, 1961.

Saurat, Denis, 'The "Modern" Style' in *N.R.F.*, edited by Justin O'Brien, London, 1958.

Segalen, Victor, 'Les Synthèses de l'école symboliste', *Mercure de France*, 1902.

Strauss, Richard, et Rolland, Romain, *Correspondance; Fragments de Journal*, 1951.

CHAPTER 6

Bellaigue, Camille, 'Salomé', *La Revue des Deux Mondes*, 1 June 1907.

Berggruen, Oskar, 'Concerts à l'Exposition 1900' [Vienna Philharmonic Orchestra conducted by Mahler], *Le Ménestrel*, 24 June 1900.

Boutarel, Amédée, 'Mahler', *Le Ménestrel*, 23 April 1910.

Bruneau, Alfred, *A l'Ombre d'un grand cœur*, 1931.

Casella, Alfredo, 'Mahler', *La Revue S.I.M.*, 15 April 1910.

Dietschy, Marcel, 'Claude Debussy et André Suarès', *Revue Musicale de Suisse Romande*, Lausanne, No. 3, 1963.

Durand, Jacques, *Souvenirs d'un éditeur de musique*, vol. II, 1925.

Gauthier-Villars, Henri (Willy), 'Salomé', *Le Mercure de France*, 1 June 1907.

Gide, André, *Journal, 1889–1939*, Bruges, 1939.

Indy, Vincent d', 'La Quatrième Symphonie de Mahler', *La Revue S.I.M.*, 1 February 1914.

Laloy, Louis, *La Musique retrouvée*, 1928.

Landormy, Paul, 'L'Etat actuel de la musique française', *La Revue Bleue*, 2 April 1904.

Lockspeiser, Edward, 'Mahler in France', *Monthly Musical Record*, London, March–April 1960.

Mahler, Alma Maria, *Gustav Mahler: Memories and Letters*, translated by Basil Creighton, London, 1946.

Ponnelle, Lazare, *A Munich: Mahler, Strauss, Busoni*, 1913.

Revue S.I.M., La, July–December 1910. (Including supplement on French Festival at Munich.)

Ritter, William, *Etudes d'art étranger*, 1906.

—— 'Mahler', *La Revue S.I.M.*, 15 November 1908.

Rolland, Romain, *Chère Sofia: Lettres de Romain Rolland à S.B. Bertolini Guerrieri-Gonzaga*, 1959.

Santoliquido, Francesco, *Il dopo Wagner: Claude Debussy e Richard Strauss*, Rome, 1909.

Stefan, Paul, *Gustav Mahler: ein Bild seiner Persönlichkeit in Widmungen*, Munich, 1910.

Symons, Arthur, 'Richard Strauss', *Le Mercure Musical*, 15 November 1907.

Szeps, Berta, *My Life and History*, translated by J. Sommerfield, London, 1938.

Vallas, Léon, *Les Idées de Claude Debussy*, 1927; English translation by M. O'Brien, *The Theories of Claude Debussy*, London, 1929.

CHAPTER 7

Bax, Sir Arnold, *Farewell my Youth*, London, 1943.

Debussy, Claude, Letter to the Queen's Hall Orchestra, *Musical Times*, London, March 1908.

Doret, Gustave, 'Lettres et billets inédits de C. A. Debussy', *Lettres romandes*, Geneva, 23 November 1934.

Evans, Edwin, 'Pelléas et Mélisande', *The Musical Standard*, London, 29 May 1909.

Gui, Vittorio, 'Debussy in Italia', *Musica d'Oggi*, Milan, December 1932.

—— 'Debussiana' in *Battute d'aspetti*, Florence, 1944.

Hirschberg, Leopold, 'Claude Debussy', *Signale für die musikalische Welt*, Berlin, 1912.

Huneker, James Gibbons, *Bedouins*, New York, 1920.

Karatygin, V. G., 'Pelléas et Mélisande', *Muzykalnyi sovremennik*, Moscow, no. 4, 1915.

Knosp, Gaston, 'Claude Debussy', *Neue Zeitschrift für Musik*, Leipzig, 1905.

Liebich, Franz, 'Claude Debussy and his music of legend and dream', *The Musical Standard*, 20 February 1904.

Liebich, Louise S., 'Pelléas et Mélisande', *The Musical Standard*, 29 May 1909.

Pfeilschmidt, H., 'Pelléas et Mélisande', *Die Musik*, Berlin, May 1907.

Specht, Richard, 'Neue Werke' (Debussy, Scriabin etc.), *Der Merker*, Vienna, December 1910.

—— 'Arnold Schoenberg. Eine Vorbemerkung'; 'Pelléas et Méli-sande [of Debussy], *Der Merker*, June 1911.

Symons, Arthur, 'French Music in London', *The Saturday Review*, London, 14 December 1907.

—— 'Claude Debussy', *The Saturday Review*, 8 February 1908.

Wellesz, Egon, 'Die jüngste Entwicklung der neufranzösischen Musik', *Der Merker*, 15 May 1911.

Wood, Sir Henry J., *My Life of Music*, London, 1938.

CHAPTER 8

Debussy, Claude, *Lettres inédites à André Caplet*, 1957.

Eliot, T. S., 'Edgar Allan Poe et la France', *La Table Ronde*, December 1948.

Gatti-Casazza, Guido, *Memories of the Opera*, New York, 1941.

Lefebvre, Louis, *Charles Morice*, 1926.

Lhombreaud, Roger, *Arthur Symons*, London, 1963.

Lockspeiser, Edward, *Debussy et Edgar Poe*, 1962.

—— 'Debussy's Concept of the Dream' in *Proceedings of the Royal Musical Association*, London, 1962–3.

Mellerio, André, *Odilon Redon*, 1913.

Morice, Charles, *La Littérature de tout à l'heure*, 1889.

Poe, Edgar Allan, *Poésies complètes*, translated by G. Mourey, 1889; second edition with an introduction by J. H. Ingram, 1910.

Redon, Arï, editor, *Lettres à Odilon Redon*, 1960.

Symons, Arthur, 'A French Blake: Odilon Redon', *The Art Review*, London, July 1890.

Wilson, Edmund, 'Poe at Home and Abroad', in *The Shores of Light*, New York, 1952.

CHAPTER 9

Allan, Maud, *My Life and Dancing*, London, 1908.

d'Annunzio, Gabriele, *Gabriele d'Annunzio e la Musica*, Milan, 1939.

Astruc, Gabriel, *Le Pavillon des fantômes*, 1929.

Cohen, Gustave, 'Gabriele d'Annunzio et le Martyre de Saint-Sébastien', *Mercure de France*, 16 June 1911.

Courtney, William Leonard, *Rosemary's Letter Book*, London, 1909.

Ghéon, Henri, 'D'Annunzio et l'Art', *Nos Directions*, 1911.

Lesure, François, 'Debussy et le XVIe siècle', *Hans Albrecht in Memoriam*, Kassel, 1962.

Martyre de Saint-Sébastien, Le, Special number of *La Revue Musicale*, 1957.

Orchestre de la Suisse Romande, Geneva, article by Robert Godet in programme of 28 January 1928.

Rhodes, Anthony, *The Poet as Superman: A life of Gabriele d'Annunzio*, London, 1959.

Tosi, Guy, ed., *Claude Debussy et Gabriele d'Annunzio: Correspondance inédite*, 1948.

Traversi, Camillo Antona, *Gabriele d'Annunzio: Curriculum vitæ*, vol. 2, Rome, 1934.

CHAPTER 10

Blanche, Jacques-Emile, 'Souvenirs sur Manet et sur Debussy', *Le Figaro*, 22 June 1932.

—— *La Pêche aux souvenirs*, 1949.

—— *Portraits of a lifetime*, translated and edited by Walter Clement, London, 1937.

Eimert, Herbert, 'Debussy's Jeux', *Die Reihe*, No. 5, Bryn Mawr, Pa., 1959.

Grigoriev, Sergei Leonidovich, *The Diaghilev Ballet*, London, 1953.

Harvey, John W., *The Eurythmics of Jaques-Dalcroze*, London, 1917.

Jamot, Paul, 'Salon d'Automne (Art Russe)', *Gazette des Beaux-Arts*, January 1907.

Jaques-Dalcroze, Emile, *Souvenirs*, 1942.

Laloy, Louis, *La Musique retrouvée*, 1928.

Lesure, François, 'Debussy et Stravinsky', *Musica d'Oggi*, Milan, June 1959.

Lifar, Serge, *Serge Diaghilev: An Intimate Biography*, New York, 1940.

Martin, Auguste, *Claude Debussy: Chronologie de sa vie et de ses œuvres*, 1942.

Mauclair, Camille, 'Karsavina et Mallarmé', in *La Religion de la Musique*, 1928.

Nijinsky, Romola, *Nijinsky*, London, 1933.

Nijinsky, Romola, editor, *The Diary of Vaslav Nijinsky*, London, 1937.

Souris, André, 'Debussy et Stravinsky', *La Revue Belge de Musicologie*, vol. XVI, Brussels, 1962.

Stravinsky, Igor, *Chroniques de ma vie*, 1935; English translation, *Chronicle of My Life*, London, 1936.

Stravinsky, Igor, and Craft, Robert, *Avec Stravinsky*, 1958.

—— *Conversations with Stravinsky*, London, 1959. (This is a translation of an abridged form of *Avec Stravinsky*.)

—— *Memories and Commentaries*, London, 1960.

—— *Expositions and Developments*, London, 1962.

White, Eric Walter, 'Stravinsky and Debussy', *Tempo*, Nos. 61–2, London, 1962.

CHAPTER 11

Casella, Alfredo, 'Claude Debussy', *Monthly Music Record*, London, January 1933.

Debussy, Claude, *Lettres à deux amis*, 1942.

—— *Lettres inédites à André Caplet*, 1957.

Dietschy, Marcel, 'Claude Debussy et André Suarès', *La Revue Musicale de Suisse Romande*, June 1963.

Gauthier, André, editor, *Debussy: Documents iconographiques*, Geneva, 1952.

Jankélévitch, Vladimir, *L'Ironie ou la bonne conscience*, 1950.

Jullian, Philippe, *Dictionnaire du Snobisme*, 1958.

Lesure, François, editor, *Correspondance de Claude Debussy et de Louis Laloy*, *La Revue de Musicologie*, 1962.

Martineau, Henri, editor, *Correspondance de Claude Debussy et Paul-Jean Toulet*, 1929.

Newman, Ernest, *Wagner as Man and Artist*, London, 1925.

Peyre, Henri, *Literature and Sincerity*, London, 1963.

Suarès, André, *Debussy*, 1922.

Symons, Arthur, *The letters of Charles Baudelaire to his Mother*, London, 1928.

CHAPTER 12

Besse, Clément, *La Musique allemande chez nous*, 1916.

Brogan, Sir Denis William, *The Development of Modern France*, London, 1940.

Caine, Sir Thomas Henry Hall, editor, *King Albert's Book*, London, 1914.

Chastenet, Jacques, *Jours inquiets et jours sanglants*, 1957.

Debussy, Claude, *Lettres à son éditeur*, 1927.

Laloy, Louis, L'Ode à la France', *Musique*, 15 March 1928.

—— 'Debussy', *Revue des Deux Mondes*, 15 July 1932.

Lesure, François, editor, *Catalogue de l'exposition Debussy*, 1962.

—— 'Lettres inédites de Debussy', *Candide*, 21 June 1962.

—— 'Cinq lettres de Robert Godet', *Revue de Musicologie*, 1962.

Liess, Andreas, *Claude Debussy und das deutsche Musikschaffen*, Würzburg, 1939.

Rolland, Romain, *Journal des années de guerre*, 1952.

Slonimsky, Nicolas, *Music since 1900*, New York, 1949.

Vuillermoz, Emile, *Claude Debussy*, Geneva, 1957.

CONCLUSION

Almendra, Julia d', *Les Modes grégoriens dans l'œuvre de Claude Debussy*, 1948.

Ansermet, Ernest, 'Le langage de Debussy', *Feuilles Musicales*, Lausanne, June–July 1962.

Boulez, Pierre, 'La Corruption dans les encensoirs', *Nouvelle Revue Française*, December 1956.

Brailoiu, Constantin, 'Pentatonismes chez Debussy' in *Studia Memoriæ Belæ Bartók Sacra*, Budapest, 1956.

Danckert, Werner, *Claude Debussy*, Berlin, 1950.

Gervais, Françoise, *Etude comparée des langages harmoniques de Fauré et de Debussy*, 2 vol., 1951.

Jakobik, Albert, *Zur Einheit der Neuen Musik*, Würzburg, 1957.

Jankélévitch, Vladimir, *Debussy et le Mystère*, Neuchâtel, 1949.

Kecskeméti, Istvan, 'Debussy's last sonatas', *Revue Belge de Musicologie*, Brussels, vol. XVI, 1962.

Linden, Albert Vander, 'Debussy, Octave Maus et Paul Gilson', *Revue Belge de Musicologie*, vol. XVI, 1962.

Ruwet, Nicholas, 'Note sur les duplications dans l'œuvre de Debussy', *Revue Belge de Musicologie*, vol. XVI, 1962.

Schnebel, Dieter, 'Tendenzen bei Debussy', *Die Reihe*, Bryn Mawr, Pa., No. 6, 1960.

Wartisch, O., *Studien zur Harmonik des musikalischen Impressionismus*, Erlangen, 1934.

INDEXES

INDEX OF WORKS
GENERAL INDEX

INDEX OF WORKS

SKETCHES AND PROJECTS

GENERAL INDEX